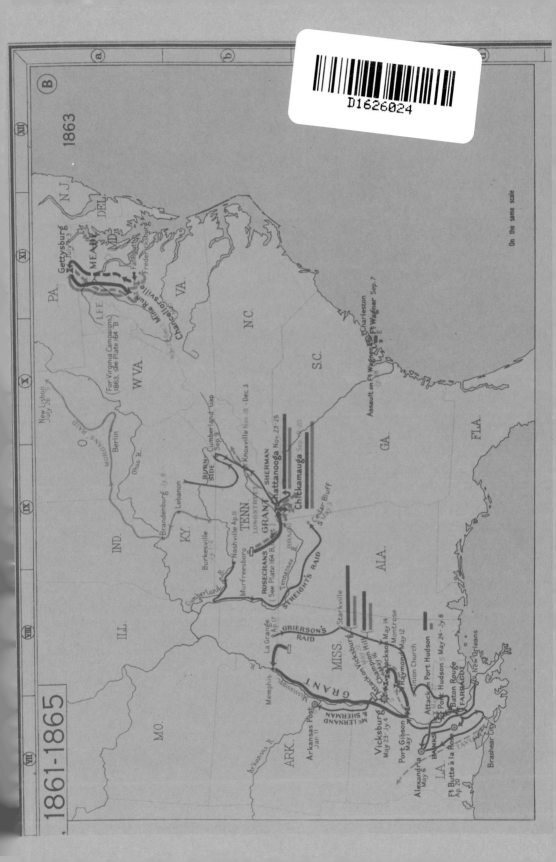

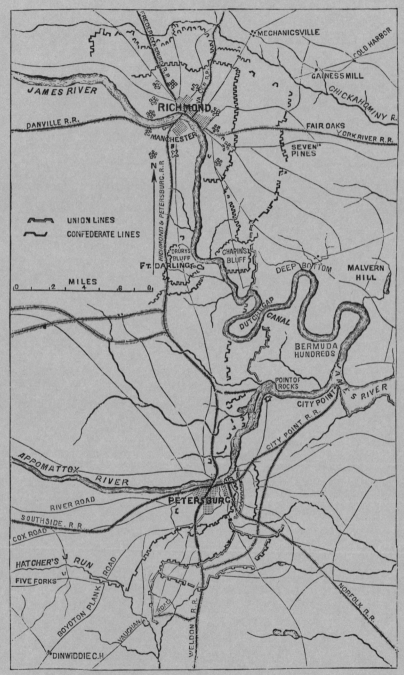

THE LINES AT PETERSBURG AND RICHMOND.

HOUSE UNDIVIDED

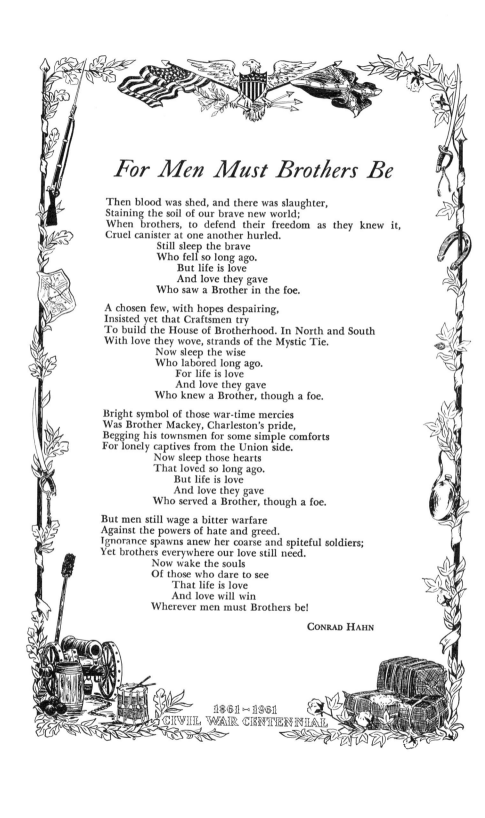

For Men Must Brothers Be

Then blood was shed, and there was slaughter,
Staining the soil of our brave new world;
When brothers, to defend their freedom as they knew it,
Cruel canister at one another hurled.
      Still sleep the brave
      Who fell so long ago.
        But life is love
        And love they gave
      Who saw a Brother in the foe.

A chosen few, with hopes despairing,
Insisted yet that Craftsmen try
To build the House of Brotherhood. In North and South
With love they wove, strands of the Mystic Tie.
      Now sleep the wise
      Who labored long ago.
        For life is love
        And love they gave
      Who knew a Brother, though a foe.

Bright symbol of those war-time mercies
Was Brother Mackey, Charleston's pride,
Begging his townsmen for some simple comforts
For lonely captives from the Union side.
      Now sleep those hearts
      That loved so long ago.
        But life is love
        And love they gave
      Who served a Brother, though a foe.

But men still wage a bitter warfare
Against the powers of hate and greed.
Ignorance spawns anew her coarse and spiteful soldiers;
Yet brothers everywhere our love still need.
      Now wake the souls
      Of those who dare to see
        That life is love
        And love will win
      Wherever men must Brothers be!

CONRAD HAHN

1861 ⊷ 1961
CIVIL WAR CENTENNIAL

HOUSE UNDIVIDED

The Story of
Freemasonry and the Civil War

By

ALLEN E. ROBERTS

*. . . Lord, how oft shall my brother sin against me, and
I forgive him? till seven times? Jesus saith unto him, I
say not unto thee, Until seven times: but, Until seventy
times seven.*

Matthew 18:21-22

Macoy Publishing & Masonic Supply Co., Inc.
Richmond, Virginia

Printed in the United States of America

Dedicated to the Masons who wore the Blue and the Gray of opposing forces—but who remembered to practice without their Temples that which they had learned within—and to Kenneth, my young "warrior," for his faith in his dad.

Preface

◇◇◇

THIS IS a story that should have been written a century ago. Many of the episodes involving Freemasonry during the Civil War years have been lost in the mists of time. They will never be recovered. These pages are but a beginning of the history of that period, as it concerns Freemasonry. I hope that other Masonic historians will take up the quest to add, and if necessary, subtract, what is herein written.

The task has just begun if the complete history of Freemasonry during the Civil War is to be recorded. Each jurisdiction should, during the centennial commemoration of that unnecessary war, endeavor to have an authentic history written insofar as it pertains to its territory. In this book, my own state of Virginia could only be touched upon, as well as the others that are rich in Civil War experiences.

The question is often asked, "What has Freemasonry to do with the Civil War?" Actually, Freemasonry had nothing to do with any war, including the War of Independence. Yet, Freemasons had much to do with both of those wars that took place on American soil, for it was Freemasons who endeavored to prevent both struggles, and when they proved unsuccessful, did all they could to ease the difficulties and suffering of all involved. Members of the Craft were among the highest in command of all armies; they held top political posts, and were at the head of humanitarian agencies.

Not all good men were, or are, Freemasons. Not all Masons were, or are, good men. Patrick Henry, Thomas Jefferson, and Samuel Adams were among the Revolutionary heroes who were not Masons, and by no stretch of the imagination can they be considered anything but good men. Benedict Arnold was among the Masons who proved "bad." Early in the Revolution he had fought heroically for the independence of the colonies, but being angered by what he considered unjust treatment by Congress, he turned against his fellow Americans.

No attempt is made in these pages to analyze the various battles fought, or which side was right and which was wrong. This is an effort to write an unbiased report about Freemasonry and Freemasons during the Civil War period. Having been born in Rhode Island, and having "adopted" Virginia as my home after World War II, both sides have an equal place in my heart. It is my opinion that both sections of the United States were right to some extent, but both were wrong to a greater degree.

The form used in setting forth this history of Freemasonry during the Civil War has been considered during the more than five years spent in gathering information. Perhaps a letter I received from R. Baker Harris, librarian of the Supreme Council, Scottish Rite, Southern Jurisdiction, had much to do with the form finally decided upon. In speaking of grand lodge proceedings for the Civil War years, he wrote: "No one has done a comprehensive job on extracting such information from these sources." Believing it will help the Masonic historians who follow, I have endeavored to set forth the "meat" contained within the thousands of addresses and reports of those *Proceedings*.

There will be criticism for using so many lengthy quotes (the various articles and speeches, the reports and letters, are quoted many times in full insofar as they pertain to the period in question), but I believe they are all not only pertinent, but interesting. We cannot understand the past unless we understand the individuals who were a part of it. What they *actually* said and did is important—not what someone 100 years later *claims* they said and did.

I must make it clear that I do not agree with everything that is quoted. No one will. But every side has the right to be "heard." There were statements made then that would not have been made even a year later. The facts were not readily available a century ago. Communication was poor, and newspapers seldom printed unslanted items.

Millions of words have been written about the American Civil War, but rarely do we find anything pertaining to Masonry. One of the greatest difficulties I encountered was in knowing who were Masons—until I "discovered" William R. Denslow's wonderful volumes of *10,000 Famous Freemasons.* From that moment on my work was ten-fold easier; then other sources were made available. To my amazement I found that over 300 generals in the Union and Confederate armies were members of the Craft—plus an uncountable number of other officers and men. An appendix in this book will list many of them.

This story is written in chronological order to better understand why statements were made and actions taken in the various grand lodges, subordinate lodges, and in the field. It was deemed preferable to embody information in the text that would normally be employed as footnotes. The bibliography covers the original sources.

Not all of the Masons who participated in the Civil War will appear in these pages; that would be an impossibility. Where a known Mason appears, he will be so listed. A Mason may not be noted as such, simply because I have no knowledge of that fact. Under no circumstances will an attempt be made to class anyone as a member of the Craft just because he would enhance the name of Freemasonry. There were many, like Lincoln and Grant, who almost became Masons. Their story will be told, along with the stories of Masons like Buchanan, Farragut, McKinley, Johnson, Forrest, Morgan, and others.

The temptation to write at greater length about some of the battles and men has been strong. Several episodes have been quite intriguing. An example is John Hunt Morgan's connection with a master Confederate spy named Thomas H. Hines. Hines, at the age of 20, resigned from the staff of the Masonic University at LaGrange, Kentucky, at the outbreak of the war. He joined Morgan, and from then on the "Sons of Liberty," "Copperheads," and other Southern sympathizers in the North play prominent roles in the tale of Morgan and Hines. It was Hines who master-minded the escape from the Ohio State Penitentiary, and paved the way for many of Morgan's successful raids.

That Morgan and Forrest were considered among the best in

the Confederate forces was evidenced early in 1864. A Captain Longuemare outlined a plan to President Davis for a general uprising of the Copperhead societies in the North. Davis said he wanted good "military men" to carry out the plan, preferably West Pointers, but he would "communicate at once with Generals Forrest and Morgan"; neither had attended that academy.

The work done by David Farragut, and his naval forces deserves more than the passing notice received in this book, as do many other men who were Masons and served with valor.

There is a story about a Masonic lodge meeting between the lines during the Battle of Gettysburg. I can find no evidence to substantiate that tale. But it *could* have happened. Generals Henry Heth, C.S.A., and James Robinson, U.S.A., were both members of Rocky Mountain Lodge No. 205, Utah Territory; both took part in the fighting at Gettysburg. There were dozens, if not hundreds, of other friends and Masons on opposing sides, such as Hancock and Armistead.

ALLEN E. ROBERTS

Highland Springs
Virginia

Author's Post Script

◇◇

*H*ouse *Undivided* was published in 1961. My quest for information about the actions of Freemasons and Freemasonry during the War Between the States began six years earlier. I've often been asked what brought about this interest in that war. Here's the answer:

During a church service sponsored by my lodge, Babcock No. 322, Highland Springs, Virginia, a retired Baptist minister told a story about Joseph Fort Newton. Newton's father, Lee, had been made a Master Mason in a Confederate military lodge during the American Civil War. Later Lee was captured by Federal forces, and taken to a prisoner-of-war camp at Rock Island, Illinois. There he became deathly ill. The commander of the camp learned the elder Newton was a Mason, took him into his home and nursed him back to health. When the war was over the commander gave Newton money and a gun, then saw him safely on his way to his home in Texas.

In his autobiography, *River of Years*, Joseph Fort Newton, D.D., wrote: "This experience of my father, when I learned about it, had a very great influence upon my life, as will appear later; the fact that such a fraternity of men could exist, mitigating the harshness of war, and remain unbroken when states and churches were torn in two, became a wonder; and it is not strange that I tried for years to repay my debt to it." He later praised Freemasonry highly within and without the Craft. In addition, he took time out of his extremely busy schedule to write several books and many articles about Freemasonry.

This story haunted me for months. How many more such wonderful acts of brotherhood took place during that anything but civil war, I wondered. I couldn't erase it from my mind, so I started my search for truthful information.

The paper I planned to write for my research lodge turned into a book called *House Undivided*. It became a widely read and quoted story of Freemasonry's brotherhood in action.

Soon after its publication a Masonic degree team, based on the brotherhood expressed in the book, was formed. It was the *Virginia Craftsmen.* Its members wore a Confederate cavalry-type gray and gold uniform. From 1962 to the present it has worked in almost every State in the United States, several Provinces in Canada, Scotland and England. Its purpose, graphically portraying brotherhood in action, has been highly praised. It has continually asked its audiences to "practice without the lodge those lesson learned within."

With the publication of *House Undivided,* I seemed to become an immediate "expert" in many areas. I was invited to speak on a myriad of Masonic subjects. Most of the topics suggested I knew nothing about! This didn't appear to matter to anyone but me. It did, however, force me to learn as much about the many facets of Freemasonry as possible. This learning actually became a life-long obsession.

This obsession produced several books on various topics. My vocation was management. I was also serving on my Grand Lodge educational committee. I believed that Freemasonry had to adopt the principles of good management if it was to survive in a competitive age. Combining actual management and Masonic education, I wrote *Key to Freemasonry's Growth.* Later there were other books on leadership.

Symbolism, I learned while studying the Civil War period, was important. This brought into being *The Craft and Its Symbols*—a book for the newly raised Mason, his wife, speakers, the non-Mason, which the Macoy Company asked me to write. Freemasonry needed a comprehensive one-volume truthful story of George Washington, the outstanding Freemason of the 18th century. I had the pleasure of writing it. The phenomenal Freemason of the 20th century was Harry S. Truman. His Masonic story had to be told and I thoroughly enjoyed researching his life and recording it.

The task is not complete. There are hundreds of books that must be written if the vast scope that is Freemasonry is to be told. Much more can, and should, be recorded about brotherhood during the War Between the States.

It is now time to turn the gauntlet over to younger hands and minds.

Highland Springs, Virginia   ALLEN E. ROBERTS
December, 1989

Acknowledgments

THERE ARE some men who claim they are "self-made." They are in error, for without the help of God and thousands of individuals, no man can accomplish anything worthwhile. So it is in writing a book, whether fact or fiction. This one is no exception.

Every author and publisher listed in the bibliography, as well as many more, contributed something to this work. The Civil War ended over fifty years before I was born. What I have learned about it had to come from the writings of others.

I particularly want to thank William R. Denslow for the wealth of information he gave me about Freemasons connected with the war; for bringing the partial manuscript to the attention of his father, Ray V. Denslow, who suggested it be published by the Missouri Lodge of Research; for carrying on where his father's untimely death left off; for editing the manuscript; for working with Ovid H. Bell, the printer, who did an excellent job; for compiling the index; for the many other things he did before the book was completed.

My gratitude is extended to Gloria W. Martin who typed the manuscript, and Helen S. Jeter who checked the manuscript and corrected my many errors. I appreciate the assistance received in Missouri from Juanita D. Denslow and Nada W. Hoffman who painstakingly read copy and checked proofs, as well as Ethel M. Comstock who helped with the indexing.

Louis H. Manarin, co-editor of *Lee's Wartime Papers*, not being a Mason, checked the historical portions of the manuscript with an unbiased eye. So did Robert W. Waitt, Jr., executive secretary for the Richmond Civil War Committee. Their advice and criticism was invaluable.

My appreciation goes to the many grand secretaries who helped in so many ways; particularly my own, Archer Bailey

Gay, who interrupted his busy schedule repeatedly to answer my questions or search for a remote piece of information.

The staff of the Virginia State Library was most helpful, as always. No Masonic information was available to them, but when I needed other books or documents they made them available to me. Many times they made a search for obscure items I would otherwise have missed.

Assistance was graciously given by F. J. Anderson of the Iowa Masonic Library; William J. Paterson, former librarian for the Grand Lodge of Pennsylvania; Muriel L. Taylor, librarian for the Grand Lodge of Massachusetts; and particularly Wendell K. Walker, director of the library and museum for the Grand Lodge of New York.

Frank Blair Bishop was especially kind in giving me access to his library of books about the Civil War. The editors of several Masonic magazines were most helpful. Among them was the late Laurence R. Taylor of the *Indiana Freemason* and John Black Vrooman of *The Philalethes* who several times went out of their way to assist me. Previously mentioned is William R. Denslow, who is also editor of *The Royal Arch Mason.*

My heartfelt thanks is extended to Marcia A. Wehren for preliminary typing; Harry C. Lackner for information about Gettysburg; Clarence R. Martin, past grand master of Indiana, for a copy of his *Traveling Military Lodges;* Ray D. Smith of Chicago for sending me Masonic references found in the pages of the *Confederate Veteran;* Louis W. Bridgeman for information about Wisconsin Masonry; Bernhardt F. Wagenblast for items about Edwin Booth; R. W. Houghton for some of his notes about the war; Alexander A. Lawrence, author of *A Present for Mr. Lincoln,* for items about Savannah; W. A. Ross of St. Albans for information concerning Vermont.

My good friend, Frank A. Smith, grand junior warden of the Grand Lodge of Arkansas, suggested the title for this book. The information he gave me about his state was invaluable, as was his encouragement.

Conrad Hahn, editor of the Masonic Service Association,

another good friend, graciously wrote the poem *For Men Must Brothers Be* especially for this book. For that, and the many other things he has done for me, I am most appreciative.

I am deeply grateful to those who helped by sending articles, other items, and in so many other ways.

I must give my special thanks to my ten-year-old son Kenneth for his faith in his dad.

The understanding and patience of my wife Dorothy will always be appreciated. Not once did she complain about the books and papers strung throughout our home, or the nights spent listening to my typewriter when I should have been entertaining her. While no woman can be a Mason, we who spend so much of our time working for the Craft know that without the love and backing of our womenfolk there would be no Masonry.   A. E. R.

◇◇◇

THE MAPS used for the end papers of this book are taken from *Atlas of the Historical Geography of the United States* by Charles O. Paullin and are reproduced through the courtesy of The Carnegie Institution of Washington.

We are also indebted to the Virginia State Library of Richmond who supplied the prints for these and the other maps appearing throughout the book.

Table of Contents

Foreword

◇◇◇

THIS VOLUME on Freemasonry, Freemasons and the War Between the States is being published on the centennial anniversary of the fratricidal conflict which shook our nation and hurled brother against brother, father against son. Houses joined by the strong ties of blood were split asunder, families fought against one another, each choosing to defend the point of view which he espoused. In the midst of this bitterness, hatred and bloodshed Freemasonry stood as a monument to tempered passions, to brotherly love and to sound thinking. It was truly a *House Undivided,* as Worshipful Brother Roberts has titled his book.

There are many men who have the talent required to write a book but such a work as has been produced within the covers of this volume reflects a high degree of patience for it involved the sifting of a variety of legends and traditions which the years have built around both Freemasonry and the Civil War. Brother Roberts has done this quite successfully. He has carefully separated fact from fiction and has spent years in extensive research through many volumes, records and letters which cover this period of history. Thus he has been able to substantiate by documentary evidence the many incidents which he quotes in full.

He has written the factual story of brotherly love in action. Thus he has shown the Freemason as faithful to his country on the field of battle but ever ready to extend the hand of brotherly love to the fallen member of the Craft. He has recorded the words of men who have gone on to their reward but who still speak to us from the printed page, using their own words rather than giving voice to his thought as to what they might have said on these occasions. As is always the case, the author has disproved some of the lore of this great conflict, but we are richer because he has placed the stamp of authenticity on so many of our beloved legends.

The records of the several Grand Lodges of the United States for the years 1859-1861 indicate that the Masonic mind was running in safe channels; that our leaders felt brotherhood to be a more powerful issue than that which was debated generally on the street corner and in the Congress. Our Masonic leaders of a century ago were sure that the issues of their day could be settled if our people would but exercise the statesmanship of brotherhood. Alas, the public mind did not run in the same channel and our nation resorted to the force of arms, spilling much of the blood of the finest young men of our nation.

Brother Roberts has not dealt with the war as a cause to be defended, rather he has related the facts as he has found them and given his readers the unvarnished truth as he has discovered it. His book is the product of years of research and recording, of much correspondence, of journeyings and many hours of conversation concerning the events of that most tragic era in our national history. Time has clothed this conflict and its heroes in a patina of gallantry and nothing which the author has written in these pages detracts one whit from their reputation.

It is our hope that both Mason and non-Mason will enjoy the work which Brother Roberts has produced and find in his book a treasure of factual information on that great tenet of Freemasonry—*Brotherly Love.*

ARCHER B. GAY, PGM, *Grand Secretary,*
Grand Lodge AF & AM of Virginia

HOUSE UNDIVIDED

II. *Of the* CIVIL MAGISTRATE *supreme and subordinate.*

A Mason is a peaceable Subject to the Civil Powers, wherever he resides or works, and is never to be concern'd in Plots and Conspiracies against the Peace and Welfare of the Nation, nor to behave himself undutifully to inferior Magistrates; for as Masonry hath been always injured by War, Bloodshed, and Confusion, so ancient Kings and Princes have been much dispos'd to encourage the Craftsmen, because of their Peaceablenefs and *Loyalty*, whereby they practically anfwer'd the Cavils of their Adverfaries, and promoted the Honour of the Eraternity, who ever flourish'd in Times of Peace. So that if a Brother should be a Rebel against the State, he is not to be countenanc'd in his Rebellion, however he may be pitied as an unhappy Man; and, if convicted of no other Crime, though the loyal Brotherhood muft and ought to difown his Rebellion, and give no Umbrage or Ground of political Jealoufy to the Government for the time being; they cannot expel him from the *Lodge*, and his Relation to it remains indefeafible.

III. *Of*

The foregoing is a copy of Section II of the Constitution of Masonry as written by James Anderson for the Grand Lodge of England, and adopted by that grand lodge and printed on "this 17th Day of January, 1724." It was the article most frequently quoted in Masonic circles throughout the Civil War.

CHAPTER I

The Years Before

◇◇

*. . . Masonry hath been always injured by War,
Bloodshed, and Confusion . . . ever flourish'd
in Times of Peace.*

JAMES ANDERSON

THE FOLLY of war and all forms of violence has been recognized by Freemasons from the beginnings of the Craft, but blundering edicts of powerful, though ill-advised rulers, have forced even peace-loving men to leave their homes and loved ones to fight for a cause they felt just.

For at least 14 centuries the blood of Freemasons has mingled with that of other men and women upon the ground of this planet called "Earth." Even in this supposedly enlightened age there are threats of more wars.

No living person knows when Freemasonry began. Many of the symbols of the organization go back to the very childhood of civilization; back to the days when the written word was rare, if it existed at all. During the Middle Ages and the rise of Gothic architecture are found two distinct classes of Masons: the Guild Masons, who, like the Guild carpenters or weavers or merchants, were local in character and strictly regulated by law, and the Freemasons, who traveled from city to city as their services were needed to design and to erect the marvelous churches and cathedrals which stand today inimitable in beauty.

The operative Freemasons were the artists, the leaders, the teachers, the mathematicians, and the poets of their time. In the beginning only craftsmen were admitted to the Order, but as learning was difficult to achieve, and scholarly men rare, it was but natural that such men should apply and be accepted, not as operative craftsmen, but as "accepted" Masons.

3

The Accepted Masons gradually became the majority in many of the lodges, particularly in England in the 17th century, when the erection of great buildings was brought to a stand-still with the coming of the Reformation. The organization known as "Freemasonry" was in danger of being extinguished. To prevent that, the members of the lodges that met at the Goose and Gridiron Alehouse, the Crown Alehouse, the Rummer and Grapes Tavern, and the Apple-Tree Tavern, met at the latter's Lodge room on June 24, 1717, and formed what was to become the first of many grand lodges of Speculative Freemasons.

The *Regius Manuscript,* the oldest known Masonic document, written about 1390 A.D., dates the Craft in England from the time of Athelstane, 924 A.D. There is strong evidence that the date was closer to 597 A.D., when Augustine visited the Anglo-Saxons as a missionary, reportedly bringing several *Liberi Muratori* (Freemasons) with him.

From the beginning of Freemasonry to the present, Masons have passed through wars, conflagrations, and persecutions. The Craft has been hurt, sometimes almost extinguished, only to spring back stronger than ever.

War gave birth to the Masonic Service Association in 1919. It was formed in Cedar Rapids, Iowa, by a group of dedicated Masons who saw the need for an adequate method by which American Freemasonry could function unitedly to give aid and relief to the distressed in times of emergency. No central agency was in existence, as each grand lodge was, and is, an entity in itself. During, and after, World War II the service it rendered to military personnel, both men and women, whether or not they were connected with Masonry, more than justified the trust of the founders and its supporters.

While no such organization existed during the Civil War, the unity of Freemasonry was still apparent. Lodges met within the sound of guns and the din of battle. Masons wearing blue, joined hands with those clad in gray, in peace and harmony. The sounds of war were stilled while Southern Masons buried their brothers from the North. Grand lodges in the North sent money to grand lodges in the South to help destitute families where the scenes of battle were vivid. Masons of both sections

4

were merciful angels about the prison camps. Churches and other organizations were torn apart, but Masons had been taught toleration and helped one another. And when the war was over, it was Freemasonry that helped to heal the wounds of ill-will and aided in bringing the North and the South together.

The early history of Freemasonry on the American continent is shrouded in darkness. When the first lodge was formed no one knows, and although an eminent Masonic historian, J. L. Gould, states that a Masonic lodge was held in Newport, Rhode Island from 1658 to 1742, other historians are skeptical. Benjamin Franklin, who was some three years away from being a Mason, wrote in the pages of his newspaper in 1730 that there were "several Lodges of Freemasons" in Pennsylvania. A lodge was formed in Boston, Massachusetts at least as early as 1733. The same year a lodge came into existence in Norfolk, Virginia, according to John Dove and William Moseley Brown, two Virginia historians.

From the 1730's on, Freemasonry in the colonies of the "New World" made great strides. The Craft went about its business, adhering to its ancient laws which would not permit religion and politics to enter the lodge. But Masons, as individuals, took an active part in community activities. The Masonic lodges were the units of community life in which men who cherished freedom most, associated themselves to face the issues of survival and progress.

For years the people in the 13 colonies had been dissatisfied with the attitude of the English rulers. They were particularly irritated about what they termed "taxation without representation." Masonic historians have often wondered whether there would be a nation called "The United States" if those rulers in Great Britian had followed the practice of the Grand Lodge of England. No tax was ever levied on any lodge outside of England by that grand lodge. The money it received from the lodges in the colonies went into its charity fund, and that money was strictly donated.

A crisis in Boston was reached when three large Indiamen, loaded with tea, dropped anchor in Boston Harbor. Governor Hutchinson, who knew the sentiments of the people, did nothing to ease that crisis. After a lengthy conference with his advisors in the Old South Church, on the evening of December 16, 1773, the governor announced that the tea would be unloaded, sold, and the tax thereon collected. The tax-conscious citizens rebelled! Samuel Adams greeted that decision with, "This meeting can do nothing more to save the country!"

To Griffith Wharf came the "Mohawk Indians," from the *Green Dragon Tavern*—home of St. Andrew's Lodge! The "Indians," comprised of the members of that lodge and members of the North End Caucus, dumped 342 chests of tea into the harbor. The march away from suppression was started with Masons like Paul Revere, whom a poet named Longfellow was to make immortal; Dr. Joseph Warren, who was to fall at Bunker Hill; and John Hancock, who was to *boldly* sign a paper that could have been his death warrant, the Declaration of Independence. Their deeds, and those of a host of other Masons during the Revolution, have been covered extensively by Masonic historians.

Freemasonry was destined to survive another crisis and to help give the United States the best form of government ever contrived by man. (It is claimed that more than 30 of the delegates to the Constitutional Convention were Freemasons.) But the enemies of the Fraternity continued to work against it. They put forth their greatest efforts during the anti-Masonic craze that started in 1826 and lasted for more than 20 years.

The Craft had hardly recovered from that affair when another great calamity struck—Civil War!

The spirit of brotherly-love instilled in Freemasons was in existence during the trying decade prior to the war. Many Masons were responsible for the series of compromises made during the 1850's, which stilled for a time the talk of secession. But those compromises were to end in failure. Part of the reason they were unsuccessful is summed up in this paragraph by Harold V. Faulkner:

One cause of the failure of compromise was undoubtedly the passing from the scene of the older statesmen, those able political leaders who had risen to power in the nationalistic era following the War of 1812. Van Buren had retired from national politics, and

6

Benton had lost his seat in the Senate in 1851. Clay died in June of 1852 and Webster in October of the same year. Compromisers anxious to preserve the Union were still to be found in national politics, such men as Douglas of Illinois, Marcy of New York, Bell of Tennessee, and Crittenden of Kentucky, but in the end it was the radicals of the North and South who were to prevail. Among the younger and ardent antislavery politicians of the North were Charles Sumner of Massachusetts, William H. Seward, formerly Whig governor of New York, and Salmon P. Chase of Ohio. Opposed to them were Southern secessionists of the type of Barnwell Rhett of South Carolina and J. A. Quitman and Albert G. Brown of Mississippi, who were joined in the late fifties by such former Unionists as Jefferson Davis of Mississippi and Robert Toombs of Georgia.

Nine of the men named by Faulkner were Masons: Thomas H. Benton, Henry Clay, Stephen A. Douglas, Lewis Cass, John Bell, John J. Crittenden, John A. Quitman, Brown, and Toombs. Two of them had been grand masters; Clay of Kentucky, and Cass of both Ohio and Michigan. At least one, Seward, was a violent anti-Mason and had served in the New York State Senate as a member of the Anti-Masonic Party from 1830-34. Another, Jefferson, was known to be friendly to Freemasonry and his father, Samuel, and his brother, Joseph, were Masons.

During 1854, Senator Douglas, after a ten year struggle, managed to have the Kansas-Nebraska Bill pass the Congress. That bill wiped out the Missouri Compromise by permitting the settlers to decide whether the area was to be free or slave. Both sides rushed people into Kansas, and bloody fighting raged. More than 200 persons were killed and property damage ran into the millions. The passage of that bill was a stupendous blunder, for it hastened the bloodshed between the North and the South.

The agitation continued unabated. Each state had its champion for the other section's cause. Masons as well as other citizens were among both groups. All concerned felt they were in the right.

Long before 1860 some of the Southern states made it clear they would secede from the Union if the Northern states won control of the national government. The people of the South felt the North had won when Abraham Lincoln was elected president. He won the election by defeating three Freemasons —Stephen A. Douglas, John C. Breckinridge, and John Bell.

His election caused this declaration on December 20, 1860:

The union now existing between South Carolina and other States under the name of the United States of America is hereby dissolved.

To help prove that South Carolina had become a separate nation, the *Charleston Mercury* headed all items from New York, and other Northern cities, as "Foreign News." As 1860 came to a close, one star was missing from the union of the North American states.

The action of South Carolina caused Henry M. Phillips, grand master of the Grand Lodge of Pennsylvania, in his annual address December 27 to say:

. . . I am compelled, brethren, by a sad but imperative necessity, to call your attention to another subject, to which Masons cannot be indifferent, and which, I doubt not, is frequently in your thoughts—I mean the present condition of our country. A year ago, on my installation as Grand Master, I took occasion to say to you, *"you should* repress any attempt whatever, made to weaken or to *destroy the bond of union* that binds together in the brotherhood of liberty the whole American People. I speak thus to you because the spirit of *strife and discord* is about our country." I then had an instinct of approaching danger, and I desired to warn you and to awaken in you such an apprehension of peril to existence of the Union, to the preservation of the liberties, and to the safety of your institutions, as would make you, in every relation of life, exert and use your influence to avert the political evils which selfish strife and ambitious discord were calculated to engender. At this time, alas, the danger is imminent—the Constitution of the United States, framed by the wisest body of men that was ever assembled, has been violated, and the Union of the States—the model government of the world—*the* land of liberty—the only asylum for the persecuted and oppressed of all the nations of the world, is now in danger of disruption and producing a civil—a fraticidal war. To our brethren throughout the nation we make an affectionate and a Masonic appeal to practice out of the Lodge those principles of forbearance, generosity, conciliation, charity and brotherly love they are taught within it, to unite as a brotherhood to preserve the glorious work in which so many of our honored brethren participated, and to aid in restoring the peace, harmony, good will and friendly relations that should exist among the whole American people.

John Dove, chairman of the committee on foreign correspondence for the Grand Lodge of Virginia, took note of the turmoil in the country, and ten days before South Carolina seceded, wrote:

> . . . The devout Mason had, at this moment, real reason to be thankful to his Grand Master that, while outside the Masonic Temple, the lowering clouds and muttering thunder of discordant factions are now seen and heard in form and tone, at which the patriot's heart stands aghast and almost riven with apprehensions of the future, he had graciously permitted to infer, that his gracious and priceless boon has been vouchsafed to us for some wise and beneficent purpose—it may be, to be instrumental in allaying the angry tumult of popular frenzy? Let, then, the three hundred thousand patriotic Masons, good and true, of the United States, unite in fervent prayer to our Heavenly Grand Master, that he may be pleased to will that this bitter cup of tribulation may pass from this once-blessed and happy nation, and that the angry passions of popular prejudice may yield to the softening influence of brotherly love and friendship. Let us unite in heartfelt orisons to invoke the spirits of WASHINGTON and WARREN, our almost sainted Brothers, to intercede for us in restoring our distracted country to peace and harmony, and make her again what she once boasted of being, the asylum of the oppressed in every clime, a beacon light for all nations.

All through the years before the strife that was to pit father against son, and brother against brother, Freemasons, and all other right thinking men and women, worked to prevent war. The fanatics on both sides won—the citizens of the United States lost.

CHAPTER II

Freemasonry Seeks Prevention Of the Catastrophe

◇◇◇

> *War is the greatest plague that can afflict humanity; it destroys religion, it destroys families. Any scourge is preferable to it.*
>
> MARTIN LUTHER

THE COMPLETE story about the acts of Freemasons, in lodges and as individuals, during the trying years prior to the outbreak of hostilities, will never be learned. What was said and done can only be told in part, for until recent years much that could have been written was not. While Masonry has few secrets, far too much is never recorded in the minutes of the subordinate lodge.

Grand Master Love S. Cornwell, during his annual address to the Grand Lodge of Missouri in 1856, spoke with great foresight:

This is a year of universal political excitement; our whole country seems to be convulsed to its very center; questions of policy are agitated that seem to tend directly and speedily to a dissolution of the union of these States. The Constitution and laws are frequently set at defiance and trampled under foot, parties are being formed of every political cast, and our country filled with secret political and benevolent societies; demagogues, through religious fanaticism, are endeavoring to elevate themselves to honor and distinction, by the agitation of questions that should rarely ever be discussed, expecting to ride upon the whirlwind, and guide the storm that will place them in a position they are frequently poorly qualified to fill. *The great trouble will be that the storm may not only carry them, but also the innocent, into civil war, anarchy and confusion.*

10

It will be well, my brethren, for us to look at the great mission of Masonry, and learn our duty. Masonry requires of its devotees, "that they be peaceable and quiet subjects of the country in which they reside; never be concerned in plots and conspiracies against the government, but to conform cheerfully to its laws." They also are bound by their tenure to obey the moral law. Where, then, is the Mason who will disregard those wholesome tenets of our institution?

Where is the Mason who will suffer himself to be drawn into those angry discussions that may cause his blood to mingle with that of his brothers?

Where is the Mason, who will so far disregard the great moral taught him from the use of one of the great lights of Masonry first presented to his vision in a Masonic Lodge, as to "let his passions or prejudices betray him beyond due bounds?" If we have any such within our jurisdiction, let me say to my brother, reflect, return, and again place your feet upon a basis, "that makes all men honorable who conform to its precepts."

* * *

Is our glorious Confederacy under which we have flourished threatened with dissolution? Let Masons do their duty, and all the powers of earth, together with all the machinations of evil men, cannot cause this noble edifice to shake. Look what a bond of union, extending from Maine to Florida, from Massachusetts to Oregon, all "bound by their tenure to obey the moral law, and to be obedient subjects to the Constitution and laws of the land in which they reside." Where is the Mason who does not regard the perpetuity of our union as a paramount question? Who would not shed his blood, if necessary, to uphold and sustain its Constitution?

These things being true, who doubts the perpetuity of our government? Is there a Mason hailing from the land of the Puritans, who so far forgets his duty as to set laws at defiance, and attempt to propagate his political creed by force of arms, although advised by that course by the degenerate sons, desecrating the sacred desk of their Puritan fathers? Or is there a Mason hailing from the sunny South, proverbial for honor, generosity and benevolence, that is willing to sacrifice this temple of freedom, upon the altar of ambition? No, rather let all Masons who enter upon the political arena, carry emblazoned on their banners the wreath of lily work speaking peace, and the emblem of right hands joined, denoting fidelity to our common country. Let us not, my brethren, indulge in harsh epithets towards each other, although we may be found connected with all political parties; let our truly Masonic virtues never be

11

lost sight of, let no motive cause us to swerve from our duty, violate our vows, or betray our trust.

From the annual addresses of many grand masters, and the committees on foreign correspondence, we learn that Cornwell was not the only one concerned with what was taking place in the political arena, although he was among the few who saw a civil war within the foreseeable future.

Grand Master R. R. Rees, during the annual communication of the Grand Lodge of Kansas, October 20, 1856, opened his address with these remarks:

Through the kindness and under the protecting care of overruling Providence, we are permitted to assemble once again in Grand Communication, and though the past Masonic year has been one of turmoil, or contention, and of angry conflict in the outer world, yet peace and quietude have reigned within the retirement of our Sanctum. . . .

During the same communication, William Walker read a letter from the Grand Lodge of New York, dated August 22, 1856 which referred to the blood being shed because of the passage of the Kansas-Nebraska Bill.

The Lodges of Free and Accepted Masons of the City of New York send to their brethren in Kansas Territory their fraternal greetings and salutations. Hearing, continually, with painful emotions, of the political convulsions and social disorders that distract that distant land, avail themselves of this occasion of tendering their heartfelt sympathies to their western brethren in the midst of their troubles. Amidst the bitter contests that once raged between the Guelphs and Gibolines—amidst the sanguinary outbreaks and lawless acts so fearfully raging amongst you, let our time-honored, our ancient Temple be kept uncontaminated with the surrounding atrocities—maintain its purity and moral grandeur amidst the warring elements.

Let her do her kind offices in mitigating the severities of civil war, which in the days of other years, have marked her career through far more fearful and protracted scenes and come out unscathed, unsullied, and without "the smell of fire upon her garments," and stood forth luminous, the admiration of the moral world.

That sanguinary conflict was described by J. M. Pelot, M.D.,

12

grand lecturer and grand orator, of the Grand Lodge of Kansas, in an address before that grand lodge, October 18, 1859:

... A man may be a Mason who would respond to the cry of distress, or relieve the destitute, with as much alacrity as any of us, and yet be brutal in the extreme to all else than his brethren. Witness the case of Tecumseh, viewing with pleasure the inhuman butchery of his traditional enemies; and yet how quick was he, on seeing the mystic sign, to command: "Let the slaughter cease!" ... What beautiful illustrations are exhibited, in scenes of war, of the strength of the mystic tie! With us in Kansas, it was the only link that bound together Americans of opposite politics, though the same Anglo-Saxon blood coursed through their veins. It was not an uncommon spectacle to see brethren arrayed against each other, with arms in their hands, "meeting on the level and parting on the square," with mingled emotions of pain and gratitude towards the Institution that conferred the high privilege of joining hands. Our history is rich in illustrations of this kind, but I can only relate a few that came under my personal observation.

In August, 1856, when the citizens of Lawrence and Lecompton met only at the point of the bayonet, I had the honor to accompany Acting Deputy Grand Master, O. C. Stewart, to Lawrence, for the purpose of instituting the lodge and installing the officers at that place. We saw numbers of armed men, and heard numbers of prisoners who had been arrested for encroaching on the bounds of a *corps d'armee,* and without that universal passport, which Masonry gave us, we certainly would have shared the prisoner's tent. But we were not molested nor insulted in our peaceful mission, and the brethren received us hospitably and parted with us fraternally.

On what was thought to be the eve of a great battle, a certain commander-in-chief of one party blundered into the camp of his adversary. Of course he was detained a prisoner of war, until it was discovered that he was a Mason, when he was immediately released and escorted beyond the reach of danger.

A Colonel who had rendered himself conspicuous, was, after a hard fought battle, taken prisoner and conducted to headquarters for court-martial, when it was confidently expected that his life would pay the forfeit of his unenviable notoriety. An officer who knew him to be a brother declared that he would die before the prisoner should be injured. The court sat, and for some *inexplicable* reason, his judges were lenient and the prisoner was released. I heard a judge whose court was broken up and whose life was spared only by the interposition of his Masonic brothers.

I saw a poor fellow brought into camp as a spy. He protested

13

his innocence, and pled to be allowed to return to his unprotected wife and children, who were suffering in his absence. But all in vain. Finally he resorted to a mystic sign, when the commander saw the force of his arguments and turned him loose.

Many of us, brethren, who sit around this altar today, occupied a far different position toward each other four years ago. It may not be deemed good taste nor propriety to indulge in such personalities; but I cannot see the objection. I would that Freemasonry in Kansas has a history worthy of her noble fame, and such examples of Brotherly Love, Relief and Truth were spread upon the eternal record. Whatever the past may show, however, the present calls forth the most hearty congratulations on your brilliant success and the happy future that is before you.

Unknown to Pelot, that happy future was to last for less than two years from the day he spoke.

The grand master of Georgia, William S. Rockwell, was also optimistic on October 26, 1859, in his annual address:

I am gratified to announce the continued prosperity of the Order within our own limits; and so far as appears from the Proceedings of the Grand Lodges of the Union, unbroken harmony now reigns among them all. The various schisms and dissensions once painfully disturbing the peaceful current of Masonic events, are now composed and set at rest; no longer the vivid topics of earnest and exciting debate; their huge and darkening forms, as they loom up among the recollections of the past, warn us emphatically how easy it is for even brothers to disagree, and what fatal results can flow from an obscure and trivial source. Let us remember and rely upon the doctrine which Israel's royal psalmist teaches: "Abundant is theirs who delight in the law of JEHOVAH; they shall never be made to stumble."

Another "schism" that was to plague the grand lodges of the Confederate States and the United States all through the Civil War was on the horizon. Rob Morris, a past grand master of Kentucky, had formed an organization known as the "Conservators" with the idea of giving to all American Symbolic Masonry a common ritual. That organization had a hectic life; most grand lodges frowned upon it. Many of them felt it was an organization within Freemasonry whose members were to infiltrate and command every grand lodge in America. Others believed Morris was sincere; that the idea was patriotic and

14

generous. It flourished, or appeared to, during the early years of the war, but died when the war came to a close.

On February 22, 1860, James Buchanan, president of the United States, and a past master of a Pennsylvania lodge, joined the Grand Lodge of the District of Columbia in the dedication ceremonies of the equestrian statue of Washington. During the service the gavel that was used by George Washington when he acted as grand master at the laying of the corner-stone of the capitol of the nation, was presented to President Buchanan. He had this to say:

I perform this act of pious devotion, not in the name of the people of the North, of the South, the East or the West—not in the name of those who dwell on the waters of the Atlantic, or of the far Pacific, but in the name of the whole American people, united, one and indivisible, now and forever. [Applause] May the God of our fathers preserve the Constitution and the Union for ages yet to come. May they stand like the everlasting hills, against which the tempest from every quarter of the heavens shall beat in vain. In a word, may they endure as long as the name of Washington shall be honored and cherished among the children of men. [Renewed and prolonged applause] May Washington City, which he founded, continue throughout many generations to be the seat of government of a great, powerful, prosperous and united Confederacy. Should it ever become a ruin by a dissolution of the Union, it will not, like the ruins of Balbic and Palmyra, be merely a monument of the vanity of human greatness, but it will teach the lesson to all the dwellers upon earth, that our grand political experiment has failed, and that man is incapable of self-government. May such a direful disaster to the human race be averted, and in the language of SOLOMON, at the dedication of the Jewish Temple, "May the Lord our God be with us as he was with our fathers. Let Him not leave us or forsake us." [Applause] May this be the prayer of all present, and may each one return to his home in heart more determined to do his whole duty to God and his country, than when we assembled here today.

People from all over the country were present at that dedication, and it would appear from their applause during the president's speech, which was Masonic in spirit, that unity was what was desired by everyone above all else.

Rev. Thomas Taylor, grand orator of the Grand Lodge of Tennessee, in October, 1860, said:

15

Now is the time when every true Mason should seek to guide the Ship of State with a well-directed hand, and be sure to mingle his lessons of prudence in all he says and does.

I must be permitted to say, that should our nation remain prosperous and happy—should her gates be enlarged and her stakes be strengthened—it will be done by Masonic hands, by principles embodied in our Order. It is my opinion, that when the last political cord shall be broken, there will be one still stronger uniting us together, which is indissoluble.

Few of Taylor's listeners realized how prophetic his last sentence was to prove during the trying years ahead.

On the fifth of November of the same year, Albert Pike presented his credentials as representative of the Grand Lodge of Kansas Near the Grand Lodge of Arkansas to his grand lodge, meeting at Little Rock:

I am glad to present these credentials now . . . when clouds and shadows form ominously over the Republic and darken even the peaceful calms of Masonry with doubts and dismay. These greetings that I convey to you are proof that the strong ties of Masonic obligations, Masonic affections and Masonic brotherhood, are not yet, like so many others, snapped asunder, but that they still endure and there is yet peace, and calm, and harmony around our holy altars, though the elements without are gloomily ominous of disaster and the atmosphere is oppressive as when an earthquake is near at hand. I am sure that all these brethren will unite with me in the earnest, anxious wish, that some power may say to the tumultuous waves, "Peace! be still!"—that the bonds of friendship and good neighborhood may be re-knit and strengthened, and anger and recrimination cease, and that all the great moral and social influences of Masonry may be exerted, honestly and unceasingly, for the restoration of harmony, the maintenance of peace, and the performance of duty. And may it not be the evil fortune of any of us, . . . to live to see the dark and fearful day when our great chain of brotherhood shall be broken and shivered into fragments, never again to be united.

To which the grand master of the Grand Lodge of Arkansas, Elbert H. English replied.

We most heartily concur in the statement that, while the political relations existing between the States are unfortunately being weakened, and the calmest and wisest patriots are looking with fearful forebodings to the result of the impending crisis, the fraternal relations existing between the members of the Masonic family should

16

be strengthened and preserved, so that CHARITY and HUMAN-ITY may ameliorate the untold *evils* that will inevitably follow, should God, in His providence, permit the Union of the States to be severed!

Six months and one day later Arkansas was to join her sister states of the South and enter the fight against that union she truly wanted to preserve. Later, it was only through those ties of brotherly love that the Masonic library of a Confederate general, Albert Pike, was saved from destruction when the grand master of Iowa, a Federal colonel, placed a guard about the building to keep it from being burned.

The Grand Lodge of North Carolina held its annual communication on December 3, 1860. Within the address of the grand master, Lewis L. Williams, was this:

While we would implore Him to stay the hand of wild fanaticism and sectional strife which threatens disaster and destruction to our country, we would return our heartfelt thanks that no sectional divisions have been permitted to enter our sacred portals. Let us, then, invoke the Genius of Masonry to endue us with that spirit of brotherly love which will lead us to a discharge of those high duties entrusted to our care with that noble emulation of who can best work and agree.

The strife going on in the political field did not go unnoticed in Virginia, where the grand lodge met in annual communication on December 10. Grand Master John R. McDaniel speaks about it:

While strife and discord rage without our beloved Institution, all within is calm and peaceful, and regularly and steadily adding to its members and increasing in usefulness—diffusing its benefits and blessings as the great regulator of the passions and propensities of the human heart, when applied in accordance with the principles laid down in the "Great Light," which is the rule and guide of a Mason's faith and practice.

The Grand Chapter, Royal Arch Masons of Virginia met on December 13 in Richmond. Of the impending struggle and the events leading up to it, John Dove wrote:

... But if separation must come, if the Bird of Jove is driven from his splendid eyrie, let him not be harrowed with the mortifying re-

17

flection, as he flies to some mountain height to die, that his own wing furnished the feather which gave the deadly aim of the envenomed arrow. But rather, when we have exhausted every effort at compromise and reconciliation, and the very last ray of hope is about departing from the patriot statesman's vision in the western horizon, and the black and rayless night of anarchy is about to shroud his mind with gloomy forebodings of the future, which God only can see—let not this night close in . . . but let us agree to separate amicably, as brothers, each traveling a different road, and each having a different aim and end to accomplish amongst the great family of nations.

Dr. Winslow Lewis, grand master of the Grand Lodge of Massachusetts, told his grand lodge on December 27:

Go on, brothers, in the cultivation of every noble and manly quality. Let the pure principles of our Order rule and regulate your lives; let justice, temperance, mercy, truth and charity, be the prevailing sentiments of your hearts, and let those hearts be warm and kindled so that

> "Friend, parent, neighbor, first it will embrace—
> Your country next, and next all human race.
> Wide and more wide, the o'erflowing of the mind,
> Take every creature in of every kind.
> Earth smiles around, with every bounty blest,
> And Heaven beholds its image in our breast."

Later it was announced that the following letter was sent on the same day the Grand Lodge of Virginia was meeting in its annual communication:

Boston, Dec. 10th, 1860.
M W G. Master of the Gd. Lodge of Virginia.
Dear Brother.

The period has arrived (alas! that it should ever be so.) when it behoves every one who has lived and flourished under the benign influence of our glorious Union, to exert his best endeavors to obviate that sad impulse which threatens its dissolution. In the relations of fellow-citizens of a wide spread republic, our efforts have proved ineffectual. Fanaticism is the predominate demon, and the ties which have bound the South and North so long together, which carried them shoulder to shoulder in the days of our fathers, and have continued them in their prosperity as a United Nation, are now in preparation to be severed.

Is it too late to avert the calamity? Is there nought remains of

18

conservatism to be tried? Have we not an institution which binds us together not only as fellow citizens but as Brothers, and as Brothers can we lacerate those pledges, the foundation of our Faith and Practice? Therefore may we not look to it as a strong element to allay the bitter anguish of these dark days in our Nation's history?

It was my good fortune to visit Richmond with a band of our Order, and to witness and feel the mighty operation which cemented the hearts of all the participants on that occasion.

The influences of meeting are ineffaceable, the impress indelible, with such feelings of so powerful a fraternization, how disunion must pall the hearts of those whose affections as Brothers are so warmed towards those so dear to them in Virginia, and as one I was resolved to pour out my own, and to express to you what I deem to be the predominate sentiment in Boston, if not in the whole jurisdiction over which I have the honor to preside, and I assure my dear Brother, that we cling to you, not only as Brothers, but as Fellow-citizens; and may that evil day be far removed, when Virginia and Massachusetts, the States which gave to our country a *Washington* and a *Franklin* and to Freemasonry two of its brightest lights, shall be found opposed as enemies, and severed as components of United States.

May God avert that terrible issue: and may He instill into the hearts of all of our Order the observance of that precept of His Holy Word, that first before to every neophyte in Freemasonry: "Behold how good and how pleasant it is for Brethren to dwell together in unity," and may all under your fraternal jurisdiction, demonstrate by their acts, that in the "Old Dominion," as well as among ourselves of the "Old Bay State," union as fellow citizens, and Brotherly Love as Masons, shall now in this, the perilous hour, as heretofore under the days of prosperity, be their aim and Resolve. "So mote it be."

Fraternally yours,
WINSLOW LEWIS, M.D.
Grand Master

That letter, when it was read in the Grand Lodge of Massachusetts, was greeted with:

Great favor and elicited warm and hearty responses from the Brethren, and especially from Col. Ruggles of Virginia who was present as a visitor. It was also voted that the sentiments of the letter be adopted as the sentiments of the G. Lodge, and that it be spread upon the records, and a copy sent to each G. Lodge in the Union. The vote was taken by the Brethren rising and was carried with but two negatives.

Grand Master John R. McDaniel of Virginia answered that letter 11 days after South Carolina had seceded from the Union:

Lynchburg, Dec. 31st, 1860

Dr. Winslow Lewis, Grand Master of *Massachusetts, Boston:*

MOST WORSHIPFUL SIR AND DEAR BROTHER—Your very kind and fraternal favor of the 10th instant came duly to hand, and would have met with an earlier response had I been physically able so to do. By a fall a few nights before, I strained my right wrist and broke both bones in my right arm, which caused me much suffering. I am, and shall be for some time yet, unable to use it.

I most cordially unite with you in mourning the threatened destruction of our once glorious Republic.

It is sad to think of it, the Stars and Stripes, the emblem of the noble patriotism of the heroes of the Revolution, and which has ever since floated in triumph, both on sea and land, wherever it has been thrown to the breeze, should now, by internal dissensions, be torn into shreds and "scattered to the four winds of Heaven."

As a body we can do nothing; but did every individual brother possess, and yield to the dictates of so true and fraternal a heart as beats in your bosom, much could be done as individuals—indeed this state of things would never have existed. Masonry teaches us to be "quiet and peaceful citizens, and cheerfully to submit to the government of the country in which we live." The tenets of our profession teach us to "render to every man his just dues"; but alas! Puritanical fanaticism seems to be the order of the day; constitutional rights are trampled under foot, and the same mad career which attacked our beloved institution in former times, is now leveling its shafts at our country. Can the shield of Masonry avert the deadly thrust? I fear not; but it may do much to weaken its force. Let each individual brother, whether at the North or at the South, feel the awful responsibility that rests upon him, and apply to his conduct the Plumb, the Level and the Square, and whatever they dictate as right, that do, and do it with a will.

The Masonic fireside, and in the body of the respective Lodges, are the places to correct this evil. There impress upon them the duty of going forth as individuals, exerting the influence of its teachings as good and true Masons should.

No Mason should be ostracised for his opinions in religion or politics when within proper bounds. The atheist is excluded, as so should be the enemy of his country.

I do not propose to discuss the questions which now agitate the country, but rather pursue the truly Masonic spirit of your letter, and seek means by which to allay the excitement.

Gladly would I co-operate in any proper way to effect the object,

20

but in all sincerity and unfeigned regret, I say that all is now in vain. The Union is beyond doubt dissolved, and the only hope that remains is, that a peaceful separation may be effected, and the conservative element of both sections may so exert themselves, as to secure the most friendly relations; so that whilst we may not be able to live as one family, we may nevertheless continue forever good neighbors.

The blood of the Old Confederacy is upon the intriguing and unprincipled politicians, and the wolves in Christian clothing. They are welcome to the honor of their achievements. Masonry, pure and genuine, bearing the impress of our "Great High Priest," I trust, will remain unshaken, and whilst it cannot shield our beloved country from the impending storm, yet secure in our existence, we can continue to live in the full existence of Brotherly Love without regard to geographical bounds or political divisions.

Your friend and brother,
JOHN ROBIN McDANIEL, G.M. of Va.

Although South Carolina had seceded and hope of a peaceful settlement between the North and South appeared to be doomed, John J. Crittenden was not ready to see the Union destroyed. He, like his predecessor Henry Clay, believed wholeheartedly in compromise. He hopefully submitted a parcel of compromises to the senate, which, when turned over to a Committee of Thirteen, was killed.

Crittenden, the white-haired Kentucky Freemason, was backed by two other Masons, the "little giant" Douglas, and the "fire-eater" Robert Toombs. The Republicans on the Committee, with the endorsement of Lincoln and his "let there be no compromise" statement, killed what the New York *Tribune* called "the most considerate and conciliatory" proposal of "our opponents."

The abolitionists like Wendell Philips and William Lloyd Garrison, who hated the Constitution of the United States, and the Southern fanatics like Robert Barnwell Rhett, Edmund Ruffin, and William Lownders Yancey were about to win their fight to precipitate "a little blood-letting."

Although they fought for peace until the eleventh hour, Freemasonry and Freemasons could not prevent the catastrophe. The few fanatics, knowing their time was limited, forced the conflagration that came close to destroying the Republic of the United States of America.

21

CHAPTER III

Tragedy

◇◇

The entire decade was one of tragedy. One in which brother spilled the blood of brother for four long years on the fields of battle.

ARCHER BAILEY GAY

WITH THE dawn of the new year, legislatures in several states opened in special sessions. The results of their deliberations were not kept from the people, for the General Assembly of the State of Virginia, meeting in Richmond, on January 8, 1861, left no one in doubt as to Virginia's course with the passage of this resolution:

1. Resolved by the general assembly of Virginia, that the union being formed by the assent of the sovereign states respectively, and being consistent only with freedom and the republican institutions guaranteed to each, cannot and ought not to be maintained by force.

2. That the government of the Union has no power to declare or make war against any of the states which have been its constituent members.

3. Resolved, that when any one or more of the states has determined, or shall determine, under existing circumstances, to withdraw from the Union, we are unalterably opposed to any attempt on the part of the federal government to coerce the same into reunion or submission, and that we will resist the same by all the means in our power.

On January 9, the day that Mississippi became the second Southern state to secede from the Union, the Grand Lodge of Vermont started its annual communication. The grand master, Philip C. Tucker, took note of the foreboding clouds on the horizon:

We meet, upon the present occasion, with a cloud of gloom hang-

22

ing over our beloved Country. One of the stars in our national flag has been torn from its place; our flag itself, as to one portion of our national soil, no longer spreads its folds to the breeze, to typify to all eyes the unity of national freedom, but where it once proudly waved now appears the palmetto and the rattlesnake, sad substitutes indeed for that glorious banner which has heretofore commanded respect in every country where human foot has trod, and in every sea which has borne upon its waves the keel of an American vessel. We are a divided republic, and the last resting-place of republican liberty on earth is no longer one and indivisible. The cannon which perform the bloody mission of war stand charged with the missiles of destruction, desolation and death, their mouths pointed to each other, and the lighted portfire for their discharge is holden by the hands of *brethren,* waiting only for the first discharge from either side. The picture is soul-sickening to every true lover of his country—to every friend of freedom throughout the earth. . . .

There are no symbolic rattlesnakes, either in our Masonic textbooks or upon our master's carpet. One glorious *Star* may be found at the center of our tesselated pavement and a *galaxy* of them in our Masonic canopy.

The committee on foreign correspondence made its report that same evening, before any of the Masons meeting in the Masonic Temple at Burlington, Vermont, knew of Mississippi's action. That report was closed with these words:

. . . Thus throughout the length and breadth of the land, prosperity prevails. Even though now our Southern horizon seems to be overcast with the black clouds of political fanaticism, yet, by the kindly spirit which pervades our brotherhood from Northern frosts to Southern skies, we firmly believe its unseen influence will gradually temper these temporary waves of madness, and make our whole country abide forever and ever, the light, the admiration, the blessing of the world.

After that report was adopted, the grand lodge was "called from labor to refreshment" until the next morning at eight o'clock. The members then met with the other citizens of Burlington to discuss the happenings in the South.

The Grand Lodge of Michigan met in annual communication on the same day as Vermont. Grand Master W. L. Greenly, also took note of what was taking place without the temple, and hoped that, "When all efforts at conciliation shall have failed, our beloved Order, powerful alone for good, may, by a united effort throughout the length and breadth of our land, bring about that harmony which alone can save our common country."

Florida broke relations with the United States on January 10, the day the Grand Lodge of Vermont "resumed labor." Alabama followed on the 11th. When the Grand Lodge of Florida met in annual communication on the 14th, the state was an independent nation. D. C. Dawkins, the grand master, reminded his brethren: "Our deliberations have nothing to do with steering the Ship of State, or of planning or promoting the objects or desires of any political, commercial, or other association, appertaining to the affairs of government."

Before Georgia had seceded on the 19th, her troops had seized Fort Pulaski in Savannah harbor. Two days later, the Grand Lodge of Mississippi met at Vicksburg, a name soon to become well-known throughout the world. The turmoil in the South had its effect on that grand lodge. A past grand master was called on to preside due to the absence of the grand lodge officers, who were attending to "important state business."

North Carolina, by a referendum vote, refused to call a state convention, on the 24th, but on the 26th the Louisiana State Convention adopted an Ordinance of Secession. Texas followed on February 1, the last of the states to break away from the Federal government before all hope of peace was destroyed.

The United States steamer *Star of the West* was fired upon as it entered Charleston harbor shortly after dawn on January 9. It was carrying reinforcements for Major Robert Anderson, a member of Mercer Lodge, No. 50, New Jersey, and commander of the forces in the harbor. The fire from a battery on Morris' Island set the people of the North to demanding of President Buchanan that he send troops into South Carolina to protect and reinforce Fort Sumter. They wanted "action," "but just what 'action' he could have taken is not made to appear," Robert S. Henry states. "He had left but two months of office when states began to secede. The United States, as has so often been the case at critical times, was caught unprepared, with a

24

tiny army of 16,000 men scattered over thousands of miles of frontier."

Among the scattered troops of the United States were those at Camp Floyd, Utah Territory, under the command of a Mason named Albert Sidney Johnston. It appeared that the Mormons had been defying the laws and burning the records of United States district courts. Judge George P. Stiles, one of the district judges, submitted an affidavit to that effect to the president in 1857. Early in 1858, President Buchanan ordered troops into Utah Territory and they settled on Camp Floyd as their headquarters.

Among the officers and men at the camp were several Masons. They wrote to the Grand Lodge of Missouri requesting a dispensation to organize a Masonic lodge, to be called Rocky Mountain Lodge. On March 6, 1859, the dispensation was granted by the grand master of Missouri, Samuel H. Saunders. John C. Robinson was named master; Henry W. Tracy and Carter L. Stevenson, senior and junior wardens.

General B. M. Thomas, of Dalton, Georgia, who was a lieutenant at the formation of Rocky Mountain Lodge, No. 205, furnished an account of the building in which the lodge met:

Our Lodge room was built of adobe brick. . . . We had men detailed to saw timber into plank, in the hills nearby. The saws worked vertically with men above and below the log, to alternately pull and push the saw. Our buildings were roofed with those planks and covered with dirt. We had no floor, yet in that room was generated the noble brotherly influences which softened the horrors of war [the Civil War] throughout the length and breadth of our country. . . . The windows of our Lodge room were on the north and south sides and were very high up the walls—more for ventilation than light. . . . The dimensions were about 60 x 30 feet, walls of adobe, covered with plank. . . .

The Lodge, unlike some of the military lodges that were to follow, was extremely careful of the men it accepted, but even so, 162 degrees were conferred in a single year! The equivalent of making 54 Masons! H. W. Tracy, the acting master, believing that would cause "some discussion at [the] meeting of the grand lodge" wrote, "In explanation of the matter would state that many of the parties desiring admission had been kept waiting for the granting of a dispensation since the arrival of the troops . . . in Utah, which caused many applications on the night of our first meeting, which has continued to this time. But one thing I can assure you, grand lodge cannot boast of better material than this lodge has engrafted upon our ancient and honorable institution."

In the latter part of 1860 and early 1861 the unrest in the country was being felt in Utah Territory. On December 27, 1860 the secretary of Rocky Mountain Lodge, Richard Wilson, "Sargent, Co. C, 4th Art.," wrote to the grand secretary of the Grand Lodge of Missouri and enclosed the annual returns. He called attention to the vacancy in the office of senior warden, which had been occupied by Henry Heth. He evidently explained that Heth had resigned to cast his lot with the South, for on June 17, 1861, Heth was made a colonel of Virginia Infantry, commissioned a brigadier-general in January, 1862, and in May, 1863, he became a major-general. He and John C. Robinson, who was to become a Union major-general, opposed each other during the battle of Gettysburg. Both men, as well as others from this lodge, were to distinguish themselves during many battles of the Civil War.

The Grand Lodge of Missouri was to hear no more from Rocky Mountain Lodge, No. 205. Its members were scattered throughout the country, but the effect that lodge left on Masonry will never be forgotten.

Masons and well-meaning citizens continued to hold out hope for a peaceful settlement of the difficulties existing between the two great sections of the country. A "Peace Convention" called by Virginia met in Washington on February 4, but could accomplish nothing. On the 9th, Jefferson Davis was elected president and Alexander H. Stephens, who had fought to keep Georgia in the Union, vice-president of the Confederate States. They were inaugurated at Montgomery, Alabama on the 18th.

John B. Floyd, a member of St. Johns Lodge, No. 36, Virginia, Buchanan's Secretary of War, was accused of transferring rifles to Southern arsenals. He demanded and received an immediate trial, and a committee from the house of representatives completely exonerated him.

Brigadier General Pierre Gustave Toutant Beauregard, who is thought to have been a Mason and Knight Templar, arrived at Charleston to take charge of the preparations for reinforcing the harbor against an expected attack from Federal forces on March 3, the day before Lincoln was inaugurated the 16th President of the United States.

As Buchanan had done, Lincoln waited. He had no choice. The Confederate States did not, however. Calls were issued repeatedly for militia, and work went on in Charleston. One by one the arsenals and forts that belonged to the United States surrendered, without bloodshed, to Confederate forces.

All thoughts were focused toward Fort Sumter, a ledge on a man-made isle formed of granite blocks obtained from New England, protecting a harbor in South Carolina. Anderson, the Federal commander of the fort, could do nothing but watch his former pupil and brother Mason, Beauregard, surround his garrison with armament. Lincoln's cabinet was in almost complete accord about the wisdom of giving up the fort, but not so Lewis Cass who had been secretary of state under Buchanan. When Lincoln hesitated to supply Fort Sumter, he resigned in protest. Earlier Cass had said, "I speak to Cobb and he tells me he is a Georgian; to Floyd, and he tells me he is a Virginian; to you, and you tell me you are a Carolinian. I am not a Michigander; I am a citizen of the United States."

On the 9th of April, the state department in Washington refused to receive the Confederate state commissioners. Anderson was asked to surrender his fort on the 10th, and on the 11th a final demand for capitulation was made. He refused. Early in the morning of the 12th, a fleet of United States vessels arrived off the bar of Charleston harbor. At 4:30 a.m., as the first gray light of dawn appeared on the horizon, a shell from the howitzer battery on James Island, under the command of Captain George S. James, was fired. The resulting holocaust was reported extensively by the Charleston *Courier,* on Saturday, April 13. That report contained this paragraph:

We dare not close this brief and hurried narrative of the first engagement between the United States and the Confederate States, without returning thanks to Almighty God for the great success that has thus far crowned our arms, and for the extraordinary preservation of our soldiers from casualty and death. In the fifteen hours of almost incessant firing, our enemy one of the most experienced and skilful of artillerists, no injury has been sustained by a single one of our gallant soldiers.

Throughout the war men on both sides were to call upon God for assistance. He was to be thanked for victories, and in defeat asked to make the next battle a victory. Ministers and priests in the North told their congregations they had God on their side; Southern churchmen said the same. Among them were Masons like Thomas Starr King, a Unitarian clergyman, who spoke throughout the country on the importance of upholding the Union, and James H. Otey, an Episcopal bishop of Tennessee, who took the opposite view.

Not a man was killed on either side during the bombardment of Sumter, but on Sunday morning, as Major Anderson and his men left the fort, the United States flag was raised to receive the national salute of 100 guns, and a gun on the 50th round burst, killing one and wounding five. Private Daniel Hough was the first of nearly 500,000 to die in a war that claimed more American lives than any previous war, or of the three great wars that were to follow; a war that began with the commanding officers on both sides Freemasons.

An era that had been a war of words had ended—a shooting war had begun.

CHAPTER IV

Stalemate

◇◇

*I would urge . . . that we look on this great
struggle not merely as a set of military operations, but as a period in our history in which
the times called for extraordinary degrees of
patriotism and heroism on the part of men and
women of both the North and the South.*
DWIGHT D. EISENHOWER

THE FIRING on Fort Sumter and the surrender of Major
Robert Anderson caused the threatening war to become a
reality. The Confederate government became enraged when
Lincoln called for troops in the number of "75,000, in order to
suppress said combinations [Confederate States] and to cause
the laws to be duly executed."

To that proclamation, B. Magoffin, the governor of Kentucky, replied: "Your dispatch is received. In answer, I say emphatically, Kentucky will furnish no troops for the wicked purpose of subduing her sister southern States." The governor of
North Carolina, John W. Ellis, a Mason, telegraphed the President that he could not respond to the call for troops, as he had
doubts of his authority and right to do so.

Governor Isham G. Harris, a member of Paris Lodge, No.
108, replied: "Tennessee will not furnish a single man for
coercion, but fifty thousand, if necessary, for the defense of
our rights or those of our Southern brothers." The governors
of Virginia, Maryland, Arkansas, Missouri, and Delaware, also
refused to furnish troops for the Federal government.

Elsewhere the sentiment was entirely different. Governors
and citizens hastened to answer Lincoln's call, and feelings were
anything but calm throughout the country. At a meeting in

29

Jersey City, a fellow demanded the striking down of every Northern man who advocated secession, and all "traitorous newspapers." His statement led another man to propose that the people call upon the proprietors of the *American Standard* there, "The editor of which had so much maligned the Government, and make them hoist the American flag, or make them leave town." That proposition was received with tremendous cheering, and cries of, "Let's do it tonight!"

The citizens of several border states did not agree with their governors' action in refusing to send troops, but not so those in Arkansas, Tennessee, and North Carolina. In Virginia on April 17, the general assembly stated: "That said constitution of the United States of America is no longer binding on any citizen of this State." The vast majority of the people upheld that declaration on the 23rd of May, but the Western counties declared their independence from their mother state and formed another which they called "West Virginia." The Grand Lodge of Virginia thereby suffered the greatest numerical loss in Masons of any state in America because of the Civil War.

Lincoln called for a naval blockade of all Southern ports on April 19. On the same day, the Sixth Massachusetts Regiment, with Colonel Edward F. Jones, a Mason, arrived in Washington, after fighting its way through the streets of Baltimore.

From Utah Territory, Mrs. Maria Gove, wife of Jesse Gove, a member of Rocky Mountain Lodge, No. 205, wrote to her sister on May 1:

We have received no orders as yet, but are in a great state of excitement to know what is to be done with the troops here. Our last Pony Express brought intelligence that Col. Smith had command of troops in Washington, that Virginia had seceded, the mob in Baltimore killing some of the Massachusetts men, etc., all of which enraged us beyond measure. We have very spirited and almost quarrelsome discussions with Virginians, and with those who glory with the South in their rebellion.

A number of Virginians here are now talking of going to defend their State, and it is high time for them to leave. . . .

I have hung a flag up in my parlour. I never was so proud of my being a Northerner [New Hampshire], and I tell all who come in they must salute the stars and stripes.

30

Grand lodges throughout the country, and Masons as individuals, were doing everything within their power to bring about peace. If that was to prove unsuccessful, they hoped to be able to mitigate the horrors of an all out war. Among the many letters written was one from the Grand Lodge of Tennessee, and sent to every other grand lodge:

GRAND LODGE OF TENNESSEE, FREE and
ACCEPTED MASONS
Nashville, May 1, 1861

MOST WORSHIPFUL SIR AND BROTHER:

In addressing you this communication, we are sure no apology need be offered. The unhappy circumstances under which our country is now laboring are such as to arouse the deepest feeling of every heart. But recently occupying a position of proud pre-eminence among the Nations of the earth—the hope of the lovers of civil and religious freedom—we find her now apparently upon the verge of a conflict of arms, that unless speedily arrested will form a dark and bloody epoch in the history of the human race. From the contemplation of the horrible spectacle of State arrayed against State, friend against friend, and even brother against brother, we shudderingly look around for some means of escape from the dire calamity that seems so certainly impending over us as a people. With deep mortification, and sorrow, and dread, we look into the dark gulf of human passion, we see its billows heaving with fearful excitement, and, horrified by the sight, we instinctively raise our feeble arms and in hopelessness of spirit, exclaim, *Great God, is there no help in this time of need? Who may stay the wrath of the whirlwind?*

For the causes that have led to the unparalleled spectacle now presented to the world, it is no province of ours to inquire. That wrongs have been committed by both parties to the dreadful combat that seems to be so rapidly approaching, we are not called upon to admit or deny. The causes and the wrongs will be fully judged by the future historian, and when this page of impartial history is written—the dark record of a nation torn by contending factions—rent asunder by animosities engendered by fierce conflicts and the rage of battle—precious lives destroyed, with ruined cities and devastated firesides—tears of bitter anguish will fall upon the leaf of a nation's disgrace, and if possible blot it out forever.

While it is no part of our duty to investigate the causes that have produced the present state of antagonism in political affairs, neither is it our province to suggest a remedy. But as Masons—as members of a common brotherhood—as brethren bound together by fra-

31

ternal ties that are not broken save by the hand of death, we can safely appeal for a cessation of the unnatural strife that is now raging around us, and whose surging billows threaten to overwhelm all in a common destruction. We therefore confidently appeal to the five hundred thousand Masons of our land to step forward, and pouring the oil of peace upon the troubled waters of civil war, roll back the raging tide, and in one united demand make their voices heard in arresting the terrible havoc of fraternal strife. Is it possible, that in this enlightened age—this age of Christian progress, of advancement in all the arts and sciences of civilized life—there are none to step forward whose voices shall be sufficiently potent to stay the madness of the hour, and *compel* a peaceful solution of the issues now presented for the consideration of a people whose freedom has been the pride and boast of an admiring world? Shall the alternative be presented, of section arrayed against section—shall we be compelled, both North and South, to listen to the tread of armed legions, whose swords are even now ready to leap from their scabbards for the purpose of being bathed in the blood of those who should, by every tie of interest and consanguinity, be linked together in bonds stronger than those forged of brass and steel? And when the contest is ended—as end it must—what will be gained by the victors? What mind will be able to count the cost of thousands upon thousands of precious lives sacrificed in the horrible contest, the cries of the widows and orphans rising night and morn to Heaven—mothers weeping in bitter anguish over the dead bodies of loved ones laid in the dust by the hands of a merciless destroyer —blackened ruins of once happy homes—devastated fields, where once peace smiled upon the industrious husbandman—the helplessness of childhood even affording no barriers to the destructive march of contending armies. And then, end as it may, the victory will be attained at a sacrifice of human life that will cause the stoutest heart to tremble in deepest anguish. Let the battle once commence, and who may live to see its termination?

Considering all these things—the blessings of peace, and the horrors of domestic war—is there no appeal that can be effectual for peace? Will you not add your earnest efforts for a peaceful solution and settlement of all the questions now agitating the minds of the people of every section? We appeal to you, and through you to the thousands of Masons in your jurisdiction, to stop the effusion of blood while yet they may. We make no suggestions as to how this shall be accomplished. As Masons we make no decision as to who is right or wrong, or as to the proper course to be pursued for securing the object we have so deeply at heart. Restore peace to our unhappy country, and surely Heaven will bless every faithful effort towards its accomplishment.

But if all efforts fail—if every appeal for peace shall be thrust aside—if the sword must still be the last resort, and accepted as the final arbiter—we beseech the brethren engaged in the awful contest to remember that a fallen foe is still a brother, and as such is entitled to warmest sympathies and kindliest attentions. If war cannot be averted or turned aside, let every brother use his utmost endeavors, and, as far as lies in his power, rob it of some of its horrors. While each is true to his sense of public and patriotic duty, on which ever side he may be arrayed, we earnestly urge that he shall also be true to those high and holy teachings inculcated by our Order.

Praying that God, in His infinite mercy, may yet incline the hearts of His people to ways of peace and paths of pleasantness, and that He may dissipate and disperse the storm-cloud of destruction which seems to hang so fearfully above us, we subscribe ourselves, faithfully and fraternally, in the bonds of Masonry.

JAMES McCALLUM, K.T.
M.W. Grand Master of Grand Lodge

The other grand lodges agreed whole-heartedly with Tennessee. Among them was Pennsylvania, which referred the letter to a special committee headed by Richard Vaux, who sent the following reply:

REPLY OF THE R. W. GRAND LODGE OF PENNSYLVANIA
ANCIENT YORK MASONS, TO THE R. W. GRAND
LODGE OF TENNESSEE, A. Y. MASONS.

To the Right Worshipful Grand Master, Deputy Grand Master, and Officers and Members of the Grand Lodge of Tennessee:

Your circular letter of last month, addressed to the Right Worshipful Grand Lodge of Pennsylvania, was received and read at a Quarterly Communication of that body, held at Philadelphia on the third of the present month, and referred to the committee of correspondence.

On behalf of the Right Worshipful Grand Lodge of Pennsylvania, we are entrusted with the duty of considering and answering it.

Brethren: Masonry is as old as government. It constitutes a government in itself. Its origin, principles, organization and administration are to be found in loyalty, obedience, hope, charity and love. It is operative everywhere, because its foundation can be laid among mankind wherever mankind exist. Resistance to, or disobedience of, any of these principles is not permitted in Masonic sovereignty. Masonry could not exist a moment, it would not have lived longer

33

than languages, races, and empires, if it had tolerated insubordination or rebellion against its authority.

Masonry teaches lessons for all peoples, and all times, and all epochs in history, past or future. Every Masonic principle, all its virtues, each of its benefits, have been sanctified by time. They have been ripened into good fruits by the aid, approbation and support of the wise, virtuous and patriotic of every commonwealth.

Masonry is a sovereignty and a law unto itself. Wherever existing, it is occupied with the permanence, universality, and integrity of its own organic laws and usages. It has excluded all but its own members from participation in its affairs. It knows nothing but the principles and teachings of its faith. Masonry has relations only with such as are bound together by the ties of its brotherhood. It regards the rise and fall of empires, the disturbances in states, the wars of contending nations, and rebellions and revolutions in commonwealths or among peoples, as calamities arising from causes to which Masonry is a stranger. The proud position of the brotherhood is to stand aloof from such evils, without partiality and without participation. The mission of Masonry is not either imperilled or hindered by such conditions of society. The claims of a brother are not dissolved by war, pestilence or famine; the tie, once formed, is only sundered by death. In gloom and despair, in want, distress and peril, the life of Masonic principles is neither endangered nor attacked. The roar of the whirlwind cannot render the cry of a brother inaudible; nor the darkness of civil war prevent the destitution of a brother from being seen.

As to the present deplorable state of the country, Masons cannot fail to have opinions as to the cause that produced it. It is to be feared that some of our brethren are in arms against the union of the States; others, are in the ranks of its defenders. Taught by the history of the Order, that resistance to its government is indefensible, they have carried these principles into the formation of opinions on the present crisis in our national history. But while Masons, as individuals, have been thus influenced and are acting in harmony with such views, Freemasonry is a silent, unimpassioned, abstracted observer of events. It is hardly possible that a fraternity which has on its roll the names of the fathers of American liberty and independence could be other than deeply impressed with the present relation between heirs of such a glorious inheritance.

Brethren—These are the thoughts we cannot bridle, and almost force their way without the will, and to which your circular letter has given utterance. The Right Worshipful Grand Lodge of Pennsylvania, for which we speak, fraternally salutes you, and the brethren under your jurisdiction. One of the earliest and most consistently followed duties of this Grand Lodge, had been to stand by, and defend, our ancient landmarks. Those who are familiar with its history know, she has gone through trials in support of this organic article of Masonic faith. In times of prosperity and peace, but little courage is required to perform duties ever so imperative. Now, or whenever this, or any Masonic duty is to be discharged in the face of stern exigencies or unaccustomed perplexity or peril, the Right Worshipful Grand Lodge of Pennsylvania, hopes and believes she will not be found less faithful nor more unwilling than any of her sister sovereignties of the Craft, around the world.

Brethren—We, with you, deplore the present unnatural and deeply distressing condition of our national affairs. Civil strife cannot be the outgrowth of the principles and victories of that great epoch in the history of mankind, known as the war of "1776." We have a hope and a faith, that the God of our Fathers will behold their children in their affliction, and be merciful, bless, protect and preserve them, and to say to them, "Peace, be still!" But if this whirlwind threatens to overwhelm us, yet in this last extremity, the still small voice of Masonic faith will be uttered and heard, saying, Brethren, there is help at hand in this time of need.

Brethren, thus we feel justified in answering your cry to the craft, contained in the circular letter sent to us. We feel it just and proper to conclude these thoughts, with the reiteration of the views we presented to the Right Worshipful Grand Lodge of Pennsylvania, in December, 1860. We do it the more willingly, in order to attest the sincerity of our present sentiments. We do it the more earnestly, to indicate that the Right Worshipful Grand Lodge of Pennsylvania, has carefully watched the course of our country's troubles, and pointed in advance to the panoplied protection which Masonry holds over the brethren of all lands.

"Surely your God is our God; your faith our faith; your landmarks our landmarks; your joy our joy; your prosperity our satisfaction. Then let us unitedly work together for the preservation and perpetuity of a common inheritance. It may be, thereby we will aid in maintaining unity, peace and concord, among the brethren and citizens of united sovereign States in our glorious Union. If all bonds should be broken, all ties rent asunder; if discord, dissension, and disruption, shall mark the decline and fall of the most wise and wonderful of the governments of mankind, let the Masonic temple, in all States, kingdoms, lands, peoples or confederacies, be common refuge of an indestructible Masonic fraternity."

On behalf of the Committee of Correspondence of the Right Worshipful Grand Lodge of Pennsylvania.

RICHARD VAUX, Chairman.

Philadelphia, June 13, A.L. 5861

From the beginning of the Civil War, Masonry was hurt by

events over which it had no control. An example took place in Arkansas.

In the 1840's, the Grand Lodge of Arkansas was informed that many grand lodges throughout the country were "establishing schools for the education of the children of our deceased [or] indigent brethren, and extending light and knowledge to many who otherwise might have remained in ignorance and poverty." Among the grand lodges praised for their schools were: Alabama, Georgia, Florida, Iowa, Kentucky, Maryland, Mississippi, Missouri, New York, North Carolina, Ohio, Texas, and Virginia.

After years of work, the Grand Lodge of Arkansas opened Saint John's College of Arkansas in October, 1859. It progressed steadily until the first of May, 1861, when "Mr. Lincoln's proclamation of war upon the South came, and there was a call to arms, the larger students, prompted by that ardent and impulsive patriotism common to our youth, laid aside their books, deserted the College, and rushed into service, and the president and professors with a cooler, but equally determined patriotism followed the boys to the war; and the trustees were compelled to close the college. . . . Our College but shared the fate of most of the colleges in the southern country."

Six years were to elapse before the college again opened, for Federal troops occupied Little Rock and took over the building for a military hospital. That occupation did not end until the spring of 1867.

The Confederate forces abandoned the city of Alexandria, Virginia, on May 5, 1861, and Federal troops occupied it on the 24th. The change in the control of the city was to cause strained feelings between the grand lodges of the District of Columbia and Virginia for several years. That commenced in 1862 when Theodore G. Palmer, George W. Knabb, E. H. Delahay, and others, petitioned the Grand Lodge of the District of Columbia for a dispensation to form a lodge to be known as "Union Lodge." The petition stated there was no lodge working in Alexandria and no charter for a lodge anywhere to be found; they were cut-off from communicating with the Grand Lodge of Virginia, and "the Grand Lodge of Virginia forbids those working under its jurisdiction to recognize or hold Masonic intercourse with Masons who adhere to their allegiance to the Union."

The grand master of the District, Charles F. Stansbury, called his grand lodge into special communication on February 12 to consider that petition. On the 15th, after much discussion about jurisdiction, and the rights and wrongs of the matter, the grand lodge voted to let Stansbury issue the dispensation when he was satisfied that the conditions required by his body had been complied with. They were, and he issued that dispensation on the 22nd.

Alexandria Washington Lodge, No. 22, the lodge of which George Washington had been charter master, had been ransacked and forced to disband. Of the three men named on the petition in the District's *Proceedings,* only one, Edward H. Delahay, was listed as a member of the former Lodge in the *Proceedings* of Virginia for 1860.

The statement made about the Grand Lodge of Virginia prohibiting her Masons from fraternizing with Northern Masons was a rumor that circulated far and wide throughout the war. As will be seen, Union Masons, when captured or hospitalized in Virginia, kept their affiliation secret through fear of reprisals.

Actually, no grand lodge issued any such order as that attributed to Virginia, although some came close to it. The misunderstanding reverted back to the years before the Civil War began.

During the year 1850, the Grand Lodge of New York, "by a compact and resolutions" affected a union with the "St. John's Grand Lodge" of that state, a body that was considered "clandestine" by every grand lodge in communication with the Grand Lodge of New York. In 1849, before this union, a group of Masons in New York, led by Isaac Phillips, broke away from the original grand lodge and formed one of their own styled the "Phillips Grand Lodge." In 1858, a union was effected between the two bodies, and in the same year the Grand Lodge of Virginia objected to the manner in which the two were united. Virginia claimed the members of the rival grand lodge should be "healed" (made legal) before they could be recognized as Masons. In 1860, the deputy grand master of the Grand Lodge of New York, John W. Simons, stated in a report that there was "a great diversity of opinion" about what the term "healing" meant. He "finally adopted as the safest plan for all concerned, a remaking" of those who had been members of the St. John's body, so he did just that.

The Grand Lodge of Virginia contended Simons was correct, and the members of the Phillips Grand Lodge should be treated in like manner. A lengthy report was made in the Grand Lodge of Virginia in 1858, and while no specific action was taken, subordinate lodges in Virginia refused to let Masons from New York enter their lodges. A definite statement had to be forthcoming from their Grand Lodge, so the following resolution was presented and adopted:

Resolved, That the Lodges and Masons, under the jurisdiction of the Grand Lodge of Virginia, are hereby forbidden and prohibited from holding converse on the subject of Free Masonry with any person hailing from the State of New York, or in any other manner extending Masonic intercourse and recognition towards them; and this Grand Lodge feels it to be its imperative duty to discontinue all Masonic intercourse with the Grand Lodge of New York, until such time as the difficulties now existing in New York shall be adjusted in accordance with strict Masonic law and usage, as laid down by M. Wor. Jno. W. Simons, the present Grand Master, while acting as D.G. Master.

Resolved, That this regulation shall have full force and effect from its adoption, and continue in operation *until* the Grand Lodge of New York shall revise the union of 1858 with the Phillips' Grand Lodge, and adjust a settlement on the principles and "conditions set forth," when "the matter of the St. John's Grand Lodge was finally disposed of in June, 1860."

> JOHN R. PURDIE
> JOHN DOVE
> LEWIS B. WILLIAMS
> POWHATTAN B. STARKE

The resolution adopted by the Grand Lodge of Virginia pertained only to Masons from New York; it was adopted well over a year before there were any Confederate States of America, and before hostilities had started. During the war, the Masons of Virginia overlooked that resolution, as a report made to the Grand Lodge of New York in 1866, when the grand lodges of

New York and Virginia resumed fraternal relations, by Joseph D. Evans, a past grand master, clearly states:

In this connection may be noted as worthy of remark, that the brethren of both jurisdictions have never ceased, during this interval of legal alienation, to obey the humane promptings of their nature, and the teachings of Freemasonry, in alleviating the physical agonies of a suffering brother, and in other respects fulfilling the duties imposed upon them as Masons. Nor were the occurrences rare, calling into lively exercise these moral virtues, as can be attested in hundreds of instances which have transpired in various ways during the heart-rending trials of the late civil war. The estrangement, therefore, if estrangement it may be called, partook more of a jurisdictional or diplomatic character, than of one affecting materially the personal relations of a brotherhood mysteriously linked together by the indissoluble chain of the mystic tie.

The destruction of friendly relations between the North and the South was noted and commented on by grand lodges from Maine to California. Josiah H. Drummond, grand master of the Grand Lodge of Maine, told his members on May 7, 1861:

The roll of the drum, the shrill note of the fife, and the heavy tramp of armed men are heard in our streets. We almost listen to hear the thundering cannon, the tread of hostile armies, and the din of a conflict between brothers, endeared to each other by a double tie, common descent, and the bonds of our Fraternity. But our duties cannot be winked out of sight, nor evaded. On the very threshold of Masonry, we are taught that our duties as Masons will not interfere with the duties we owe to our country; that we are to be quiet and peaceable citizens, true to our country.

* * *

May the Supreme Grand Master above, if consistent with his holy will, so order things, that peace may soon be restored among us; that our country may again resume her march in power and prosperity, with not a single star blotted from her banner, not a single stripe erased; and especially that this experiment of a free government, to which the eyes of the oppressed of the whole world are so anxiously looking, may not be made an ignominious failure by the insane folly and madness of those whose solemn duty it is to maintain it in its integrity.

In California, May 14, the grand master, N. Greene Curtis, told his grand lodge:

How sad and gloomy the reflection that in a portion of our beloved fatherland, warriors are on the tented field and bayonets are bristling; that the citizens of our common country are arrayed against each other, awaiting the deadly shock of arms. Let us invoke Almighty God to speedily end the unnatural conflict, and spare the effusion of human blood. May the good angel who has so long hovered over the destinies of our country, so temper the hearts of the rulers and the people, that civil war may be averted. . . .

The Grand Lodge of Indiana met on May 26, its deliberations disturbed by the shrill sound of the fife and the rattling of the drum. The regular step of a long line of well drilled soldiers was plainly audible, as were the commands of the non-commissioned officers. A look from the windows disclosed only scenes of preparations for war; the baggage trains being loaded with munitions; the troop trains being filled with men to hurry them on their way to the fields of deadly strife. Many a heart in that grand lodge was heavy with the thoughts of their Masonic brethren who were boarding those trains, and would never more meet with them in Indiana. That thinking gave rise to the submission, and adoption, of this resolution:

Resolved, That those engaged in the rebellion are truly censurable for violating their vows and striving to destroy the best government under which Masons were ever permitted to assemble; and that, until they return to their allegiance, and are legally healed by the laws of the government they have so wrongfully abused, we will cease to regard them as true and worthy Masons.

That resolution, adopted in the heat of the moment, was carried out only in isolated instances. Other heated, and quite often un-Masonic statements were made by grand masters and committees, but in almost every case cooler heads took over and much that was said that should have remained unsaid was stricken from the record, because the grand lodges, as a whole, would not adopt "harsh patriotic" statements.

The grand master of Missouri, Marcus H. McFarland, on May 27, summed up the general feeling of Freemasons in connection with the Civil War:

Our fraternity embraces the whole in bonds of charity; as Masons we know no North, no South, no East or West; yet we know our country and brotherhood everywhere. Peace and harmony are the mission of our order. Whatever individuals may feel to be their duty as citizens let us not forget our brotherhood. Let no bitter personal animosities spring up among us. Let us remember the fraternal cord and its duties. We can do much to assuage the bitterness of the present with all men, and especially with those of our own household. May the God of Love keep you all in harmony and brotherly love.

Anthony O'Sullivan, the grand secretary of Missouri, asked:

Can we arrest this great misfortune? Are the teachings of Freemasonry, if practiced, sufficient, if not to cause our brethren to be united, at least to induce them to practice those beautiful tenets of our order—brotherly love and relief. We firmly believe that if we were more deeply impressed with the sublime lessons taught in Masonry; if we could realize in all their force and comprehension the covenants which bind us together, Freemasonry would as of old exercise a potent influence. On the tented field, in the heat of battle, and by the couch of the dying soldier, in all the trying and varied scenes of a soldier's life, when all of the earth is about to fade from the dying gaze, the warm grasp and the loving tones of the craftsmen's voices as they whisper a word of prayer, would be felt and recognized, and the spirit would pass to the throne of God with the halo of Masonic prayer surrounding it as with a glory. In view, then, of the perils which encompass us, how important it is that the Masonic sentiment should be cultivated and strengthened. Let us then endeavor to practice that first great lesson taught us—to subdue our passions. . . .

The Grand Lodge of Rhode Island met on May 27, two days before Jefferson Davis was to receive a tremendous welcome in Richmond, the city that was to become the capital of the Confederate States of America. Grand Master William Gray, prayed:

Let us return thanks to the Supreme Ruler of the Universe, for the many blessings we have received, both as a Lodge and a people, during the past year; and let us invoke a continuation of Divine favor upon us and our beloved country, whose perpetuity as a union is now threatened; and may the dark cloud overhanging and involving in darkness the future prosperity of our country and its institutions be speedily dispelled; and peace, fraternity and brotherly love, once more take possession, not only of all our brethren, but the whole people throughout the country.

41

The hope of a peaceful settlement of the political differences between the two great sections of the country was still apparent as the month of May ended. That hope was to end as passions broke their bounds.

CHAPTER V

The Battles Begin

◇◇◇

While churches, and sects, and creeds are rent asunder, their members denouncing each other in language anything but Christian, and too many of their ministers fallen low—very low, Freemasonry, like an Egyptian pyramid, looms up grandly above and beyond the shallow devices of little men. . . .

ANTHONY O'SULLIVAN

THE QUESTION of how to treat those on the opposite side of the struggle plagued every organization in America. On June 4, George Armstrong, grand master of Nebraska, indicated he was perplexed when he spoke to his grand lodge:

The right of secession, or the propriety of dividing the Union into separate confederacies, are questions not within the province of a body of Masons. But, until these questions are determined, and the bloody and fratricidal contest which is now convulsing our beloved country, is ended, we should be guarded in our affiliations with the Masonic organizations of those States who have lifted their bloody hands against the civil authorities, trampled in the dust the banner of the country to which they have pledged their allegiance, and have set on foot the most unnatural and unholy conflict that has ever disgraced a civilized nation.

That statement was brought about by a communication he had received from the Grand Lodge of Louisiana asking for the appointment of a member as representative of that grand lodge, near the Grand Lodge of Nebraska. Although Nebraska had not adopted the "Representative System," he wondered if states in "open rebellion against the government" could "fraternize" with those who were not. His grand lodge also wondered; consequently it was June 19, 1867 before a grand master of Ne-

43

braska (Robert W. Furnas) recommended the adoption of such a system. His members concurred in his recommendation.

William R. Penick, grand master of Missouri, spoke along that same vein when he ruled:

I have decided lately, that a traitor to the Government of the United States is not entitled to Masonic burial, or any other benefits of Masonry.

Penick was a brigadier general of the state militia, and his grand lodge took that into consideration when his statements and decisions were reviewed in 1862. The members agreed that a Mason in good standing, from whatever part of the world he may be from, is entitled to a Masonic burial. The committee, to whom his address had been referred, closed its report with this:

Looking alone to the future welfare and prosperity of our noble fraternity, and expressly disclaiming any discourtesy to our Grand Master, for whom we have the highest sentiments of regard and respect, we would therefore recommend that that portion of the address, together with so much as refers to the manner of the death of our late brother, Past Grand Master B. W. Sharp, be laid upon the table and omitted from the published proceedings of this Grand Lodge.

Freemasonry was not the only group in a dilemma, for the *Rebellion Record* quotes the following from the New Orleans *Catholic Standard:*

Let no Southern child be educated outside the limits of the Confederate States. We have excellent schools and colleges at Richmond and Norfolk in Virginia; at Charleston and Columbia in South Carolina; at Savannah and Augusta in Georgia; at St. Augustine in Florida; at Mobile in Alabama; at Bay St. Louis, Pass Christian, Sulphur Springs, Vicksburg, and Natchez in Mississippi; at Fort Smith, Helena, and Little Rock in Arkansas; at Galveston, New Braunfels, San Antonio, Brownsville, and Liberty in Texas; and at St. Michael's Grand Coteau, Vermillionville, Thibodeaux, Donaldsonville, Natchitoches, Avoyelles, Alexandria, Shreveport, Iberville, Algiers, and New Orleans in Louisiana. The social bonds between us and the Catholics at the North have been severed by them. We acknowledge them no longer as our countrymen. They and their institutions have no claims upon us.

The Methodist Episcopal Church had split North and South

in 1844 over the political questions of the day. It took 95 years for a union to take place. With the start of the war the Presbyterian Church was torn in two, as was the Baptist Church. The question of who was right and who was wrong; whose side God was on, and who were the better Christians, agitated all sects for many years. Some of the differences have never been reconciled.

While Masonry could not escape the political issues of the decade, breaches in relations were few and isolated. As soon as hostilities were halted, any bitterness that had arisen abated.

There were tears in the eyes and hearts of many a grand master as he addressed his grand lodge as to the happenings in the political arena. Typical of that group was Grand Master Thomas H. Benton, Jr., of Iowa, who spoke to his grand lodge on June 4, 1861:

> The present unhappy and distracted state of the country is a source of deep regret to every true mason, and no portion of the community have, perhaps, been more constant in their desires, and untiring in their exertions to avert the impending storm. As masons, and as citizens of the State, the ancient charges clearly define our duties. I would say, therefore, to brethren throughout our common country, read these irrepealable laws of masonry, think of your obligations, and then determine your line of duty, and may Heaven aid you in making that determination.
>
> I have long contemplated with deep emotion, in the distance, what is now a stern reality, and have labored, though feebly and ineffectually, to avert the awful crisis. It has been my good fortune to press the fraternal hand in various parts of our country, from New England to Texas, and from the Atlantic to the Missouri. This consideration alone were sufficient to enlist my undivided energies in word and deed to perpetuate the friendly relations once so common among us as a people.

Benton was to prove the sincerity of his remarks a short time later, when as the occupation commander of Little Rock, Arkansas, he placed a guard of Union troops about the home of Albert Pike, a Confederate general, to save his valuable Masonic library from destruction. That act has been cited throughout the years as one of the greatest examples of Masonic love during the Civil War.

On the same day that Iowa met, the grand master of Texas,

45

John B. McMahon, was considering the feasibility of cancelling their annual communication, because, "All our people are preparing for, or already engaged in conflict." He reconsidered, and on the 10th of June the communication was held as scheduled with all of the grand lodge officers present and 131 lodges represented. That was the largest representation Texas was to have for a number of years.

Two days later, the Grand Lodge of New Hampshire met, and Grand Master Aaron P. Hughes, told his members:

> I have sometimes felt that the great misfortune that has befallen us might come, and if it did that there was one body of men that could do much to reconcile the difficulties that exist more in imagination, in my judgement, than in reality. The angry passions of men have much to do with the present critical position of our country; and, as Masons, we are in duty bound to make every exertion to assuage the storm that is now desolating our land. The institution of Masonry has its members in every part of our country, and it can more readily reach them than any organization in the world.
>
> We have no right to meddle or interfere with the political affairs of the nation, but whenever any question arises that affects the Institution of which we are members, it is our duty to consider it. That the precepts taught by Masons have always tended to soften the hearts of men, is a truth that every brother will assent to.

The fighting in Virginia was becoming more tense, particularly in the Western counties that had broken away from their mother state. The Union troops, under Major General George B. McClellan, a Mason, were in the process of securing a considerable portion of Virginia for the Federal government. They had driven the Confederate troops to a place called Carrick's Ford, where the first high ranking officer on either side was to die in battle.

At the ford, Robert Selden Garnett, brigadier general, C.S.A., asked his aide, Colonel William B. Taliferro, a member of Bortetourt Lodge, No. 7, Virginia, and who was to become grand master of that state in 1874-75, for ten good marksmen, with which to hold their position. The colonel sent back a whole company. A short time later, while showing Sam M. Gaines, who had just risked his life to save a wounded man, the "proper bearing of a soldier under fire," Garnett was mortally

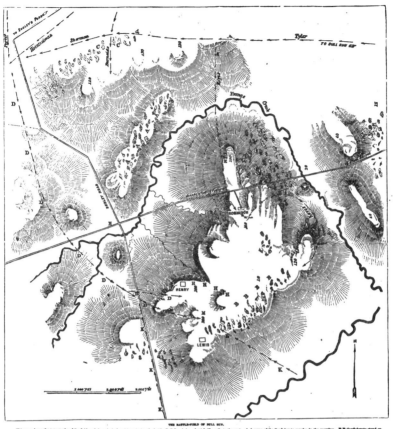

THE BATTLE-FIELD OF BULL RUN.

This map shows the topography of the field, and the principal positions during the battle, Bull Run being about half a mile to the east. A A scene of the Confederate repulse in the morning. B B Confederate stand on the southern edge of the plateau. C C Burnside withdrawn from the action after the fight of the morning. D D general line of advance of the united columns of Porter, Heintzelman, and Sherman upon the Confederate right. E E Keyes's movement after the separation of his brigade from that of Sherman, of Tyler's division. H H final advance of the Confederates. K K advance of the last Confederate re-enforcements. M Mill where Griffin's and Ricketts's batteries were disabled. N Sykes's stand with the regulars after the rout. The figures denote the elevation above the level of Bull Run.

wounded, and as the Federals reached him he died. His body and belongings were returned to his family.

Less than ten days later, several high ranking officers on both sides of the struggle were to lose their lives at a place called Manassas, better known as Bull Run. The *Masonic Monthly,* Boston, published an eye-witness account of one phase of what transpired there:

The awful disaster at Bull Run occurred on the 21st of July, 1861. It was a beautiful Sabbath day, though oppressively hot. The Frst [First] Ohio, under Colonel M'Cook, in a brief lull of the battle, was prostrate upon the ground, panting in utter exhaustion. The joyful thought echoed along the lines, "The day is ours! The rebels are running!" The Ohio troops sprung to their feet and with parched lips gave new wings to the cry. They could not, however, cross the Run until the pioneers [Engineers] had hastily constructed a bridge. While waiting, a young officer, subsequently Colonel W. H. Raynor, went, in company with two sergeants, a short distance to the left to get some water. Just as they had reached the much coveted stream they heard a trampling through the thick underbrush of the forest, followed by that unearthly savage yell with which our troops afterward became so familiar, and a squadron of rebel horsemen came thundering down upon them, crashing and roaring like an avalanche. Bewildered and almost stunned by the sudden onset, Colonel Raynor instinctively drew his pistol and fired, just as a buckshot from the foe struck his instep and numbed his foot. He dropped upon his knees behind a large tree, and gazed with awe and admiration upon the appalling scene. The snorting and trampling of the excited horses, the demoniac yells of the men, the rattling fire from their pistols and carbines, all blending with the roar of the battle raging around, seemed like the phantom of a delirious dream.

One of the horsemen, who had already fired his piece, at Raynor, swung his carbine in passing in lieu of a sabre, and brought it down with all his force upon the head of the wounded soldier. A few scintillations of light flashed through his eyes, a pang of acutest anguish shot through his brain, and he fell senseless to the earth, apparently dead. After the lapse of some time he was brought slightly to consciousness by some one tugging at his clothes. In utter bewilderment he raised himself upon his elbow, and found that a rebel soldier, who was stripping the dead, had already taken possession of all his accoutrements, sword, pistol, canteen, and cap, and was endeavoring to get off his coat. The robber was so terrified at his sudden resurrection, as of a corpse, that he sprung upon his horse and disappeared in the forest as though a ghost were pursuing him.

As Colonel Raynor gradually regained his senses, and recalled what had happened, he found that the rebel cavalry had swept over him in their impetuous charge, had apparently met a repulse, and had retired in as great haste as they had made the onset. He staggered to his feet by the aid of the tree which had protected him from being trampled to death, and while standing, covered with blood and half-bewildered, the woods all around being still filled with the exchange of hostile shots, he saw two rebel horsemen approaching. One said: "There's a Yankee, bring him along!" They immediately rode up to him, and the two powerful men seized him by each wrist, and dragged him violently between them for some distance, until the woods partially sheltered them from our fire, which was quite severe. As Colonel Raynor was thus forced along he saw several rebels drop from their horses, struck by our bullets. At length he was lifted upon the horse in front of one of his captors, and carried behind the shelter of a small hill, where several of the rebel wounded had been collected. Quite a group gathered around the prisoner, cursing him in the strongest epithets of denunciation they could coin. But their victim, faint from his wounds, suffering excruciating pain and deadly sick, closed his eyes and paid no heed to curses or questions.

This silence enraged the rebels. One drew out a formidable knife, saying: "Let us cut out his cursed abolition tongue; he's got no use for it." Another struck him a violent blow with his clenched fist. A feeble effort of the half-dead captive to resent the insult provoked peals of derisive laughter. At the same time another rebel came up, covered with blood and with his right arm in a sling, and presenting, with his left hand, a pistol to the head of their helpless prisoner, exclaimed, with one of the most brutal oaths: "This is the infernal hound who shot my horse and gave me this broken arm, I'll kill him!" In the attempt to execute his threat he fired his pistol. But another at the instant struck up the assassin's arm, so that the ball just passed over his head into the tree against which he was leaning. This cowardly act raised quite a commotion, and several cried out vehemently against it, declaring it to be shameful to kill a wounded prisoner. Others, however, defended the act, contending that every prisoner should be instantly put to death. "What did he come down here for," they exclaimed, "but to kill us, steal our slaves, ravish our women, and destroy our property? Don't they all deserve hanging?"

In this hour of weakness, pain, and despair, death seemed not an unwelcome visitor; and the bleeding captive almost regretted that the ball had not pierced his brain. He was, however, soon lifted upon a horse behind a rebel soldier, and conveyed about four miles to the Junction. The battle was still raging at Bull Run, and many fresh rebel troops were met hurrying to the field. Our blood-stained captive, almost blinded with weakness and pain, was assailed with the most profane abuse, and many a wish was expressed to try the effect of a bullet or a bayonet-thrust through his heart.

It was early in the evening when they reached the Junction, and the captive was taken to a stable, where quite a number of the wounded rebels had been conveyed. His guard, a kind-hearted man, immediately sought a surgeon to examine his wounds. The surgeon, as he looked at him, said disdainfully, "Why that's a Yankee; let him wait; enough of our own men to attend to now!" Another surgeon was found who was more compassionate. His wounds were washed, and he was made as comfortable as the circumstances would permit. The generous guard, J. H. Lemon, of Radford's Cavalry, truly acted the part of the good Samaritan. He got some ice, pounded it up in his own handkerchief and tenderly bound it around the throbbing brow of his captive. He inquired if he had any money, evidently intending to give him some if he were destitute. In reply to Raynor's earnest expression of gratitude, he said:

"I only hope to get the same treatment from your men if I ever fall into their hands. If you will relieve the distresses of a suffering brother Mason when in your power, I shall be well paid."

As he said this he pointed to a Masonic pin in Colonel Raynor's shirt-bosom, and hastily mounting his horse rode away, leaving the wounded soldier in pain and despondency, surrounded by the dying and the dead. In the morning the captive was removed to another barn, where he found some twenty Union officers, and learned for the first time the extent of our calamity. All these prisoners were then transferred to a train of cars to be taken to Richmond. The constant arrival of fresh captives delayed the departure of the train until after noon. All Monday night, and until the evening of Tuesday, the train crept slowly along, being constantly impeded by trains from Richmond crowded with troops hastening to reinforce Beauregard's rebel army.

The same *Monthly* reprinted an extract from a private letter that had appeared in the *Democrat:*

When the Union troops marched to Manassas, I accompanied them. I did not go as a soldier; I had no interest in the result of the conflict personally, and less politically, than most of those who were there. Having lived all my life in Maryland, I preferred that the troops with whom I marched should be defeated; but my preference was not strong.

There was one place on the field where the dead covered the ground. More than one place, without a doubt, but one place where I stood, at eight o'clock in the evening. It was a ravine, a valley, rather, through which ran a small stream. For the first time in my life I realized the force of the expression, "Rivers of blood." The water of the stream ran red in several places along the margin.

The firing had ceased. The Union troops were in full and disorderly retreat, and the Confederate forces pressed on after them. The wave of war was heard rolling in the distance.

Of the multitude who lay upon the ground, only a few could receive immediate attention.

One man, requiring instant help, a surgeon requested me to assist him in performing an operation necessary to save his life. While lending the assistance asked, my heart was pained with the cries for help which arose all around me. One poor fellow in particular, wearing the Union blue, chilled the blood in my veins by the piercing agony of his cries. I could not see distinctly why he suffered so dreadfully. And no one appeared to assist him.

Bringing no one to his relief by shrieks, he suddenly ceased, save a smothered groan, which he was unable to suppress, and commenced giving the masonic sign of distress. This he repeated several times, when three men (I did not myself understand the signal at the time) left Confederate soldiers whom they were assisting, and went to his relief. They bore him off the field, and saw him properly cared for. This incident I witnessed as I stood in that frightful valley, and recognized, for the first time, the power and beauty of the mystic tie.

Jesse Gove, a member of Rocky Mountain Lodge, No. 205, wrote a highly critical letter from his "Camp on Platte River, August 22, 1861."

Today I saw the Senate confirmations of the new appointments and promotions. My heart fails me, almost, when I reflect on the suicidal policy of the administration. I wrote you long before these appointments were made predicting what would be the policy pursued, and you now see some of the results of my worst fears. Why was an attack made on Bull's Run? God help them, lawyers, merchants, loafers, etc., made to command masses of men, when they do not understand the first rudiments of a squad drill. How should they know? Do you suppose it possible for any man to be taken inexperienced from the desk and given a brigade or regiment of men and understand how to use them? It is like putting into the hands of a novice a watch and tell him to take it apart and clean it and set it arunning again. If there is anything capable of mathematical calculation to be learned only by thorough theoretical and practical knowledge, it is the manoeuvring of men in military tactics, the step, cadence, wheel, deployment, and massing, distance to be moved in a given time, etc., all go to make up the minutia of tactics. Now how, provided the word of command is committed from the book, in God's name can any man know or understand the results of a movement without long experience and practice, the use of arms, range of piece, effect of shots at given distances, etc.? But why say anything about it? War is a science, and unless the government stops short and lays aside this damned party preferment, to the exclusion of merit and skill, we shall be defeated though our men are as numerous as the sands of the sea. Now what was the idea of attacking the rebels in front at Manassas? There was this view open to every military man, and that is this: it might have succeeded or it might have not: in any event a great sacrifice of human life must have been the result. Victory or defeat, but a defeat was as probable as a victory with the material at hand. Then why hazard the attack? What did their major and brigadier generals know? They were given a large mass of men, and, like the man who drew the elephant in a lottery, did not know how to use them. It requires the head and ability and experience of military men to manoeuvre large bodies of men. The time when to move and the moment to strike all go to win a victory or provoke a slaughter. These men from inexperience knew not how to get their men on or off the field. A double line for which 50,000 human lives will have to be sacrificed. It will cost every man of that number to recover the defeat.

From the remarks McClellan made when he was given command of the army, he agreed with Gove, at least in part. But Gove was not through writing about this battle, for on September 13 he again wrote to his friend, Rolfe, back in New Hampshire, from a "Camp Near O'fallon's Bluff, Platte River":

. . . The leaders of the government started out with the idea that the moral effect of calling out three or four hundred thousand men would intimidate the rebels and counteract the wide spreading rebellion and bring them to their senses. But the rebels foresaw that they were not soldiers, nor could they be until drilled and disciplined. The fact of their being officered by men inexperienced was a point to them gained. They fortified Manassas, and provoked an attack, and how well they judged of our weakness let the "Bull Run" answer.

This attempted moral effect on the part of the government served to strengthen the rebels. It afforded them the very facts they wanted

51

to go before the people and rally them to arms, and so well did the Confederate States respond that 60,000 rebels appeared at Manassas as quickly as a corresponding number of Federal troops fortified themselves on Arlington Heights. [The National Park Service states, "The Federal strength of the battle was 35,732, losses 2,708; Confederate strength 31,810, losses 1,982."] This advantage there was that they had the best troops and the best officers, they were behind fortifications, impregnable to veteran troops. What then could you expect of undisciplined troops?

There is another feature in their movements that has been lost sight of. After capturing all the forts, animals, and their armaments, almost the first step taken then was to capture small parts of the army, thinking thereby to cripple the resources of the government by paroling its best officers. This has thus far succeeded admirably. How many officers and soldiers there are now on parole! The fact of the matter is simply this, that while the government held the cards the rebels finessed, until, thus far, they have the most points in the game.

I am wandering from the point I started to arrive at. In the want of discipline and efficiency growing out of inexperienced officers has it occurred to the government that a mutiny is as easy to provoke as that stampede from Manassas?

From a "Camp on Spring Creek, Kansas, Sept. 30, 1861," Gove continued his complaints about the Federal government and its method of promoting officers he considered inferior:

. . . Can you wonder, then, that officers, especially those born in the border states, feel chagrined and mortified at being overlooked and ill treated in these matters? In times of peace no officer would stay in service twenty four hours, but would resign and trust to the country for justification. It is here on this point that the government treats the army with impunity. It was small at the commencement of this trouble; the exigencies of service called for thousands and tens of thousands of men; new fledged generals were made from the field, the counter, and the desk, broken down resigned officers taken up and put in high places, and the army officers were left in the shade. They fought a battle before Washington with the militia, commanded by inexperienced officers, and the mention of the dastardly cowardice of these same generals and other officers is enough to sicken one at heart. A disgrace that the country will never outgrow even though it wins a thousand victories. I have seen it compared to Bunker's Hill. Bunker's H--l! Had the poor ignorant devils led the men half as gallantly as did the militia generals of that day the run would have been forward instead of backward, and they would have been ahead in the advance as they were in the retreat.

Captain Jesse Gove was commissioned colonel of the 22d Massachusetts Volunteers, November 9, 1861, and was killed while leading his men in battle at Gaines' Mill, Virginia, June 27, 1862.

Henry Kyd Douglas relates the following episode that happened during the Battle of Manassas which tells of the birth of a name and the death of a Mason:

General Bee [Bernard B. Bee, Jr., a Texas Knight Templar], his brigade being crushed, rode up to him [Jackson] and with the mortification of an heroic soldier reported that the enemy was beating him back.

"Very well, General," replied Jackson.

"But how do you expect to stop them?"

"We'll give them the bayonet!" was the brief answer.

Bee galloped away and General Jackson turned to Lieutenant H. H. Lee of his staff with this message, as it came to Colonel Allan [Lt. Col. William Allan].

"Tell the colonels of this brigade that the enemy are advancing; when their heads are seen above the hill, let the whole line rise, move forward with a shout and trust to the bayonet. I'm tired of this long-range work!"

It was about this time that Jackson was shot in the finger. The storm swept toward us. Bee was back with his brigade but could not stay the onset. His horse was shot under him as he tried to rally and hold his men. At that supreme moment as if by inspiration, he cried out to them in a voice that the rattle of musketry could not drown,

"Look! There is Jackson's brigade standing behind you like a stone wall!"

With these words of baptism as his last, Bee himself fell and died; and from that day left behind a fame that will follow that of Jackson as a shadow.

Jackson later told Douglas that he believed a defeat would have been less disastrous than the victory at Manassas for the Confederates as it set the North to preparing for war in earnest.

Many men were left wounded and dying on the field of battle. George W. Dame in his history of Roman Eagle Lodge, No. 122, Danville, Virginia, writes about one:

Two days after the first battle of Manassas, the 18th Virginia

Regiment, commanded by Colonel Robert E. Withers [Grand Master of Virginia, 1871-72], was in camp near the battle grounds of the 21st. when the pickets brought in as prisoner a member of the 12th. Brooklyn Regiment of Zouaves, captured near their picket line the night before. He was of course brought up to headquarters and examined by the Colonel, to whom he rather reluctantly stated that the Colonel of his regiment, who was severely wounded, was concealed in the woods near the point at which he was himself captured, and offered to guide a party to his place of concealment, as he said he knew he would die unless he could receive surgical aid. A detail of men was sent out with a small wagon to bring in the wounded Yankee. They soon returned with Colonel Benjamin Wood, who was a near relative (brother or cousin) of the Honorable Fernando Wood, M.C. of New York, who was suffering severely from a gun-shot wound of the pelvis. While conversing with him, Colonel Withers . . . observed a Masonic pin on the bosom of Colonel Wood . . . finding that the prisoner was indeed a brother in distress, Colonel Withers countermanded his first order to convey the wounded officer to the field hospital at the Lewis House and had him carried into his own tent, which he surrendered to him and his attendant who had been paroled to wait on him.

Dame further states that the surgeon from Colonel Wood's regiment was paroled to assist his colonel, and when he was able to be moved safely, he was transferred to a hospital at Charlottesville where members of the organization called "Freemasonry" again saw to his comfort. He later stated he would never "fight again the men who had so generously befriended him," a statement made after he had been promoted to the rank of brigadier general. The Fernando Wood mentioned by Dame was a member of Eastern Star Lodge No. 227, New York City. In a message to the common council on January 7, 1861, he recommended New York should become a free city. He did not want to lose either the Northern or Southern trade.

The shooting at Manassas was over; the war of words that was to last for a century or more had begun, and Lincoln, as though in answer to Jackson's prophecy, replaced McDowell with a Mason named George B. McClellan.

CHAPTER VI

The North and South Dig In

◇◇

I pray that in these exciting times, when men and states seem to be running into insanity, the Masonic institution will be conservative, as of old, intermeddling not with questions which do not concern it and retain the respect and admiration of the world.

HORACE S. ROBERTS

McCLELLAN, immediately upon assuming command of Union forces, let it be known what he thought of the army as it had been and was. He claimed that they were uninstructed, undisciplined, demoralized, commanded by poor officers and that drunkenness was common. He instantly started instruction for them and, by constant demands for more men, tripled the number of men in his forces.

While McClellan built his army and fortified the capital, the naval blockade of Southern ports was intensified under the command of such Masons as David G. Farragut, John R. Goldsborough, Henry H. Gorringo, Lois A. Kimberly, John W. Philip and William D. Porter. The ultimate results of the success of their blockade were to prove disastrous, not only for the South, but for the Federal troops who were taken prisoners and confined in Southern prison camps. While food and clothing were kept out of the South, so were badly needed medicines and surgical instruments.

The action in the political arena and on the fields of strife received varying degrees of praise or condemnation from the different orders of Masonry. Soon after the outbreak of hostilities the Grand Chapter of Maine met in its annual convocation and Grand High Priest Moses Dodge, told his brethren:

Our National Constitution, framed by our fathers many of whom were pledged at the altars of masonry, and were brethren of those who fought in our revolutionary struggle for liberty, brethren of Washington, Warren and Lafayette—this constitution, which heretofore has bound us together as one people, which we regard as the supreme law of the land, and which every mason is solemnly bound to support and maintain is now in danger of being thrown aside as an "unholy thing," and its provisions disregarded. And while evil passions seem to have warped the judgment of many in our land, in some localities "madness rules the hour."

In view of this threatened peril, what is the duty of each member of this great union and brotherhood, which has embraced in its fold a Franklin, a Jackson and a Clay; whose members are citizens of all sections of our common country; who have no balance of power to maintain between North and South; and who know no Mason and Dixon's line to divide them; and who, if true to their masonic teaching, must be far the most powerful conservative element in this nation?

Every mason throughout this entire land, whether resident in our own state or Texas, South Carolina or California, is a brother, and bound to us by the most sacred ties. Can we, then, be bitter foes forgetting the kind relations that should ever exist between the members of our beloved Order everywhere; cease to "love one another"; forget the lessons of self-denial, justice, prudence and patriotism, taught us in the Lodge, and be found arrayed as enemies, brother against brother?

Say, can the South sell her share in Bunker's hoary height?
Or can the North give up her boast in Yorktown's closing fight?
Can ye divide with equal hand a heritage of graves?
Or rend in twain the starry flag that o'er them proudly waves?

Can ye cast lots for Vernon's soil, or chaffer mid the gloom
That hangs in solemn folds about our common Father's tomb?
Or could ye meet around his grave as fratricidal foes,
And wake your burning curses o'er his pure and calm repose?

During the same convocation, which occurred in May, the report on foreign correspondence was written by Cyril Pearl. About the struggle he wrote:

The hour of trial and the national perils are now upon us; and the interests of humanity now summon every man and every mason to his post of duty. Sectional strife has culminated in civil war, and a nation is rushing to arms. The country of Washington is in the throes of civil war, and the city called by his name is now tred by marshaling hosts who rally to protect a national capital from invading armies rallying for its destruction, and the overthrow by violence of the government which was founded and sealed with the blood of noble martyrs, led by him to death, or, as we had fondly hoped, to a deathless victory. By what seems to us an inexplicable infatuation, seven of the states so lately called united, have been hurried by their leading statesmen into revolt against the government founded by Washington and which, almost in its infancy, had become the wonder of the world.

Another misfortune is, that the two great sections of the country, and the political parties that govern them, have too long and too persistently misunderstood each other, and too fatally misled the people who had looked to them for light and direction. Conservative men, christian men, engrossed in their varied enterprises, have been too ready to leave the affairs of the government in the hands of those who aspired to its honors, and its official trusts and spoils; so that all at once we are roused from fatal slumber by the battle-cry and the maddening march of revolting legions.

On the field, drama of varying degrees was unfolding. One scene took place when a company of the First Iowa Regiment, in August, 1861, was sent to guard a railroad bridge at Mozeille Mills, Missouri, which, according to rumor, was scheduled to be destroyed by guerrillas. Soon after arriving and setting up a camp site, the captain was given a letter that had been taken from a mule that wandered into camp. On opening it he read the words, written with a feminine hand, "The Temple of Jerusalem was destroyed on the first Friday before the full moon." He turned to his men and stated, "The guerrillas will attack the bridge tonight."

The men were ordered to take every precaution to drive off the attackers when they arrived, and they did. They chased them to a farmhouse which the guerrillas set on fire with the occupants, a woman and two children, still inside. That was evidently done to divert the Federal company, but the soldiers were able to capture three of the party that had set the fire. Among the three was a boy with an Irish brogue, about sixteen, and well dressed.

A "drum-head court-martial" sentenced them to be executed as a lesson to the other guerrillas in the neighborhood. The boy pleaded for his life, but his pleas went unheeded. Then a girl of about eighteen burst upon the scene, clasped the boy in her

arms, and exclaimed, "Oh soldiers! oh Holy Mother! gentlemen! for the love of Jesus, do not kill him. He is innocent, he
is my brother!"

The *Masonic Monthly* adds a strange ending to the story:

The girl at length was removed. When two soldiers advanced and
unloosed her grasp upon her brother, her scream, her appeals to all
for mercy, were terrible. They had dragged her but a short distance
from him, when, looking back, and seeing a black handkerchief
already tied over his eyes, with one wild frantic scream, she flung
the soldier from her, and bounding back to her brother, tore the
handkerchief from his eyes, and again enfolded him in her arms.

As the soldiers were again removing her, the coat-sleeve of one of
them was torn during the struggle, and her eyes fell upon a breast-
pin that he had fastened upon his shirt sleeve, perhaps for concealment and safety. In an instant all physical powers were relaxed, and
in a calm, subdued, and confident tone of voice, she observed as she
pointed to the pin, "Soldiers, let me make one more effort for my
brother."

The soldiers, startled at the strangeness of her manner, unloosed
their grasp upon her, and in a moment she bounded away to her
brother, shielding his body again with her person at the very moment that the guns were descending to receive the word "Fire!"
Turning her back to her brother, and facing the file of soldiers, she
stood forth a stately woman. There was no scream, no tear, no
agonizing expression, but, calm, and erect, she swept the field with
her eye, and then advancing three steps, she gave the grand hailing
signal of the Master Mason. None but masons among those soldiers
observed it, and there were many of them in that command, who
now stood mute with astonishment at the strange and mysterious
spectacle before them. There was a grouping of the officers for a few
minutes, when the captain came forward, and in a loud voice said,
"that owing to the distress and interference of the young woman,
the execution would be postponed until nine o'clock the next day."
The guard was then ordered to be doubled, and a strict watch kept
over the prisoner during the night.

Notwithstanding this precaution, it was discovered in the morning that both the boy and his sister had made their escape; in what
way they accomplished it has been a mystery with the company
from that time to this. During the early part of the evening, there
was a meeting of the masonic members of the company at the captain's quarters, where the girl was examined, and found to have
passed all the degrees in masonry, to that of a Master Mason. Where
or how she had acquired these degrees, she declined to say. She and
her brother had been in the United States but about ten weeks,

58

having come from Ireland for the purpose of purchasing a farm, intending when they had done so, to send for their mother and younger brother. The boy did not know that his sister was a mason, and only knew that his father, when living, was Master of a lodge in their native town of Ireland.

Of this story the Editor of the *Masonic Monthly*, in January 1869, writes:

This incident, which we copy from the *Evergreen*, we remember hearing at the time it occurred. We have no doubt there is considerable truth in the narrative. Our contemporary says of it: A correspondent, we do not know whether or not he is a mason, has sent us the following exceedingly well-told sensation story. Improbable as it is, the tale is worth reproducing in our columns. The author, who resides at Guttenburg, in Clayton County, was one of the war correspondents of that able paper, the *Chicago Tribune*, and forwarded this story from Helena, Arkansas, January 17, 1863.

During the annual convocation of the Grand Chapter of New Jersey in September, Grand High Priest Thomas J. Corson, told his members:

But even now, while we are congratulating ourselves on the present prosperity of our Order, a wail of sorrow and deep anguish is heard from Maine to California, from the Atlantic to the Pacific, which sickens the heart and saddens the soul of every true mason. We behold those who were but recently affectionate brethren and Companions, now engaged in an internecine and fratricidal war. Our beloved country is in peril, the horizon of our future is clouded in doubt and darkness, and the stoutest heart is appalled. Wicked and unprincipled demagogues, led on by unholy ambition, are seeking to destroy the government, and rend to fragments that union, to establish which a Washington fought and a Warren fell, which cost us the most precious blood of our forefathers, and under which we have attained a national greatness and prosperity unparalleled in the history of the world.

* * *

We have eulogized the characters of Washington, Franklin, Warren, *"et omne id genus,"* as true men and masons, because they boldly battle for truth, right and justice; and future masonic orators will include the name of Robert Anderson in this bright galaxy, as a true man and mason, because he nobly and bravely defended his country's honor. We honor such patriots, and we trebly honor the patriotism that prompted them to lay wealth, position, and all that is dear to the human heart, upon the altar of their country, as a willing sacrifice to duty.

Early in September an innocent looking building made of plain brick with a shingled roof and wooden gables, was the scene of a battle in Lexington, Missouri. Painted on the gables was the square and compasses enclosing the All Seeing Eye. That building was a Masonic college which had been erected by the Grand Lodge of Missouri almost 20 years before the outbreak of hostilities. It was located on a high hill over looking the Missouri river and the city of Lexington. Because of the strategic location, Colonel James Mulligan of the 23rd Illinois, chose the building as his fortress. On September 11, intrenchments were thrown up all about the city and the building. On the 12th, the Union forces held, although surrounded and beseiged by an overwhelming Confederate force under General Price, which was estimated to be between fifteen and thirty thousand men. For several days thereafter, there was a lull in the battle with only intermittent exchanges of artillery. On the morning of September 18, about nine o'clock, the attack was renewed by the Confederate forces. They advanced upon the college building behind hemp bales, which had been soaked with water to protect the men from the hot shell from the cannon in the college building. One of the participants described the action:

With plenty of coal and men to ply the bellows, the shot were readily super-heated. The gun, with a charge of powder in place, was then quickly wheeled out in range, and, with proper elevation, aimed at the big eye on the college gable. The hot shot then dropped into the cannon, on contact with the powder, was instantly sent out again on its mission. Several balls going through the gable, struck the rafters and fell to the floor below, as we calculated they would, but the vigilant soldiers at once caught them and threw them out of the window. Other shots perforated both the gable and the roof, and a few over-shot the building altogether, speeding far up the river.

The battle continued all day on the 19th, and during the afternoon a past grand master of the Grand Lodge of Missouri, Colonel Benjamin W. Grover, received a mortal wound.

On the 20th, with water and ammunition gone, Colonel Mulligan was forced to surrender. The victor in this battle was Gen. Sterling Price, a Mason, who, when he returned Mulligan's sword, said, "I cannot see a man of his valor without a sword," and ordered his men to in no way insult or harm the men who had been vanquished.

A Confederate participant had this to say about the results of the battle:

Our brilliant achievement at Lexington was barren of results save to demonstrate the fact that the sentiment of Missouri was not in harmony with the secession movement. General Price devised, and executed, the expedition with the hope and expectation that he could reach the central part of the state—the wealthy slave-holding section—with a respectable force, an opportunity would be afforded the people there in sympathy with the southern cause to join him; and that they would flock to his standard with such unanimity as to enable him to hold his position until reinforcements were sent him by the Confederate government. It was a delusive hope. He planned well, but the substantial Missourians were more interested in the conservation of their property and scalps than in sacrificing anything for the defense of any mere abstract principle. Yet when it became known that the garrison of 2,640 Union men had surrendered, large contingents of Missouri chivalry did rush into Lexington, frantic with enthusiasm and loud in their vapory declarations of loyalty to our cause. They came pouring in —large land owners, the slave holders, the chronic office seeker and moth-eaten politicians—in force as to seriously tax the resources of our commissary department. They were with us, but first must return home to arrange their business affairs and set their houses in order. Then came word that the Federals were on their way to dislodge us, and our recruits began to scatter. Some of them remained with us—for awhile. General Price left Lexington with an army of 22,000 men, two-thirds of whom were unarmed and unorganized. He crossed the Osage, going south, with barely 12,000; and less than 8,000 of us went into winter quarters at Springfield, to be hustled out by the Federals in January, and driven in wild flight down into the hills of Arkansas.

The governor of Missouri, Hamilton R. Gamble, a Mason, was doing all in his power to save the state for the Union, which helped account for the citizens not being "with" the Confederates.

Jesse Gove was in a camp in Spring Creek, Kansas, on September 30, 1861, when he wrote about the affair at Lexington, Missouri, to his friend Rolf:

By the last advices from the East, we hear of the fall of Lexington, Missouri. It seems extraordinary that General Price could have appeared at that point with sufficient force to take that place after two or three days fighting. It can be accounted for in no other way than that among the new fledged generals roaming around Missouri, each was waiting for the other, and while they were hesitating, Lexington was taken; and we now hear of Generals Pope, Lane, Hunter, Sturgis and others all marching to its relief just in season to be "too late." If no better generalship is displayed in Missouri in future, than characterized recent movements the rebels will have a foot-hold not easily displaced. We get but little news of late indeed as we approach the borders the items of news become more meagar and beautifully less. I fear to hear of the fight on the Potomac. I have great confidence in Gen. McClellan but the most I hear of him is in making his staff Generals in getting undeserving subalterns promotion.

While the battle around the Masonic College in Lexington was raging, a happy note was struck in a Masonic hall in Minnesota—a baby was born in the lodge room! Samuel Adams owned a general merchandise store in Monticello and rented the upstairs portion to Monticello Lodge, No. 16. On the night of September 15, 1861, because the living quarters at the rear of the store were crowded, Mrs. Adams was moved into the lodge room.

Soon after the expectant mother was settled in her new quarters, Dr. James W. Mulvey, the junior warden of the lodge, was hurriedly called. He brought into the troubled world Henry Rice Adams. The baby was to grow up to have a Masonic career as unusual as his place of birth. Twenty-three years later he was made a Mason in the room in which he was born. In 1903 he became grand master of Masons in Minnesota. On March 30, 1927, he was fatally stricken while attending a communication of Minnesota Lodge, No. 224. A highly successful Masonic life ended as it had started—in a Masonic lodge.

From Lexington General Price moved to Neosho, Missouri, where he protected Claiborne Jackson and 49 members of the

Missouri legislature during their secession meeting in the Masonic hall there. That session declared on October 28: "war exists between Missouri and the Federal government and is incompatible with the continuance of our union." The statement was greeted with cannon fire and shouts of joy from Price's men. There was only one thing wrong with the "Ordinance of Secession" adopted in the Masonic hall in Neosho—the governor and his legislators had been declared "fugitives" before they left the capital. But Richmond recognized it; so did thousands of Missourians.

An article by Colonel R. M. Kelley contains an excellent example about how Masons and members of the same family were split in their political thinking:

The military situation in Kentucky in September, 1861, cannot be properly understood without a brief sketch of the initial political struggle which resulted in a decisive victory for the friends of the Union. The State Legislature had assembled on the 17th of January in called session. The governor's proclamation convening it was issued immediately after he had received commissioners from the States of Alabama and Mississippi, and was followed by the publication of a letter from Vice-President Breckinridge advising the calling of a State convention and urging that the only way to prevent war was for Kentucky to take her stand openly with the slave States. About this time the latter's uncle, the Rev. Dr. Robert J. Breckinridge, an eminent Presbyterian minister, addressed a large meeting at Lexington in favor of the Union. The division of sentiment is further illustrated by the fact that one of his sons, Colonel W. C. P. Breckinridge, followed his cousin into the Confederate army, while another son, Colonel Joseph C. Breckinridge, fought for the Union. The position of the Union men was very difficult. They knew that Governor Magoffin was in sympathy with the secession movement and that the status of the Legislature on the question was doubtful. The governor had under his orders a military force called the State Guard, well armed and disciplined, and under the immediate command of General Simon B. Buckner, a graduate of West Point.

Robert Breckinridge was a member of Lexington Lodge, No. 1, Kentucky, as was his son, William; John belonged to Des Moines Lodge, No. 41, Burlington, and Good Samaritan Lodge, No. 174, Lexington, from which Lodge he was suspended in

1861, and not reinstated until 1871. Simon Buckner, who was to become a Confederate general, was also a Mason.

On October 1, 1861, the grand master of Iowa, Ira W. Buck, told his grand lodge:

One year since, we met while our country was at peace at home and abroad. Now we meet in the midst of preparation for war, and not far removed from the roar of cannon, the blast of the bugle, and the horrid, unearthly din of carnage and battle. One year since, we beheld the familiar faces of friends we shall never see on earth again.

The Grand Lodge of Tennessee met on October 7, 1861, and the war upset its plans so much that the proceedings of the grand lodge for that year were not printed until February 1, 1902, and were taken from the minute book in the office of the grand secretary at Nashville. Grand Master James McCallum, during the 49th annual communication in Nashville told his grand lodge:

But while we have so much to be thankful for, we meet, Brethren, under most extraordinary circumstances. As citizens, as members of the body politic, we have cause to mourn; we are passing a most fearful crisis. The horrors of war are upon our land. Twelve months ago, we could look out from this beautiful temple, the freest and happiest people on earth. But alas! A change has come over us. The government organized by the Father of His Country, and which we so fondly called *our government,* is in hostile array against us. The *Constitution* framed by our forefathers, and under whose wise provisions we have lived and were so prosperous and happy, no longer protects us. The *Union,* which we cherished with more than filial regard, is no more.

It is not the province of Masonry to inquire into the causes which have led to our national troubles, nor to suggest a remedy. But we cannot be indifferent to the fact that our civil relations with those around us, and with whom we lately mingled as Brethren in the sacred temple, have so sadly changed since our last Annual Communication. Let us, then, as Masons, humbly bow before Him in whom we have put our trust and implore His *wisdom* to direct us, His *strength* to support us, and His *arm* to defend us.

On the question of granting charters to the military lodges, the grand master had this to say:

Military or Traveling Lodges have been long sanctioned by the

Grand Lodges of England and Scotland; they have been authorized chiefly at long established military posts, or to troops in foreign countries, enlisted for a term of years. In this country they have been resorted to only in times of war. Army Lodges, or Traveling Lodges, existed in the time of the Revolutionary War, in the War of 1812, and in the War with Mexico. Since the commencement of the present war, they have been authorized in South Carolina and by New York and Connecticut, and perhaps other States. In this State, the question is comparatively a new one, and is not without difficulties. If our troops were in permanent forts or barracks, or if they were in a foreign country, where we recognized the jurisdiction of no other Grand Lodge, the question would present fewer difficulties. Our troops have volunteered for but one year. They are mostly in States, the jurisdictions of whose Grand Lodges we respect, and in whose bounds we can not establish Lodges without violating their rights. Some of the troops are still in our own State, and to create Lodges in the vicinity of other Chartered Lodges and make Masons of material in their bounds, without consulting them, would be in violation of long established principles.

He closed his address with these words:

In conclusion, Brethren, pardon me for reminding you, in view of our national troubles, that *Masonry* is founded on the great social maxim that "whatsoever ye would that men should do unto you, do ye even so to them." It consists in the regulation and enforcement of certain moral and social duties between its members, as rational and social beings; it has nothing to do with forms of government or religion; it knows no party, no sect or creed. The virtues it inculcates, and the duties it enjoins, lie at the foundation of all social happiness, and commend themselves to all good men in every country, without regard to its form of government or religion. Changes in these do not affect the relation of the parties; they are still bound to be true to the teachings of the Order. I therefore most earnestly and fraternally entreat you, in the trying ordeal through which we are passing, to exercise forbearance toward each other; and may the Supreme Ruler of the Universe guide and protect you, and those whom you represent, and keep you in the bonds of brotherly love.

The horrors of civil war prevented the Grand Lodge of Tennessee from meeting in annual communication at its stated time in October, 1862.

On the 15th of October a letter was read to the members of the Grand Lodge of Kansas from the grand master, George H. Fairchild, in which he apologized for being unable to be present. He asked the brethren for their indulgence for being unable to carry out their recommendations of the previous year, because of "the fact that I have been so much engaged in the discharge of the duties of the positions of trust that I hold at home, and the time I have felt called upon to lend for the defense of our country."

Richard R. Rees presented his credentials and was received as the representative of the Grand Lodge of Illinois near the Grand Lodge of Kansas. Among the things he told the Grand Lodge of Kansas were:

You, my brothers, have grown up as masons amid the conflicts of party strife and animosity, yet the clangor of arms has been with you, but the tocsin that sounded upon the hills of your new born State to call together a band of brothers bearing the olive branch of peace. But the dark cloud of war has lowered not only over Kansas—the startling roll of the alarm drum, and the shrill blasts of the bugle calls to arms the *stalwart* sons of our country, from Maine to Florida. Our common country heaves like the mighty ocean tossed by the fearful tornado. Friends are severed, the ties of kindred rent assunder, hatred burns in the bosoms of those that were wont to embrace each other in true affection.

> Alas, how slight a cause may move
> Dissension between hearts that love
> Hearts that the world in vain have tried,
> And sorrow but more closely tied;
>
> That stood the storm when waves were rough,
> Yet in a sunny hour fell off,
> Like ships that have gone at sea
> When heaven was all tranquility.

But 'tis not ours to censure or applaud; this we leave to the forum, the hustings, ensanguined field. Ours is the resting place of the wearied soldier, the seafarer and the husbandman. We ask not his nativity, nor do we care to know his bias. It is enough that he subscribes to the fundamental faith of masonry. How e'er the fate of revolutions turn we are admonished that our Order knows no bounds, of Kingdoms, States or Empires—from the clad regions of the Northern Seas, through all the varied climes of earth to the Antarctic Ocean, we are brothers, inseparable, through all the changing scenes of time our greetings are sincere, and we will fondly hope that this system of inter-communication shall continue to dispense its social blessings, while timeworn masonry shall live.

On the same day, the Grand Lodge of Ohio met in its annual communication and George Rex, acting grand master, had this to say:

In this deplorable crisis in our affairs, it becomes us, as Masons, to determine what is our duty to our country, our brethren and ourselves. In addition to the fealty, the loyalty and the attachment which every citizen owes to his country, it is enjoined upon every Mason, as his first and highest duty, to be true to his country and just to his government. We may not, as Masons, enter into any political controversy as to the cause of the present lamentable condition of affairs; but we may, nay, it is our duty, not only as Masons, but as citizens, to remember that our country and its constitution are in imminent danger, and that we are bound by every tie of honor, love and duty to defend them, and to maintain inviolate their safety and the honor of our flag.

Our duty to our brethren, which is second only to our duty and devotion to God and our country, is the duty of love, which bids us in the hour of triumph to remember mercy, and amid the strife, the tumult and the roar of battle, to be ever ready to extend the helping and protecting hand to a fallen foe.

On October 21, the grand master of Kentucky, Lewis Landram, told his grand lodge:

We have met under circumstances of a peculiar character. Our beloved commonwealth is the theater of civil strife, and where a few months since all was peace and quiet, the stirring drum and deep-mouthed cannon now breathe forth their tones of war. It is with no ordinary feelings of sadness that we look upon these empty seats, once filled by brethren from distant parts of our noble State; and, whilst we can but mourn the absence of many of those we have been accustomed to meet, we can but trust, that amid all the vicissitudes of life, they may ever prove faithful to the trusts confided to their care. It may be that we, in common with our fellow citizens, have wandered from the path of duty, and been forgetful of our obligations to God, our neighbors and ourselves; have failed to look to that higher source of strength, whence cometh all blessings.

During October, the Grand Chapter of Royal Arch Masons for Minnesota met, and the grand high priest, R. S. Alden, told his members:

Companions: We have fallen upon troublous times. At this second commemoration of our organization, we see our beloved country torn and convulsed with civil war. Though this is not the time or the occasion to advert to the causes which have led to and continued this unhappy strife, I cannot pass over in entire silence an event of such profound significance, which enters so largely into our daily thoughts and plans; so vitally affect all our interests, and is pregnant with such vast results to the political status of our country and the principles of free government throughout the world. Suffice it here to say, that as Royal Arch Masons, we have the proud and satisfactory consciousness that no word, or act, or teaching of any Chapter of either of the United States in which they exist, has hastened, or even remotely tended to bring about the deplorable evils which oppress us. We meddle with no political organizations, have no sectional objects to promote, nor can revolutions, dismemberment of states, or even the overthrow of civil government, and the prevalence of anarchy, sunder these indissoluble ties which bind the hearts of the royal craft in a beautiful and eternal union.

On the 5th of November, the grand master of the District of Columbia, Charles F. Stansbury, told his grand lodge:

I have felt on stranger shores, the thrill of patriotic pride and pleasure pervading every fibre of my frame, at the sight of the glorious ensign of our country, as it floated from the peak of one of our grand ocean monarchs, while entering some foreign harbor on its mission of peaceful commerce, or proclaimed from the masthead the nationality of some frowning man-of-war. . . . Every prompting of my will coincides with my clear Masonic duty to support and defend it. I hope to die—as I shall try to live—a Mason; but above and beyond all other hopes, is the heartfelt aspiration that I may retain to my latest breath, and transmit unimpaired to my children, that proudest title that humanity can boast—the title of an American citizen.

At the same communication, the committee on foreign correspondence wrote:

Let me here do justice to brethren of our Fraternity in Western Virginia, who promptly disclaimed all sympathy with the unmasonic course pursued by those in the eastern part of the State. . . . Had all Masons, north and south, been true to these teachings, the calamities of civil war would have been avoided, and Albert Pike would not now be engaged in the diabolical purpose of arming the fierce and bloodthirsty savages with tomahawk and scalping knife to carry desolation and death to our homes and firesides, and to destroy the Government that has so long fed and protected them.

68

The committee was referring to the fact that General Albert Pike and Colonel Douglas H. Cooper, in the fall and winter of 1861, organized three regiments of Indians from the Choctaw, Chickasaw, Cherokee, Creek, and Seminole nations or tribes, for service in the Indian Territory.

Even in far-off California, the effects of the Civil War were being felt among civilians and the Masonic lodges. In some cases lodges were split and new ones formed in an endeavor to keep Masonry alive and civic feelings out of the lodge. That situation was not peculiar to California alone, for in Wisconsin anti-Southern feeling had been running high since 1857, and one lodge refused to request a charter. The lodge was Nemadjii of Superior, which had been granted a dispensation in 1856. Later the Grand Lodge of Wisconsin received a report that some of the officers of Nemadjii Lodge, being Southern sympathizers, withdrew their association with the other members. Their withdrawal dealt a death-blow to all hope of forming a lodge that would prove successful, and Nemadjii Lodge was never to become a reality.

During the first three years of the Civil War in Wisconsin, six lodges were forced to give up their charters because of the number of their officers and members being in the Union forces. Nineteen new lodges were chartered during the same period, making that the first boom period in the history of Wisconsin Masonry.

In Missouri, a state where there appeared to be as many people that felt as strongly for one side as the other, many anomalous situations arose. Among them was a difference of opinion concerning the re-elected master of Clarksville Lodge, No. 17, J. W. Hemphill, who, in April, 1861, was re-installed by Rev. L. R. Downing. During that installation, the master refused to assent to certain ancient charges, according to a letter sent to the district deputy grand master, John F. L. Jacoby, who was also a member of Clarksville Lodge, by the junior warden, secretary, and junior deacon of the lodge. The grand master, William R. Penick, ordered his deputy to investigate the charges. He found that the master had assented to all of the charges of installation, but readily admitted he had certain political reservations of his own, and those he planned on retaining. He denied the right of the deputy to go into those. Jacoby removed the master from his office, and on November 16 he took the charter of the lodge away, stating a plotter against the government had been present in the lodge on the 9th. The "plotter" was a member of the lodge who had served as an officer with Sterling Price.

The Grand Lodge of Missouri acted. The committee to whom the matter was referred, without any evasion, reported:

The Grand Lodge and every grand officer, as such, are prohibited by all the teachings of our noble institution from any interference in the heart-rending strife now desolating our beloved country. We do not mean that multiplied ministrations of charity and kind offices to suffering and distressed brethren, whether engaged upon the one side or the other shall cease—for these ought to be everywhere redoubled with the single inquiry, is the brother in distress? It is not for us who have preserved relations of loyalty to our government to pronounce sentence of outlawry upon beloved brothers, who, wherever they may be, are doubtless as conscientious in their actions as we claim to be in ours. If they are in error, they are still our brethren; and they have the same equal right with us, as Masons, to determine their own political destiny, and we are not constituted their judges. We may grieve that so many of our brethren entertain conflicting political sentiments that lead to civil war and carnage; but as Masons we hope the day will never come when our lodge rooms will be closed against a worthy brother on account alone of such conflicting opinions.

The Grand Lodges of England and Scotland, with reference to our ancient brethren who rebelled against the former government, repudiated the power which a District Deputy in Missouri dared to exercise. Every standard Masonic authority upon Masonic law has expressly repudiated it. The ancient charges and regulations reproduced in our Book of Constitutions, repudiate it; and every impulse of intelligent Masonry condemns it. But in the case under consideration the brother had returned to his home and business. He had laid aside the flashing implements of war for the white robes of peace and, as it appears from the evidence, had given his parole of loyalty and bonds for good behavior. How unkind, therefore, to seek to close against him the doors of Masonry! Brotherly love and charity are mere names—Fraternity must at all times inspire us.

The grand lodge then acted upon a resolution declaring the

acts of the district deputy illegal, which the members approved and the charter was restored to the lodge. The committee took the grand master gently to task:

Your committee would further report that as to the portion of the address which refers to the decisions of the Grand Master, we can but express our admiration of that candor which prompted him to admit that they were of a "political" character, and as, in the opinion of your committee, the spirit and genius of our great order forbid, and its rules and regulations expressly prohibit, the consideration of anything of a political or sectarian character. Taking warning from the unhappy fate which has befallen other great and commendable institutions, by a departure from the strict course which their legitimate objects rendered necessary, and desiring to steer clear of that great rock which has rent asunder the church of God itself, and is now shaking from center to circumference the great temple of republican liberty, which, for more than three-quarters of a century, has been the admiration of the world, we can but conclude that the introduction of that portion of the address was unfortunate for our Grand Lodge, and that discussion or publication of it would be fraught with great evil to the fraternity at large.

The committee recommended that the political portions of the grand master's address be laid upon the table and omitted from the published proceedings, because it was "Looking alone to the future welfare and prosperity of our noble fraternity." The recommendation was adopted.

A thousand miles away a letter was written by an officer in the Federal army:

Fort McHenry, Md., November 25th, 1861

Hon. John S. Berry,
   M. W. Grand Master of the
     Grand Lodge of F. and A. M.
      Of the State of Maryland.

M. W. Sir and Brother:

The 3d Regiment, New York Volunteers—to which I am attached —encamped in June last at Camp Hamilton, Va., some two miles from Fortress Monroe, and about one mile from the village of Hampton.

This village had been deserted by its inhabitants, a short time previous to our arrival, and in such haste as to leave libraries, furniture, etc., exposed to the pillage and plunder of the hordes of negroes who congregated there immediately on the departure of the citizens. Much valuable property had been taken and destroyed by them.

Learning that there was a Masonic Hall in the place, and fearing for its safety, I reported the fact to Major General Butler, and obtained from him an order to take "a sufficient force, proceed to Hampton and take possession of such property belonging to the Masonic Order, as was thought proper, and report to him."

In accordance with this order, Col. S. M. Alford, commanding the 3d regiment, provided a detachment commanded by Captain John E. Mulfold, W. M. Mystic Lodge, No. 131, N. Y., Capt. John G. Butler, Central City Lodge, No. 315, Syracuse, N. Y., and Lieutenant William E. Blake, S. W. Excelsior Lodge, No. 195, N. Y., accompanied the detachment.

The property thus found, I have retained in my possession, hoping that a favorable opportunity might present itself to forward it directly to Richmond. But not having had such an opportunity, I take great pleasure in transferring the effects to you for safe keeping, subject to the order of the Grand Lodge of Virginia. Since taking this property, the hall, together with the entire village was destroyed by fire; and my associates with myself congratulate ourserves that we were the humble instruments in rescuing the Records and Warrants from that conflagration.

When this property shall be returned to our brethren in Virginia, please convey to them our fraternal regards, and say that although we come in defense of our just rights—as we honestly believe—still we come not to wage war upon an Order expressly founded to inculcate the exercise of *Brotherly Love, Relief and Truth.*

> With great respect,
> I remain fraternally,
> > J. H. CHASE,
> > Lt. and R. Quartermaster,
> > 3d N. Y. Vols.,
> > and P. M. Temple Lodge,
> > No. 14, Albany, N. Y.

The lodge in Hampton was St. Tammany Lodge, No. 5, which was chartered in 1759, 19 years before the Grand Lodge of Virginia was founded. That lodge had suffered through three wars, the War of Independence, the War of 1812 and the Civil War. It survived them all and continued to prosper and remain strong.

The sentiments expressed by Chase in his closing paragraph were later to be officially expressed in General Order No. 38, of General Butler's department:

Whereas the Government of the United States in its efforts for the preservation of the Union, is not warring upon charitable benevolent organizations, and certain proper, worthy and responsible persons representing the Masonic Fraternity have requested to be placed in quiet possession, as trustees, of the property of the same in this city [Newburn], it is ordered—

I. That all the buildings and appurtenances of the said Fraternity be immediately turned over to the following named persons: A. A. Rice, J. B. Knox, and W. L. Crowell.

II. The above-named trustees will give a proper receipt for the property to the Provost Marshal of North Carolina.

The correspondence committee of the Grand Lodge of Maryland commented on the letter received with the property of St. Tammany Lodge:

It is, my brethren, most gratifying to have in this the evidence, that, even when engaged on the battle-field, in the deadly strife of war, we do not forget our Masonic ties, or the duties we owe to the brethren of our noble and time-honored Order. It serves to convince us, that there lives in the hearts of all *true* Masons those fixed principles that will prompt them, when the din of battle shall have ceased, and brother no longer stands in strife against brother, contending for what each believes to be right, to gather in fraternal love around the Masonic altar, deeply deploring the necessity that brought them into collision, and invoking our Supreme Grand Master in behalf of a brother's welfare.

On each side of the contending armies, we have heard of noble instances, in which the tenets of our profession have been faithfully and beautifully exemplified, demonstrating that Masons do not forget that they are *brethren;* and that the lessons they are taught, to aid, support and protect each other, live in their conduct.

Reminded as we are, my brethren, of the mutability of all things earthly, that empires crumble and fall, nations fade and pass away, family ties are riven and social relations severed, surely these things should not fail to indelibly impress us, that there is a more enduring state, a higher, nobler trust, the state to which our highest hopes aspire, *"the Kingdom which fadeth not away,"* and the object of our firmest trust, our common Father, God.

The grand master of Alabama, Stephen F. Hale, was unable to be present when his grand lodge met in its annual communication on December 2. He was serving in the Confederate army near Centerville, Virginia. A letter he had written two weeks earlier was read, in which he apologized for being unable to attend to his official duties during the year he had been grand master. His civil duties had included "1st, as a Commissioner from the State of Alabama to the State of Kentucky; then a representative in the Legislature of my own State; next a member of the Congress of the Confederate States; and since about the middle of June last, I have been in the military service of the country, in the State of Virginia."

Hale was mortally wounded "in the Great Battle before Richmond" and died in that city on July 18, 1862. Suitable resolutions were ordered prepared at the annual communication of 1862, and it was readily agreed that "his brilliant intellect" would be keenly missed in "the bar, the legislature and the congress hall, and the Lodge of which he was at once the member and the ornament."

When the Grand Lodge of Virginia met on December 9, 1861, the members were unaware of what had transpired in Maryland. The grand master, John Robin McDaniel, issued a harsh edict to his members, which was softened by his closing remarks:

We are permitted again my dear brethren, to assemble within "This sacred retreat of Friendship and Love." It is not as formerly we come from our quiet firesides, but from the turmoil and strife of a dismembered country.

The lowering cloud, so threatening in its character at your last Grand Annual Communication, soon after burst in its fury, involving our country in sectional warfare, and which has since been waged with unrelenting bitterness. Occasionally the gloom may have seemed to abate its *wrath*, but it was only to increase in strength, to renew the conflict with redoubled *force*.

It is with saddened hearts that we find that the baneful influence of this bitter strife has extended to and taken root with our Grand Jurisdiction. Upon the call of the roll, "silence prevails" in many Subordinates. We deeply deplore the absence of many brethren, whom we have been wont to greet with the most fraternal and social feelings.

We know that many who are absent are in the ranks, battling for our *rights* and our family altars, and let us in Charity at least hope, that many, if not all, located in disaffected portions of our State, are absent from military restrictions, and not from any estrangement of Masonic feelings, and that when the glad tidings of peace shall be sounded throughout our now oppressed land, when we shall have gained our independence, and have taken our stand amongst the nations of the earth, we trust, at least, then we shall see our Western and North Western brethren again in their places, united once more around our Holy Altar, joining in thanksgivings and praises to our Supreme Grand Master, for all His inestimable gifts; for the will and the means of resisting oppression, and, more especially, for His protecting hand, which guided us safely through our troubles.

War—dreadful war—brings with it many a scourge—truly may it be said to be "the times that try men's souls." It is well calculated deeply to exercise the Masonic's mind—brother meets brother in deadly *strife*. The principles of Masonry are outraged. By whom? Each may, and doubtless will, accuse the other. The battle-field is no place for discussion. Our country calls and our first duty under God is to obey. If our soil be polluted by an invader's tread, be he Mason or Profane, drive him back. We are bound to protect our property, our families and ourselves. Should the Square and Compass glitter on the breasts of an advancing *foe*, use it as a mark, and bring the invader to the dust. He fights under false colors; he violates the fundamental objects of the Order; he is unworthy of your confidence and protection; he uses the symbols of the Order for mercenary purposes and would prostitute its Holy principles. A true Mason invades the rights of no man; on the contrary, espouses the cause of the oppressed.

The battle over, visit the field of carnage and give the most extended scope to your Masonic feelings—administer to the sufferers all the comforts at your command; treat kindly those whom the fortunes of war have thrown in your power, regarding that a fallen and prostrate foe is no longer our enemy; but conquered, he should excite our pity. An unresisting *foe* should soften the asperities of our nature, and entitle him at our hands to the exercise of that most exalted attribute of Diety—*Mercy*.

These are the teachings of Masonry; the exercise thereof, the fruits—blending most happily in the true Masonic character the *valiant warrior* and the *good Samaritan*.

The Grand Lodge of Pennsylvania met on St. John the Evangelist's Day, December 27, and the grand master, John Thomson, alluded briefly to what was transpiring in the political arena:

... If I allude to the troubles that now distract and divide this once united and happy country, I do it in a Masonic spirit, though, alas, I fear that Masonry is powerless to still the whirlwind or allay the storm that now hovers o'er us. Yet, if Masonry is powerless to heal and unite this bleeding and distracted nation, it is also at the same time powerful to relieve, commiserate with, and succor individual brethren on either side, engaged in this fratricidal strife.

In war, as well as in peace, the Masonic duty, and the Masonic privilege, are alike binding and reciprocal. By the ancient constitutions of Masonry, a brother, even when engaged in rebellion against his country, is still to be considered as a Mason; his character as such being indefeasible. Then whenever opportunity offers, let us show ourselves true to our teachings, by mitigating the sufferings and alleviating the distresses that follow in war's dread train, for such *is* the mission of Masonry.

On the same day, a letter was read to the members of the Grand Lodge of the District of Columbia, the offer accepted, and a unanimous vote of thanks tendered by them:

Washington, D. C., December 27th, 1861
To the Most Worshipful Grand Master Officers and
Brethren, of the District of Columbia
MOST WORSHIPFUL SIR AND BRETHREN: We the undersigned, R. W. Charles DeCosta Brown, M.D., of New York, and P. M. Joseph B. Alexander, M.D., of New York, would most respectfully inform this Grand Body of the District of Columbia, that through the solicitations of many prominent Masons of the State of New York, viz: R.W.P.G.M. John J. Crane, M.D.; R.W. James M. Austin, M.D. G. Secretary of the city and State of New York and many others, we have opened an office, No. 410 Seventh Street, Washington, for the purpose of embalming and preserving the bodies of such brother Masons, citizens or soldiers who may be so unfortunate as to die or be killed, while at the seat of war and away from their families and friends.

Our process is that of the celebrated Professor Brother Sucquet, of Paris, by which all the distinguished personages who have died in France for a number of years past have been preserved, and is now endorsed by the whole medical faculty of New York, as the only method by which a dead body can be perfectly preserved with life-like expression for all time, and without change of color or feature. The process is simple—that of merely injecting the whole body from one small artery with a powerful antiseptic fluid which contains no arsenic or other poison, and which instantly arrests decomposition and gradually hardens the body into a marble like mass.

The truly sympathetic heart must immediately appreciate the advantage of having the body of a deceased friend or relative returned to its sacred home free from the taint and ghastly discolor of a decaying corpse.

By our system persons dying away from their homes can be returned to the bosom of their friends in as perfect condition as at the day of their death, and can be thus retained for months or years without the necessity of immediate burial, as a corpse embalmed by us presents all the appearance of sleeping life, rather than the gloom of death.

We therefore humbly pray that this Grand Body will take cognizance of that fact, and all Subordinate Lodges to whom this shall become known, and that they with Masons generally will notify us immediately of the demise of any brother Mason, whose body they may wish to preserve by embalmment, and such bodies we pledge ourselves to embalm and preserve free of cost and without other charge, or professional fees, when recommended by any Lodge of the District.

Yours in the Mystic Bond,
DR. JOS. B. ALEXANDER,
CHARLES DECOSTA BROWN,
No. 410 Seventh Street
Washington, D. C.

The year 1861 ended and found Masonry affected but little by the events that had transpired since the beginning of the year. Feelings were strained in some cases; the work in a few lodges was interrupted, but the full effects were to be felt in the succeeding years. The annual communications of all grand lodges were held as scheduled and the legislation passed and words spoken were, as a whole, surprisingly tolerant, a situation that was to exist throughout the conflict. Masons on the field had proven their patriotism to the side on which they fought, but they also had proved that the teachings of Freemasonry were more deeply lodged in their hearts than anyone would have suspected months earlier.

CHAPTER VII

Gunfire on the Tennessee River

◇◇

And see the rivers how they run
Through woods and meads, in shade and sun,
Sometimes swift, sometimes slow,
Wave succeeding wave, they go
A various journey to the deep
Like human life to endless sleep!

JOHN DYER

A NEW YEAR dawned and with it the peacefulness of a whole section of the country was brutally disturbed. Rivers were literally turned red with the blood of brothers and friends, and those rivers were running in the wrong direction for the South. They were open channels for invasion, poor for Southern communication, a situation the Federal armed forces was to exploit to the fullest. The flooded condition of those rivers during the winter of 1861-62 was to prove an undisguised blessing for the people who continued to hold allegiance to Washington. A harsh war was to become more harsh.

In the capital of the Federal government George McClellan was laying the foundation for an army that was to be great, celebrated, and well organized. Twenty-five miles away in Manassas, Virginia, Joseph E. Johnston was endeavoring to do the same with the Confederate forces. He was to do an excellent job with what he had, but men and supplies in the South were limited. Guns, powder, and bullets were so scarce that the noise for celebrations had to be confined to the beating of drums.

Affairs in the West were no better for the Confederates. Albert Sidney Johnston was given command of the forces between the Alleghenies and the Mississippi. He, who was considered one of the ablest soldiers of the Confederacy, was forced to

78

establish the best military line possible under existing conditions. That military line had to stretch over 300 miles from the mountains to the Mississippi, and before spring it was to be penetrated repeatedly.

An Ohio Mason wrote some of his war experiences for the *Cincinnati Masonic Review:*

At the battle of Stone[s] River [December 30, 1862 to January 3, 1863], Major V——— deployed his battalion as skirmishers on the left of the line. Through some fatal mistake of one of the generals, the line at that point was withdrawn, and the Major, together with Captain C———, were taken prisoners by the enemy. A hurried march, a few days of temporary prison life, and they were huddled into Salisbury.

After some months of captivity, they seized a favorable opportunity and escaped. Days of hunger and nights of weary travel over the mountains of North Carolina, and they were again within sight of the Stars and Stripes, when a party of Confederates again took them prisoners. "There in a lonely mountain pass," said Major V——— to me, "without a friend or hope, the days passed wearily indeed. In one of the cells of the county jail, Captain C——— and I, the only inmates of the room, both Masons, made in the same Lodge, spent many an hour that *otherwise* might have been pleasant, in social song and converse.

"I wore on the lapel of my coat, a small masonic breast-pin, merely to be fashionable with Masons (largely represented) in the great Army of the Union. One day our guard, a bitter enemy, pacing back and forth before our cell, suddenly stopped before the door, looked at me for a moment, unlocked the door, and ordered me to come out and follow him. In a little room adjoining he became satisfied that I was a Mason, and I with him, and I vouched for Captain C———. The Lodge met that night, and our newly found brother got exempt from duty, went to the Lodge, and told the story of our captivity, when a committee was appointed to visit us. They came the next day—three of them,—were introduced, and in the usual manner, examined us as Master Masons. They were satisfied, and we received promise of assistance.

"General A———, the commandant of the post, and a Mason, was appealed to; he gave us the freedom of the town on our parole, and many were the little favors we received."

The Major and the Captain learned an attempt was going to be made by the Union prisoners to escape, so they returned to prison rather than violate their parole. Several days later, they, and 200 other prisoners managed to break out of the prison. Many weary days later they reached Federal troops. But that did not end the Major's story. He went on to tell how his life was saved:

Once since then, in battle, the enemy charged upon my line with bayonets. The line wavered, fell back, and I alone was destined to be a victim. *Literally* the bayonet was at my breast, in the hands of one who was to me a perfect demon, so intense was his feeling of hatred at the time, when an exclamation of agony attracted his attention, the bayonet was lowered, and I was saved. Politics would have hung me, the Church failed me, but the grand old principles of our glorious Order secured to me life, happiness, and freedom.

Early in January a Mason named David G. Farragut was contacted and requested to take command of a Federal naval force whose ultimate goal was to capture and secure New Orleans. Farragut was a Virginian who early in the war had been asked to take charge of the Confederate Navy. He had refused, choosing to remain with the government he had served since 1810 when he had entered the navy at the age of nine. He accepted the challenge and went on to build a strong naval attacking force from vessels of all descriptions and sizes.

In far away Vermont, the committee on foreign correspondence reported to its grand lodge on January 8, 1862:

Our unhappy national troubles form the burden of many Grand Master's Addresses, and yet we rejoice to find that every Grand Lodge has acted, in regard to them, dispassionately, and in an eminent spirit of conservatism.

Though we, as Masons, are firm and decided in our support of this glorious Government, still we are not yet ready, even in this wicked rebellion against the "powers that be" of a large section of the country, to inculcate amongst us a spirit of retaliation or revenge. Let us rigidly live up to the requirements of justice, but do not let us fling away the mantle of charity; for the day may not be far distant when our misguided brethren of the south may see the folly of their ways, and return, repentant, to the loyalty they once professed.

Stilman Blanchard, grand secretary and chairman of the correspondence committee for the Grand Lodge of Michigan, on the same day, reported to his grand lodge in much the same vein:

With respect to the political condition of the country, we have found the brethren of the various jurisdictions, as it were, holding their breath, and depreciating the strife, and while disclaiming either their right or their duty as *Masons* to enter the conflict, yet we find a disposition on the part of our brethren in other jurisdictions to acknowledge the brotherly tie, and as much as in them lies, to soften, both by precept and example, the asperities naturally engendered by the lamentable state of facts now existing.

The grand master of Michigan, Horace S. Roberts, stated in a letter from "Annapolis Junction, Maryland, January 4th, 1862," he must "be absent when the roll of our Grand Lodge is called for the first time in 12 years." He closed his letter with a prayer that Masonry would do all it could to retain the respect of the world. His grand lodge apparently felt as he did according to this report, made by a special committee, and condensed for the *Proceedings* by the Grand Secretary:

The committee heretofore appointed on the state of the country, reported that they had had the subject under consideration, and while they deeply deplored, as every Mason must, the present unhappy and disturbed condition of affairs, they were strongly of the opinion that it was neither the duty nor policy of this Grand Body to give any expression of views on political questions which deeply agitate the nation at large, and upon which Masons were divided in sentiment and feeling. It had always been the policy of the Order to refrain from interference in questions of National and State politics, because upon all such questions Masons are divided in opinion, and because the discussion of such themes is calculated to irritate the passions and disturb that perfect harmony which should ever exist between the members of the fraternity. A different course of action would not only lead to dissentions among ourselves, but would soon destroy the universality of the institution, and render our principles sectional in their influence, and operation. For these reasons the committee were decidedly opposed to any expression of opinion as to the causes or motives which had produced the present troubles of our country. It was sufficient for them that we knew our duty and had the disposition to perform it fearless of consequences. At the same time the committee did not wish to be misunderstood. As Masons, they had been taught to revere government, and be true and loyal citizens, and it was not without sorrow and regret that they witnessed the effort that was making to destroy what they considered the noblest and best government on the face of the globe. But as it was not the province of Masons to discuss political, or questions of State policy, we must content ourselves with endeavoring to keep whole the bonds of union which still subsisted between the members of the craft in every part of our country, and leave to others the discussion of mixed questions of politics.

The committee closed their report with the fervent hope that peace might speedily be restored to gladden thousands of hearts, and make happy thousands of homes. The report was unanimously adopted and ordered printed.

Later, the grand lodge upheld Francis Darrow, then grand master, who, when deputy grand master, refused several petitions for the formation of military lodges. Then the grand lecturer reported:

To some of the Lodges, my visits were peculiarly welcome, and renewed instruction to the brethren, of more than ordinary importance, owing to the fact that the officers elect were absent from their halls, in obedience to the requirements of our national government, for volunteers, to sustain the integrity of the Union. The active duties of the Lodges, in the meantime, devolved upon those who were not well prepared for the emergency, and who, therefore, desired the aid of the Grand Visitor and Lecturer.

Amid the great political trials of our country, it gives me pleasure to state that the interests of our Order have been maintained with commendable zeal by the faithful of our household; indeed, our Lodges are dearer to us now than ever, for there we find order, and unity, and peace.

While some of our noble brothers, whose cordial greetings we miss on this occasion, are battling for the overthrow of anarchy, and the preservation of law, on fields as extensive as the nation itself, others, on fields less extensive, but equally sacred, are laboring to support the same principles at home.

The same conditions were prevalent throughout the country. Many lodges had lost their officers and well-informed members to the armed services, both North and South. The faithful few at home were exerting every effort to keep their lodges alive, and their success was amazing. More new lodges were formed during the war years than gave up their charters. The membership in Freemasonry increased to a greater extent during the four years of war than during any similar period in its history.

That was to give rise to much concern from grand masters in every state. They feared the quality of the new Masons would be lessened because of the large numbers petitioning the organization. Those fears, in general, were to prove groundless.

The grand master of Florida, D. C. Dawkins, on January 13, told his grand lodge:

When we last met in Grand Annual Communication in this hall, our beloved country was the scene of immense and fearful national troubles, which, soon after, engulfed the nation in a bloody, and, I fear, long to be protracted war. And my first official act, after the close of the Grand Lodge, was to grant, on the 13th of May last, a dispensation to a sufficient number of Florida Volunteers, at Warrenton, near Pensacola. Our Worthy Grand Lecturer, Brother James Ellenwood, being present when the dispensation was received, instituted the Lodge, and which, I am informed, has been attended with happy and useful fraternal results. This evidences the fact, that our brethren, though clothed in the habiliments of war, and subjected to the hardships and privations of the camps, in defense of their country's liberty, yet they have lost no zeal for the Institution, which they delighted to advance and to honor.

His deputy grand master, Henry J. Stewart, sent a letter from "Camp Wynn's Mill, near Yorktown, Va., December 27th, 1861," in which he said he, too, had issued a dispensation for "a Regimental Traveling Lodge."

A Virginian, and Mason, who had remained with the Federal government, and whom that government viewed with suspicion, proved his worth at Mill Springs, Kentucky, on January 19 and 20. That man was George H. Thomas, who General Don Carlos Buell had sent against the Confederate forces of Zollicoffer, who was killed early in the engagement, and George B. Crittenden. Thomas, with a small force, handled the situation so well that he won an ample victory. The victory was so complete that it reached the president, who sent congratulations to the forces, but no where in that congratulatory message did Lincoln mention the name of Thomas.

With Thomas' victory, the Eastern part of Kentucky was cleared of Confederate troops. General James A. Garfield, a Mason, had the command of Humphrey Marshall bottled up near Big Sandy, so their presence was ineffectual.

Early in February, the value of the navy was firmly established. Near noon on the 6th, gunboats steamed up the Tennessee to endeavor to capture a poorly located fort. So badly was Fort Henry situated that it fell two hours after the engagement started. Its commander, General Lloyd Tilghman, had only kept up the hopeless battle to enable his garrison to escape to Fort Donelson on the Cumberland, 12 miles away. The extensive damage done by the gunboats during their bombardment was reported by Admiral Henry Walke:

When I took possession of the fort the Confederate surgeon was laboring with his coat off to relieve and save the wounded; and although the officers and crews of the gunboats gave three hearty cheers when the Confederate flag was hauled down, the first inside view of the fort sufficed to suppress every feeling of exultation and to excite our deepest pity. On every side the blood of the dead and wounded was intermingled with the earth and their implements of war. . . . But few of the garrison escaped unhurt.

Among the Masons who took part in the capture of Fort Henry was William D. Porter who commanded the *Essex*. He, along with John A. Logan and Edwin S. McCook, also Masons, was to go on to the more heavily fortified and manned Fort Donelson. There they were to fight with, and against, dozens of other Freemasons.

Among those Masons was General Lew Wallace, one of Grant's divisional commanders. He was the Lew Wallace who was to write one of the all-time best selling novels, a story he was contemplating writing even during the Civil War. But it was not until a chance meeting with Colonel Robert G. Ingersoll, a man who had earned the title of "The Great Agnostic" that he decided, as he wrote later, "to bring Christ into the story I was writing. I resolved to fill the book with accessory incidents which should tend to give the reader an idea of the moral, social and political condition of the world at that period; out of which shrewd minds might evolve one of the most powerful arguments for the divinity of Christ."

Not even Wallace could have foreseen the results of *Ben-Hur;* a work that was to be read by thousands of people throughout the years; a work that was to become a motion picture that was to receive the acclaim of the entire free world; a picture that on April 4, 1960, was to receive more awards from the Academy of Motion Picture Arts and Sciences than any other film in its 32 year history (except *Gone With the Wind,* a Civil War story); a picture that was directed by another Mason, William Wyler, a member of Loyalty Lodge, No. 519, California, and for which he was to receive his third "Oscar."

In an article about "The Capture of Fort Donelson," Wallace proved his remarkable insight of human nature:

A peculiarity of the most democratic people in the world is their hunger for heroes. The void in that respect had never been so gaping as in 1861. General Scott was then old and passing away, and the North caught eagerly at the promise held out by George B. McClellan; while the South pinned its faith and hopes on Albert Sidney Johnston. There is little doubt that up to the surrender of Fort Donelson the latter was considered the foremost soldier of all who chose rebellion for their part.

* * *

Having taken the resolution to defend Nashville at Donelson, he [Johnston] intrusted the operation to three chiefs of brigade—John B. Floyd, Gideon J. Pillow, and Simon B. Buckner. Of these, the first was ranking officer, and he was at the time under indictment by a grand jury at Washington for malversation as Secretary of War under President Buchanan, and for complicity in an embezzlement of public funds. As will be seen, there came a crisis when the recollection of the circumstance exerted an unhappy influence over his judgment. The second officer had a genuine military record; but it is said of him that he was of a jealous nature, insubordinate, and quarrelsome. His bold attempt to supersede General Scott in Mexico was green in the memories of living men. To give pertinency to the remark, there is reason to believe that a personal misunderstanding between him and General Buckner, older than the rebellion, was yet unsettled when the two met at Donelson. All in all, therefore, there is little doubt that the junior of the three commanders was the fittest for the enterprise intrusted to them. He was their equal in courage; while in devotion to the cause and to his profession of arms, in tactical knowledge, in military bearing, in the faculty of getting the most service out of his inferiors, and inspiring them with confidence in his ability—as a soldier in all the higher meanings of the word—he was greatly their superior.

The battle for the fort was costly for both sides. Grant had

85

decided upon taking it by force rather than having his troops enter upon a siege. With all hope of reinforcements arriving to assist them gone, the Confederate generals determined, "it would be wrong to subject the army to a virtual massacre, when no good could result from the sacrifice, and that the general officers owed it to their men, when further resistance was unavailing, to obtain the best terms of capitulation possible for them."

General Wallace's narrative continues:

Both Generals Floyd and Pillow acquiesced in the opinion. Ordinarily the council would have ended at this point, and the commanding general would have addressed himself to the duty of obtaining terms. He would have called for pen, ink, and paper, and prepared a note for dispatch to the commanding general of the opposite force. But there were circumstances outside the mere military situation which at this juncture pressed themselves into consideration. As this was the first surrender of armed men banded together for war upon the general government, what would the Federal authorities do with the prisoners? This question was of application to all the gentlemen in the council. It was lost to view, however, when General Floyd anounced his purpose to leave with two steamers which were to be down at daylight, and to take with him as many of his division as the steamers could carry away.

General Pillow then remarked that there were no two persons in the Confederacy whom the Yankees would rather capture than himself and General Floyd. . . . As to the propriety of his accompanying General Floyd, the latter said, coolly, that the question was one for every man to decide for himself. Buckner was of the same view, and added that as for himself he regarded it as his duty to stay with his men and share their fate, whatever it might be. Pillow persisted in leaving. Floyd then directed General Buckner to consider himself in command. Immediately after the council was concluded, General Floyd prepared for his departure. His first move was to have his brigade drawn up. The peculiarity of the step was that with the exception of one, the 20th Mississippi regiment, his regiments were all Virginians. A short time before daylight the two steamboats arrived. Without loss of time the general hastened to the river, embarked with his Virginians, and at an early hour cast loose from the shore, and in good time, and safely, he reached Nashville. He never satisfactorily explained upon what principle he appropriated all the transportation on hand to the use of his particular command.

Colonel Forrest was present at the council, and when the final resolution was taken, he promptly announced that he neither could nor would surrender his command. The bold trooper had no qualms upon the subject. He assembled his army, all as hardy as himself, and after reporting once more at headquarters, he moved out and plunged into a slough formed by backwater from the river. An icy crust covered its surface, the wind blew fiercely, and the darkness was unrelieved by a star. There was fearful floundering as the command followed him. At length he struck dry land, and was safe. He was next heard of at Nashville.

General Buckner, who throughout the affair bore himself with dignity, ordered the troops back to their positions and opened communications with General Grant, whose laconic demand of "unconditional surrender," in his reply to General Buckner's overtures, became at once a watch-word of the war.

Fort Donelson was surrendered on the morning of February 16 by Buckner to a man he had befriended eight years earlier. After Grant had resigned from the army, he was stranded without the funds necessary to return home. Hearing of his plight, Buckner went to his aid and gave him the necessary money. The strangest of all wars saw a virtually unknown general, U. S. Grant, win from a friend the greatest victory the Federal forces had attained.

The victory was great without question. The Tennessee was opened to Federal vessels and Johnston's left was cut from his center. But perhaps the greatest calamity for the South was the loss of one-third of its coal supply and large amounts of iron-ore.

Brigadier General Stephen A. Hurlbut, a Mason, who was to be promoted to major general for meritorious conduct at Shiloh, was placed in command of the fort, and the troops moved up the Tennessee River.

General Pierre Beauregard, who disagreed wholeheartedly with the secretary of war, Judah P. Benjamin, as many other Confederate generals were to do, was ordered to join Albert Johnston in Kentucky. That order caused angry words between General Joseph Johnston and the secretary of war. The former felt that the removal of Beauregard was a great mistake.

Early in February, Beauregard arrived in Nashville where he stopped to make public addresses in the Masonic auditorium. He joined with Father Abram Ryan in encouraging the Tennesseans not to give up hope for the cause they considered just.

Whether or not their words were heeded made no difference. Nashville was occupied by Federal troops the day following Jefferson Davis' inauguration as the first, and last, president of the Confederate States of America, and Andrew Johnson, a Mason, was made military governor of Tennessee.

George Washington's birthday fell six days after the capture of Fort Donelson and the Confederates celebrated it by inaugurating the permanent government in Richmond. The ceremonies took place at the foot of the equestrian statue of Washington, the cornerstone of which had been laid by the Grand Lodge of Virginia on February 22, 1850. The same grand lodge had dedicated it only four years before President Jefferson Davis received the oath of office in the midst of a large group of citizens which included the clergy, members of the press, members of his cabinet, city and state officials, and "the Masons and other benevolent societies."

Davis was inaugurated the president of a country that was to be recognized by no political entity. The government of the United States never dealt with it except militarily. The European countries, which at one time looked in favor on the Confederacy, after the fall of Donelson, turned away from the group of states that had formed a country. The Confederate commissioners, under their secretary of state, Robert Toombs, continued doing what little they could toward obtaining recognition, but to no avail.

With the action of the war being stepped up, many grand masters felt it would be well to remind the Masons under them of their Masonic obligations to each other and to everyone in general. On March 21, 1862, Grand Master David Ramsey of South Carolina wrote:

Wisdom, Union, Strength

From the Grand East of Charleston, this twenty-first day of March, in the year of Light, five thousand eight hundred and sixty-two, the Most Worshipful Grand Master in South Carolina, to all under his jurisdiction, Masters, Fellow Crafts and Entered Apprentices, sends greeting:

Brethren:

The Grand Lodge, anxious for your prosperity and desirous that

88

as members of the great mystic family, you should preserve in unfaded brightness the light of Masonry which had been entrusted to your keeping, did heretofore address an encyclical letter of advice and admonition. In the last Grand Communication, moved by like feeling, it made request of me to direct another letter unto the same purpose.

I republish and affirm the former letter for your guidance in all respects therein set forth; as to other general doctrines, my brethren, the Masters of Lodges will admonish you; it is your duty, and should be your pleasure, to hearken diligently and observe their precepts. Special matters remain concerning which I have to charge you. Walk circumspectly in the present evil time, ever mindful of solemn undertakings on your part in the presence of Almighty God: Be faithful in observance thereof towards all and singular the brethren, whether these be met in Lodges dedicate, or only known to you by divers means, in darkness or light; in health or sickness; in wealth or want; in peril or safety; in prison, escape or freedom; in charity or evil-mindedness; armed or unarmed; friend or seeming foe, and as to these, most certainly as towards brethren, when masonically met on, by or with all due and regular intercommunication and intelligence. You have registered words which cannot be unspoken or recalled, antedating as they will survive all disturbance among men and turmoils in State; words which in fullest force and meaning should be ever present unto you in thought, utterance and deed. Time with its affairs will soon to every one be past. We are at labor for a short while only in the work of Him who hath no respect of persons, building us, if meet, into another and an enduring temple; if vouchsafed unto us to be so edified, it will never be regret to remember any good deed done in the name of a common Master and Father to whatsoever brother, even him whom the profane would call an enemy. If we do good to those who love us and do good unto us, what more do we than other men? I charge every one of you, in the name of our Supreme and Universal Master, to be mindful how you are bound in certain duties whereunto you have called Him to witness your obligations and performance who will hereafter judge. I charge you, in His great name and in view of His final day, suffer not the disputes and broils of men to impair the harmony which has existed and will exist throughout the fraternity: for whether or not you put to shame the teachings of our Craft, they cannot be annulled: not, despite evil members who may pain us, can the body of our faithful brotherhood be annihiliated or destroyed, even so much as paralyzed.

Let us not hear among us that there is war, that strife and dissension prevail; as Masons it concerns us not.

Speak no ill of your brethren; if you have aught against one, suffer not your anger to get the mastery of your troth. If any, deeming that their personal desires of advancement or gain have been hindered by a brother, clamor unto you, heed them not when they speak apart: consider that it were unmasonic and unmanly to take amends by backbiting and slandering: harken not to such, nor be covetous, joining together and complotting, whereby brethren unheard and undefended, may be injured. There are such among you, of such make not further observation than to shun their errors. Except unto themselves, blame them not for speaking, nor blame those of whom it is spoken: Listen not to the one, nor repeat to the other; let the great Searcher of Hearts alone decide on right or wrong. Judge not when one accuses and the other is absent. You do gravest wrong as men not even called Masons, should you act on partial judgments severally formed. Nevertheless, should this wrong be done unto you, forgive even when misjudged, forgive as you hope to be forgiven. Above all things, give no cause of offense; see that your brother has no just complaint against you; walk erect and upright, in fact as well as appearance—Masons. Remember wherein to be zealous to give aid, counsel, protection; lend attentive ear, preserve a faithful breast, having withal a ready and true heart. If it be ill to speak evil, how much more is it to do evil.

It were useless to write unto you save to remind you of these things, and but for my office-sake I should not warn or counsel or commend, for speaking without vain humility, I best know how much I have of error and regret, how much I have to learn and listen: I was constrained to write, and that not as one having authority of himself, but such as was placed in his hands to write doctrine approved among us at all times.

I laud and honor you, brethren, for many things, and chiefly forasmuch as you have been diligent in your work of faith, hope and charity. You have been and are constant in well doing; some among us have gone astray, but even these wandered from our fold and erred not within its sacred bounds; their condemnation is of themselves and not of us. You may say without boastfulness that you have fulfilled your undertakings in your Lodges unto all whencesoever coming in our common name. So continue and not for praise of men, but looking forward to the time when your example will confirm future good deeds in good or evil days, and also looking forward beyond all times to the well-done of our Master who is in Heaven.

And may the Supreme Grand Architect of the Universe ever have you in His holy keeping. May brotherly love prevail, and every moral and social virtue cement you in the bonds of peace and fellowship.

DAVID RAMSEY, Grand Master of Masons

90

Before that letter could be mailed, Halleck was planning new offensives to keep the Confederates off-balance. Early in March, General Samuel R. Curtis, a Mason, arrived in Missouri in an endeavor to end Confederate resistance in that state. On the 7th he met another Mason at Elkhorn Tavern. There he was to defeat Sterling Price in a battle that was to be known as Pea Ridge.

In that battle Indians under the command of General Albert Pike participated. They were to be charged with scalping and mutilating the dead on the field; charges that were to give the Northern press a field day. About that charge Wilie Britton wrote:

General Pike, hearing of the scalping, called on the surgeon and assistant-surgeon of his field-hospital for reports, and in their reports they stated that they found one of the Federal dead who had been scalped. General Pike then issued an order, denouncing the outrage in the strongest language, and sent a copy of the order to General Curtis. General Pike claimed that part of the Indians were in McCullouch's corps in the first day's battle; and that the scalping was done at night in a quarter of the field not occupied by the Indian troops under his immediate command. After Pea Ridge the operations of the Confederate Indians . . . were confined, with few exceptions, to the Indian Territory.

Among those wounded during the battle was General Francis J. Herron, a member of Mosaic Lodge, No. 125, Iowa. He was to recover and continue active throughout the war.

On the 8th, the day the Battle of Pea Ridge ended, another Mason, General John Hunt Morgan, raided the suburbs of Nashville. That was the beginning of many such raids that were to destroy millions of dollars worth of Federal military stores. He was to capture and burn dozens of railroad trains, tear up tracks, and burn bridges, continually harrassing Northern officers until his death on September 4, 1864, near Greeneville, Tennessee.

In the East on the same day, March 8, a cumbersome raft-like affair called the *Virginia* steamed up Hampton Roads on a trial run, but its commander, Commodore Franklin Buchanan, sent the workmen ashore, deciding to attack the Federal vessels lying at anchor across the channel. She rammed the *Cumberland* cutting a large hole in her side, then headed for the *Congress,* which struck her colors after an hour's battle. Aboard the *Congress* was Joseph B. Smith, a member of National Lodge, No. 12, District of Columbia. When his father, a rear admiral, heard of the ship's surrender, he exclaimed, "Then Joe is dead." He was!

The success of that iron-clad sent Washington into consternation, but the next day John Ericsson's "tin can on a shingle," commanded by John L. Worden, a Mason, met the *Virginia.* The ensuing battle lasted for over six hours and revolutionized naval warfare for all time. While the battle between the *Monitor* and *Virginia* was a draw, actually it saved the blockade, making it safe for George McClellan to continue with his plans to destroy the Confederate capital in Richmond.

A week later McClellan loaded 400 vessels with his troops and started down the Potomac for his goal, the Peninsula between the James and York Rivers. From that "jumping off place" he hoped to reach Richmond—and he was to come within hearing distance of the church-bells.

On March 5, the siege of Yorktown was begun, and on the 6th the first day of the Battle of Shiloh, or Pittsburg Landing was fought. Of that battle, and an event leading up to it, one of the participants wrote for the *Freemasons' Monthly:*

Just previous to the battle of Shiloh, last spring, the 3d. Ohio cavalry, commanded at the time by Lt. Col. Murray, took possession of Lawrenceburgh, Tennessee. The people of the place were understood to be all Secessionists, and the Lt. Col. ordered his men to search all the houses, arrest all the men, and take possession of all guns and other arms—being careful to protect the women and children from all harm and insult. While this was going on, Col. Murray rode down the street, and, while in front of the Masonic Hall, noticed that some of his men had been in the Lodge-room and taken possession of some articles belonging to the Lodge. He immediately ordered them to return every article to its place, and then placed a guard at the door to protect the hall from future violation. His proceeding, unknown to him, was observed by a Mason—a rebel soldier disguised in citizen's dress.

As the troops were to bivouac in town during the night, Lt. Col.

Murray proceeded to post his pickets a mile or two from the town, and accompanied them himself, to see that all was properly done. This accomplished, he rode back to the town alone, unconscious of any danger.

A few days after occurred the battle of Shiloh, and among the captures made by the 3d. Ohio Cavalry, was a rebel surgeon—a Mason. Bro. Murray took his parole in the evening, until morning, allowing him to remain and sleep with him in an out house. During the evening Col. Murray and the rebel surgeon were made conscious of each other's Masonic character, and the conversation became free. The surgeon inquired if he was not in command at the taking of Lawrenceburgh? On being answered in the affirmative, the surgeon told him that he was there also; that while he (Col. Murray) was engaged stationing his pickets, a squad of rebel soldiers stationed themselves in ambush on the road by which he would return, determined to shoot him as he passed. As he approached the spot, the rebel soldier (first alluded to above) in command of the squad recognized him as the officer who had protected the Lodge-room, and stationed a guard at the door for its protection. He immediately ordered his men not to fire, but let him pass in safety, naturally and truthfully concluding that he was a Mason. By this sudden interposition the lieutenant-colonel escaped with his life, although he himself was at the time totally unconscious of danger.

Another article about the battle from the same magazine is of Masonic significance:

At the terrible battle of Pittsburg Landing, or Shiloh (as it was subsequently called), Capt. G. A. Strong, belonging to one of the Michigan regiments, was fatally wounded on Sunday, the 6th of April. Captain Strong was a Mason—a Knight Templar. . . . When he received the fatal [sic] wound and fell on the battlefield, he had on his person a fine gold watch, and wore a Masonic breast-pin, set with brilliants. A Captain of a company of Texas rangers approached him, as he lay on the ground, and discovered the Masonic emblem on his person. Knowing that the wounded officer would be robbed, and perhaps murdered, if left where he had fallen, the Texan had him carried to a tent, where he bound up his wounds as well as he could, furnished him with water, and took means to protect him from insult and robbery. The battle was still raging, and was renewed on the next day, Monday, when the National troops succeeded in repulsing the rebel army, and in recovering the ground, tents, etc., they had lost on Sunday. On Tuesday, Captain Strong was found in the tent where the Texan officer had left him, still alive and fully sensible, and with his valuables safe

93

upon his person. . . . It was observed by one, who gave an account of this occurrence, that "a Mason, though a rebel, and in arms against his government, *could not* do otherwise than protect and aid his wounded, dying opponent, with such a talisman of peace intervening between them."

CHAPTER VIII

Military Lodges Flourish

◇◇

> *During the Civil War the Masonic ties stretching from the Northern Armies into the Southern Forces were the only bonds which continued to unite the opposing sections of the country and the fraternal courtesies exchanged between the brethren in the two armies were so extensive as to make that one of the Knightliest of wars.*
>
> F. P. STRICKLAND, JR.

THE CAUTIOUSNESS of the general in command of Union forces was a source of concern to President Lincoln and the North. The House of Representatives took a different view by adopting a resolution of thanks for securing results "with but little sacrifice of human life." In the South his "inaction" was met with derision and wry humor. The *Rebellion Record,* with no apologies to William Shakespeare, published one such item written by "A Daughter of Georgia" prior to the Federal advance up the Peninsula—entitled "McClellan's Soliloquy":

> Advance, or not advance; that is the question!
> Whether 'tis better in the mind to suffer
> The jeers and howlings of outrageous Congressmen;
> Or to take up arms against a host of rebels,
> And, by opposing, beat them?—To fight—to win—
> No more: and by a victory, to say we end
> This war, and all the thousand dreadful shocks
> The flesh's exposed to—'tis a consummation
> Devoutly to be wished. To fight, to win,
> To beat! perchance be beaten;—ay, there's the rub;
> After a great defeat, what would ensue!
> When we have shuffled off the battle-field,

Must give us pause; there's the respect
That makes calamity a great defeat.
But shall I bear the scorn of all the North,
The "outward" pressure, and old Abe's reviling,
The pangs of being scoffed at for this long delay,
The turning out of office— (ay, perchance,
When I myself might now my greatness make
With a great battle?) I'd not longer bear
To drill and practice troops behind entrenchments,
But that the fear of meeting with the foe
On dread Manassas, from whose plains
Few of us would return—puzzles my will,
And makes me rather bear the ills I have,
Than fly to other which are greater far.
These Southerners make cowards of us all.

The importance of railroads was realized by both sides at the beginning of the war. On the same day that Lincoln declared a state of rebellion existed, he assumed control of some of the Northern railroads. Railroad officials were appointed government agents. In the South, directors of the railroads met and offered the Confederacy the services of their systems.

Early in 1862, Daniel C. McCallum, a member of Valley Lodge, No. 109, Rochester, New York, was appointed military director and superintendent of railroads for the Federal government. The organization he established had much to do with the final outcome of hostilities.

Railroad bridges, tracks, yards, shops, and rolling stock were prime targets for raiders, cavalry, and soldiers throughout the war. The supply lines *had* to be disrupted.

A Federal spy named James J. Andrews set out to destroy the railroad connecting Atlanta, Georgia, with Chattanooga, Tennessee. Accompanying him were soldiers from three Ohio regiments. The accounts vary as to how many started on the venture, but there were 20, including Andrews, who boarded a train drawn by a 4-4-0 type, woodburning locomotive called the "General," at Marietta about 5:00 a.m., April 12, 1862.

The Northerners did not ride the north-bound mail train far as passengers. At Big Shanty (now Kennesaw, but the Georgia Legislature may change it back to Big Shanty), while the other passengers and the crewmen were eating breakfast, Andrews and his group stole the "General" from under the eyes of a Confederate army camp. William Pittenger, one of the raiders, wrote: "the little train darted away, leaving the camp and station in the wildest uproar and confusion. The first step of the enterprise was triumphantly accomplished."

Andrews had postponed the raid by 24 hours. That appeared to spell the difference between success and failure. It failed. Rain, extra trains, and the tenacity of the conductor, William A. Fuller, combined to defeat the raiders' plans to destroy the bridges along the way.

Fuller, on foot, with a hand-car and the aid of two engines, the last one named the "Texas," frustrated Andrews and his raiders by staying so close they had no time to do more than cut telegraph wires, lift up a couple of rails, and stock up on wood and water for the "General." About 18 miles south of Chattanooga the engine ran out of steam. Fuller "recaptured" his engine; the Confederate soldiers who had accompanied him on the last leg of the chase captured the raiders.

Andrews and his men were placed in jail in Chattanooga. Among the prisoners was Marion A. Ross, of who Pittenger wrote: "Ross was a Freemason, and some of the members of the fraternity visited him and gave him assurances of friendship, together with some small sums of money, which he generously used to procure us all a little greatly-needed addition to our food."

Later, Ross, Andrews, and six other raiders were executed as spies. The others were never brought to trial. At their first opportunity they attempted to escape by attacking their guard in "broad daylight." All but six were successful, and those six who were recaptured were exchanged in March, 1863.

Whether the raid was sensible military-wise has remained a controversy throughout the years. General James B. Fry, chief of staff to General D. C. Buell, wrote: "I do not hesitate to express the opinion that if the raiders had succeeded in destroying every bridge on their proposed route it would have produced no important effect upon Mitchel's military operations, and that he would not have taken, certainly would not have held, Chattanooga. Hence, it is my opinion that Mitchel's bridge-burners took desperate chances to accomplish objects of no substantial advantage."

President Lincoln and the Federal congress felt differently. All of the survivors of the expedition were the first to receive the newly created Congressional Medal of Honor. They also received promotions. With the exception of Andrews, who was a civilian, and one soldier whose relatives could not be located, all of those who had died were awarded the medal posthumously.

After five days of bombarding Forts Jackson and St. Philip at the mouth of the Mississippi, Flag Officer David G. Farragut ordered the vessels under his command to heave up their anchors at two o'clock on the morning of April 24. An hour later his ships were under fire by Confederate shore batteries, gunboats, and rams. "In one hour and ten minutes after the vessels of the fleet had weighed anchor, the affair was virtually over." The boldness of Farragut's feat was something the Southern forces had not expected, and he went on to take New Orleans, paving the way for a Mason named Benjamin Butler to become a most unpopular man in that city.

Butler's unpopularity started on April 29, 1862, when he reported to Secretary of War Edwin M. Stanton concerning what he found when he entered New Orleans:

I find the city under the dominion of the mob. They have insulted our flag—torn it down with indignity. This outrage will be punished in such manner as in my judgment will caution both the perpetrators and abettors of the act, so that they shall fear the *stripes* if they do not reverence the *stars* of our banner.

A short time later William B. Mumford was condemned to death for that "crime" and hanged, while "more than a thousand spectators stood around the gallows . . . they looked on in astonished and profound silence."

On May 15, Major General Butler issued "General Orders 28"; the order that was to earn him the title of "Beast":

As officers and soldiers of the United States have been subject to repeated insults from women calling themselves ladies, of New Orleans, in return for the most scrupulous non-interference and courtesy on our part, it is ordered hereafter, when any female shall by

98

mere gesture or movement insult, or show contempt for any officers or soldiers of the United States, she shall be regarded and held liable to be treated as a woman about town plying her avocation.

He later defended his order by claiming the real ladies of New Orleans did not interfere with his troops; the prostitutes, and would be "street-walkers," would spit in his soldiers' faces, call them "monkeys" and other terms not so lady-like.

Butler remained a controversial figure throughout the war. To some, he was cruel, a despot, and everything unsavory; to others he was an efficient administrator.

An amusing episode occurred between David G. Farragut and Winfield Scott Schley, who was to become a member of Benjamin B. French Lodge, No. 15, Washington, D. C., as recorded in the pages of Volume 4 of the *Little Masonic Library:*

When Farragut assembled his fleet at the bar of the Mississippi River, he found it necessary to jettison part of the cargo of the *Colorado* and of the *Pensacola* in an effort to get them through the shallow water. He succeeded in getting the *Pensacola* over but not the *Colorado.* Schley's little ship (the gunboat *Winona)* was particularly useful in these maneuvers. Several Confederate gunboats (the *Ivy,* the *Manassas,* etc.) not infrequently came within range while reconnoitering but never lingered very long after a shot was fired.

On one occasion Farragut sent Schley up to the head of the pass for observation and very soon heard heavy firing. He signalled Schley to cease firing and return but Schley did not obey. When the *Winona* returned Farragut sent up a signal, "Commanding Officer, come aboard." Schley often said afterwards that he confidently expected a court-martial. Farragut met him on the quarterdeck of the *Hartford* and administered a severe reprimand during which time Schley kept glancing nervously at the yardarm as if afraid he might be hanged there. He said he never felt so mean or ashamed in his life. When Farragut had finished his reprimand, he said, "Now, young man, come into the cabin with me, I have something more to say."

Schley followed him into the cabin. As soon as the door was closed, Farragut produced a bottle of sherry and two glasses, held up a glass of wine and exclaimed: "Young man, if I commanded a gunboat and got into a mixup with the enemy, and was getting the better of him, I'll be damned if I'd see a signal, either!"

The first valley campaign by "Stonewall" Jackson was started on May 4, and on the same day Yorktown was evacuated after an elaborate and monotonous siege of a month, during which all sorts of implements of war were brought up to surround the town. Joseph Johnston fell back to Williamsburg before McClellan could open fire with his tremendous siege batteries. On the next day the Federal troops drove the Confederates out of Williamsburg after a sharp battle. Almost 1,000 miles away, at Lebanon, Tennessee, another reverse was suffered by the South when Morgan's cavalry was defeated.

In Connecticut, where Alvan P. Hyde addressed his grand lodge, on May 14, the sounds of war could not be heard, but what had transpired was noted:

> The year that has just passed has been a year of trial and sorrow to our beloved country. The fell destroyer, Death, has overtaken many of our brethren, upon the battlefield, in the camp, and in the hospital, and has filled our land with grief and mourning. This terrible civil war is still raging, desolating our country, and causing brothers of different jurisdictions to meet each other in battle array, instead of their friendly contention that has heretofore existed between them, of striving "who can best work or best agree." Yet within the limits of our jurisdiction—in marked contrast with the bitterness, turmoil, and strife, that surrounds us—the affairs of our Order have been eminently peaceful and prosperous.

The grand master of Rhode Island, Ariel Ballou, told his grand lodge that Masonry should be careful not to place itself in such a position that its enemies could claim it had political aspirations. Any convention of Masons throughout the country, he felt would "place our order in a false position, and render it open to the charge of being a selfish and political institution of which our enemies would not be slow to avail themselves." He was referring to a convention that had been proposed to try to pour oil on the troubled waters in the country.

On May 21 the New York *Times* reported: "Commodore [John R.] Goldsborough with the *Susquehannah,* the *Wachusett,* the *Dacotah,* and the *Maratanza* moved up the James River, Virginia, to reduce two batteries on the south shore, and found the batteries abandoned." Goldsborough was a Mason.

General George Stoneman, a Mason, made a balloon reconnaissance from Gaines' Mill on the same day. He reached an altitude of 500 feet and had a complete view of Richmond "with the aid of a glass."

The First Maryland, commanded by John R. Kenly, a Mason, was attacked on May 23 at Front Royal, Virginia, by Jackson's forces. Nathaniel P. Banks, the commanding general, also a Mason, on being informed that the Confederates planned to encircle and destroy his army, retreated through Winchester and into Maryland.

In Mississippi on the same day, Nathan B. Forrest took time out from harrassing the Federals to answer a letter received from a member of his Lodge, Angerona, No. 168, Memphis, Tennessee. The contents of that letter, taken from the collection of Ralph Newman, indicates that Forrest's education was limited:

Corinth Miss May 23 1862

D. C. Trader

Sir your note of 21 ins is to hand I did not fully understand the contents and ask for information the amount you ask for is it for a publick contrabution or is it for my dues due the log [Lodge] I wish you to give me the amt due the log from me as you did not State it in your notice or the amount asked for I had a small brush with the Enamy on yesterday I suceded in gaining thir rear and got in to thir entrenchments 8 miles from hamburg and 5 behind farmington and Burned a portion of thir camp at that place they wair not looking for me I taken them by Surprise they run like Suns of Biches I captured the Rev Dr Warin from Illanois and one fin Sorel Stud this army is at this time in front of our Entrentchments I look for a fite soon and a big one when it coms off Cant you come up and take a hand this fite wil do to hand down to your children I feel confident of our success

your Respct/N. B. FORREST

To/D. C. Trader/Memphis Tenn

The grand secretary of Missouri, Anthony O'Sullivan, whose home was in St. Louis, on May 26, 1862, wrote:

It is known to the members of the Grand Lodge that the section of the country in which I reside has been visited during the past year with the horrors of civil war, and as may be readily conjectured, many Masons were found in the ranks of the contending armies. It was my misfortune to witness some of the sufferings occasioned by this unnatural strife, and I thank God that it was in my power to do some little good for my wounded and suffering

101

brethren; and while I regret to state that many, claiming to be Masons, hailing from this and other jurisdictions, failed in their duty as such, I found others who clearly comprehended their position, and acted accordingly. Of these brethren, I take pleasure in mentioning the names of Col. WYMAN, Capt. BLANCHARD, and Lieut. WILLIAMS, of the 13th Illinois, and Lieut. BUCK, of the 36th Illinois; also Col. MILLS, of the 24th Missouri, formerly of Hampden Lodge, Springfield, Massachusetts. These brethren, while they discharged their duties as soldiers, never forgot their covenants as Masons. Many of my brethren have good reason to be thankful to them for protection in person and in property. May they be gratefully remembered by the Fraternity.

O'Sullivan later took to task another writer of foreign correspondence who had written phrases which the Missourian considered un-Masonic. He likened some of those expressions to what was then occurring in France during the "days of the Reign of Terror."

Andrew G. Curtin, governor of Pennsylvania and a Mason, issued an order stopping the enlistment of three months' volunteers and congratulated the people because "the emergency which seemed to require them" had passed. Two months later he was to issue a proclamation calling for more troops. Subsequently, he was to institute a system of caring for the children of men killed during the war, and thereafter be known as "the soldiers' friend."

On May 30 Corinth, Mississippi, was evacuated by Beauregard, leaving the city to the forces of Halleck. The next day, McClellan's forces, after crossing a winding, swampy stream called the Chickahominy, had arrived in sight of the church spires of Richmond. Johnston, expecting McClellan to be reinforced by McDowell, which was never to happen, attacked the Federal forces near Seven Pines, and Fair Oaks Station.

Late in the afternoon of May 31, General Johnston was wounded. The wound was severe enough for President Davis to replace him. At two o'clock on June 1 General Robert E. Lee was given command of the Army of Northern Virginia.

A daring strategist named "Stonewall" Jackson was the reason President Lincoln stopped General McDowell from reinforcing McClellan. With 19,000 men, Jackson, through brilliant maneuvering, bottled up Fremont with 15,000 men, as well as Banks with about 19,000, and kept McDowell at Fredericksburg with a force estimated at 40,000.

Among the Generals fighting with Jackson in the Shenandoah Valley, was Turner Ashby. Henry Douglas, who fought with Ashby, describes him as:

A man of striking personal appearance, about five feet ten inches tall, with a well-proportioned figure, graceful and compact, black eyes, black hair, and a flowing black beard. His complexion was of the darkest brunette, so dark that a Federal scout whom he once shot with a pistol declared he had been shot by a Negro. His face was placid not stern; even his smile was shadowed with a tinge of melancholy. . . . Riding his black stallion, he looked like a knight of the olden time; galloping over the field on his favorite war horse, his white one, eager, watchful, he was fascinating, inspiring. Altogether he was the most picturesque horseman ever seen in the Shenandoah Valley—he seemed to have been left over by the Knights of the Golden Horseshoe.

As the sun set in the west on June 6, covering the Blue Ridge Mountains with a deeper blue, one that was almost purple, Turner Ashby, the daring Confederate General, and a well-liked Mason, lost his life. Two days before the battle of Cross Keys, Ashby, with a small group of his men, endeavored to drive off a Federal advance party. During the skirmishing, with his horse shot from under him, a bullet pierced his heart, and in the arms of his friend, Lieutenant James Thurston, he breathed his last.

Rev. James B. Avirett, the chaplain of Ashby's brigade, and a Mason, states his body was taken to Port Republic where all through the night saddened men went to pay tribute to the man they all loved. On June 7, all that was mortal of Ashby was moved by train to Charlottesville, Virginia, where it was buried in the cemetery of the university.

There it remained for four years, when it was "disinterred by the Faculty and Students of the University of Virginia," to be taken to Winchester, Virginia, where it was to find its final rest in the Stonewall Cemetery, October 25, 1866. Avirett, in describing the reinterment, wrote, "The Masonic Fraternity, representing 15 Lodges, and numbering 300 members, under the marshalship of Col. L. T. Moore," preceded the hearse to the grave where, with 10,000 people looking on:

The Masonic ceremonies over the body of General Ashby were very interesting and impressive, and immense throngs of people were stilled to silence by the solemnity of the scene. The District Deputy Grand Master, Joseph S. Carson, delivered the Masonic Exhortation, and the Worshipful Master, Wm. R. Denny, of Hiram Lodge, No. 21, deposited in the lamb-skin or white apron, which he remarked was an emblem of innocence and the badge of a Mason; also, the evergreen or sprig of acacia as an emblem of the immortality of the soul, were deposited in the grave by all the brethren present of the fraternity, after which the Worshipful Master consigned the body of their brother, Turner Ashby, to the grave —"earth to earth—ashes to ashes—dust to dust." The Masonic services were then concluded with prayer by the Chaplain, Rev. J. B. Avirett, who, it may be remarked, was the Chaplain of the "Ashby Brigade."

That Ashby was a hero to the South was proved when the *Richmond Whig* just one week after his death published a poem written by John R. Thompson entitled "ASHBY":

> To the brave all homage render,
>   Weep, ye skies of June!
> With a radiance pure and tender,
>   Shine, oh saddened moon!
> Dead upon the field of glory,
>   Hero fit for song and story,
> Lies our bold dragoon.
>
> Well they learned, whose hands have slain him,
>   Braver, knightlier foe
> Never fought with Moor nor Paynim—
>   Rode at Templestowe;
> With a mien how high and joyous,
>   'Gainst the hordes that would destroy us
> Went he forth, we know.
>
> Nevermore, alas! shall sabre
>   Gleam around his crest;
> Fought his fight, fulfilled his labour;
>   Stilled his manly breast:
> All unheard sweet nature's cadence,
>   Trump of fame and voice of maidens:
> Now he takes his rest.

104

Earth, that all too soon hath bound him,
  Gently wrap his clay,
Linger lovingly around him,
  Light of dying day,
Softly fall the summer showers,
  Birds and bees among the flowers
Make the gloom seem gay.

There, throughout the coming ages,
  When his sword is rust
And his deeds in classic pages,
  Mindful of her trust,
Shall Virginia, bending lowly,
  Still a ceaseless vigil holy
Keep above his dust!

The Editor of the *Amherst Cabinet* (Massachusetts) tells about an incident that happened after a battle at James Island, South Carolina:

Maj. Sissons of the R. I. 3d was bearer of a flag of truce, accompanied by three officers, all happening to be Masons. The rebel officer that came down to meet them happened to be a Mason also. Maj. Sissons remarked, "I suppose by *the tools you carry* I have the honor of meeting a Craftsman, as well as an enemy in war?" The rebel officer replied—"You do, and I am happy to meet you as such, and regret that circumstance compel us to meet in any other manner than the former—but such are the fortunes of war."
. . . The rebel officer sent after some more Masons, and they cracked a bottle of wine and drank "to the health of the craftsmen, whether in *peace* or in war."

On June 3, the Grand Lodge of New York met in its annual communication, and the grand master, Finlay M. King, speaking to the South, condemned the Confederacy. Of Abraham Lincoln he stated:

He is not of my choice any more than he is of yours. Anticipating and proclaiming with my feeble voice some of the troubles which now threaten the destruction of the Union, I did all I could, in my capacity as a citizen, to prevent his election, as did, I venture to say, one-half of my constituents, but he was elected! Abraham Lincoln, by the voice of the people, by the fiat of the Constitution, and by the decree of Almighty God, is the President of the United States, and I bow with all deference and due solemnity, as all good Masons ought to bow, to the majesty and power and irrevocable decrees of these authorities.

Concerning military lodges, he said:

Different opinions are entertained in regard to the propriety of granting dispensations or warrants for the organization of Lodges in military departments in any case; but in my opinion it is difficult to conceive of circumstances which would present stronger claims for the exercise of a kindly and fraternal course toward our brethren engaged in the maintenance of the integrity of our nation than the present. Masonry upholds the country of its adoption by its direct teachings, and still more by its great conservatism.

It teaches its votaries to be peaceable citizens, and cheerfully to conform to the laws of the country in which they reside; to pay a proper respect to civil magistrate, to work diligently, live creditably, and act honorably by all men. It is a peaceful, social, humane organization, scattering blessings wherever it goes.

One of the nine military lodges authorized by the Grand Lodge of New York throughout the war years was the National Zouave Lodge, U.D., organized in May, 1861. Of that lodge and its existence at Fort Monroe, Virginia, one Mason wrote:

Here all passion was laid aside, and with them frequently met the gray clad soldiers from the South, a prisoner within our military lines, but a brother within our Masonic limits.

Within our crowded walls the private soldier and the general officer met on the level of equality, to part when the Lodge was closed on the square of discipline. Here the beautiful tenets of our institution tempered the rough and rugged life of the soldier, stimulated his patriotism and nerved his heart for the dangers and trials in the path before him.

A list of traveling military lodges compiled by Clarence R. Martin, the grand master of Indiana in 1943, indicates there were 94 in the Northern armies and close to 150 in the Southern armies. Indiana led the list for the North with 37; Texas with more than 50, and Virginia with 28, were the leaders for the South. The number of members these lodges had will never be known. For the most part, the records kept were poor and inadequate. The grand lodges that had issued dispensations, or in some manner permitted them to work, in but few instances, never heard from them during or after their existence.

Many of the jurisdictions, both North and South, refused to have anything to do with granting dispensations, warrants, or charters, to military lodges. Josiah Drummond, grand master of Maine, in 1863, gave his reason for refusing the petition to form a lodge in the 9th Maine Regiment, then stationed at Fernandina, Florida: "There is the danger of admitting to the Order men who have lived all their lifetime with the sound of the gavel of a Lodge, and who could not gain admission at home, where they are best known."

Joseph Fort Newton, in his autobiography, *River of Years*, writes that his father had been made a Mason in a military lodge, and during the course of a battle he, a Confederate from Texas, was captured by Union troops. He was subsequently taken to Rock Island, Illinois, where he became deathly ill in the prison camp there. He was able to let a Union officer know he was a Mason, and that officer, himself a Mason, took him to his home, nursed him back to health, and when the war was over, gave him money, and a gun, and saw him off for Texas.

Newton added: "The fact that such a fraternity of men could exist, mitigating the harshness of war, and remain unbroken when states and churches were torn in two, became a wonder; and it is not strange I tried for years to repay my debt to it."

In 1861, the grand master of North Carolina said he had "received several applications from brethren serving in the army, for Dispensations, empowering them to open Lodges in their respective camps." He had refused all such requests "believing the policy would be detrimental to the Order." He felt he was in an excellent position to determine the ill effect of such Lodges "having been in camp the greater part of the present year."

A special committee appointed to consider the part of his address that concerned military lodges, differed with him. "Your committee sees no sufficient reason why seven brothers in the army, are not as capable of governing and conducting a Lodge, as they would be at home," it reported. The arguments set forth by the committee were so strong, the grand lodge adopted its report.

Although the grand master received at least two requests

for the formation of military lodges in 1862, he refused to grant them. He reasoned they would be infringing "on the jurisdiction of the Grand Lodge of Virginia," on whose soil the petitioners were fighting. He was pleased to inform his members "that the petitioners subsequently applied to the Grand Master of Virginia, who granted them a Dispensation, and the Lodge thus established is prospering."

Again in 1863, the grand master of North Carolina refused to grant dispensations for the formation of lodges in the army. Once more a special committee took issue with its head. Consequently, in 1864, the grand master granted "military dispensations" to "J. E. Avery Military Lodge No. 1, 6th N. C. Troops, Hoke's Brigade; Z. B. Vance Lodge No. 2, 40th Reg't, Heavy Artillery, N. C.; Vance Brothers' Lodge, No. 3, 43rd N. C. Troops, Daniel's Brigade; Lodge in 3rd N. C. Cavalry, No. 4; Chicamauga Lodge, 21st Regiment, No. 5; J. C. McDowell Lodge, 1st N. C. Battalion, No. 6."

At least one of the dispensations was never acted upon. "No. 4" was transferred to Lee's army in Virginia and the men felt they "had no right to work on the soil of another state." On December 5, 1865, all military lodges were ordered to surrender all of their records "to the Grand Secretary" of North Carolina.

Massachusetts lost no time in permitting military lodges to be organized, for on May 6, 1861, Bay State Army Lodge, in the Third Regiment, was granted a dispensation. That was the first of six to be issued before 1861 ended. Ten were granted during the war.

One of the ten was for McClellan Army Lodge No. 6, attached to the 43rd Massachusetts Volunteers, where there were "at least a hundred Masons . . . including most of the officers." The two top ranking officers, Colonel Charles L. Holbrook and Lieutenant Colonel John C. Whiton, along with the chaplain, "Rev. Dr. J. M. Manning, Surgeon Wm. H. Bradley and Adjutant James M. Whitney," were made Masons "at a special meeting of Columbian Lodge, A.F. & A.M. of Boston on Monday evening, September 29, 1862, just before the command left for the South." Eleven days later, the grand master of Massachusetts, William D. Coolidge, issued a dispensation for the formation of McClellan Lodge.

With "a large attendance of Masons" looking on in Boston on August 4, 1864, McClellan Lodge surrendered its dispensation to the Grand Lodge of Massachusetts:

The ceremonies of the occasion . . . took place in Corinthian Hall, which was decorated with the regimental flags of the 43rd, and was well filled with members of the Lodge, who appeared in full uniform and regalia, and the friends of the regiment, among whom were a large number of the past members of the Boston Light Infantry.

The Worshipful Grand Master Parkman, together with the Grand Lodge, visited Corinthian Hall in a body, and formally received the Dispensation, and discharged the officers. It was a novel sight to witness all the official chairs filled with members in full military uniforms.

The acts and records of the McClellan Lodge were reviewed, and showed that during the six months in which it was in working order at Newburn [New Burne, N. C.] over forty members were initiated.

During the evening, a magnificent silver pitcher was presented by the Lodge to their Worshipful Master, Capt. Thomas G. Whytal, and a beautiful silver goblet to the Secretary, Lieut. James M. Whitney. The presentation speeches were made in a very happy manner by the Senior Warden, Capt. Wm. B. Fowle, Jr., and the recipients of the splendid gifts made appropriate responses.

Only forty-five lodges were represented when the Grand Lodge of Texas met on June 9, 1862. The grand master, George W. Van Vleck, gave a graphic picture of what was happening in the country:

Since our last Annual Communication, our entire land, from the Atlantic to the Pacific, has been convulsed by a struggle, the gigantic proportions of which amaze the world. Fierce and bloody conflicts have occurred upon our soil, and between armies that, but a short time ago, regarded each other as brothers. The whole country is now but little less than one grand encampment of armed soldiery. The workshops stand still, the daily pursuits of life are suspended, and the courts of justice are closed. The shrill notes of the war trumpet, the roll of martial music, the array of streaming banners, and the more terrible sounds of musketry, the clashing of steel, and the deep-mouthed cannon is heard in every State and on almost every plain, speaking death and destruction to every hill and valley.

Thousands are daily rushing to the battlefield, and almost every man has become a soldier. Our once prosperous and happy country has almost become desolate. War, with all its trials, suffering and carnage, sweeps over our loved country.

A great republic has been overthrown, fertile plains turned to barren wastes, great cities transformed to encampments for the soldiers—and many towns reduced to ashes by the folly and rage of man. How long these unfortunate things will continue none can tell. We can only struggle on fiercely and determinedly, leaving it with the God of battles to decide the issue, and trusting faithfully in His power and in His will to deliver us from tyranny.

But while this great contest is waging, our cherished institution, Masonry must, like all things else in our land, suffer greatly from the confusion and desolation that surrounds us. The benevolent task of Masonry has ever been to enlighten and bless, to build up and preserve what ignorance, ambition, avarice and revenge combine to destroy. She has never been engaged in any of the bloody conflicts and guilty wars which have caused this destruction.

The grand lecturer of Texas, C. K. Stribling, reported:

I started soon after the close of your last Communication in the discharge of the duty assigned me, and would have continued devoting my whole time and ability to the work, but for the dismal cloud that arose, threatening to overshadow our national horizon, echoing thunder peals amidst the clash of arms and the terrible roar of mighty cannon. Startled by the alarming news of the evacuation of Bowling Green and Nashville, and the fall of Fort Donelson, the shrill cry "to Arms! to Arms!" rang like a clarion voice throughout our land and country, awakening the martial spirits and patriotism of the Southern people to drive back the bristling bayonets of the Northern legions.

I ceased labor and on the 24th of March, in obedience to my country's call, I grasped the implements of war and hastily repaired to the tented field.

Passions were aroused more during the first year of the war than in the latter years, at least in Masonic circles. The discussions that had taken place in grand lodges, and in the proceedings of some of them, caused many brethren to view with alarm the harshness then prevalent. G. W. Washburn of the committee on foreign correspondence for the Grand Lodge of Wisconsin reported on June 10, 1862:

110

. . . And when we pronounce the sentence of excommunication against our brethren, and undertake to place them beyond the pale of recognition for other than purely Masonic reasons, we expose ourselves to like indignities at the hands of others, and jeopardise the prosperity, if not the very existence of our institutions.

The States in rebellion *have a government,* perhaps not one of their own election—to us a gross and palpable usurpation, but nevertheless *a government which exercises unbounded sway over its people, and the only power which can be dignified by the name of government in fact. To whom, then, do the Craft in those States owe their allegiance? To our minds the question does not admit of doubt, and we assert the broad doctrine that Masonry has for them no word of censure, no sentence of excommunication, no rebuke to administer, and no punishment to inflict.*

We do not take issue with our brethren as to the soundness of the political doctrines they assert, nor dispute the proposition that a Mason may not raise his hand against his Government, *but we claim that he cannot excuse himself in doing so upon the assumption that the Government under which he lives is not the rightful government, but is a base and violent usurpation.*

On the following day, the Grand Master of New Hampshire, Aaron P. Hughes, took a somewhat different view when he stated: "The question now is, shall this government, with all its attendant blessings, be destroyed? I can not doubt that there is any difference among all true men. I know there is but one sentiment among Masons, and that is, the 'Constitution as it is, and the Union as it was,' must and shall be preserved, cost what it may." He undoubtedly was referring to the Masons holding allegiance to the Federal government; not to those whose Constitution had been written but a short time earlier.

The historian of Mount Vernon Lodge, No. 4, Providence, Rhode Island, writes about a Masonic funeral that was held in his state:

. . . On June 22, 1862, Colonel John S. Slocum's body, with that of Bro. Sullivan Ballou of Morning Star Lodge of Woonsocket, who fell in the same battle [Bull Run] was laid at rest in Swan Point Cemetery, where both were buried with impressive Masonic ceremonies . . . under the direction of Grand Master Ariel Ballou.

111

CHAPTER IX

From Swamps to Mountains

◇◇

> *When I would recreate myself, I seek the dark-*
> *est wood, the thickest and most interminable,*
> *and to the citizen, most dismal swamp. I enter*
> *a swamp as a sacred place*—a sanctum sanc-
> torum.
>
> THOREAU

McCLELLAN moved his forces to the south bank of the Chickahominy. There he entrenched his troops from that river to White Oak Swamp, and pleaded for reinforcements. Allan Pinkerton had led the commander to believe 200,-000 Confederates were protecting Richmond.

Lee, wanting to know his enemy's strength, sent J. E. B. Stuart to find out. Stuart and his cavalry pleased the South and shocked the North by riding completely around the entire Federal Army.

While both sides were strengthening their positions, General Robert E. Lee sent Major W. R. Mason to call on General Mc-Clellan. Lee's wife and daughter, Mary, had been caught within the Federal lines at the "White House." Mason was escorted to the Union commander, who gave him a hearty welcome, fed him "a dinner of the best," and offered to ride through the lines with him and the ladies. The offer was declined by Mrs. Lee as "entirely unnecessary."

After the battle at Fair Oaks, violent storms increased the difficulties for both sides. The swamps were made virtually impassable without bridges, and they were difficult to build until the rains stopped on the 20th of June. Immediately afterwards the momentum of transferring the Federal forces to the south side of the Chickahominy was stepped up.

In the meantime Lee had sent a message to Jackson in the Shenandoah Valley asking to meet him secretly in Richmond. The meeting took place on the 23rd in the home of the Dabb family on the Nine Mile Road. There Lee, D. H. and A. P. Hill, Longstreet, and Jackson discussed the strategy they hoped would drive McClellan away from the Confederate capital.

While the Confederate generals were meeting, the *London Times* reported that the civil war in America had reached a point where it was a scandal to humanity and had become a war of extermination. The article went on to state that the "excited railers" on both sides might think there was no alternative but to let a flood of blood pass over the land. The *London Herald,* a few days later, "declared the Union a nuisance among nations."

About the flood of blood mentioned by the *Times,* a correspondent for the *Cincinnati Commercial* reported on July 2, at the close of the "Seven Days' Battles": "The soil of Virginia *is* now sacred. It is bathed with the reddest blood of this broad land. Every rood *(sic)* of it, from Upper Chickahominy to the base of Malvern Hill, is crimsoned with the blood of your brave brethren."

The first of those battles took place at Mechanicsville, or Ellerson's Mills, on June 26. At three in the afternoon, no word having been received from Jackson, A. P. Hill attacked the Federal forces, and found a practically impregnable wall. Until dark the battle raged, the Confederates charging and being repulsed with terrific losses. When night ended the fighting, it was found that the union losses totaled 361, but a single Confederate unit, the 44th Georgia, lost 335.

At three in the morning of the 27th, the Federal forces withdrew to a point east of Powhite Creek. At 12:30 in the afternoon the battle of Gaines' Mill, or First Cold Harbor, was started. Darkness had almost fallen before General Pickett's brigade, "headed by 'Old Ironsides' (18th Virginia), broke Porter's linc just west of Watts house."

The *Commercial* report said the onslaught all afternoon was terrible, and about six o'clock "the conflict seemed to grow fiercer than at any previous time." Close to an hour and a half later "the left gave way, the center and finally the right was also pressed back. . . . It is certain we were beaten in strategy and in grand tactics." About the Federal commander, General D. H. Hill was to write: "General Fitz John Porter, who commanded the Federals at Cold Harbor, handled his 40,000 men with an ability unsurpassed on any field during the war."

Among those cited for bravery was a Mason, Colonel Alfred Iverson, a U. S. Senator from Georgia, who in that capacity led the secession movement in the Senate. During the final charge he fell, wounded while leading the 20th North Carolina.

Before dawn on the 28th the Federal forces were entrenched at Goldings farm where the Confederates attacked. General Winfield Hancock was "equal to the occasion, and the enemy was driven back." That evening General McClellan told his corps commanders they would begin a movement the next day to the James River.

On the day of the Battle of Golding's Farm, the military governor of Tennessee, Andrew Johnson, ordered five clergymen imprisoned in Nashville for refusing to take the oath of allegiance to the Federal government.

At dawn on the 29th, General McClellan's forces were on the road. "Thousands of cattle, of wagons, an immense train of artillery, intermingled with infantry and great troops of cavalry, choked up the narrow road."

General Lee had learned that his enemy was moving toward the James River and ordered Magruder to pursue and give battle. Magruder, fearing a Federal attack in great force, busied himself in placing his troops in the best defensive positions he could find. So Kersaw and Semmes bore the brunt of the Battle of Savage Station where General Burns successfully held the ground.

On the 30th the violent battle of Frayser's Farm, or Glendale, was fought, and General McCall captured. Although the Confederates claimed a victory, McClellan had succeeded in getting all of his forces through the swamps to Malvern Hill where a mass slaughter took place on the 1st.

The withering fire from the forces of McClellan, a Federal and Mason, held off the forces of the Confederate com-

114

manders, who were also Freemasons, Wise, Armistead, Magruder, Toombs, and others. D. S. Freeman wrote of the Confederate attempt to take the hill: "It was not war; it was mass murder. . . . Valor could not conquer those perfectly served batteries on the crest. . . ."

The next day the Federal troops reached their destination—Harrison's Landing, where the guns of the Union gunboats could protect them and where Lee gave up the chase.

On July 9, 1862, the grand master of Canada, T. Douglas Harrington concluded his address to his grand lodge by alluding to the devastation taking place across the border:

And now my brethren, I would . . . bespeak your serious attention as loyal subjects and Freemasons of no insignificant numbers, to the unhappy and unnatural war still devasting the neighboring country, and causing bloodshed, misery, and the cutting asunder of the very closest ties of cosanguinity and friendship.

You all must remember how nearly this country was recently involved in the convulsions, and who can foresee what is to happen! It is our *duty* as fellowmen, and our *privilege* as brethren, to pray and hope for peace, and a return to its normal condition of that powerful republic, between whom and us there is only an imaginary geographical line of separation. But whatever the womb of futurity may bring forth (if peace, so much the greater reason for gratitude to the G.A.O.T.U.) remember, that *the defense of their institutions, their homes, and their altars against foreign attacks, is a duty incumbent on the inhabitants of this Province.*

I quote the language of the Representative of our Sovereign to the Parliament of this Province. Cast your eyes southward on Mexico—contemplate what is popularly termed the Old World, and think how small a spark would fire the combustible there stored.

Then, having the signs of the times before you, while earnestly desiring for the sake of suffering humanity, that the storm will be stilled by that Power, who can alone say with authority, *"Peace! Be still!"* read, study the fourth chapter of Nehemicah in our *first Great Light,* and ponder at the same time as Freemasons, on the symbolic significance of the *"Sword and Trowel."* While we look steadily and fearlessly in the face of probabilities and dangers, still happily at a distance, and which may not appear nearer, while we determine to perform our duty if our country is menaced, let us never forget, brethren, that the tie of Freemasonry—the mystic tie—has acted as a curb on human passions; has alleviated the miseries of warfare, and that, as well in turmoil as in tranquility, we are all bound to acknowledge a brother's claim, no matter what his country when preferred in difficulty, danger or distress.

On the same day, the first reports of the raids in Kentucky by the Confederate General John Morgan reached the Northern newspapers. Morgan reported to General E. Kirby Smith on July 30, according to the *Rebellion Record:*

He [Morgan] left Knoxville, Tennessee, on the fourth, with about nine hundred men, and returned to Livingston, in the same state, on the twenty-eighth instant, with nearly twelve hundred men, having been absent twenty-four days, during which time he traveled over a thousand miles, captured seventeen towns, destroyed the government supplies and arms in them, dispersed about fifteen hundred home guards, and paroled nearly twelve hundred regular troops. He lost in killed, wounded, and missing, of the number he carried into Kentucky, about ninety.

On July 11, 1862, two days before Nathan Forrest drove the Federal forces out of McMinnville, Tennessee, he used the farmhouse of William Lusk, a fellow Mason, as his headquarters. During the day he paroled four Union soldiers who had been captured in civilian clothes.

One of the parolees returned the following day with an advance troop of Federal cavalry to point out the house that had been Forrest's headquarters. They left when the main body arrived. The commanding officer rode up to Lusk and asked: "What time of the day, sir, did General Forrest leave here yesterday?"

Lusk replied with a quivering voice, "I declare I don't know."

The officer said sharply, "Sir, your memory is damned short! Didn't he leave here precisely at twelve o'clock?" And he raised his pistol to the farmer's head. Lusk made a Masonic sign; the gun was lowered; the officer jumped off his horse, grasped the farmer by the hand, and the two of them, with arms around each other, stood by the gate until the army had passed.

Typical of the many accounts of blockade-runners captured while trying to supply the needs of the South, was this account in the *Rebellion Record:*

116

The steamer *Tubal Cain* was seized as a prize by the United States gunboat *Octarora* this day [July 24th] having on board a cargo of small arms, salt, saltpetre, military buttons, shells and various other goods suitable for a Southern market.

Many of the communications held by military lodges have been lost for all time, but a portion of one was preserved in the Richmond *Dispatch* of July 25, 1862:

Masonic Celebration.—The first anniversary of the battle of Manassas was celebrated at Dill's farm, at General Whiting's head-quarters, near Richmond, Virginia, by the Bee Lodge of Masons. [Virginia Military Lodge granted Dispensation February 24, 1862.] A procession was formed at Dill's and marched thence, preceded by a brass band, to the farm of Mrs. Schermerhorn. Arrived there, proceedings were initiated by prayer by Rev. Dr. Duncan. An oration, an eulogy on the death of the gallant and lamented brother Barnard E. Bee, Brigadier-General, C.S.A., who fell at Manassas, was then delivered in feeling and appropriate language by Rev. Dr. Stewart, an Episcopalian clergyman, of Alexandria, Virginia, who, it will be remembered, was driven from his pulpit by the hirelings of Lincoln for declining to pray for that individual. The procession returned to Dill's farm, where the exercises of the day were concluded.

The following day General Price asked the residents of Quitman, Missouri, for shoes and "yarn-socks." He asked "every white woman in the state to knit at least one pair of socks" for his army, offering to pay seventy-five cents for each pair.

In the deep South, harassing action continued, for John C. Breckinridge attacked Baton Rouge, Louisiana, on August 5, and was repulsed by the forces of Colonel Thomas W. Cahill, the Federal commander, "after a fight of four hours' duration and of great severity." Breckinridge complimented his men and told them: "The inability of the *Arkansas* to reach the scene of conflict prevented the victory from being complete; but you have given the enemy a severe and salutary lesson."

On August 8, General Lovell H. Rousseau, at Huntsville, Alabama, claimed "lawless bands of robbers and murderers" were firing into railroad trains. In order to eliminate that, he ordered that preachers who were "active secessionists" be placed on board such trains. His *"Special Order No. 54"* went on to state: "When not on duty these gentlemen shall be comfortably quartered in Huntsville."

The next day, at Cedar Mountain, about three miles from Culpeper Court House, Confederate forces under General Thomas J. Jackson attacked the Federal forces under General John Pope. General Nathaniel P. Banks' Second Army Corps was given the task of holding back Jackson's troops. Of that action, Pope in his official report wrote: "The behavior of General Banks' corps during the action was very fine. No greater gallantry and daring could be exhibited by any troops. I cannot speak too highly of the ceaseless intrepidity of General Banks himself during the whole of the engagement."

After the battle the Confederates retired to a position behind the Rapidan River and waited for Robert E. Lee. Pope returned to Culpeper Court House and from there to Rappahannock Station, when he learned Lee was about to attack him before he could receive reinforcements. From August 16 to September 2 the second battle of Bull Run, or Manassas, was fought, the heaviest fighting taking place on the 29th and 30th.

On the evening of the 30th Pope ordered his forces to fall back to Centerville. On the 2nd they were drawn back to "the intrenchments in front of Washington." And Lee prepared to invade Maryland.

Among the men left behind at Manassas during the Federal retreat were three members of the Tenth Regiment New York Volunteers. Captains Robert A. Dimmick and Thomas D. Mosscrop, and Corporal Edward A. Dubey were severely wounded, and for two days their cries for help went unheard. During the period they assisted each other to the best of their ability.

Just as all hope seemed gone, Captain Hugh Barr of the 5th Regiment of Virginia Riflemen, as he was attending wounded Confederates, stumbled upon the Federal soldiers. While aiding them he noticed a Masonic emblem on the shirt of Mosscrop, and redoubled his efforts to save the three men. A surgeon was summoned, removed the shot, and dressed the wounds of the enemy. They were taken by Barr on the following morning to the Van Pell house, which was being used as a hospital, and when their wounds had healed sufficiently, they were sent to Washington, D. C.

Nineteen years later, the three New York Masons recorded for posterity the kind act of the Virginia Mason, who, regarding a fallen foe as a friend in need, did all in his power to save their lives.

Not all of the Masons who were in that battle of August 30 were as fortunate. Among those who were killed was Horace S. Roberts, the immediate past grand master of Michigan. He had been commissioned a colonel on April 28, 1862, and led his regiment in the battles of Mechanicsville, Gaines' Mill, Savage Station, White Oak Swamp, and Malvern Hill. At Second Bull Run, or Manassas, a minnie ball ended his life, and his body was never recovered. It rests, buried in the trenches in the companionship of those whom he loved and beside whom he had fought. His last words before the battle were typical of the man, "I trust Michigan will believe that I tried to do my duty."

On August 29 and 30 the forces of Brigadier General Mahlon D. Manson, a Mason, were attacked by the troops under Confederate General E. Kirby Smith near Richmond, Kentucky, "resulting . . . in a defeat of the Nationals."

One of the many Masonic funerals that were conducted during the war was recorded in the *Rebellion Record:*

The funeral of Col. George W. Pratt, of the New York 20th Regiment, took place at Albany today [September 14th]. It was one of the largest assemblages ever seen in that city on a similar occasion. It was attended by the Governor and staff, the 10th and 25th Regiments, deputations from Masonic orders, and a number of distinguished strangers from New York and elsewhere.

In a lengthy article, *Freemasonry on the Battlefield,* written by John Edwin Mason, K.T., for the *Masonic Monthly,* General Lee's invasion of Maryland is described. It is a flowery, heart-on-the-sleeve, example of the journalism of that time and leaves no doubt as to the allegiance of the author.

The Grand Army of the Potomac in September, 1862, had bivouacked on the banks of the beautiful, serpentine Monocacy, in Maryland, and were eagerly pressing forward to meet the invading

119

foe, who had just crossed the Potomac, proud and defiant, with the avowed determination to conquer and to subdue the North, and pay off the army on State Street, in Boston.

The long lines of glistening bayonets bathed in the warm September sunlight of Maryland, dotted here and there with batteries of field artillery in position, and unlimbered for action, told the whole story that either the banks of the Monocacy or the banks of the Antietam beyond, must witness the greatest conflict of modern times. There peaceful rivers, slowly winding their way to the sea, must be crimsoned by the blood of the men who speak the same language, owe allegiance to the same country, and once loved the same dear old flag.

Our skirmish line had flanked the lovely little city of Frederick three miles from the Monocacy, and was driving the rebel hordes from their plunder in the loyal and patriotic little city to the mountains beyond. The long, gray lines so easily and plainly seen with the field-glass were receding westward, and seeking an asylum in the impregnable ravines of South Mountain.

As the sharp crack of the rifles on our skirmish line grew fainter and fainter as they advanced, the grand army with measured tread, and manly bearing, with bands playing, and colors kissing the welcome evening breeze, marched into the quaint old city of Frederick. Our bands struck up "Maryland, my Maryland," when two Union regiments from Baltimore, overjoyed to think their sister city was rescued from the iron heel of rebel usurpation and oppression, forgot their military discipline and broke forth with the wildest hurrahs, and with deep, rich bass and falsetto voices echoed all along the streets—

> "We will conquer with the sword,
> We will drive the rebel horde,
> Maryland, my Maryland."

If anyone doubted the love for the old flag which slaveholders professed to have, or Maryland citizens had cherished, they could doubt it no longer—the whole population turned out en masse to greet us. The aged, with tottering step and dim eyes, grasped us by the hands, and with eyes fixed on heaven, invoked God's choicest blessings on us. The young and middleaged shouted themselves hoarse, waved their Union flags as they cheered, throwing their hats high in the air, dancing while wild with excitement, and shouting in the most boisterous manner.—Ladies of all ages waved their handkerchiefs, threw kisses at our sun-burnt soldiers, and several imprinted their lips on our young heroes, seeming to forget that they were the "horrid Yankees" of years gone by. Citizens were rushing about with pails of lemonade, and even giving out their

120

choice wines in bottles to the soldiers as they passed triumphantly through the city.

We left the patriotic city of Frederick alive with delight, and each soldier was inspired with a desire to fight the rebel hosts that had been plundering these people because of their loyalty for the old flag. To die for such noble people would seem to be a pleasure. We marched to Middletown and bivouacked for the night, sleeping on our arms ready for action at a moment's notice. All were expecting a great battle at daylight, but during the night the entire rebel army on our front had retreated to a strong position in their rear on the crest of South Mountain. This delayed action for several hours.

It was high twelve when the continuous crack of musketry on the skirmish line indicated that our forces had discovered the chosen position of the rebels. Two hours later our field artillery began to shell the woods beyond our skirmish line which skirted the base of the mountain. In the cornfields near the base of the mountain, our skirmishers found the rebel infantry massed. The smiling face and noble form of the gallant BURNSIDE was everywhere seen forming the line of battle, while his staff was on different parts of our line getting the corps into position. His chief of artillery rides up and salutes for orders.

"Order all the artillery to open with shell, cannister, and case shot when the infantry charge," said our brave Gen. Burnside, as he dashed forward to the front line of battle.

"Clear that cornfield at the point of the bayonet," said Gen. Nagle as he executed his superior officer's order and pointed to a dense cornfield within easy musket range.

As the sun was retiring beyond the crest of the mountain, drawing after him his curtains of gold and crimson, as he sunk to rest beyond the dense foliage on the mountain summit, the roar of artillery shook the ground, and at the same instant the long lines of gleaming bayonets were flashing in the air, as the Federal infantry charged on the rebel lines secreted in the tall, waving corn. Gray uniforms began to be seen showing their heels to the "Yanks," and soon their whole line retreated in disorder and confusion from our advancing, gallant heroes in blue.

Up the side of South Mountain the Union army charged, driving the rebels at the point of the bayonet, until they rallied on a strong natural position on the crest of the mountain, placed their reserved forces in line of battle, and here the battle of South Mountain was fought. Continuous and impetuous charges were made on their lines, but not until almost dark did they at last give way, and victory perched wherever "old glory" waved.

Just at twilight, as we had gained our brilliant victory, two

121

brother Masons were about to salute each other, when the bullet from a rebel sharpshooter pierced one of them and he fell. The word was hastily passed along the lines "Reno has fallen!" In revenge for the killing of one of our favorite commanding generals after victory has been achieved, and firing nearly ceased, our lines poured a deadly fire into the ranks of the rebels within musket shot and the action again commenced along the lines.

When night had drawn around her sable mantle, and the roar of battle ceased, and all was still save the groans and low moaning of the wounded and dying lying on the field, two Generals again embraced each other; they were Brig. Gen. Samuel D. Sturgis and our dying hero, Maj. Gen. Jesse L. Reno. They were classmates at West Point, but there was something stronger than early friendship that bound them together. *It was Freemasonry.*

"Are you mortally wounded, Jesse," said Gen. Sturgis, as he embraced and kissed with tenderness the form he loved so well. "I am dying, Sam," said the expiring General, as the death rattle choked his utterance and cold sweat covered his brow.

The final disposition of everything on earth which he possessed, the last words to loved ones at home, and all the final arrangements for another world, were hastily made in a few moments between these brother Masons. His spirit crossed the river of death to the other shore, where rebellion is known no more forever, and where rebels, who once set up a kingdom of their own in *Hades,* are debarred from the sacred privileges of heaven.

Major General Reno, the true and sincere Mason, died as Masons love to die, on the battlefield, offering up his life to his country as the best gift of man to his native land. His last words were tributes of praise to Freemasonry and to his brother Masons.

Skirting a forest on the summit, where a dense growth of underbrush obstructed rapid movements, the dead and dying in both blue and gray lay thickly scattered over the ground, where a bayonet charge had been executed with decisive success. Death had reaped a rich harvest here.

The groaning and low moans of the severely wounded were painful to hear. As the battle was over, and no action would probably ensue until daylight, I determined to assist the wounded on the field we had just charged over and taken from the enemy. It was very dark and difficult to tell the rebel from the Union wounded as they mixed together on the field.

I was passing through some very dense underbrush, giving water from my canteen to the wounded, and assisting the "stretcher-bearers" to take the worst cases from the field, when someone sitting against a tree uttered in a clear, distinct voice the never-to-be-forgotten words accompanying the sign of distress among Masons. In

122

a moment I was by his side, with my hand grasping his, proffering any aid in my power. A drink of cold water from my canteen was his first request, and then I bathed his wounds with the remainder of the water I had. He was shot through the right leg and also through the shoulder, the latter wound being very painful. I tore away the skirts of his coat and with my handkerchief bound up his wound to stop the blood, for he was quite weak and evidently bleeding to death.

When I had succeeded in stopping the blood from flowing he seemed to revive and in a nervous manner asked me if I knew who I was attending to so kindly. I told him I did not have the honor of knowing and really cared very little to know as long as he was a *Mason.* He replied in a very desponding manner, "I am Col. C——— of the ——— South Carolina Regiment, instead of being a Union officer as you supposed."

I replied that I was happy to learn his name and as it was so very dark I could not tell the color of uniforms and knew not rebel from Union wounded.

"I will call the stretcher-bearers and have you taken to our hospital," I added.

"What, me!" said the rebel officer, speaking as if taken wholly by surprise. "Yes sir, YOU," said I emphatically. "I am not entitled to any such treatment," said he in a very decisive manner.

"You are entitled to *all* I can do for you, and to the kindest care and treatment our field hospitals afford," said I, "because you have proved to me you are a *Freemason.*"

He tried to speak but something choked his utterance. I thought it was blood from his wound, but he afterward told me it was his attempted utterance suddenly surprised by kindness which captured his finer feelings and led him a willing captive into a Masonic ambuscade.

The stretcher-bearers were found and he was carefully taken to the nearest field hospital, where a surgeon had charge of it, who happened to be a Mason. I asked of the surgeon, as a personal favor, that this rebel officer might receive the best attention and if any expenses were incurred to charge them to me. A convalescent was detailed to take charge of him, his wounds were carefully dressed, nourishment was given him, and I lay down to catch an hour's sleep before the hard duties of the morrow summoned me hence.

Morning dawned on that bloody field of battle. The crest of South Mountain was lighted up with gold and crimson sunbeams chasing each other among the deep, dark foliage of those grand old forests. The sunbeams kissed the suffering heroes in blood and dirt lying on the ground without a covering, and fell sadly upon the

123

pale faces locked in the cold embrace of death. Ere this same sun would fall behind the distant Alleghanies many in pain and agony would pass beyond the blue heavens into which they were gazing, where soldiers die no more. The cross and the crescent, the square and the compass, the blue and the gray, would all be gathered together where the lamb and the lion would lie down together, where peace would be eternal, and war be known no more forever.

The whole command was to move at sunrise, but the rebels had again retreated from our front during the night and taken up a strong position on Antietam Creek. It was high twelve before the reconnaissances in force found the position of the enemy, so we lay all the forenoon, expecting the next moment to move.

Just before noon, I went back to the hospital and found Col. C. much refreshed and looking quite cheerful. He grasped my hand and kissed it, and the tear of a manly soldier stood in his eye, hardly daring to fall. I never can forget the flash of those dark Southern eyes as he said:

"Please tell me for what reason you have been so kind to me?"

I replied, "Because you are a Freemason—yes, a Royal Arch Mason."

"I have taken in the old Granite State the same oaths that you have in a sunny Palmetto State, and we are therefore companions until death. Nothing on earth can separate us, or our attachment for each other. In war as well as in peace we are still the same. While thrones and republics are tumbling, and the world changing day by day, *we, as Masons,* are now and ever will be the same without change. I love and respect you as a brother, and as you would peril your own life to save mine, I ask you if I have done any more than was my duty to you as a Royal Arch Mason?"

He gave way to considerable emotion as this reply was made, but added with much sincere feeling:

"But I have been fighting against you, and all such as you for a year, and aiding in all ways in my power to kill you."

"Then go and sin no more," I added, "for this you should feel ashamed as a Mason. It is your country and not your State you have sworn to support and be a good citizen in, and you have been trying to subvert the best government ever framed by man, and blessed by Almighty God. It has done you no injury, but has watched over and protected you, as faithfully as a brother Mason. It has protected your life and property, and you owe it a debt of gratitude. Return, then, to your allegiance, and be as true to your country as you have been false. It is your duty *as a Mason.*"

With one hand in mine and the other on his heart he said: "I swear by the God who has so kindly made you the instrument for saving my life, that if these wounds do not prove mortal, I will never be found in our army again." And turning to the surgeon, who was just then coming up, "I will never cease to love the flag I honored in boyhood, until we three, or three such as we, meet together in heaven."

The author adds this postscript to his story:

In the summer of 1864, while many of our officers were under our own artillery fire in Charleston, and our privates in prison were being starved in a systematic manner, which will stand on the pages of history as the most atrocious crime of modern times, a citizen of Charleston might have been seen, going at all hours and in all places to these prisons and slave-pens where our soldiers were confined, and giving them the best that Charleston market afforded. All the delicacies were faithfully given to the sick and suffering, and surgical aid was often called at his own expense. He would often sit all night by the side of some sick or dying soldier, and watch over him with the tenderness of a mother. His countenance became familiar to all imprisoned in Charleston, and he was often asked why he dared perform such duties, being a native South Carolinian. He never gave a satisfactory reply. All imprisoned in Charleston will remember him as a ministering angel, a nameless hero, *who was wounded in the right leg and severely wounded in the shoulder.*

The *Freemasons' Magazine* records another incident of the Battle of Antietam, an engagement which has been claimed as the bloodiest of the war:

The day after the battle of Antietam the 5th New Hampshire formed the picket line along the edge of the cornfield where Richardson's Division fought. The reserve was in one edge of the corn, and the pickets about middle way of the field concealed in the corn, as the sharpshooters of the enemy fired on all who undertook to walk around on the battle field at that locality. Early in the morning one of the wounded rebels who lay just outside the pickets called one of the N. H. men and handed him a little slip of paper, on which he had evidently with great difficulty, succeeded in making some mystic sign with a bit of stick wet in blood. The soldier was begged to hand the paper to some Freemason as soon as possible, and he took it to Col. E. E. Cross of his regiment. The Colonel was a Master Mason. He sent for Capt. J. B. Perry, and several Brother Masons in the regiment, told the story, and in a few moments four "Brothers of the mystic tye" were crawling stealthily through the corn to find the Brother in distress. He was found, placed on a blanket, and at great risk drawn out of range of the

125

rebel rifles, and then carried to the 5th N. H. hospital. He proved to be First Lieutenant Edon of the Alabama volunteers, badly wounded in the thigh and breast. A few hours and he would have perished. Lieut. Edon informed his Brethren of another wounded Mason, who, when brought out, proved to be a Lieutenant Colonel of a Georgia regiment. These two wounded rebel officers received the same attention as the wounded officers of the 5th and a warm friendship was established between men who a few hours before were in mortal combat.

Another Confederate wounded at Crampton Gap, South Mountain, was James H. Camp. He shouted the Masonic words of distress and a Federal officer responded: "Brother, what can I do for you?" Camp asked for water. The officer sent two of his men for it. They returned loaded down with canteens for the wounded Confederate and his companions. The Union officer remained with Camp until help arrived to take care of his wounds.

After the Battle of Antietam, Lee recrossed the Potomac and settled down in Winchester, Virginia. There was no real pursuit by McClellan; he was content to remain on the other side of the river.

Although the decline of the Confederacy began with the unsuccessful invasion of the North, the Confederate Senate passed a bill furnishing the South with a seal. The Richmond *Whig,* on September 25 described it as:

In the foreground a Confederate soldier, in the position of charge bayonet; in the middle distance, a woman with a child in front of a church, both with hands uplifted in the attitude of prayer; for a background a homestead on the plain with mountains in the distance, beneath the meridian sun; the whole surrounded by a wreath composed of the stalks of the sugar-cane, the rice, the cotton, and the tobacco-plants, the margin inscribed with the words, "Seal of the Confederate States of America," above and "Our Homes and Constitution" beneath.

At Corinth, Mississippi, on October 4, General Van Dorn and the Confederate Masonic generals Price and Mansfield Lovell attacked the Union forces under the command of General Rosecrans. "The loss on both sides was very severe, and particularly in officers."

126

The Confederate troops marched into Kentucky, fought the Battle of Perryville and several smaller engagements, and marched back to Tennessee prior to the annual communication of the Grand Lodge of Kentucky. That set the state into such confusion that a constitutional quorum of lodges was not present on October 20. The grand master, John B. Huston, in order to open his grand lodge, suspended the charters of 138 lodges that had failed to comply with the requirement of the grand lodge. Another roll-call then found a quorum present. Huston, in his annual address, said:

Again we are taught among the first lessons in Masonry that it unites upon the principles of brotherly love men of every country, sect, and opinion. Shall we then, of the same country, perhaps of the same kin, allow our political opinions, however we may differ, to estrange, divide and disunite us? I trust not. If we admit any other theory we destroy the universality of Masonry, or sectionalize it, and it becomes as chamelion like in its hues, as the various shades that characterize the different nations, or political organizations of the earth.

No, my brethren, Masonry was informed on a broader principle than this, and our ancient brethren wisely determined that no political or religious distinctions should ever limit its boundless charity. It is peculiar to no country but common to all. It recognizes no religion, but that unfaltering trust in the Omnipotent Being who created the world and all things therein—the Grand Architect of the Universe—by whose unerring square the blocks we offer must at last be tried, and who will reward us according to our merits.

Let us then leave all these subjects where our forefathers placed them—"outside the Mason's door." Let each of us resolve, that though civil strife may sever all natural, social, political and even religious ties, yet so far as we can avert it, there is one tie it shall not break—*the mystic tie.* Yes, my brethren, let us resolve anew, that there shall be at least *one* tribunal, where the cries of suffering humanity shall not be disregarded—where the distressed of "every country, sect and opinion," may prefer their suits and not appeal in vain. Then, even though it should be the fate of our noble institution, as it seems alas! likely to be that of all others of human origin, to perish amid civil strife and social convulsions; still, however much we may grieve over the ruin, we will have the proud consolation to know, that we at least did not with iconoclastic hand, inflict a single blow upon the sacred temple.

Charles F. Stansbury, grand master of the District of Columbia, told his grand lodge on November 4:

It is scarcely to have been expected that in a year of internecine war, almost upon the very theatre of military operations, and in the presence of contending armies, the affairs of the Fraternity should have been conducted with the same regularity, and on precisely the same principles, as in times of domestic tranquility.

We cannot ignore a Masonic brother because he comes from any particular quarter of the world, or holds any political or religious creed different from our own, unless such creed is inconsistent with Masonry. He must have committed some offence which would justly subject him to suspension or expulsion, before we can repudiate his claim upon our Masonic sympathy and charity whenever he is in a situation to need them. Hence, the action of any body of Masons in assuming to cut off from Masonic fellowship those who are arrayed on the one or the other side of the present unhappy contest in our country, is in the highest degree unmasonic and reprehensible. Masonry is ancient, universal, and unchangeable, or it is a sham and a farce. Its principles are to be derived from a study of the ancient landmarks, and no deviation from them is to be countenanced.

However, close as was the relationship which existed among all members of the Masonic fraternity, a rift in the ranks was soon to make itself apparent.

On the day preceding the meeting of the Grand Lodge of the District of Columbia, the Grand Lodge of Colorado met at Central City, and, declaring the "Conservator's Association" a corrupt organization, adopted the following resolution:

Hereafter no Grand Officer, and no officer of any subordinate Lodge, shall be installed until he shall have made a solemn pledge, in open Lodge, that on his honor as a Mason he repudiates and condemns the said association.

Fires that had been smoldering had begun to break into flames and to cause a division in the ranks of Freemasons more severe than the war.

CHAPTER X

The Conservators

◇◇◇

> *It would be interesting for us to know what might have happened should the Civil War not have occurred just at the height of the movement. It is our opinion that the Civil War, intervening as it did, prevented the dispute from becoming any more bitter than it did; the war sapped the resources of the Conservators and occupied the attention of Grand Lodges to such an extent that the attacks made upon the Association were probably lessened in character.*
>
> RAY V. DENSLOW

FROM THE TIME of George Washington, who was proposed as a good prospect for a general grand master of Masons in America, until the present day, there have been movements for the establishment of a national "general grand lodge." Most such movements were primarily designed to bring a uniformity in the ritual throughout the country.

In Washington on March 9, 1822, a convention was held with the avowed purpose of laying the foundation for a general grand lodge. Although the much respected Henry Clay of Kentucky was behind the movement, his grand lodge, as well as many others, turned a deaf ear to the proposal.

The next major convention took place after the "Morgan Affair" had passed from the Masonic scene. It was the Baltimore Convention of 1843. Its results were fairly successful, for it did set up a uniform standard or "work" which some grand lodges adopted, most of them with some reservations.

Then a man named Robert Morris appeared on the scene with an organization that was to plague every grand lodge in

129

America during the trying days of the Civil War. That organization was styled "Conservators of Symbolical Masonry," although it became better known simply as "The Conservators."

Rob Morris, the founder and "Chief Conservator," was initiated in Oxford Lodge, No. 33, Mississippi, on March 3, 1845, at the age of 26. Three years later, according to one of his friends, he started to inquire, "either personally or by correspondence, with every elderly Mason known to have been bright in his earlier days." In all, he "conferred with more than 50,000 Masons . . . [and] visited nearly 2,000 lodges." He was elected grand master at Lexington, Kentucky, on October 11, 1858, and less than two years later started his "Conservator" movement, for which he was to be condemned by his grand lodge, as well as many others throughout the United and Confederate States.

Ray V. Denslow, in his book, *The Masonic Conservators,* writes:

The Conservator movement without "Mnemonics" would have been a failure; its use was the key to whatever success it may have had as an organization. Instructors in Masonic ritual were few; Grand Lecturers were a rarity, and few lodges ever received the assistance of qualified instructors; the brethren were clamoring for some method whereby they might become proficient in Masonry.

The "key" or "code" which put all of the exoteric, as well as the esoteric, work into a form that could be read by anyone possessing the key that untangled the complicated system, aroused the ire of most of the grand lodges. Leverett B. Englesby, the grand master of Vermont, on January 14, 1863, stated: "To no man's sleeve should Masonic or any other faith be pinned. Our traditions are verbal—not written—transmitted from mouth to ear, and so handed down."

During 1863, a committee of nine appointed by the Grand Lodge of Michigan conferred with Morris on several occasions, and on January 14, 1864, submitted a lengthy report which indicated it had made an exhaustive search for the facts about the "Conservators." It concluded "the scheme to be unlawful, unmasonic, and opposed to the real interest of Masonry." The

130

committee then listed a summary of the 12 points of the obligation of a full "Conservator":

1. To secrecy.
2. That every document furnished the candidate as a member of the Conservator's association, whether written or printed, is to be considered as between himself and the Chief Conservator; that no one is to have any access to any such document, to be informed of its allusions or existence, except those directly accredited by the Chief Conservator.
3. To answer and obey all summonses and orders of the Chief Conservator, and of such as may be duly accredited by him, without question as to the object or intent thereof.
4. To aid and help all Conservators in distress or in need of help, with advice, money, information, service, or in any other way, in preference to any other persons, and especially in any way that will advance the interests of their association.
5. That the great end of the Association shall be constantly kept in view, and uniformity of work, upon the basis prescribed by the Chief Conservator, commonly called the Webb-Preston system, shall be strenuously urged, to the exclusion of all other systems.
6. Every Conservator is bound to use all his influence to obtain and hold the first three offices in his Lodge; to teach the Morris system and no other, and to seek by every available means to obtain possession of the Grand Lodge so as to compel all Lodges to adopt and use the above named system of work.
7. To root out all the old Masons, who adhere to any other system, from office; to depreciate and dimish their influence, seduce them to their support, when necessary or advisable, by giving them unimportant offices; to create divisions and jealousies among them; to attack them and drive them from all participation in the business or counsels of the Craft.
8. To menace and threaten all brethren who will not submit to their terms; to aggravate and persistently annoy them until they commit some indiscreet act, so that they may take advantage of the same.
9. To make use of power when obtained to propagate the system of work dictated by the Chief Conservator, and to break down every Lodge that stands in its way.
10. To keep all secrets communicated by Conservators, without exception, let their character or objects be what they may.
11. To insist everywhere, and at all times, that the system of the Chief Conservator is the only true system, and that all other systems are illegitimate.

12. Not to assist in the making of a Conservator, who had not previously declared, in writing, that he will fully conform to all the rules of the order.

The report of the committee was adopted, as was the following resolution:

Resolved, That any attempt, by any person or body of men, to introduce or teach any change of our long established lectures, is unconstitutional, unmasonic, and deserves the most severe reprehension, and is by this Grand Lodge strictly forbidden within this jurisdiction.

While the vast majority of the grand lodges fought Morris and his movement, he was not without his defenders. Members of every grand lodge then in existence, except Colorado, District of Columbia, Oregon, and Virginia, had anywhere from one to more than one hundred "Conservators" among them. Indiana had by far the most members of the movement, and Illinois, Iowa, New Jersey, and New York had more than 100. The states with only one or two included Delaware, Florida, Georgia, Maine, Maryland, Rhode Island, and Washington, according to a partial listing of the membership. The adverse publicity kept the full list from ever being published, but it is estimated that more than 3,000 Masons became "Conservators" during its five years of existence.

Shortly after the close of the war, on June 24, 1865, the life of the "Conservator" association ended, but its influence went on for several years. Ray Denslow believes there are many states that follow closely today the ritual of the Mnemonics, although the movement did not accomplish its avowed purpose, which was uniformity of ritual. Some grand lodges, which during the Civil War condemned Morris and his coded ritual, use the method they then abhorred to teach the Masons of their jurisdictions today.

The movement, born on June 24, 1860, could not have picked a more inopportune time for its purpose, for less than a year later the country was embroiled in the strife that has come to be known as the Civil War. Masons were uprooted from their homes and sent from state to state. Those who had become "Conservators," or who leaned toward Morris, were unacceptable to those who felt he was trying to become a Masonic dictator. The unkindly feelings were sharper between those for and against Morris than they were between the Masons of the North and South.

Many grand lodges adopted resolutions forbidding their members to associate with "Conservators"; no grand lodge adopted a resolution forbidding Masons from either the North or South to meet in Masonic fellowship. A few grand masters *did* try to have such an edict enforced, but did not succeed. Far more grand masters rebuked individual lodges and Masons for refusing to admit members on the opposite side of the conflict.

The renunciation oath of the Grand Lodge of Missouri was harsh:

I do solemnly declare, on my honor as a Master Mason, that I have never belonged to the so-called Conservators' Association; that I do not now belong, to the same; and that I do, and will, forever denounce and repudiate the system, and all connected therewith.

The following year, realizing the harshness of the above, it was changed to a milder form.

In 1861, Rob Morris had been elected an honorary member of the Grand Lodge of Michigan; in 1864, that grand lodge rescinded its action of three years earlier. From Maine to Oregon, Robert Morris and his Conservator movement was condemned. Thousands of unkind words were written about him; as were hundreds of words of praise. With the end of his dream for a uniform ritual came the end of the bitterness he had invoked. Gradually what he had attempted to do was erased from the minds of Masons, and as his poetry again appeared, he was received in many of the grand lodges that had refuted him. Typical was the warm welcome he received in Missouri in 1886 from a grand lodge that had once considered him a traitor.

Today, Robert Morris is best known as the "Poet Laureate of Freemasonry," and as the author of a ritual and founder of the Order of the Eastern Star.

An excellent example of the split caused by Morris and his "Conservators" is reflected in a letter written on July 13, 1863, from Pilot Knob, Missouri, enclosing the following petition to the Grand Lodge of Nebraska:

To the Most Worshipful Grand Master of Nebraska:

The undersigned Master Masons in good standing in the several lodges to which they belong, having the good of Masonry at heart, respectfully petition you, the Most Worshipful Grand Master of Nebraska, to issue us a dispensation to meet and work as a traveling lodge of Master Masons, and to do all lawful business pertaining to Masonry.

We are induced to make this application for the following reasons, viz.:

First. We are placed in a situation where we cannot meet with a regular organized lodge for months together.

Second. The Grand Lodge of Missouri has passed resolutions requiring all who visit their lodges to take an extra oath, which in our opinion does not in the least appertain to Masonry.

Third. We have many in our Regiment who are anxious to become members of our Ancient and Honorable Order whom we consider to be good and true men and who will do good work in our order with pleasure to themselves and honor to our fraternity.

We respectfully recommend the following named brothers to act as our officers:

W.M. Lee P. Gillette; S.W., R. R. Livingstone; J.W., S. M. Curran.

G. W. Wilkinson, Omadi Lodge, No. 5, Nebraska; Lee P. Gillette, Western Star Lodge, No. 2, Nebraska; S. M. Curran, Capitol Lodge, No. 3, Nebraska; F. L. Cramer, Nodaway Lodge No. 140, Iowa; J. P. Murphy, Nodaway Lodge No. 140, Iowa; Wm. L. Jaycox, Taylor Lodge No. 156, Iowa; R. C. Jordan, Capitol Lodge No. 3, Nebraska.

The grand master of Nebraska, G. H. Wheeler, after "consultation with many of the Brethren . . . concluded to grant the dispensation, knowing well that the interests of the Fraternity would never be allowed to suffer." He felt assured of that because the man appointed as master (Gillette) was grand lecturer of Nebraska, the man charged with seeing that the ritual selected by that grand lodge would be adhered to. Thus Monitor Lodge U.D. came into being, to exist from July 20, 1863 until June 21, 1866. It was a lodge composed mainly of men who had fought at Forts Henry and Donelson, Shiloh, Corinth, and other engagements in the area.

134

Ray V. Denslow, a Past Grand Master of Missouri, and author of *Civil War and Masonry in Missouri*, writes, "The old record book of Monitor Lodge U.D. is now one of the treasured possessions of the Grand Lodge of Nebraska and as time passes on, and the brethren who engaged in the internecine conflict pass from the scene of action, these records become more and more valuable and interesting." That record book shows that the lodge met in Ironton, Pilot Knob, St. Louis, and for the last time on Missouri soil, at Rolla. Batesville, Arkansas, on January 13, 1864, was the next scene of the meetings of the lodge.

Denslow further writes, "During its stay in Confederate territory we find the lodge occasionally visited by officers and members of the Confederate Army, and many instances are recorded which verify the sincerity of the Masonic tie during that stirring period." He later writes about the "Masonic spirit" of the man who was the first senior warden, and who served repeatedly as master, Colonel R. R. Livingston, who, after taking over command of Northeast Arkansas, issued the following proclamation:

Ordered to assume command of the District of Northeastern Arkansas, I have come among you clothed with authority to protect the loyalty and summarily punish all violations of the laws of war.

I am not here to ask you what you have done in the past; your actions in the future, more than your past conduct, shall serve as a basis for my guidance.

To the noble sons of Arkansas, who have stood true to the old flag amid all the vicissitudes of this deplorable war, I extend the warm right hand of fellowship. To those who have already repented of their folly in resisting the best and most powerful government on earth, I shall afford protection; and to such as are now in arms, but are anxious and willing to return to their allegiance to the United States, I promise security in the enjoyment of those inestimable blessings, which only the Government I represent can bestow upon her citizens.

Let the strong reasons of good men be exercised to recall the misguided, who still persist in a fruitless and ruin entailing struggle against fate.

Be advised in time—forego the course of bootless warfare you

135

have carried on in detached and unwarranted hands against the Government—return to your firesides and the bosoms of your families, and as far as my power lies, I will protect you and yours from harm.

I ask and shall expect the full support of all good men in restoring peace to your desolated district. The hearty co-operating of law and order loving citizens in suppressing lawless bands, by information as well as by appealing to the erring, is essential to your own safety, and is demanded.

Robert R. Livingston, who had received the degrees in Masonry in Plattsmouth Lodge No. 6, Nebraska, served that lodge as master for a number of years, and went on to become grand high priest of the Grand Chapter of Nebraska. He organized the Nebraska State Medical Society, and was its first president. He later served as its secretary for several terms.

The Masonic spirit of Livingston and the other members of Monitor Lodge proved no error had been made in granting a dispensation. The good it did throughout the balance of the war will never be known, but that it helped an untold number of Masons and non-Masons is without question.

CHAPTER XI

Masonry Blamed for the Draft

◇◇◇

*I cannot tell how the truth may be; I say the
tale as 'twas said to me.*

Sir Walter Scott

THE RECORDS of Osaukee Lodge, No. 17, Port Washington, Wisconsin, for November 10, 1862, state:

The Lodge room was entered by a mob this day and the Master's carpet was destroyed and other property injured. The records and most of the Lodge papers were saved. The immediate cause was the general feeling against the draft which was to take place this day, many believing that Masons were the cause of the draft. This day will long be remembered by many as the day of the "Great Ozaukee County Draft Riot."

The damage to the lodge was so extensive it was more than a month before it could be used. Troops finally had to restore order in the county, for a mob also wrecked the courthouse. They chased the commissioner, Benjamin Pors, from one place to another and destroyed more private property on their way.

On November 13 the *Milwaukee Sentinel* carried the following:

The resistance to the draft in Ozaukee County has assumed quite a serious aspect. Early on Monday morning, the day on which the draft was to take place, processions came into the village and paraded the streets with banners on which was inscribed "No Draft." At a predetermined signal, (the firing of two cannons), they marched to the courthouse where they found Commissioner Pors had just commenced operations. The mob immediately attacked the courthouse, the commissioner fled, a part of the mob pursuing him and assaulting him with stones, brickbats and other missles until he took refuge in the post office. The other part continued their assault on the courthouse and destroyed the papers and other

137

machinery connected with the draft. The commissioner having escaped the hands of the rioters, they turned around and wrecked vengeance upon several eminent citizens, who had been counseling obedience to the law. Among those assaulted were S. A. White, the county judge; L. Towsley, the district attorney; Judge Downs, registrar of deeds, and A. M. Blair, a leading lawyer.

The rioters then commenced to destroy private property. The house of Commissioner Pors, Mr. Loomis and Mr. Blair were sacked. The house of Commissioner Pors was also visited with particular vengeance. The furniture was smashed and dumped out on the street—jellies, jams and preserves were poured over Brussels carpet, and ladies apparel torn to shreds.

Each of the men listed in the newspaper account as having been victims of the mob were Masons; all except Pors were members of Ozaukee Lodge; Pors was a member of Astra Lodge, and after the war became a member of the former.

That draft riot was among the first that was to take place throughout Northern states. The drafting of men for armed service did not meet with favor anywhere. While September 3, 1862, was set as the day for the first drawings, it was not strictly adhered to. The Federal government did not take the initiative, and many of the governors kept postponing the inevitable. Even at the end of the year some states had held no drawings.

A new business came into being because of the draft—substitute brokers. James A. Garfield, a Mason, describes that business:

What is a substitute broker? A man who establishes an office and offers to furnish substitutes for different localities. He pays bounties and gathers men in gangs for sale, and when the committees of any town are hard pressed to fill up their quotas they send to the substitute broker and buy his wares at exorbitant rates. He gets men for comparatively a small bounty and sells them at enormous prices to the districts that are otherwise unable to provide to fill their quotas. The results have been that men in all parts of the United States have been compelled to see their sons bought and sold by these infamous substitute brokers.

What has been described as the greatest riot in American history broke out on July 13, 1863, in New York City. Soon after drawings for the draft had started, street fighting raged, and for three days the mob took over the city. What had started out as opposition to the draft turned out to be opposition to everything and everyone. The draft riot widened into a race riot; Negroes were hunted down and murdered on the streets; anti-administration men destroyed the property of the administration supporters; the malcontents ran wild. Estimates vary from 74-1,200 killed; from several hundred wounded to six or seven thousand. The property damage has been estimated at $1,500,000.

Among the men who were finally successful in quelling the riots was William T. Coleman, a Californian who was in New York on business. Having had experience as a vigilante leader, he was requested by the governor to organize the law-abiding citizens, which he did with such success he became known as "The Lion of the Vigilantes." During the same year, he was made a Mason in Holland Lodge, No. 8, New York City.

The South had its troubles with the draft also. Although the Confederate Congress approved a system of conscription on April 16, 1862, it never became successful because of the strong states rights feeling among the people. The substitute market reached big business proportions in the Confederate states, as it did in the Union. It is claimed that those who would serve in place of those who were supposed to serve received fees ranging into the thousands of dollars. Anonymous advertisements were constantly carried in the newspapers similar to the one that appeared on May 3, 1862, in the *Southern Confederacy,* Atlanta, Georgia:

A SUBSTITUTE WANTED!

A substitute wanted for the war. Call at the store of Brown, Fleming & Co., Masonic Building, a few doors below the Trout House. Call at once. A liberal sum will be paid.

Many of the men who had been drafted deserted both armies in wholesale lots. Those who were substitutes were the worst offenders. General Lee wrote to President Davis stating that desertions were so numerous "nothing will remedy this great evil which so much endangers our cause except rigid enforcement of the death penalty in future cases of conviction." It was a penalty that Davis was extremely reluctant to enforce.

The battle of Fredericksburg began on December 11, when General Burnside, who had succeeded McClellan, ordered his 147 heavy guns to fire into the town. It ended by Burnside ordering his men back to the opposite side of the Rappahannock.

On the 13th the Federal troops charged the heavily entrenched Confederates. Six times they formed and charged; six times they were repulsed with staggering losses in dead and wounded—almost 13,000.

The Freemasons' Monthly Magazine tells of a conversation that took place at the end of the battle:

Capt. Marchand of Philadelphia, wounded at Fredericksburg, before dying, said to an attendant: "I do not want to go home to die." The attendant responded, "I should wish to be with my friends. Don't you, Captain?" The response was: "Yes, but if paroled and sent home, when death is morally certain, the enemy will get a well man in my place, and my government and country will lose one in any event. So I will stay here." Captain Swearengen, at his own expense, spent twenty-five dollars for head-board, etc., for his brave Masonic Brother. In the Libby burial ground, at Richmond, set apart for the burial of deceased federal soldiers, the stranger will read the touching memorial of this brave Mason.

The same magazine carried another story about another one of the hundreds of Masons who participated in the fight:

At the battle of Fredericksburg, Captain T. B. Wearengen, General Mead's Adjutant General, was wounded through the lungs, badly bruised, and was found *senseless on the field* by a North Carolina Confederate officer, who, believing him to be a Mason by a jewel on his person, had him carried to a house used as headquarters, called a surgeon to dress his wound, which was thought fatal; yet by the kind care and watching of the craft he was soon able to proceed to Richmond. His blankets were returned by half-naked, blanketless soldiers, and nothing taken from him.

Previous to the battle, the home of Fredericksburg Lodge, No. 4, the lodge in which George Washington had received his degrees over 100 years earlier, was broken into. The silver jewels, made in Scotland, and used during Washington's initiation, were stolen as were many other items of value. Years later, most of what had been stolen was returned after they had fallen into the hands of Masons who realized their worth.

While Burnside was preparing to attack Fredericksburg, the Grand Lodge of Virginia was meeting in Richmond. The grand master, Lewis B. Williams, noting the many vacant places, stated:

> Knowing the cause of the absence of our brethren—that they are engaged in defending their firesides and their altars from a merciless invasion and from a relentless and vindictive foe—I approve their absence, and we should, by all honorable means, sustain and support them in their noble and manly efforts to maintain the rights and liberties of our beloved country.

A letter from Rockingham Union Lodge No. 27 was read, which informed the grand lodge that their lodge had been mutilated by men "led by a Mason." The committee to which the matter was referred said they wanted more information "as to whether General Fremont" was a Mason, and "if he actually knew his men were desecrating that lodge hall."

Williams said: "Since the last meeting of this grand body, seven dispensations or warrants have been granted for military or traveling lodges." That action met the approval of his grand lodge. The proceedings of only seven states had been received, all Confederates.

The Grand Lodge of Pennsylvania had the same difficulty according to Richard Vaux, chairman of the foreign correspondence committee, who reported on December 27 that no grand lodge proceedings had been received from any of the Confederate States during 1862. That was a source of deep concern to the chairman. He made an impassioned plea for the continuation of brotherly love and the right hand of fellowship, and hoped the lodges would seal the break that had been made in fraternal relations. He closes his report with these words:

> With the most sincere regard and fraternal salutation to your Committee and yourself—clothed in that solemnity of feeling which this subject suggests, and trusting to the God and Father of all for that fortitude, strength and wisdom which makes man a patriot, and Masons good and true.
>
> I am your brother,
> In the bonds of Freemasonry,
> RICHARD VAUX

141

The loss of postal service between the states arrayed against each other was a problem that vexed more than Masons. Friends, relatives, and families went for months without hearing from each other.

The break in mail service occurred early. On April 2, 1861, before the firing at Fort Sumter, the Confederate States of America published a proposal to bid for the manufacture of postal stamps. That was answered by three New York firms plus one each in Philadelphia, Newark, Baltimore, and Richmond. The Richmond firm got the job, but throughout the war the lack of stamps was a major problem to the Confederacy.

On June 1, the Postmaster General, John H. Reagan, a member of Palestine Lodge, No. 31, Texas, took over control of all mail in the Confederacy, and on the same day, his counterpart for the United States, Montgomery Blair, issued a proclamation suspending mail service in the Southern states.

Reagan, in his *Memoirs,* writes of the trouble he had in operating his department:

The Confederate Government experienced much difficulty and delay in sending and receiving foreign mail on account of the blockade of her ports. Such mail matter was carried by the blockade-runners, and by other means through Cuba, Bermuda, Nassau, and sometimes through Canada and Mexico, arriving at its destination in this round-about way, if at all. After reaching port in some one of the above named places in going out, the mails were generally transferred to vessels of neutral nations, mostly English and French; and on coming in, they were generally brought to some of those places by foreign vessels, and then transferred to blockade-runners.

The difficulties attending the operations of the postal service multiplied as hostile armies pierced farther and farther our lines. After the fall of Vicksburg and Port Hudson, communication between Richmond, the seat of government, and the country west of the Mississippi River became extremely uncertain. . . .

Chapters could be written on the expedients to which we were driven to get the mails back and forth across the Father of Waters, which was now patrolled throughout its length by the armed vessels of the enemy. The river was crossed in rowboats, usually under cover of night and at many points, and in this manner the letters of wives to husbands and of mothers to sons who were serving in the army, went forward to their destination; and in return came papers and letters from the front to the anxious ones who bore the brunt of sufferings at home, who lived lives of sacrifice that the cause for which they struggled might be furthered.

The leaders in the Federal government were determined to forge a speedier communication system between the East and West. The Pony Express was utilized on a daily basis instead of weekly, or spasmodically. The rapidity with which they delivered the mail has been attested to time and time again, in spite of difficulties encountered with Indians and guerilla attacks. That continued until the overland telegraph line was completed late in 1861. The North never suffered as badly as the South communication-wise.

Many communications for the South were carried by blockade runners under difficult and dangerous conditions. Moses Drury Hoge, a Presbyterian clergyman in Richmond, Virginia, used them to bring Biblical publications from England to the Confederacy. In December, 1862, he left Charleston aboard the *Herald,* later to be renamed the *Antonica,* for a shipment of 10,000 Bibles, 50,000 Testaments, and 250,000 other books. He managed to return them safely, but two years later the ship he was aboard was captured and his books jettisoned.

During October, 1863, Hoge left Bermuda aboard the blockade runner *Advance.* When it approached the Southern coast it was spotted by a Union sailor, and had to run through the entire Federal blockading fleet in broad daylight to reach its port. Past a hail of shrapnel, shell, and solid shot the speedy vessel fled. The people lining the shore cheered lustily when the little ship, without receiving a scratch, reached the safety of the guns of Fort Fisher. A few moments later it tied up in Wilmington, North Carolina.

Throughout his lifetime, Moses Hoge worked for his God and his fellowman. He counted among his staunchest friends many of the Masons in his community, and his desire to become a member of the Craft was fulfilled as he lay dying. The minutes of a lodge in Richmond, Virginia, tell part of the unusual story:

A Called Communication of Dove Lodge, No. 51, was held in the office of the Grand Secretary in the Masonic Temple, corner Broad and Adams Streets, in the City of Richmond on Tuesday evening, November 22nd A.L. 5898, A.D. 1898. . . . The W.M. announced that the Lodge had been called for the purpose of conferring the degrees upon Rev. Moses D. Hoge, D.D.

The M.W. Grand Master [R. T. W. Duke, Jr.] stated that in consequence of the physical disability of the Rev. Moses D. Hoge, D.D. that he would repair with the Lodge to the residence of the petitioner, and that permission was given the Lodge under dispensation which he personally granted to meet at the residence and without charter.

Moses D. Hoge, Jr., met the lodge at his father's residence on "the northeast corner of Main and 5th Streets." The grand master then conferred three degrees in Masonry, "dispensing with such portions of the ceremony as in his opinion the physical condition of the candidate required."

Upon the completion of the ceremonies, the master of Dove Lodge appointed Dr. Hoge a chaplain of said lodge, but he was never able to perform the duties assigned to that office. His illness kept him confined to his bed until January 6, 1899, when he passed to the Great Beyond.

CHAPTER XII

Brotherhood in Action

<><><><><><><><><><><><><><><><><><><><><><><><><><><><><><><><><><><><><><><><>

True friendship is a plant of slow growth, and must undergo and withstand the shocks of adversity before it is entitled to the appellation.
GEORGE WASHINGTON

THE FIRST engagement of the year 1863 resulted in a Confederate victory. It occurred at Galveston, Texas, on the night of January 1 when John B. Magruder, the new commander of the Confederate forces in Texas, determined to open that port to Southern trade.

The five Federal vessels in the harbor were engaged with artillery fire while land forces advanced to the wharf where the Northern troops were stationed. E. A. Pollard describes the action:

As the morning advanced, our fire still continuing, the long-expected cotton-boats came dashing down the harbour, and engaged the *Harriet Lane,* which was the nearest of the enemy's ships, in gallant style, running into her, one on each side, and pouring on her deck a deadly fire of rifles and shot-guns. The gallant Capt. Wainwright fought his ship admirably. He succeeded in disabling the *Neptune,* and attempted to run down the *Bayou City.* The Confederate boat adroitly evaded the deadly stroke; although, as the vessels passed each other, she lost her larboard wheelhouse in the shock. Again the *Bayou City,* while receiving several broadsides almost at the cannon's mouth, poured into the *Harriet Lane* a destructive fire of small arms. Turning once more, she drove her prow into the iron wheel of the *Harriet Lane,* thus locking the two vessels together. Followed by officers and men, Commodore Leon Smith leaped to the deck of the hostile ship, and after a moment of feeble resistance she was ours.

A short time later "the small Federal force which held the

145

wharf, perceiving that they were abandoned by the fleet, surrendered as prisoners."

Captain Wainwright, and his second in command, Lieutenant Lea, of the *Harriet Lane*, were killed. Ironically, Major Lea was among the boarders from the *Bayou City*, and for the first time in two years he was to meet his son, only to find him among the dead on the deck of the Federal vessel.

The following day, the minutes of a Lodge in Galveston record:

Harmony Lodge No. 6 of Galveston. Lodge of Emergency to bury the dead, held January 2, 1863, A.L. 5863. . . .
Lodge of Master Masons opened in due form. The presiding W.M. stated that he had called this Lodge of Emergency after consultation with the brethren, for the purpose of interring with the rite of Masonic burial the body of the late Capt. I. W. Wainwright, late commander of the U. S. Navy and in Command of the U. S. S. *Harriet Lane,* "the body now being dead at the Ursuline Convent" who was killed in action while bravely fighting his vessel when it was captured "by the blessing of God" by the forces of our Confederate government on the morning of the last inst. in our Bay in front of this City, that Messrs. Stone, Plunkett, Penrose and other Officers of that vessel, now prisoners of war; had made themselves known as Master Masons, and vouched that the deceased was a regular Master Mason known to them in good standing as such that they asked nothing for themselves as Masons, but in behalf of their late Commander and brother, they besought at our hands a Masonic burial, upon which it was resolved that the members of this lodge, appreciating the spirit and force of Masonic ties, will not allow their feelings and prejudice and love of righteous cause to obliterate from their hearts and minds the merciful teachings of the Order; that it does not conflict with their duties as patriotic citizens to respond to calls of mercy by a prostrate political foe, or to administer the last rite of the Order to the remains of a Mason of moral worth, although yesterday they met as an armed enemy in mortal combat in which the deceased parted with his life; that the action of the Past Master and brothers presiding "who is also the officer charged by the General Commandery with bringing the dead officers of the enemy" be and is approved.
Whereupon the Lodge was called to bury the dead. A public procession formed in which appeared both friends and foes wearing the insignia of the Order, and accompanied with a proper military escort under command of Col. and Brother H. B. Debray,

among which was the Major General Commanding J. Bankhead Magruder, the body of Bro. Wainwright was borne to its grave in the Episcopal Cemetery where it was deposited with the rites of Masons and military Lodge called from burying the dead and closed in due form.

The master of that lodge, P. C. Tucker, was a major in the Confederate Army and on the staff of General Magruder, at the time of the funeral.

When the Grand Lodge of Texas met in June, the grand master, Samuel Mather, commented on several Masonic incidents that had been brought to his attention:

The Federal army in the destruction of property at Hampton Court House saved the property of the Lodge, and returned it safely to its custodian under a flag of truce; so too, when Brother Wainwright fell on the deck of the *Harriet Lane* in her defence, his remains were interred by the brethren of Harmony Lodge, No. 1, at Galveston, with masonic honors; and a singular spectacle was presented of the prisoners of war who were captured by our forces, and belonging to the Order, marching in procession with the brethren, as though for a time a truce had been proclaimed and the clang of arms was to be heard no more. Many incidents have taken place on the high hills and low valleys of New Mexico and Arizona, which will be collected ere long for the press. One only need be referred to at present, which was a fraternal meeting in a Lodge at night of members of both armies, who met on the level, and next day were in deadly conflict on the battle-field. Much suffering has been alleviated, charity has been extended to the wounded and sick, death has often been prevented, and a surrender made under the mystic sign.

In far away Florida, D. C. Dawkins, the grand master, took note of what had been occurring in his state:

I once left home with a view of visiting all the Lodges in the East and Middle sections of the State; but soon seeing the delapidating influences of war, which are felt by our most fortunate and favored Lodges, I deemed it unnecessary to visit others, and make a useless attempt to revive a new zeal in less favored regions, while the sole and all-absorbing subject is war.

The localities of some of our Lodges on the coast are now possessed by the hostile invaders of our country. Some of our zealous brethren in these localities were fortunate enough to escape and

147

bring away their Lodge Jewels, Charters, furniture and ornaments, while others have lost all their fixtures.

The Holy Bible, that inestimable gift of God to man, which we, as Masons, acknowledge to be the rule and guide of our faith, has been torn from its sacred position on Masonry's Holy Altar, dishonored and desecrated by the vile persecutors of truth, liberty and justice. The mystic square and compass, by which we are symbolically taught to square our actions and circumscribe our desires and passions—the Lamb Skin, our emblem of innocence and the badge of a Mason, more ancient than the golden fleece or Roman eagle, more honorable than the star and garter or other order of King, Prince or Potentate of earth—our distinctive jewels, and beautiful and significant ornaments, and the Master's collection of sublime and mystic symbols, have all been subjected to immoral and profane desecration and destruction by our cruel and hostile enemies.

Though reflections upon these sad things are painful and melancholy, they are nought when compared with the loss of some of our most zealous brethren and best citizens, who have fallen casual victims of the enemy's sword.

The W. Master of Amelia Lodge has forwarded me a communication relative to the unfortunate condition of that Lodge, and the death of our lamented brother, George W. All, a member of this Grand Lodge, who fell at the battle of Seven Pines. . . .

. . . The families at home of many of our brothers in the service, and of our slain and wounded in the various battles, are also proper objects of our fraternal care, assistance and protection.

The widow's cry and the orphan's wail are loudly heard and deeply felt in many portions of our country, which should forcibly remind us of our duty to do all we possibly can to relieve their distresses.

I pray God that this unnatural and cruel war may soon terminate in our happy deliverance from our cruel enemies.

The Grand Lodge of New Jersey met on January 21 and the grand master, Isaac Van Wagoner told his members:

May a grateful people ever remember those who have thus fought and died; ever minister to the wants of those who have thus been injured; and, while they live, cherish and esteem those who have survived the horrors and carnage of the battle field.

Yet, during this unnatural contest—one where brother has met with brother, friend has met with friend in the deadly conflict, where the fiercest and most ungovernable passions of the human heart have been excited and brought into action—numerous instances are on record of the benignant influences that the teachings of Masonry have produced on the minds of its votaries. The heart-stirring revulsion of bitter and deadly feeling, caused by the utterance of the talismanic words, "I am a Mason," has saved many a gallant brother's life, relieved his sufferings when wounded, ministered to his wants when needed, and alleviated the miseries of his captivity. Thus, under the most adverse and unpropitious circumstances, the guardian angel of Masonry watches over, guards and protects those who have been duly initiated into and become Masters of the sublime mysteries of "the fraternity."

On February 3, the day the Confederate attempt to recapture Fort Donelson failed, the Grand Chapter of New York met, and the grand high priest, George H. Thacher, referred to the peace and harmony that prevailed in his state:

What is true of us, is, in the main, equally applicable to most of our sister jurisdictions, not excepting those of the states which have withdrawn their allegiance from our National Government. If anything were wanting to demonstrate the wholesome influence of masonry upon those who have been admitted to its fellowship, we need only contrast the condition of our Order with the turmoils and confusions and contentions which beset and bewilder us in almost all other walks and departments of life. Those whose hearts have not been touched by the magic power, nay, I will not say by the magic power, but the eternal fire that falls from heaven upon the mystic altar, know nothing of the sublime faith with which the true mason gazes upon the turbulence of the outer world, and that, too, when he is himself an actual participant in its conflicts. Nor can they understand why it is that, in the hour of general peril, when the very foundations of society seem to be breaking up, an institution, composed of men of different political and religious sentiments, of different associations and positions, preserves within itself such perfect accord, and hold its members together with such strong bonds of unity and friendship. They are amazed at the undeniable fact that this institution, unlike others that have appeared and passed away, has, for so many centuries, survived the convulsions and wrecks of states and empires, has withstood both political and religious persecutions aimed directly against itself, and that it still remains as firmly established as are the everlasting mountains upon their base.

On the following day, Horace Chase, of the Grand Chapter of Wisconsin, wrote:

It is a happy and consoling thought that freemasonry has contributed nothing in bringing about the present deplorable condition of the country. Whatever may have been done or said by individuals to imbitter friendship and engender hatred, nothing can be charged to the fraternity as encouraging or countenancing either.

The Grand Lodge of Louisiana met on February 9, and the grand master, John Quincy Adams Fellows, said:

[I] shall hope, as you all must, that by the lapse of another year, the Grand Lodge will assemble in full quorum—that peace and harmony may prevail throughout the land, and that Freemasonry may again flourish. May our Grand Master above grant this our humble prayer.

The grand secretary, Samuel M. Todd, wrote:

Since the occupation of this city by Federal forces, I have received communications from but few county Lodges. . . . At the destruction of Donaldson, by the Federal fleet, the Masonic Hall at that place was burnt, and the furniture and property of Perkins Lodge No. 150, utterly destroyed, although earnest remonstrance was made by some of the members of the Lodge against the barbarous act. It is to be hoped that none of those engaged in the destruction of this Masonic Temple were members of our great fraternity.

About the "Relief Lodge" of New Orleans he wrote:

The rule adopted at the commencement of hostilities "to grant no assistance to able-bodied men, who had no families depending upon them, but to reserve our charities for the widow and orphan," has been strictly carried out. It is with regret that we perceive the editor of a Northern Magazine [*Freemasons' Monthly*], published ostensibly as a "Masonic" work, in reviewing the proceedings of the Grand Lodge for 1862, apply the following remarks to our report of last year: "We wish we could say as much of the report from the Relief Lodge given a few pages further on. Besides the bad taste and temper in which it is written, it reveals the discreditable fact, that relief was refused poor Brethren, who were desirous to return home to the North, on the breaking out of the rebellion, in order that, being unable to get away, they might be driven by their destitute condition to enlist in the rebel army. Such a spirit is fiendish—not Masonic."

This is a gross misrepresentation; no Brother hailing from a Northern jurisdiction, desiring to return home, was ever refused assistance by the Relief Lodge, and we defy any one not blinded by prejudice to place such an interpretation on the language of our report. To show still more the unfairness of the criticism, the editor does not give a single extract from the report which he so severely censures.

During 1862 Freemasons from Connecticut, Georgia, Kentucky, Maine, Maryland, Mississippi, New York, South Carolina, Texas, England, and France, were assisted by this New Orleans "Relief Lodge."

During the Battle of Douglass' Church on April 13, 1863, Captain Gray was ordered to counter-attack and take no Federal prisoners. But he disobeyed the command. While charging up the hill toward what had been Freeman's Battery, he aimed his pistol at a Northern trooper. Before Gray could fire, the soldier made a Masonic sign. The pistol was lowered and the Federal trooper was sent to the rear.

General "Fighting Joe" Hooker, whom Lincoln had appointed to succeed Burnside, endeavored to build up the Federal forces. In April, he felt he had succeeded and on the 27th he began crossing the Rappahannock. He advanced to a farm house called "Chancellorsville" and because of the denseness of the forest referred to as "The Wilderness."

Hooker was so pleased with what had transpired he issued a message to his troops which stated: "The operations of the last three days have determined that our enemy must ingloriously fly or come out from his defenses and give us battle on our own ground, where certain destruction awaits him."

Instead of pursuing his enemy, Hooker pulled his advance troops back to Chancellorsville on May 1, the first day of the battle. Lee's forces pushed forward, maintaining a close contact, and three days later, against odds of two to one, he drove the Union army back across the river.

The dead and wounded amounted to more than 21,000 on both sides. Perhaps the severest was suffered by the South as it included the wounding of "Stonewall" Jackson, who died on May 10, 1863.

On May 5, the day Hooker arrived on the other side of the

Rappahannock, Josiah Drummond, the grand master of Maine, in his comments on the condition of the country said:

Indeed, the ties of our brotherhood seem to be almost the only ones that have not been broken between the contending parties. And these have been strained almost to breaking. The Grand Lodge of Virginia, in the first mad excitement of the conflict, disowned all Masons in her jurisdiction, who should adhere to the Union, and pronounced them masonic outlaws. But her edict was often disregarded. And within a short time, I am informed, she has rescinded it. Very many instances have occurred in which the appeal of our brotherhood has been heeded to stay the hand raised in deadly conflict against a brother.

Vicksburg was still under siege, and Grant, on his way to join the Federal forces in that city, passed through a railroad center in Mississippi. What transpired there was told by Stephen H. Johnson, the grand high priest of Mississippi.

The temporary occupation, and destruction of Jackson, the constitutional seat of the Grand Chapter, by a portion of the Federal Army, furnishes mortifying evidence of a profound, inhuman depravity, which it was reserved for that body of men (?) to develop! Who, not content with the general destruction of the city, entered the temple devoted to Masonic purposes, and instigated either by cupidity, malice or rapine, or by all of them together, so destroyed or eviscerated its archives as to leave but imperfect traces of the recorded transactions of this Grand Body. This, to most human institutions, whose existence mainly depends upon *written* laws, rules and regulations, would be almost an irreparable disaster. Not so with ours. Although subjected to unpleasant inconvenience and loss, yet thanks to indestructible principles that underlie the foundation of Freemasonry to the *lex non scripta* deposited in the breast of each faithful member, he can smile at the impotent rage of its enemies, laugh at the incendiary's torch, the vandalic barbarity of the ignorant, the rapacity of the robber, and the prying curiosity of the unprincipled coward.

Another episode that occurred about the same time in Mississippi was told years later by Frank Brame. His father and elder brothers were in the Confederate Army, and he was therefore living alone with his mother near West Point. He tells of an event that occurred prior to Nathan Forrest's intervention:

In the early hours of the morning before daybreak I was sudden-

152

ly awakened from the sound slumber of a healthy child by cursing and screams, and found the room in which my mother and I were sleeping, full of Federal soldiers. Mattresses had been piled in the hallway and set on fire.

My mother was sitting erect in her bed with the counterpane pulled around her, and as I looked at her from my trundle bed I could see that she was greatly frightened, while I was simply frozen with horror, for I firmly believed we would all be killed by the soldiers. There were some fifteen or twenty soldiers in our house, and they were smashing the furniture with their carbines.

A soldier had found a small package in a bureau drawer. On opening it he looked at it for a moment and then ran over to my mother's bed and, leaning over close to her, he and she spoke in low tones for just a moment; then he suddenly left the room, leaving the other soldiers busily engaged, evidently looking for gold.

A few moments after the soldier left the room a tall, handsome man suddenly walked into the room and the soldiers all suddenly ceased their depredations and brought their hands up and stood at rigid attention. The tall man immediately ordered the fire in the hall extinguished and also ordered the premises vacated and guards placed at the several gates of the yard. Then turning to my mother he gravely bowed.

"Madam," he said, "I apologize for the rudeness of my soldiers and my purser shall assess the damage done your property and pay you for it. No further damage will be done or offered. Under orders, I am compelled to send what meat you have to headquarters, but I shall not move it before sunrise, by which time you may have your slaves put away enough for your reasonable needs. With your permission I will fodder my command in your woods lot and use enough of your corn and hay to feed the horses of my command, for all of which I will have you suitably recompensed."

Mother gave her consent and the tall officer gravely bowed and retired.

The command lighted fires over the 100-acre woods lot while all of us looked on. And just about time the cooking was fairly started Forrest's command came charging down through the woods, yelling and shouting. The Federals made a rapid back retreat through the plantation, not having time or opportunity to get back on the regular road. Two of the soldiers guarding my mother's front gate were captured and the running fight or skirmish variously called *West Point, Town Creek,* or *Wooton Hill* followed.

What the soldier had discovered was a Masonic apron "of

curious workmanship and material that had been in the Brame family since 1676."

On May 25, 1863, two grand lodges met. In Indiana, the grand master, John B. Fravel, said he had refused to let a lodge expel one of its members because he had joined the Confederate Army. The committee to which that portion of his address was referred, disagreed with his ruling, claiming he should have said: "Expel him, and expel him quickly; and should you ever catch him engaged in his unholy purposes, treat him just as you would the assassin who, in the dead hour of night, would with stealth enter your bed-chamber, and there, while carrying out his purposes of robbery, plunge the dagger to the heart of the wife reposing on your bosom." The grand lodge, choosing to side with the more moderate views of its head, refused to act on the committee's report.

During the annual communication of the Grand Lodge of Rhode Island, Grand Master Ariel Ballou told his members:

Let us keep constantly in mind that Masonry has nothing to do with the belligerents of the day, with the causes which are distracting our beloved country and upturning its institutions. Our mission is to do good to all, and injury to none, to cultivate friendship and to promote brotherly love, by practicing charity, relieving the distressed and soothing the unhappy.

In the days that were to follow there would be many opportunities for Masons to follow the advice of the grand master of Rhode Island. The pace of the war was about to be increased.

During the month of May, 1863, the Sixth Michigan Infantry was stationed at Manchac Pass, Louisiana. It was under the command of Colonel Thomas Scott Clark, a member of Eureka Lodge, No. 107, Monroe, Michigan. While at the Pass, Clark sent a detachment of soldiers to Ponchatoula to burn a bridge near the town.

The assignment was carried out successfully, and a Confederate officer, along with several of his men, was captured. Included in the plunder were the silver jewels of Livingston Lodge, No. 60. Clark immediately ordered them returned to the Lodge under a flag of truce.

The kindness of the Federal Mason has been remembered

154

throughout the years. It became an important part of the Centennial celebration of Livingston Lodge (now located in Hammond, Louisiana), in May, 1959. Representatives of Monroe Lodge, No. 27 (Eureka Lodge had merged with it in 1892), were invited to re-enact the return of the jewels. The invitation was accepted and the master of Monroe Lodge was presented with a plaque commemorating the original event.

Many similar acts took place during the war and for a hundred years after it was over. The love shown by Masons during and after the conflict, not only for members of the Craft, but for all human beings, was all that stood between a successful reunion and disaster.

CHAPTER XIII

Gettysburg and Vicksburg

◇◇◇

Theirs not to make reply,
Theirs not to reason why,
Theirs but to do and die.
ALFRED TENNYSON

DURING THE MONTH of June, the siege of Vicksburg and Port Hudson was intensified, and Robert E. Lee completed his plans for his second major invasion of the North. During the first month of the summer, 1863, many American men were to die in a war which only a few fanatics desired.

On the second of June the Grand Lodge of New York met for its annual communication. Grand Master John J. Crane added a pleasant note to a message that could have been completely gloomy:

It is with feelings of the greatest pleasure that I state the fact, that I have heard of many very gratifying instances of the exercise, on the field of battle, of the noblest traits of the human character, stimulated by the tenets and teachings of Masonry. It may be true that at the first breaking out of the present disastrous troubles, the solemn and binding behests of the Craft were forgotten for a time. Gradually a more healthful feeling asserted itself, and I believe that at the present time, if mail communications were open with the hostile States of the Confederacy, that we should still continue in the interchange of fraternal sentiments with the Grand Lodges and Masons of the States which are now opposed to the general government. It is of inestimable benefit to both parties in the present civil war, that our Masonic relations should still continue in the same healthful condition as at present. I may go still further, and say that every honorable means should be used which would have a tendency to strengthen the fraternal bond between the Masons of the North and those of the South. Those that are well need no physician. . . .

On the same day, the Grand Lodge of Iowa met with the deputy grand master presiding. The grand master, Thomas H. Benton, was absent in the service of his country. He was the colonel who, a short time later, was to place a guard of Federal troops about the library of Albert Pike.

Only 49 lodges were represented when the Grand Lodge of Texas met on June 8. The grand master, Samuel Mather, in a lengthy address about the condition of the country, said in part:

Once more we are permitted by a kind providence to assemble in Grand Annual Communication to review the past, and provide for the future welfare of the Order, and how thankful should we be that we are permitted once more to meet and deliberate in peace, when war, with all its horrors, is raging around us. . . . The States of the North, with whom we have been in years past in fraternal correspondence, our sister States of the Confederacy, and even the Mexican Republic, are all now suffering from the horrors of war unequaled in the history of the world, and although our State has felt less of the direct effects of the storm than her sisters, yet there is not a Lodge on the rolls of this Grand Body but has the dark lines of mourning around some name stricken from its membership on the battle-field, and called to refreshment by our Supreme Grand Master; but while death and desolation are all around us, we have still reason to be thankful that we have escaped as well as we have, and that the dark clouds which have enveloped us are passing away, and a bright and clear sky is beginning to shine over our glorious country, brought about by the recent victories which have crowned our armies in the battle-fields of our neighboring States. With these results before us now, we have high hopes ere long our Government will be an acknowledged power of the earth, citizens and brethren returned to the more genial arts of peace. . . . Many of the Lodges have been unable to hold their meetings, have failed for want of members to hold elections, and in fact from the numbers absent in the army, the Lodges have virtually been closed, and a consequent failure to forward returns to this Grand Body, as well as the meagre representation at this Communication compared with other years. When all these causes have passed away, and we again meet around our sacred altars, then may we sing with joy,

> "All hail to the morning that bids us rejoice,
> The Cap Stone completed, exalt high each voice,
> The temple is finished, our labors are o'er,
> And War with its horrors shall hail us no more."

157

Many, many, alas, have fallen, and we are called to mourn for some who have met us in years past in this Grand Body, but who are now called aloft from the battle-field to their reward, having ended their lives in defence of home, friends and all that was dear and sacred. Amongst the great roll of martyrs whose names at some future day should be inscribed on tablets more enduring than marble, none will be more universally regretted than Brother James Reily, of Holland Lodge No. 1 whose eloquence has so frequently thrilled our hearts with rhapsodies coming from a pure heart and radiating every one who either heard or read his sentiments, and proving in the most direct manner that altho' we are here left free and unrestrained as to our duties to others, yet we are emphatically bound by ties which cannot be ignored, and each becomes to the other "a Brother's keeper." . . .

"Sadly, sadly bear him forth to his dark and silent bed
Weep not that he's lost to earth, weep not that his spirit's fled.

On June 9, 1863, the Grand Chapter of New Hampshire, during its second day in session, heard Samuel M. Wilcox, the grand high priest, admonish his companions:

. . . We cannot, either as men or masons, be unmindful of the mighty struggle which is stirring the great heart of our nation, the magnitude of which we, I fear, who are so far from the din and carnage of the battle-field, scarcely as yet appreciate.

Prominent before us is the spectacle of a monster rebellion, wicked and causeless, striving to overthrow the sacred fabric which our fathers built and hallowed with their best blood, and to lay unholy hands upon the government which we are bound to protect and defend; a contest in which we have important duties to perform, and of momentous importance to us both as citizens and as masons. As citizens, because our very national existence is at stake; as masons, because masonry countenances no disloyalty or rebellion against the government under whose protection we live.

Set your faces like flint against all disloyalty and rebellion wherever found, for this is the duty which, as masons, we owe to God, to our country, to the fraternity and ourselves. To the fraternity and ourselves, because we are bound by every tie of honor to exemplify in our lives and conduct the lessons and charges which have been, from time immemorial, taught in our Order.

In times like these especially, let us resolve to do our whole duty as men and masons, and if any shall knowingly or wittingly fail in his duty, or prove false to the spirit of our ancient charges, purge yourselves of him so effectually that no more remembrance of him shall remain among good men or masons forever.

Among the gunboats of the United States Navy sailing the Mississippi, firing into the towns along the banks, and laying siege to Port Hudson, was the *USS Albatross.* At least two of the officers aboard were Masons; the captain, John E. Hart, and his executive officer, Theo. B. Dubois. One of the towns that the gunboat had been firing into was St. Francisville, Louisiana, situated about 15 miles above Port Hudson.

The captain had been in a delirium for several days and confined to his cabin. On June 11 a pistol shot was heard, the executive officer and surgeon rushed to the captain's cabin and found him dead. Dubois, believing Hart would want a Masonic funeral, went ashore under a flag of truce. He met two brothers, Samuel and Benjamin White, who lived near the banks of the Mississippi, and asked if there was a Masonic lodge in St. Francisville. The brothers, being Masons, retaining their membership in their mother state of Indiana, led him to the lodge. The master, S. J. Powell, was absent, serving in the Confederate Army, but the senior warden, William W. Leake, although serving in the Confederate Army, was in St. Francisville.

When informed of the request, he answered, "I am an officer in the Confederate Army. As a soldier, I consider it a duty to permit the burial of a deceased member of the army or navy of any government, even if, as in the present instance, there is war between that government and my own. As a Mason, I know it to be my duty to accord Masonic burial to the remains of a Brother Mason, without taking into account the nature of his relations in the outer world."

Dubois, in a letter, described what happened next:

On the 13th of June, with an armed funeral procession of fifty seamen, I took our Brother's remains on shore, and as we marched mournfully up the hill to the beautiful little church of St. Francisville, we were met by a procession of Brother Masons, who took charge of the coffin. Exchanging my sidearms for the snow white apron, I joined them, my men following on. We buried our Brother with Masonic honors. . . . Brother Reynolds . . . spoke affectingly of the circumstances of our Brother's death, far from his home in a strange land; and I feel sure that every Mason on the spot felt better for having done his duty towards the remains of a deceased Brother—though an enemy in war, *still a Brother.*

In a letter to the family, Dubois wrote: "The Episcopal service was read by the Rev. Dr. Lewis, Pastor of the Church of St. Francisville. . . . He was buried in his uniform."

St. George's Lodge No. 6 of Schenectady, New York, on August 13, 1863, adopted a resolution which read in part:

Resolved, That the thanks of this Lodge are due, and we hereby tender them to our Masonic Brothers of Feliciana Lodge No. 31 of St. Francisville, La., for their fraternal kindness manifested at the funeral of our deceased Brother. We recognize in their generous conduct another evidence of the universality of the principles of our revered Institution and cherish the hope that these fraternal bonds which bind all true Masons together may become a powerful agency in the restoration of our common Union.

After the war, the Daughters of the Confederacy kept Captain Hart's grave green and fresh with flowers, along with the Confederate soldiers buried beside him. In 1956, the Grand Lodge of New York took note of a remarkable episode:

On January 9th, Worshipful Eugene Baxter, Master of St. George's Lodge in Schenectady, N. Y., represented the Grand Master on a singular and touching occasion. In 1863, during the shelling of St. Francisville, Louisiana, Lt. Commander John E. Hart of the Union gunboat "Albatross," and a member of St. George's Lodge, died during the action. Under a flag of truce, a request was made of the Confederate troops for a Masonic burial. It was granted and the services were conducted by Brother W. W. Leake, a captain of the Confederate Army, who gathered together a few members of the local Lodge still in the area. The war halted while Confederate Masons buried a Brother Mason from the North in a church cemetery pock-marked with shells from the Union gunboat of Lt. Commander Hart. A wooden headplate marked the spot for several years.

This January the Grand Lodge of Louisiana dedicated a permanent marker on the grave of Lt. Commander Hart in the cemetery of the Grace Episcopal Church of St. Francisville. This incident again illustrates that not even the clash of war can supplant the bonds of Fraternal Brotherhood.

The permanent marker covered the entire grave of Hart and stated: "This monument is dedicated in loving tribute to the universality of Freemasonry."

The *Freemason's Magazine* tells of a celebration that took place on June 24, 1863:

The Masons of Beaufort [N. C.] and vicinity celebrated St. John's day in a very creditable manner. They had a procession, services in a chapel, a collation, a march to the Saxton House, and a splendid dinner there. Capt. Parker, of the *Wyoming*, formerly Deputy G. M. of N. Y., presided during the celebration; Surgeon Van Etten was Marshal, and Lieut. Col. Hall and Surgeon Hunter acted as Wardens.

A large delegation went up in the *Wyoming*, with a beautiful Masonic flag flying at the mast-head. They were received at Beaufort by the Masons there and were escorted to the Lodge room. A procession was then formed, the Brethren appearing in regalia, and carrying the emblems of the Order. The band of the 1st Michigan (colored) Regt. furnished music. At the Soldier's Chapel interesting services were performed by Chaplain S. P. Harris, who also delivered an address. The procession then marched to the Beaufort Garden, by invitation, and partook of some light refreshments, and from thence to the Saxton House, where supper was shortly after served. Capt. Parker presided in an able manner. On his right was Gen. Saxton, and among other distinguished members of the Order present were Col. Gurney, of 127th N. Y., Lieut. Col. J. F. Hall, Provost Marshal Gen., Capt. W. L. M. Burger, Asst. Adj. Gen of the Department, and many others. Gens. Foster and Harch and Admiral Dahlgren, though hoping to be present, were unavoidably detained. Toasts and sentiments, addresses and conversation, pleasantly filled up the hours.

While the Masons were celebrating, plans were reaching their final stages for the invasion of the North by the forces of Lee. Not all were in agreement with that arrangement, however. Beauregard of the Army, and Reagan of the Cabinet, felt something should be done to ease the siege of Vicksburg and Port Hudson. The plan finally approved by the Confederate War Department would send Lee by way of the Shenandoah Valley to invade Pennsylvania.

The Army of Northern Virginia, reorganized into three corps, with Longstreet in command of the First Corps, Richard S. Ewell in command of Jackson's old Second Corps, and Ambrose P. Hill commanding the new Third Corps, started moving north on June 3. Longstreet marched to Culpeper Court

House; Ewell through the Blue Ridge; A. P. Hill remained at Fredericksburg to see what Hooker would do. He was not long in finding out, for the Federal general left his encampments and moved northward toward the Potomac. Then Hill, on June 14 marched after Ewell.

Part of Lee's army arrived in Chambersburg, Pennsylvania, on the 27th of June, and from there proceeded toward Gettysburg. General Hooker, having displeased Lincoln, was removed from command of the Federal army. General George C. Meade was appointed in his place. He took command in Frederick, Maryland, and started moving his army for Pennsylvania on the 29th.

Henry Heth's division, leading the Confederate advance on the morning of July 1, met the advance forces of Meade and pushed them back through the streets of the town. On the heights near Evergreen Cemetery, General Winfield S. Hancock rallied and emplaced the Union troops.

General Lee called a halt to the fighting, deciding to wait for the arrival of the remainder of his army. That caused Pollard to write: "The failure of Gen. Lee to follow up the victory of the 1st enabled the enemy to take at leisure, and in full force, one of the strongest positions in any action of the war, and to turn the tables of the battle-field completely upon the Confederates."

During the evening of July 1 the entire Federal Army, under forced march, moved up to occupy the positions selected by Hancock and approved by Meade. Henry described the position as "strong, a line of heights east and southeast of Gettysburg, shaped like a question mark turned backward. The dot at the bottom is Round Top."

Lee's plan was to attack the Federal forces early on the morning of the second, but it was late afternoon before the Confederate lines were in position to attack. The fighting was furious, with the Confederates driving the Federals back, but only Johnson's division secured a foothold in the entrenchments on Culp's Hill. Darkness called a halt to the close, fiercely fought battle.

At dawn on July 3, the fighting resumed at an even faster

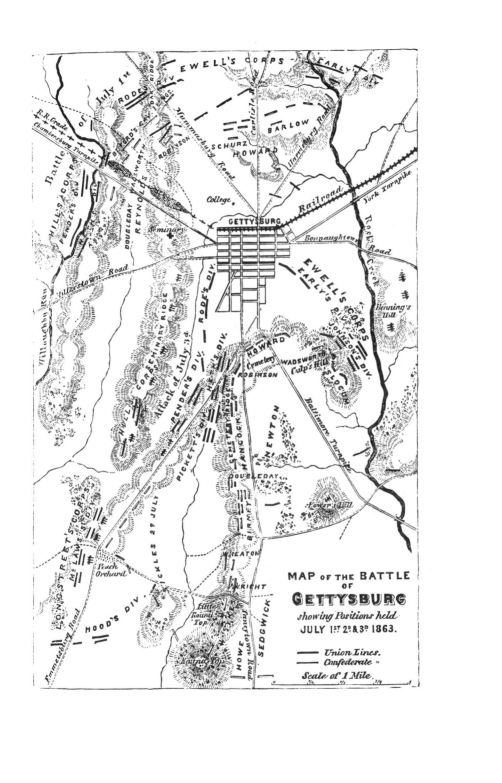

MAP of the BATTLE
OF
GETTYSBURG

showing Positions held
JULY 1ST 2D & 3D 1863.

——— Union Lines.
——— Confederate "

Scale of 1 Mile.

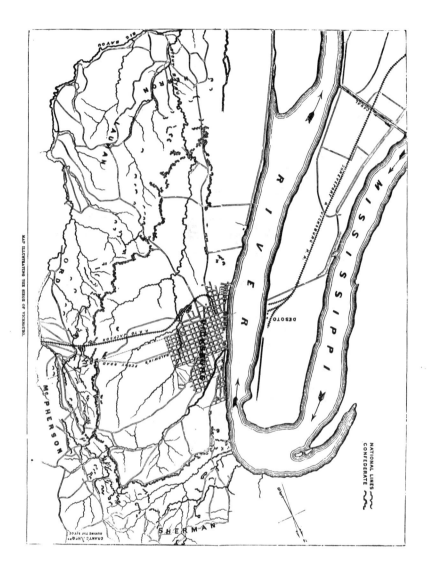

MAP ILLUSTRATING THE SIEGE OF VICKSBURG.

NATIONAL LINES
CONFEDERATE

pace and by noon Johnson was forced from the hill. That paved the way for the charge that will probably be remembered forever—the charge led by the Mason, George E. Pickett, supported by the Masonic generals James L. Kemper and Lewis A. Armistead, commanding two of the brigades, with Garnett the other. Henry Heth's division was turned over to Pettigrew, Heth having been wounded on the first day of the battle.

Twice Pickett asked Longstreet if he should advance; twice he received no answer. (Some claim Longstreet did nod his head.) Pickett then turned from his corps commander and issued the order to charge into Cemetery Ridge. Into a hail of death they charged, some reached the top only to die or make their way back down again. Thus ended the most famous infantry charge in the history of the world! The battle was over!

Among the men to reach the top was Lewis Armistead. Daniel Skelly tells that story:

> As Armistead and his men crossed the stone wall, Cushing ran his last gun forward to the stone wall and fired. Armistead rushed forward, and with his hand on the cannon shouted, "This gun belongs to me." At this moment, Armistead was struck by a ball. As he fell, he called out "I am a widow's son" . . . An officer nearby directed two men to take him to the rear on a stretcher. Armistead was taken to the Union 11th Corps hospital on the Spangler farm where, sometime that night, he died.

In an article written for the *Scranton Republican*, May 22, 1934, Charles W. Myers, K.T., writes of the friendship between Generals Hancock and Armistead, and tells about the Gettysburg episode:

> At Gettysburg, by a singular coincidence, Generals Hancock and Armistead were destined to meet again; not as comrades, but as opponents. When Pickett's division took its place in the column of assault, Kemper's brigade was on the right, Garnett's brigade on the left and Armistead's brigade in the rear, on eschelon. Although he started in the rear in command of the supporting line he, moving on foot, forged to the front, and reaching the stone wall at the "Angle" he raised his hat on his sword and said: "Give them the cold steel, boys." Advancing with a few of his men [toward] Cushing's guns, he fell mortally wounded about the same time that Cushing was killed.

Not forgetting his old comrade in arms, General Hancock, with whom he had served in the same regiment during the war with Mexico, when he fell he asked of those around him, "Where is General Hancock?" Hancock, who was wounded about the same time, was therefore unable to respond to Armistead's request to come to his side. However, Hancock ordered Brigadier General Henry H. Bingham, then a colonel and a member of his staff, to go to his former comrade in arms and minister to his wants. To General Bingham, General Armistead gave his watch and papers with the request that they be sent to his friends. As both were members of the Masonic faternity there was a mutual recognition. General Bingham had him removed to the Eleventh Corps hospital, which was on the George Spangler farm south of Power's Hill and Granite Lane, where he was laid on the floor of the kitchen with some other wounded soldiers.

During the night of the third he died . . .

Another Mason to have a memorable part in the Battle of Gettysburg was Lieutenant Stephen F. Brown, a member of Seventy-Six Lodge, No. 14, Vermont. On the march to the Pennsylvania town, the officers and men were ordered not to leave the ranks under any circumstances. When many of the men became faint from thirst, Brown took several canteens to a well and filled them with cool water. Consequently, he was placed under arrest for disobedience of orders.

When the regiment reached the field of battle, General George J. Stannard, a member of Franklin Lodge, No. 4, St. Albans, Vermont, ordered Brown released from arrest. Brown's sword was on a wagon far behind the area of the fighting, so he armed himself with a simple camp hatchet. He used his hatchet valiantly until Pickett's charge was repulsed, then he took the sword and belt of a Confederate officer who had surrendered to him. Later that scene became permanently enshrined by a monument erected near the place where he fought.

The following day, Lee, leaving behind nearly 3,000 dead and 13,000 wounded, began his retreat through the gaps in Stone Mountain. Meade pursued him until, on the night of July 13, the Confederates crossed the Potomac, never to return to the soil of the North as an army.

On the day that the Army of Northern Virginia left Gettysburg, Vicksburg, after having been under siege for weeks, fell to the forces of U. S. Grant. That story is told by John Edwin Mason, K.T., in an article entitled, "A Masonic Carnival on the Battle-Field," in the pages of the *Masonic Monthly*.

"It is believed at headquarters that Pemberton will surrender his whole army, and Vicksburg—the great Gibraltar of the Confederacy—will be ours," said Capt. H. while riding down the river bank and shouting with joy as he held his hat in his hand.

"Impossible," said I, "the news is too good to prove true."

"That is generally believed at Gen. Grant's headquarters," said he, "for I've just come from there."

"If true, wouldn't that be a glorious prize to crown all our efforts in this hard campaign," said I, as the blood thrilled through my veins and I nervously sent up a wild hurrah.

"And if they surrender to-morrow it will be on the Fourth of July—the day we celebrate," he added, proudly, and rode rapidly away, only stopping to tell the glad news to every officer he met.

We were then on the banks of the fatal Yazoo, which means in Chickasaw the "dread river of death." The sluggish waters of the Sunflower, the Yalabusha, the Tallahatchie, and the outlets of innumerable swamps in western Mississippi, here made a lazy effort to reach the great "father of waters," yet became almost stagnant with the enormous quantities of decaying vegetation that everywhere filled its channel, and myriads of insets, frogs, snakes, lizards, and here and there a monstrous alligator that lay "sunning" on the flood-wood and debris that choked its banks on every side. The putrid waters caused a stench, as that burning, blistering July sun, shown down upon them, that made their smell intolerable, and the attempt to make their waters slake the thirst our fever caused, was totally impossible. To take the poison out by boiling seemed to be one of the "lost arts." And yet we must drink this poisonous water or die of thirst—for the dry, chalky bluffs on the banks afford no water.

I had been doing my duty as Ordnance officer to the best of my ability. During the summer I had been in charge of the Ordnance stores of the 9th Army Corps, on a steamboat anchored at Snyder's Bluff on the Yazoo and at Chickasaw Bayou—twelve miles north of Vicksburg. But the fearful Yazoo malaria had filled my blood with the worst type of fever and ague, and my whole system was yearning to go North, where dame nature seemed to be pointing her index finger. The grim monster Death had been stealing a mortgage on me during the summer, and seemed about to foreclose it. It seemed as though I was not selected to die on the battle-field, wrapped in a

165

halo of glory, but to die of disease, a thing that every soldier always abhors.

Under such circumstances my personal feelings intensified the glorious news given by Capt. H. that Vicksburg would capitulate. That night, so long and gloomy, at last wore away. Each hour seemed longer than the age of brass we live in. As Aurora, goddess of the morning, kissed the first grey streaks of day that stole over these tropical bayous covered with their dense vegetation, all the animal kingdom sprung into action to usher in the coming day by gladsome tributes of praise. The sycamore, locust, cottonwood and gum trees, that lined the banks of the Yazoo, were redolent with fragrance and radiant with beauty. The holly tree with its glistening foliage shone brilliantly in the morning sun, and the magnolia with its pearly flowers festooned the drapery made by innumerable vines of every description hanging in tresses from these monarchs of the forest. Even the mistletoe, hanging so mournfully from the black walnut boughs, seemed inspired with the happiness of the occasion and waved as gracefully as the curls and tresses of a Castilian heroine.

But hark! the very earth trembles with the concussion and reverberation of our heavy artillery. Boom—boom—boom—what means this cannonading?

"It is our artillery ushering in our nation's anniversary," said brother officers on every side.

Hours pass wearily; at last an orderly came dashing down the bluffs, inquiring for me and giving the name of my boat. I met him on the plank, and hastily tore open the dispatch.

"Take your boat with all the Ordnance stores of 9th Corps at once to Vicksburg. Anchor off wharf in rear of steamer 'John H. Groesbeck.' By command of Maj. Gen. U. S. Grant."

The glorious news flashed through my mind instantly. "Vicksburg is ours—hurrah!" and the deafening cheers went up on every side. "And surrendered, too, on the Fourth of July—*hurrah*—HURRAH!"

In only an hour we were steaming out of the Yazoo into the broad Mississippi. Soon we passed the bend or curve where the iron-clad "Cincinnati" lay sunk in shallow water by rebel guns on those towering bluffs above. Soon the city of Vicksburg was in full view, bathed in a summer sunlight reflecting all the natural advantages of this impregnable stronghold—far surpassing either Quebec or Sebastopol. On the bluffs rising so abruptly from the river stands the city, like a sentinel watching the commerce of this great mart of trade. On the highest point, crowning the apex, the dome of the Court House rises, and from whichever direction you approach the city, it seems to fill the centre of the picture, exactly as the dome of the State House is first seen as you approach Boston from any di-

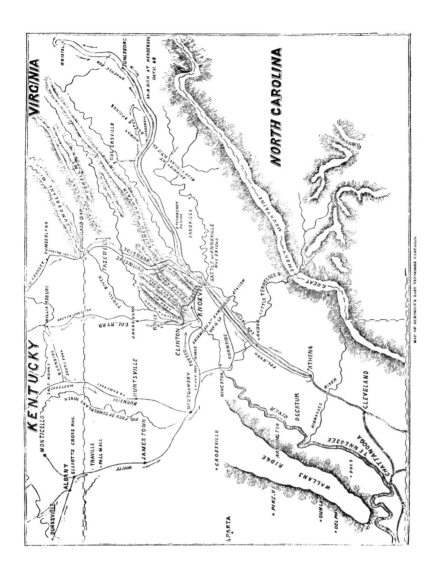

MAP OF BURNSIDE'S EAST TENNESSEE CAMPAIGN.

rection. Flanked on every side by precipitous bluffs, covered with magnificent earthworks, from which the grim rebel guns lay in position like bull-dogs showing their teeth. With our glasses we see plainly the houses all honey-combed with our shot and shell—the streets all barricaded, and all the preparations which fire-eating Mississippians had made to christen the citadel the "last ditch." But to all rebel expectations the heavens were spanning in rainbow colors on this summer morning the prophetic motto, "hope enters not here." The strongest natural fortification on the continent was ours—the great Mississippi opened again to trade and commerce, flowing untrammelled to the sea—the Southern "Confederacy" split into two fragments—the backbone broken, and "old glory" waving over the home of Jeff Davis.

On all the bluffs surrounding the city long lines of rebel infantry were in line, with stacked arms in their front, then the handsome earthworks were swarming with rebel artillerymen in their grey and scarlet—*thirty one thousand* in all, surrendered to our nation's greatest hero—"Unconditional Surrender Grant." Two hundred guns, with thirty-six thousand small arms, and vast stores of ammunition, were all ours. What a gigantic victory! How proud the nation must feel of its heroes here!

We passed alongside the "John H. Groesbec," the headquarters boat of Gen. Grant, and got permission to go ashore. We leaped on the wharf and found ourselves among the first officers who got ashore into the city, which history will make so famous. We ran toward the Court House, up the steep streets, barricaded and ploughed up everywhere with shot and shell, past the house riddled by our heavy artillery, past the adobe huts and caves in the banks where terrified children and panic-stricken women were just emerging, having learned they were safe from the leaden fire we had been raining on the rebellious city by day and by night. Just as we were clambering over the abattis protecting the Court House and its little square around it, two hundred pieces of artillery belched forth their thunder, making the ground tremble under us, and announcing that the terms of capitulation were accepted. The shock was like that of a powerful earthquake. The smoke clouded the heavens and obscured the rays of Sol. We looked through an opening to see the dome of the Court House where "Old glory" had just been placed, so we were too late to grasp the coveted honor of placing the flag of our steamboat in our hands *first* on the dome of the Court House. But we ascended to the dome and placed our flag there with an avalanche of others, that seemed as though, painted by Aurora in rainbow colors, they fell from Heaven to christen the citadel of rebellion as she renewed her vows of loyalty to the good old flag.

Amid the roar of artillery we listened, and lo! we heard a band as it came marching up from our lines playing "Yankee Doodle" *in the streets of Vicksburg!* "What a sacrilege," said a vinegar-countenanced woman near us, and she looked as though she wished to bite a file. Presently the solid, handsome form of Gen. Logan appears at the head of his Division, marching in to garrison the city. He is flanked by Gen. Grant, Gen. Rawlings and a host of "stars." Near them are the rebel Gens. Pemberton, Holmes and many others with their staffs—all paroled while in the city as prisoners of war. They enter the Court House and a general relaxation into conversation ensues.

"Whom have I the honor of addressing," said a very handsome officer in rebel uniform. I bowed courteously and handed him my card. He took my hand quickly and gave me the grip of an Entered Apprentice, adroitly following this by the sign of a Master Mason. He was a staff officer of Lieut. Gen. Pemberton. I took him aside and found by a thorough examination that he was a Knight Templar. He soon introduced me to a score or two of other staff officers for whom he could vouch, and I soon found myself surrounded by a crowd of brother Masons, all dressed in rebel uniform, whom we had been fighting for months.

The sensation was a novel one, and it was aggravated by the courteous and fraternal spirit exhibited on every side by my rebel brother Masons. They showed clearly, that while they hated me as a Yankee they loved me with true fraternal tenderness as a Mason. I was thunderstruck. The spectacle came near bringing tears to my eyes, and my heart warmed with friendship toward them after I had been so long preparing the deadly missiles of destruction to kill them with as an Ordnance officer. They told me how they had been living on mule meat and split peas, and hardly enough of these to sustain life the last week of the siege. I resolved at once that what I had on the boat should be theirs. The captain of the boat had just got a fresh lot of provisions from Cincinnati and also a box of genuine Catawba wine and plenty of ice. So I invited the entire lot of rebel officers, who were Masons, to go down on board the boat and dine with me. They looked somewhat astonished at my invitation but gladly accepted it, and *thirty-two* went with me to the boat. While dinner was being prepared I got together a few Union officers and several from the Navy whom I knew to be Masons to enjoy the scene. Some of these I had known in boyhood days in far distant New England. Officers in blue and grey sat down together in the long saloon of the steamboat and we had a real Fourth-of-July dinner of the substantials of life and many of the delicacies, ending with a huge box of Catawba wine and ice, (which these brothers in grey had not seen for two years) and all enjoyed it. Toasts were drank and responded to with great *eclat*. Every toast proposed by a

168

brother in blue would be responded to by a brother in grey and *vice versa*. No toast or sentiment was uttered to offend the pride or position of the other, and the good breeding exhibited in this respect, showed that *all* were *educated gentlemen,* as well as Masons. No reference was made to the political opinions of the other, and the *time* and *occasion* was kept out of view. Each vied with the other in courtesy and etiquette. Masonry was the theme first and last. Each, however, pledged the other to guide, honor and protect them if ever found *wandering* as *pilgrims,* which was easily understood to mean *prisoners* instead of *pilgrims.* After much wit and pleasantry, and many speeches made, and toasts drank, and congratulations exchanged the *fifth libation* was drank and all adjourned (for it was then dark) to the Masonic Hall in Vicksburg, where an impromptu Lodge was organized, with a Union officer as acting W. M. and rebel officer Senior Warden, and so alternating through the whole list. The work was of the kind that gods might envy and angels imitate. All expressed it to be the happiest hour of their lives. It was fully believed that earth never afforded a more striking scene than this. The lamb and the lion had lain down together—the sword had been beaten into Masonic jewels that were glittering before the world as positive proof that the great day of triumph had come, when enemies even in civil war had cast off their hatred, and embraced each other with true love and affection, because the bonds of *Masonry* were stronger than *all others.* Bigotry, prejudice and malice were all forgotten. In the sincere spirit of Masonry we met on the level and parted on the square. Earth has no greater joy than this. The Supreme Architect of the universe looked down upon us and blessed us. Only Masons can truly appreciate this meeting under such interesting circumstances. The world can never know the pleasure we derived from it. But this same cold and selfish world can see what a wonderful power of attraction brought together, and must learn that this cohesive power is Freemasonry. Its benign influences has made many Union officers happy when in southern dungeons and prisons, and finally led them out of captivity at an early day. *These same bonds that bind us all together in Freemasonry united the hand of General Grant with his brother Mason, Lieut. General Pemberton, who was his guest that day. This will explain what has been incomprehensible heretofore about the surrender of Vicksburg.* The future historian will take due notice thereof and govern himself accordingly. And when the good old flag shall wave over every foot of seceded territory, it will be discovered that Freemasonry has borne a prominent part in these times of war, as well as at a time when "Peace hath her victories, no less than war."

The author is in error about Grant being a Mason; he was

169

not, although this thought was prevalent throughout the war. *The Wisconsin Freemason* claims that several times he considered petitioning Miner's Lodge, No. 273, Galena, Illinois, but for various reasons did not. His father and two brothers were Masons. It is also claimed that the grand master of Illinois planned on making him a Mason "at sight," but he died before that could be accomplished.

The Masonic Temple in Vicksburg, although a prominent building, was not damaged, nor struck by a single missile, during the siege. It was used as a hospital during the time the city was held by the Confederates, and was so used after the occupation by the Federal Army. All of the records, jewels, and furniture of the Lodge were "preserved by Masons in the Federal Army" and were in use as late as 1897.

An article in the history of Washington Chapter No. 2, R.A.M., Wisconsin, tells of an incident that happened after the fall of Vicksburg:

On July 4, 1863, General Grant captured Vicksburg with some 35,000 Confederate troops. At that time I was with the 33rd Wisconsin Volunteers, under command of Colonel J. B. Moore (a Past High Priest of Washington Chapter), then a part of the 4th Brigade of the 16th Army Corps. Soon after the surrender, General Grant ordered this Brigade, with two batteries of artillery and a battalian of Cavalry, all under command of General Ransom, to proceed down the river and capture Natchez, the only point then held by the Confederates between Cairo and the Gulf. Convoyed by two gun boats, the expedition soon arrived in front of Natchez, and, after an exchange of a few shots between the gun boats and a battery on the hill, the Confederates fled and the Federals entered Natchez, and formed a cordon of camps around the city with the right and left wings resting on the river. Some two weeks after being settled in camp, two citizens of Natchez called on Colonel Moore and made themselves known as Masons. They then stated the object of their visit, saying that "three young officers of the Confederate Army had received the M. E. M. degree just before the war—that they had been captured and paroled at Vicksburg and were now at home awaiting exchange, but were very desirous of receiving the R. A. degree while at home."

The gentlemen stated that the "active working members of their chapter, Natchez No. 1, were all in the army and that there were not enough members at home proficient in the ritual to confer the degrees," ending by asking Colonel Moore to aid them in their dilemma. Colonel Moore replied by saying that while he knew there were many Masons in his regiment, he did not know if there were those who could render the necessary assistance, but that he would ascertain and report to them at an early date. After our visitors departed, Colonel Moore called to him ten such Royal Arch Masons, whom he knew, and with a few rehearsals he had an impromptu chapter sufficiently drilled to confer the degree, and so reported to our Confederate Companions of the city. A time was appointed and some fifteen or twenty Federal Companions rode down to the hall where were assembled as many more citizen Companions, members of the local chapter. The acting High Priest, who proved to be one of our visitors, requested the Wisconsin Companions to take charge of the work of conferring the degree. Colonel Moore took the East and made his assignment of workers. In due time the candidates were presented and the degree was conferred. In conducting these two-fold captives up from Babylon to Jerusalem to aid and assist in rebuilding the second temple, I could not help but wish that they might aid and assist in rebuilding the waste places of our common country. If alive, I have no doubt these Companions are now loyal citizens of our reunited country.

In the neighboring country of Canada what was transpiring on the battlefields of the United States did not go unnoticed. During the annual communication of the Grand Lodge of Canada, the grand master, T. Douglas Harrington, told his members he had been invited to attend a national Masonic convention in New York:

I thought it right to decline being present,—first, because my attendance might have been looked upon as an unauthorized interference in a domestic quarrel with which Canada has nothing to do; and—secondly, because no Southern Brethren could have an opportunity of giving an expression to their feelings.

He later spoke feelingly of the brotherly love shown between the Masons from the two sections:

With regard to the Grand Lodges of the U. S. generally, it is pleasant to notice the manifold injunctions to Freemasons under their control, to remember their Order, and to endeavor to render it subservient to lessening the misery caused by the long, bloody and unnatural strife still raging there. While all mourn for the unhappy condition of their country, and the amount of human suffering witnessed, they point out that in war, as in peace, the Masonic

171

duties and privileges alike are binding and reciprocal. No political struggles can affect the standing of a Brother, nor interfere with the mission of Masonry.

The two major defeats of the Confederates during early July found them with no offense for the balance of the month, with the exception of the raids of John Morgan in Kentucky and Ohio. There he played havoc with the Federals.

CHAPTER XIV

The War in the "West"

◇◇

When two armies confront each other in the East, they get to work very soon; but here you look at one another for days and weeks at a time.

D. H. HILL

GENERAL JOHN HUNT MORGAN kept the offense going for the South until July 26, 1863 when he, along with many of his men, was captured in Ohio.

Union forces under the command of General Shackleford had been pursuing Morgan and his men for several days, when, on the 20th, according to his report, he captured between six and seven hundred of Morgan's men, but the Confederate general managed to escape. "I will capture Morgan himself tomorrow," were the words with which he closed his report.

It was to take six days more before that capture became a reality. A correspondent for the *Cleveland Herald* wrote that Federal troops under General Brooks laid in wait along a road that Morgan was expected to travel. He did, and took to the woods when the firing commenced. The correspondent goes on to relate:

About two o'clock in the afternoon these various detachments closed in around Morgan in the vicinity of West-Point, about midway between New-Lisbon and Wellsville. The rebels were driven to a bluff, from which there was no escape except by fighting their way through or leaping from a lofty and almost perpendicular precipice. Finding themselves thus cooped, Morgan concluded that "discretion was the better part of valor," and "came down" as gracefully as the coon did to Davy Crockett. He, with the remainder of his gang, surrendered to Colonel Shackleford, who was well acquainted with the redoubtable "John," and is said to be a distant relative.

. . . Morgan retained his side-arms, and moved about freely, although always accompanied by Colonel Shackleford. . . .

Morgan's men were poorly dressed, ragged, dirty, and very badly used up. Some of them wore remnants of gray uniform, but most of them were attired in spoils gathered during their raid. They were very much discouraged at the result of their raid, and the prospect of affairs generally.

Morgan himself appeared in good spirits, and quite unconcerned at his ill-luck. He is a well-built man, of fresh complexion, and sandy hair and beard. He last night enjoyed for the first time in a long while the comforts of a sound sleep in a good bed, which was some compensation for his otherwise bad luck.

Morgan and 69 of his officers were sent to the state penitentiary at Columbus, from which on the night of November 27 he and five others, after spending more than 20 days digging a tunnel, managed to escape.

Major James Wilson, one of Morgan's officers, was more fortunate. He was sent to Johnson's Island, situated at the mouth of Sandusky Bay, overlooking Lake Erie. The first prisoners were taken there in April, 1862, and the last were to leave in September, 1865.

Shortly after Wilson's arrival in the prison camp, "they formed what was known as the Masonic mess. Every two weeks a lodge meeting was held. All in the mess were Masons and many officers in other portions of the prison were members of the fraternity."

The commander of the prison permitted the Masons to attend a lodge, and they were never molested by any of the guards, even if they remained longer than the hour set for their return. Wilson also said that the Masonic mess never knew what it was to be hungry, and gives as a reason, "it may be possible that because the officer in command of the prison was a Mason also."

A letter from the United Daughters of the Confederacy, signed by Mary Patton Hundson, was read to the Grand Lodge of Florida in 1906, asking for financial assistance to "save from desecration the Confederate grave-yard at Johnson's Island, Ohio, where lie 206 brave American soldiers and Masons in sadly neglected graves. Of the number interred there, about 152 were members of your order." The appeal was answered by that grand lodge when it sent a check for $100.

174

On both sides there were men called "guerillas" who fought independent of any command. Some were "patriotic"; more of them were robbers, like the brothers Jesse and Frank James, always in search of weak victims. The *Masonic Monthly* records an incident of a guerilla attack written by "C. H. T.":

The march of the Nineteenth Army corps from Bisland through the Teche country (as it is known in Louisiana) to Port Hudson was a memorable one, and has already become a matter of history. There were several stirring incidents during that eventful march, but only one or two of them develop the fact that there were Masons among the Guerillas of the Southwest, who continually harrassed the army of General Banks in the Teche country, and which were among the most bloodthirsty and unmerciful of all guerillas.

Lieutenant Samuel Johnson, who belonged to a Western regiment, and three of his men, were out "scouting" for food on the outskirts of the town of Franklin, where the army encamped for one week, when they discovered a fine lamb of such excellent proportions that they immediately concluded he would go far to supply a lack of rations which they had experienced for some days. Being prohibited from firing their guns or pistols, the party were obliged to chase the animal, and the latter had coaxed them some distance before they discovered that they were over two miles from camp—they were so eager for a meal of fresh meat. They concluded to shoot the fleeing lamb, and did so. All four immediately went to work to skin and quarter the carcass, and were engaged in completing the operation when the report of firearms startled them.

Lieutenant Johnson sprang up and found his men wounded and himself surrounded by guerillas, with every possible chance of escape cut off. His sword and pistols were immediately taken from him, and his legs were pinioned. A "council of war" was held to determine what should be done with him, but not before his pockets had been rifled. He looked from one face to another while they were discussing the method by which his earthly career was to be terminated. The leader was a young man of about thirty years of age, a nobly proportioned fine-looking man; and as Lieutenant Johnson eyed him more closely, he, to his great joy, discovered in him an old classmate, with whom he had graduated at Harvard College five years before. Both had taken Masonic degrees together, in Boston, Mass., and each had waited until they went to their homes (the one in Cincinnati, Ohio, and the other in New Orleans) before they joined a Lodge. Lieutenant Johnson called the attention of his former chum, Herbert Maxwell, the guerilla leader, by the usual Masonic sign of recognition. Maxwell comprehended and returned

175

the same, and turning towards his prisoner recognized his former classmate. Both, as may well be imagined, were greatly surprised, and mutual explanations followed. Maxwell ordered his men to retire a short distance, and, though some of them moved off reluctantly, they evidently knew their leader too well to disobey his orders.

On August 17, the grand chaplain of the Grand Lodge of Maryland, Robert Piggot, offered the following prayer:

We thank Thee, O! Father, that while the world without has been agitated by war and strife, our Temple has been free from discord, and blessed with peace and harmony. We thank Thee, that amid the horrors of the battle-field, and the gloom of the Lazar house, our Institution has sent her missionaries to illustrate her principles, binding up the bleeding wounds with a brother's hand, watching beside the sick bed with a brother's heart, and making *light* the prison's gloom with ministrations of Fraternal love. O God! we do thank Thee, that Thou hast permitted Masonry to exist among men, uniting them, heart with heart, by the mystic chain of Brotherhood which no human power can sunder, in prosperity and in adversity—in Palace or in Prison the same—Brothers —Friends.

Two days later a Mason died in New Orleans, but the events leading up to that time were similar to the things for which the grand chaplain of Maryland had thanked God:

... We have not learned that there were any female Masons who are members of any known lodge in this or any other country, but if there were any such institutions, or females were ever to be admitted, thousands of soldiers who were in the United States Hospital at New Orleans during the years 1863 and 1864 would cordially recommend Madame Marie Merval as a fit candidate for admission.

She was the wife of a Mason whose sympathies were with the South, though he was not of the number of venomous rebels who defied and ill-treated Union soldiers in the streets. This lady desired to aid the sufferers as far as possible, and her liege lord offered no serious objections against her visiting the hospital daily, and carrying with her dainties which were welcome to those whom she visited.

The Union-loving ladies (if the reader will pardon the digression), who were constant visitors at the hospitals, remedied many faults in the management of those institutions. For example, in the

176

St. Louis Hospital, the managers, instead of giving the soldiers the allowance of food given by the government, furnished much poorer eatables, and made a certain amount of money upon each occupant. In addition to this there were about one hundred and fifty colored men, women, and children who did the work of servants. These people were entitled to a certain sum every week; and, instead of being paid, the managers blinded them with promises thus: every Saturday night the colored individuals made their "mark" for their pay, which they never saw, and were each furnished with a handfull of tobacco (sent for the soldiers) to keep them quiet. These evils were discovered by these ladies, and they made appeals to the medical director and the military commander, who . . . took some action in the matter.

Among the patients at the United States Hospital was a member of the Thirty-Eighth Massachusetts Regiment, named James K. Spaulding, who was always accounted one of the strongest men in the regiment until he fell a scourge to the disease (chronic diarrhoea) which proved more detrimental and disastrous than bullets or cannon-balls. Just before he went to New Orleans, the Masonic brethren in that city, or a number of them, had secured a list of all Masons in the hospitals, and were taking the names of new ones as fast as they arrived. Mr. Spaulding was badly emaciated when he arrived, and was at once a subject of commiseration and assistance. He was furnished with cordials and nutritious food; and his condition improved greatly, so much so that he was able to go out, and once in a while he attended stated meetings of the Masons. On one of these latter occasions he caught a severe cold, and was once more prostrated by his disease. Everything that could conduce to his comfort was furnished him by his friends, and Mrs. Merval was unremitting in her attentions. But all was of no avail. Death had marked its victim, and on the nineteenth of August, 1863, James K. Spaulding passed from earth to that better land, just as the sun was disappearing from the western horizon. Half a dozen friends were grouped around the bedside, and after the last sad and solemn rites were over, the emaciated form was consigned to a coffin, and placed beside comrades whose lives had been given for the same cause.

The *Masonic Monthly* told the story of Mrs. Merval, and it also printed a poem, written by a Northern school teacher who had settled in Kansas, entitled, "The Fraternal Tie":

> Tired with the long day's marching,
>   A Union soldier stood
> By the banks of a rushing river,
>   In a dim old Kansas wood.

177

The gnarled roots of the oak trees
  Grew snaky along the ground;
The vines with their purple burden
  In the giants' arms were wound.

The songs of the birds in the coverts
  Came sweet to the soldier's ear;
The medley of songs in the woodland
  Gushed forth without note of fear.

The sunbeams stole through the branches
  Over the turbulent stream,
And gilded the snowy wave tops
  That fleeted away like a dream.

But scarce had these joys impressed him,
  When loud through the forest broke
The taunts and the bitter curses
  That Quantrell's guerrillas spoke.

He turned; and his deadly rifle
  Was poised in his supple hands:
"Ha, ha! we have trapped a Blue Back;
  Empty his brains where he stands."

Sharp was the click of their pistols;
  Certain the aim that they took.
Vain to contend with the ruffians;
  Fierce was the hate in their look.

He glanced at the eager bloodhounds;
  One hope illumined despair;
He tried them; a rebel sprang forward:
  "A brother! Harm him who dare."

Pistols were dropped in an instant;
  Unharmed, in the dim old wood,
By the banks of the rushing river,
  The Union soldier stood.

On August 21, Lawrence, Kansas, was again the scene of bloodshed, for many of the citizens of that city were not as fortunate as the Union soldier in the poem. A group of guerrillas, under the command of Quantrell, ransacked the buildings, and stripped the people of their valuables. The grand master of Kansas, Jacob Saqui, told part of the story to his grand lodge on October 21, 1863:

It now becomes my painful duty to bring to your notice one of those horrible occurrences at which the heart shudders, and which gives the lie to all the pretentious claims of our boasted civilization. On the evening of the 20th of August last, the town of Lawrence, in this State, presented a picture of unusual beauty. The season was delightful, summer mellowing into autumn. The quiet but prosperous little town nestled upon the bank of the broad, calm river; and the citizens, in fancied security, rested from the toil of the day. The babe smiled upon its mother's bosom. The matron counselled with her husband of his plans and purposes, or cheered his weary spirit with sympathy and affection. The maiden, yielding to the dreaminess of the hour, wandered through the realms of imagination, or warbeled, in the words of some old ballad, the inspirations of her own innocence. The aged already slept, and in dreams were young again. All were peaceful and happy. But ere morning dawned, all was terror and desolation. The flames of the burning village, which shone fitfully upon the ghastly countenances of murdered citizens, also lighted the paths of terrified women and children who, wild with alarm, sought a place of safety from the barbarous assassin. A band of barbarous murderers had made the peaceful village a ruin, red with the blood of her unoffending citizens; and among the victims were a number of our brothers and fellows. In Lawrence Lodge there are vacant places and heavy hearts.

As soon as I was convinced that the report of the Lawrence butchery was a terrible reality, and not one of the numerous sensation rumors which weary our credulity every day, I caused a communication to be addressed to each of the subordinate lodges in this jurisdiction, requesting pecuniary contributions, according to their circumstances, for the relief of our brethren in Lawrence who had suffered loss of property, and to enable Lawrence Lodge to do whatever money could effect for the bereaved widows and orphans whom the awful calamity had placed under her protection. And nobly and generously the fraternity responded to my request. It is true they did no more than their bounded duty, but the willingness and liberality with which they gave according to their ability is creditable to themselves and a practical assurance that "Charity endureth for ever."

Even though many lodges in the southern portion of Kansas had suffered at the hands of those same guerrillas, over $700 was raised to help the citizens of Lawrence. A Memorial page in the *Proceedings* of Kansas states: "MASSACRED at Lawrence, August 21st, A. D. 1863, A. L. 5863. S. M. Thorpe, P. M.;

179

J. C. Trask; J. F. Griswold; W. T. Williamson, of Lawrence Lodge, No. 6; Charles Smith, of Topeka Lodge, No. 17; L. H. Swan, of Auburn Lodge, No. 32."

At Cumberland Gap, Tennessee, Lieutenant William R. McEntire of Company A, 9th Artillery Battalion of Georgia Volunteers, disobeyed the orders of General J. A. Frazier. When the Federals surrounded the Confederates, the general ordered his men not to fire; he was considering surrendering. McEntire gave his battery orders to open fire and aimed the first gun himself. Frazier was furious; he ordered McEntire placed under arrest; an order that was not carried out, because the next day the general surrendered.

McEntire's obituary in 1920 stated: "On September 7, 1863, being a Mason, he was permitted to return to his home in Atlanta, Ga. From Atlanta he went without escort to the officers' prison camp on Johnson's Island, Lake Erie, Ohio."

On September 8, the day a Union attack on Sabine Pass, Texas, was repulsed, James Kimball of the Grand Chapter of Massachusetts, wrote: "Let it be the prayer of every Companion, that before another year rolls around the blessings of peace may shed their hallowed influences over our beloved country; that war may cease, and that our country may come forth purified and purged of those sins which have called down upon us as a nation the displeasure of the Almighty."

General Price evacuated Little Rock, Arkansas, on September 10, 1863, and Federal troops moved in. On the 19th and 20th the Battle of Chickamauga, called the two bloodiest days of the war, was fought between the Union forces of Rosecrans and the Confederate forces of Bragg.

Rosecrans had left Chattanooga, thinking that Bragg, whom he had been pursuing for almost a year, was still falling back, only to find the Confederates had turned on him and were ready for battle. For two days Bragg's men tried to drive through the Federal lines; toward the end of the second day, the Confederates were successful. Only George H. Thomas, who earned the name "Rock of Chickamauga," stood in their way; his defense helped Rosecrans escape to Chattanooga.

Nathan Forrest sent word to Bragg, on the following day,

that the Federals were retreating. He suggested strongly that the Confederates pursue them as quickly as possible. But they did not, which caused Forrest to ask, "What does he fight battles for?" The pursuit that did not take place brought the wrath of the generals in the field down on the head of Bragg. Under the authorship of D. H. Hill, and signed by many of the higher officers, a petition was sent to President Jefferson Davis, demanding Bragg's removal from command.

Davis went to the field to settle the trouble; Bragg was not removed; Forrest, who refused to serve under Bragg any longer, was promoted to major-general, and left without an army; D. H. Hill was returned to North Carolina.

The Grand Lodge of Illinois met in annual communication in Springfield, October 6, 1863. The grand master, F. M. Blair, mentioned the death of several Masons who had fallen in battle:

To those of their immediate relatives and friends who are most heart-stricken at the loss we have all sustained, we have nothing of this world's consolation to offer. We can only sincerely, deeply and affectionately sympathize with them in their afflictive bereavement. But in the beautiful spirit of the Christian theology, we dare to say, that he who "tempers the wind to the shorn lamb" looks down with infinite compassion upon the widow and fatherless in the hour of their desolation; and that the same benevolent Savior who wept while on earth, will fold the arms of His love and protection around those who put their trust in Him. Are we, brethren of the Grand Lodge, ready to enter upon the duties before us? Have we all learned to subdue our passions and improve ourselves in our Masonic duties? Let us turn our mind's eye within us, and each decide for himself whether we have deeply engraven in our hearts, Truth, which is a Divine attribute, and will assist us to regulate our conduct in such a manner that hypocrisy and deceit will be unknown among us. Have we cultivated the cardinal virtues of Temperance, so that we have a due restraint upon our passions; and Justice, which will enable us to give every brother that to which he is justly entitled?

Grand Master Huston of the Grand Lodge of Kentucky spoke in much the same vein on October 19:

Brethren of the "Mystic Tie," would it not be well for us, in these times of sore trial to our own country, of sadness and sorrow in all our borders, to search ourselves as with a lighted candle, to see how far we have fallen short of our high duties as Masons to *each other,* to our *country,* and to God. It may be that we have wandered far from the tried paths of duty. It may be that we have forgotten, in the midst of conflicting passions, to look to the only source of strength and help—to the bountiful Giver of all good— and to ask, with humble but faithful hearts, for needful help. His arm alone can bring deliverance, let us lean confidingly upon it. Brethren, I commend you, our order, and our country to His gracious keeping.

On October 27, the grand master of Minnesota, A. T. C. Pierson, explains why the communication of 1862 was not held:

Two years have passed since we met in Grand Communication to consult upon the interest of Craft Masonry in the jurisdiction of Minnesota. Two years of gloom and darkness have gone. The boom of cannon, the rattle of musketry, and the clash of arms, are receding farther and farther away from our borders, and we may reasonably hope that the time is not far distant when such sounds, so discordant to the Masonic ear, shall no longer be heard in all the length and breadth of our land. While our fields have been exempt from the deluge of blood that has marked so many others in various parts of our common country, yet have many of the brethren from this jurisdiction participated in those scenes of carnage and death that have brought sorrow and wailing in so many peaceful families.

Not a company has gone from this State but that some of our Lodges were represented in it; not a regiment but that at least one-half of its officers were members of our Order; not a Lodge in the State but that some of its officers have answered to their country's call. In some of our Lodges, one year since, all the officers had gone; in others a portion of the officers and members, and in one Lodge but three members were left. So crippled were our Lodges, that in September, 1862, I sent a circular letter to the Lodges, requesting their views as to the policy of postponing the meeting of the Grand Lodge. Of the answers received, all of the Lodges, with but one exception, recommended a postponement of the meeting. I accordingly issued my circular of October last.

He added a brighter note to the proceedings by telling his members of the actions of another grand master:

History tells us that at the first battle of Bull Run, very many of the Union soldiers were taken prisoners, and after many removals, were finally confined in New Orleans. But history does not tell us of another fact, and one, too, of which we, as Masons, may be justly proud, that M.W. J. Q. A. FELLOWS, the Grand Master of Louisiana, visited the Prisoners in their cells, administered to their wants, furnished food, medicines and attendance to the sick, undeterred by the mob, who threatened his life, and when the prisoners were exchanged and about to return home, each brother was by him presented with a suit of clothes.

The deputy grand master of Colorado presided during the annual communication of that grand lodge on November 2, because the grand master, J. M. Chivington, was out of the territory "upon pressing military duties."

John M. M'Jilton, the grand master of Maryland, informed his members on November 16, 1863 why the present war was being fought:

It is to God, our kind Father in Heaven, that we are indebted for our preservation from threatened disaster, and the peace that prevails among us. Regarding our position politically as a Southern Border State, and the interests and feelings that in past years have moved us in the management of our political relations, it is not only wonderful, but wonderfully providential, that we have not been greatly troubled by violent sectional divisions and partizan convulsions. . . . In our present unfortunate national conflict, both Religion and Masonry have failed in the effort to reach and remove the difficulty by which it has been occasioned. The working of the political machinery of our nationality by sectional agencies, that is by partizan demagogues, became too extensive in its magnitude, and too powerful in its extent to be controlled by any instrumentality that bore the standard of good-will and peace. Religion is much more to be blamed than Masonry for the sad results have succeeded the delinquencies of both. Masonry in the issue, however, is far from being faultless. Masonry bears the standard of morality, of which religion justly claims the ownership of the inspired source. When religion faltered in her Courts of Inspiration, the temple of her inspired worship, morality in the hearts of Masonic Craftsmen implanted there by the working of the Ritual, amid the secret councils of the moral tabernacle, should have come to the rescue. Masonry should have encouraged and sustained the Church and Religion by the enforcement and practice of her own high moral tenets. The Church would then have appeared as the great Light of Inspiration, not only in the proclamation, but in the encouragement and enforcement of great moral truths.

In this pursuit, Masonry would have shown herself to be what she surely is, the handmaid of Religion, and the assistant of the Church in saving the nationality from self-immolation under the control of sectionalists and partizan schemers. Neither the Church nor Masonry, neither Religion nor Morality could have admitted for a moment, in full knowledge of the fact, the working of the citizenship of this highly favored land in its progress towards the strife, and bloodshed and ruin that the pen of the historian must now record.

When Hill told Patton Anderson the armies in the East battled each other as soon as they met, Anderson replied, "Oh, we out here have to crow and peck straws awhile before we use our spurs." The spurs were used at Chickamauga, and were to be used unsparingly by Grant until he had broken the Confederate defenses. He started at Chattanooga.

CHAPTER XV

A Gloomy Year Ends

◇◇◇

To-day closes the gloomiest year of our struggle. No sanguine hope of intervention buoys up the spirits of the confederate public as at the end of 1861.
Richmond Examiner, December 31, 1863

AFTER THE FEDERALS had returned to Chattanooga, the Confederates placed it under siege, thereby employing a Union weapon. So successful was the siege, starving soldiers stole grain from the live-stock. Grant, in his report, stated: "The artillery horses and mules had become so reduced by starvation that they could not have been relied upon for moving anything."

When Grant learned of the dire condition of the forces at Chattanooga he telegraphed George Thomas to hold that city at all costs, to which Thomas replied, "I will hold the town till we starve." That appeared to be a likely possibility, for "already more than 10,000 animals had perished in supplying half-rations to the troops by the long and tedious route from Stevenson and Bridgeport to Chattanooga over Waldrons Ridge."

Through a series of orders Grant, still on crutches and in pain, managed to open short lines of supply to the beleaguered force at Chattanooga. Bragg, by permitting his Union counterpart to out-manuever him, brought about his downfall. On November 24 he lost Lookout Mountain and the following day was defeated on Missionary Ridge. Grant, Sherman, and Thomas, who had replaced Rosecrans, had "out-generalled" Bragg.

On the 26th Bragg retreated to Dalton, Georgia, where he

185

turned the Army of Tennessee over to William J. Hardee on December 2.

November, 1863, saw the birth of a new Masonic magazine, *The Masonic Monthly*, published in Boston, Massachusetts, and edited by Edward L. Mitchell. Of the struggle in the country he wrote:

In this great crisis of our country, not only have our political institutions suffered detriment, but every institution in the land has experienced the baneful and prejudicial effects of the civil war. The churches, which served, in addition to the ties of a common blood, to add the link of a common faith, have lost all control over the contending forces. They have suffered division, and have been rent asunder with a violence equal to that which has snapped in twain our political federation. The colleges, which diffused a common education among the youth of our country, have experienced this great tearing apart of North from South. Professors have ranged themselves against professors, and pupils have seceded from Alma Maters, as have their States from the Union which made them great and glorious. One institution only, amid all the strife, has retained its integrity, and its influence unbroken over its membership, in either section. Freemasonry stands out pre-eminently, a solitary pillar in the wilderness—a monument, proving, by its unbroken shaft, the excellence of its architecture, the strength of its material, and the depth and durability of its foundations. What an inestimable privilege is this to which it has been ordained!

That magazine published several articles about Freemasons during the war, such as the following, entitled, *Freemasonry: What It Has Done for Our Soldiers:*

Aside from the incalculable benefits which Masons have derived in civil and private life in all ages, there are many cases on record where, when engaged in war, members of the mystic craft were kindly cared for by, and owed their lives to, those with whom they had been striving against on bloody fields, when hundreds on both sides gave up their lives for what they deemed the right. Since the time of the Knights Templars, who "led their vassals from Europe to Palestine's plain," numerous instances have been recorded, in the annals of foreign wars, and cases wherein a Southern rebel or a Northern soldier succored each other in times of extreme danger in our own civil contest are not few or far between. Many have been placed on record, but there are many occurrences which the faithful historians would have been glad to have known, that they might add to the reputation and influence of the craft.

186

In the early part of the war a Northern (Massachusetts) officer, wounded and nigh unto death's door, was taken within the rebel lines at Richmond, and though he received much better treatment than was accorded to his fellows in later days in Libby and on Belle Isle, he did not receive that care which would have been bestowed upon him at home or in a Union hospital. He was visited one morning by his surgeon, when his wounds were less painful, and his thoughts more collected than had been the case since his fall in battle. The two soon found that they were, in one sense, of the same brotherhood, and it was not long before the wounded officer, who received closer attention and better care than before from the period referred to, was in his Northern home, among friends and kindred, blessing the day of his initiation.

A similar case, though one which was attended with far different results, occurred in New Orleans in the latter part of the war, and came under the writer's observation. A young man named James Madison, who hailed from a Western State, and who belonged to a Western regiment, was one of the gallant band, under Gen. Banks, which made the assault on Port Hudson, July 14th, 1863, which was attended with such disastrous results. Among the wounded, and numbered with the class which were never expected to recover, was young James Madison. In that charge, in many places along our line, the infantry was placed between the enemy's breastworks and our artillery, and the shells thrown by the latter passed over the heads of the foot soldiers into and over the earthworks of the enemy. At least this was the plan, but unfortunately, owing to the carelessness of those who were appointed to inspect the shells before they were used, they burst oftentimes directly over the heads of our own soldiers, and at least one fourth of those killed and wounded that day were struck by portions of what may be termed "our shells" with a double meaning. Madison had his right leg and right arm torn off, his left leg and left arm each suffered the loss of a slice of flesh and muscle, and he was also wounded in the neck, all of which wounds were caused by the premature bursting of a shell. He, or what was left of him, was conveyed to New Orleans, and placed in the St. Louis Hospital, a building which in times of peace was known as the St. Louis Hotel. The hospitals everywhere were crowded with the wounded, dead, and dying, and the surgeons and attendants were so over-worked, and had become so used to ministering to the wants of *portions* of men, that the sight of the wounded hero did not cause the feeling of pity nor any extra exertion, as would have been the case farther north. The people of New Orleans were, as all are aware, of the most determined and bitter type of rebels the South afforded, but there were a few Union ladies, who came daily to the hospital to attend to the sufferers languishing there, during the hot, stifling, enervating weather, which was then almost suffocating well men, and the effect of which on suffering, nervous soldiers, can be better imagined than portrayed in words. Madison had not lost the use of his tongue, and he was as lively as most of that class of men, who are habitually good-natured and hopeful, when surrounded with all manner of creature comforts. His case was noised throughout the city, and hundreds of people, rebels and unionists, came to see him, to exult over or pity his condition. It became known to one or two Masons that he was a brother, and from that time forth he was attended even by some of the wealthiest merchants (Freemasons) of the famous Crescent City, who guessed his every want in advance, and speedily met it in the most delicate and kindly manner possible. The hospital negroes were not allowed to attend him, and he had watchers day and night, from among the Masons, who seemed eager to perform the service. In the course of three or four months Madison recovered to an extent his new-found friends had never dreamed of when they first saw his mutilated form. He had a crutch strapped to the stump of his right arm, and his left arm and leg had been healed so that another crutch supported that side of his body. He walked with the crutches, with assistance at first, but after a little practice he could hobble alone. He went out frequently, and visited his Masonic friends in different parts of New Orleans, receiving a warm welcome in every quarter. That some of the Freemasons boasted of wine cellars containing wines of rare old vintage, was plain to be seen when Madison returned from his visits. Many times have we seen him borne into the hospital in the arms of his friends, with a jovial, beaming countenance, which showed that he had seen the bottom of many a glass of sherry, singing the songs known everywhere else as in New Orleans, and cheering the hearts of those too far gone to bear him company, who were reclining upon cots, past which his friends bore him to his own.

Radical temperance men must remember that every wounded man was prescribed wines and liquors, when such fluids could be obtained, and life was kept in many wounded heroes by this means, who eventually recovered, but might otherwise have died.

Madison had his discharge, and when he had so far recovered as to be able to travel, his Masonic brethren made up a purse for him, and parted from him with feelings of regret that they could no longer serve him, and of joy in the prospect of his soon receiving the kind care of his relatives and friends in his Western home.

We would willingly change the sequel, but we are dealing in fact and not fiction. The steamer upon which Madison embarked was blown up just above Port Hudson, and he was among a large number of wounded braves, who had stood the storm of shot and shell, been fearfully lacerated, and suffered all but death; had recovered sufficiently to cherish hopes of meeting loved ones once more; had started buoyant and happy, only to meet their final fate in the muddy waters of the Mississippi, through the direct agency of an unsound steamer. The sad end of James Madison could hardly have caused more sorrow among his blood relations than it did in the hearts of his Masonic brethren in New Orleans.

The Grand Lodge of Colorado granted a charter to Union Lodge, No. 7, on November 2, 1863. The formation of that lodge was a direct result of the conflict in opinions of the members of Denver Lodge, No. 5. The Northern and Southern sympathizers appeared to be equally divided and the dispute threatened to disrupt the communication of the grand lodge. The parties on both sides, to maintain peace and harmony, got together and agreed that Denver Lodge would recommend the issuance of a charter outright to Union Lodge.

The sympathetic act of all concerned struck a cord of fraternalism in the hearts of the members of Denver Lodge. Not a single member transferred his membership to the new lodge. A "discovery" was made that it was not necessary for congeniality for all Masons to think alike. Today, both lodges are working together in Denver, Colorado.

Two other articles in the *Masonic Monthly* are of Masonic significance, but contain no names. The first concerns a Federal naval officer captured by the Confederates:

Last Autumn [1863], an Ensign attached to one of the Federal gunboats stationed off the coast of North Carolina, was captured by the rebels. Being a member of the Masonic Fraternity, he was not long in ascertaining that an officer in command, among his captors, was a brother of the Mystic Tie. As is too often the case, on both sides, in this fratricidal war, the personal property of prisoners is very little respected by the captors. It so happened in the case of our Ensign. Of silver and gold he had none, and the possession of a quantity of it would have tended to alleviate the annoyances of captivity, and possibly secure for him the enjoyment of sundry comforts which he would otherwise have to go without. Money has wondrous charms, and can effect strange results underwhatsoever circumstances we may be placed. One day the rebel officer we have alluded to, came to acquaint our naval friend that his destination was Richmond, and the now notorious Libby Prison. After communicating this information to the Union officer, the Confederate inquired if he had any money. The reply was such as we have already hinted it would be. On receiving an answer, the rebel ex-claimed—"It will never do to start for Richmond that way"—and as he spoke, opening out a well-filled purse, he offered it to the Federal, saying—"Here, take all you require"—literally forcing on him the acceptance of its contents. There are occasions when it is impossible to refuse a favor, however much one may be disposed to decline. This was such an occasion. There was so much of candor in the manner of the rebel officer that our Ensign could not but accept the proffered kindness. In doing so he remarked, "But you will take my note for the amount?" "Not at all," was the reply; "when this trouble is over, if you have the means it will then be time enough to repay me. Perhaps, too, the fortunes of war may throw me into circumstances similar to those in which you are now placed—and then I shall only be too happy to find in you a brother who will do unto me as I have done unto you."

The incident we have above described is one of hundreds which have transpired during this war, of a nature to prove that if Masonry was powerless to avert the contest in which we are engaged, it has been most influential, in numberless instances, in alleviating the sufferings which are consequent upon the conflict.

The second article is a story that came about after the heaviest of the fighting was over at Chickamauga:

Some months since, a young man was introduced to me who had been in the army, but had obtained his discharge on account of wounds received in battle. The brother who introduced him remarked to me, "He is a Mason, I have found."

"Ah," said I "then I think it very probable he may have seen some of the practical fruits of Masonry."

"That I have," said the soldier. *"I owe my life to Masonry.* When my regiment fell back, at C---, I was left by the roadside, wounded, and weak from loss of blood. Knowing that if I fell into the hands of the rebels, who were close upon the heels of our retreating forces, my chances for recovery would be small indeed, even though I should escape being bayonetted where I lay, you may judge of my anguish as I saw our rear guard passing me. Suddenly the thought flashed across my mind that I was a Mason, and I almost instinctively made a Masonic sign. An officer, riding past at full gallop, saw and recognized it, and instantly reining in his horse, dismounted, and took my hand. We exchanged the mystic token. He hurriedly examined my wound, inquired my regiment, and remarking, 'you are a dead man if you are left here,' after several ineffectual efforts, lifted me upon his horse, mounted behind me, and, with his arm around me, galloped after his regiment. In this way I was brought to the nearest hospital—and here I am. I shall never forget what a debt I owe to Freemasonry."

The Grand Lodge of Virginia held its annual communication on December 14 as scheduled. The grand master, Lewis B. Williams, told the members:

The condition of our country has prevented the regular and stated meetings of many of our Lodges, and the representation of others in this Grand Body, which may well account for the small number of delegates from the Subordinate Lodges, without ascribing it to any want of interest in the cause and success of Masonry.

I am well assured that the principles of Masonry are as highly appreciated at this time as they have ever been; and although our Order whose tenets should command the respect and ensure the protection of every created being who claims to be a man, has been insulted and outraged by our vandal foes, yet when this bloody and cruel war shall end, it will be shown that it has been purified by the fires of persecution, and around her consecrated altars a band of brothers will assemble, renew their vows of fidelity to its principles, and go forth with new resolutions to relieve the wants and sufferings of the widows and orphans of our gallant soldiers, who have given or may give their lives in defence of the rights and liberties of their country, and more especially of those who are members of our Institution.

The grand master had issued warrants to 13 military lodges and the grand lodge confirmed his action. A special committee reported that five lodges had been ransacked by Union troops, and one by Confederates. S. S. Baxter, who was chairman of that special committee, went on to state:

Heretofore in the history of the world, wars have usually been the wars of governments; rarely the war of one people against another people. But this is emphatically, and in a more marked sense than the world has ever seen, the war of one people against another people. It differs from the social and civil wars heretofore seen in the world. Heretofore, in social or civil wars, one class or party of the community has warred against another class or party. When the successful party has established its dynasty, or the class obtained the rights struggled for, the war ended, and the State subsided into the same community under the organization effected by the war. But this is a war of States against States. In each State of the Confederacy all classes and parties are united as one man in struggling for their rights. So our adversaries seem to be united in their purposes,

191

and these purposes are avowed by their government to be, the conquest and extermination of the people of the Confederate States. The world has never before seen a great people striving as one man to exterminate another great people. This feature gives, on the part of our enemies, this war more the character of individual malice and murder than any the world has ever seen.

* * *

In no portion of the world has the Masonic fraternity been so closely united as in this. Grand Lodges existed in each State, in the most intimate and fraternal intercourse, exchanging correspondence and representations. At one time a union under one Grand Lodge was almost consummated. But during this time the right of each Grand Lodge to control all the Masonic workings in its jurisdiction was well recognized, and the boundaries of each Grand Lodge well defined. The effort of one Grand Lodge to erect or charter Lodges within the jurisdiction of another Grand Lodge, was settled to be an invasion of its rights, and the Lodge attempting to work under such illegal charter was a clandestine Lodge, and Masons attempted to be made in it were spurious Masons.

On the 15th, William H. Harman was elected grand master. One year and three months later he was to die from wounds received during a battle at Waynesboro, Virginia.

During the second week in December, 1863, Nathan Forrest moved into Tennessee for a series of raids. No strong opposition was encountered until December 24 when Colonel Edward Prince, in command of the 7th Illinois Cavalry, endeavored to stop him. He was unsuccessful and fell back to Summerville. Prince tried again on Christmas Day, found his men surrounded, fought for three hours "with terrible loss, cut his way out, and carried most of his command safely into La Grange."

During the annual communication of the Grand Lodge of Pennsylvania on the 28th, the committee on correspondence is again alarmed over the number of grand lodges that had not sent their *Proceedings*. About the condition of the country, it states:

Your Committee sincerely rejoice in the general tone which pervades all the documents submitted to them, so far as the National troubles are in any way the subject of allusion or remark in Addresses, Reports, Resolutions or other Papers. Throughout the whole there breathes a spirit of unflinching devotion to the country

192

and the Union, and of unswerving loyalty; yet the vindictiveness and unmasonic bitterness which upon occasions were shown during the first outburst of the Rebellion, and led us to think that some of our brethren had forgotten the teachings of the altar, have for the most part passed away. Such things were not to be wondered at in the beginning. That they have passed away, is cause for gratitude and congratulation on the part of the Craft, that the noble principles of the Fraternity have vindicated their claims to an elevating and ennobling and humanizing tendency.

General Butler was still having his troubles. The gas company at Norfolk, Virginia had been defying his orders for months, sealed its works, and refused to light the city. On December 29, Butler ordered the plant seized and placed in operation. It was. On the following day he ordered "several officers of his command" dismissed "for intoxication."

The Richmond *Examiner,* in an editorial on the last day of the year, saw only gloom in the year just ended and nothing but gloom for the year ahead. In summarizing 1863, it said:

. . . Meade has been foiled, and Longstreet has had a partial success in Tennessee; but Meade's advance was hardly meant in earnest, and Bean's Station is a poor set-off to the loss of the gallant men who fell in the murderous assault on Knoxville. . . . The advantages gained at Chancellorsville and Chickamauga have had heavy counterposes. The one victory led to the fall of Jackson and the deposition of Hooker, the other led first to nothing and then to the indelible disgrace of Lookout Mountain. The Confederacy has been cut in twain along the line of the Mississippi, and our enemies are steadily pushing forward their plans for bisecting the eastern moiety. . . .

Meanwhile the financial chaos is becoming wilder and wilder. . . . The cry of scarcity resounds through the land . . . no one can tell us whether we shall have a pound of beef to eat at the end of 1864, or a square inch of leather to patch the last shoe in the Confederacy. . . .

. . . Wise, cool, decided, prompt action would put us in good condition for the spring campaign of 1864, and the close of next year would furnish a more agreeable retrospect than the *annus mirabilis* of blunders which we now consign to the dead past.

In the Masonic world, prayers for a restoration of peace continued, as every grand lodge in the North and South was able to meet during the year. More lodges in the South were ransacked during the year than had been the case previously, but the feeling of fellowship had grown stronger. Masons from the North were not ashamed to fraternize with the Southern members of the fraternity. Assistance was more freely given to each other. Although the fighting had been more fierce, the brother's war became more brotherly.

CHAPTER XVI

The Beginning of the End

◇◇◇

The heart-stirring revulsion of bitter and dead-
ly feeling caused by the utterance of talismanic
words "I am a Mason" has saved many a gal-
lant brother's life, relieved his suffering when
wounded, ministered to his wants when needy,
and alleviated the miseries of his captivity.
ISAAC VAN WAGENER

THE DAWN OF 1864 found the Confederacy in dire straights. The blockade had proven so successful, clothing and all of the necessities of life were scarce. When obtainable the prices were fantastic when measured in Confederate money, valued at six cents on the dollar.

The lack of manufacturing plants was sorely felt. Even writing paper was practically non-existent; paper for the daily news was difficult to secure. Most newspapers were two-page affairs when they were printed at all. Many Southern grand lodges were unable to print their *Proceedings* until the war was over.

In the North, as well as the South, there were men and women demanding that the fighting be stopped. But many lives were to be sacrificed before their demands were met.

David O. Dodd, charged with being a Confederate spy, was executed on January 8, 1864, in front of the Masonic College at Little Rock, Ark. Three days later, Thomas Hayward, grand master of Florida, told his members he had not visited many lodges, because most of them could not work. He went on to explain:

The demand for soldiers in the field, to defend their homes from a cruel and vindictive foe, has inspired all who can leave their dear ones and repair to the field of danger and offer their lives in defence

195

of our beloved homes. This duty is felt by none more than the Masonic Fraternity. When this war is ended and the blessing of peace is again our happy lot, you will have much to do in your different Lodges to correct the vices and improprieties which generally follow a year or more in camps.

On the 13th, the grand master of Vermont, Leveret B. Englesby, was still hoping for peace:

The year has closed upon us, and as yet the long wished-for hour, the bright morning of peace, has not dawned upon the land. Many, very many desolate homes, mourning hearts, crushed hopes, are in our once happy land. God help those within those desolate homes, comfort the mourning hearts, bind up the crushed hopes. Fair, faint streaks are on the horizon's verge, as if the light would surge; may the hour soon come when the faint streaks may widen, the clouds roll up in gold and amber flakes, and the glad daylight shine.

The Grand Lodge of Michigan held its annual communication on the same day, and Grand Master J. Eastman Johnson referred to the unusual action the war had forced him to take:

During the year, I have granted dispensations to various Lodges to confer degrees upon one hundred and thirty-three candidates. In so doing, I have restricted the dispensations, in every instance, to the permission of a shorter time to act than the general rule provides, requiring the Lodges to conform in all other things to the prescribed forms. These applications have been made, in all but very few instances, in behalf of officers and soldiers of our regiments in the service of the country, at home on short furloughs, or about to enter the service. In ordinary times, the issue of so large a number of dispensations, would indicate something wrong, either in the fact, or in Masonic law. The case is extraordinary, as is the state of the country. My act can become no precedent for the future, because no such state of things can recur. Early in the year, I observed the tendencies in this direction, and endeavored to guide myself by such rule as the case seemed to require. We have been taught that Masonry was lovely in peace, and that it also had power to assuage the horrors of war, and help humanity triumph over passion. The intelligent and patriotic men who have put their lives in their hands, to help subdue the rebellion, and so restore peace, have observed a ray of light shining brightly over the excitements, the triumphs, the miseries of the battlefield. They have discovered what to them was the discovery of a new world, that this ray was the light of Masonry. Having made this discovery, they have desired to obtain that light. And toward whom could an act of favor be more worthily extended? I have deemed all these cases of emergency, and have acted accordingly.

The January, 1864, issue of the *Masonic Monthly* contained an article entitled *Freemasonry in Our National Conflict— War Incidents:*

It is a sad thought that in the civil war now desolating portions of our country, brother is arrayed against brother in the clash of arms, and many a warm heart has poured out its precious blood. But there is a redeeming thought. It is that often the mystic word, or the silent symbol has brought relief or sympathy in the trying hour. It was our fortune last week to learn two incidents in illustration. The first relates to a brother we had welcomed to the Masonic altar in a new lodge some four years ago. Now we were called to surround that altar in mourning for the deceased brother. He had died in the St. James' Hospital, New Orleans, after a hopeless illness of four months. A widow and five children were stricken by that arrow. It was our privilege to meet them at the home he had reared and near-ly finished for them, as the call of his country summoned him to her defence. What tenderness breathed through the file of letters to the dear ones at home! What devotion to the Union and its glorious flag! What heroism in the unequal conflict with disease that held him in the hospital, when his regiment left for Texas, with General Banks!

His last letter was written on the 21st of October. He was patient, hopeful, resigned. It was his desire and expectation to secure a furlough early in November, and seek recovery in the bosom of his family, but on the morning of the 5th, just past the midnight hours, he was detached by the Commander-in-Chief for nobler service in a higher sphere. Letters of exceeding tenderness announced his pro-motion to the stricken ones, both from his chaplain and a fellow-soldier, and fellow-sufferer in the hospital. But the crowning letter was from the surgeon of another regiment, one who knew him by the well-known symbols. He had found means to minister to his dying brother for the last three days, and give him fitting burial, and then to speak words of comfort to the widow and the fatherless, which will live as precious memories.

The other event is connected with the siege of Charleston. A young man from the "Forest city," was a volunteer in the besieging force at the storming of Sumter, and was wounded and carried into the city a prisoner of war. His father was a Freemason, who had worthily worn the highest honors in the gift of Masonry within his native State, and been repeatedly a representative in the general Grand Bodies. Among the counsels to his son, was the charge, in case

197

the fortunes of war should lead him into Charleston, to inquire for a brother in that city, whose name need not be published while rebellion holds carnival there. The young man, heeding a father's counsel, in his distress, sent for the brother, and disclosed his parentage, which was sufficient to secure the services of a ministering angel. Two letters have been sent by flag of truce to speak words of comfort to the stricken father and family. The first was to assure them that the son, mortally wounded, would receive every attention and aid which human skill and sympathy could supply—the second to tell the sad tale that the father and his two sons, as chief mourners, had followed to his resting-place, the dear one, and carefully marked the spot, where affection can find him when the carnage of war has given place to the bow of peace. The last written letter was the first, received, and both were filled with the overflowings of a brother's love, and assurances that spiritual counsel and consolation were given to the dying, with all that affection could do for his physical necessities. What myriads of unwritten deeds of love are seen by the eyes that slumber not, to be made manifest when the reign of passion shall have spent its force! They are now unseen and in silence preparing the cement of brotherly love, to be spread with fervency and zeal by the willing hands of worthy masters, when the erring ones shall heed the calm words of amnesty, uttered by our chief magistrate. Masonry will recognize and assert her mission then. She will be seen to have been no idle spectator amid the stern elements of the conflict.

The city where the first shot of the Civil War was fired was being bombarded by the Federal naval forces and on January 25, the Charleston *Courier* reported:

This is the one hundred and ninety-fourth day of the seige. The damage being done is extraordinarily small in comparison with the number of shots and weight of metal fired, and that creates general astonishment. The whizzing of shells overhead has become a matter of so little interest as to excite scarcely any attention from passers-by. We have heard of no casualties. Some of the shells have exploded, and pieces of the contents picked up, which, on examination, have been found to be a number of small square slugs, held together by a composition of sulpher, and designed to scatter at the time of the explosion.

On the same day, Benjamin Butler ordered Mrs. Jennie Graves out of Norfolk and to City Point because "her sympathies are with the South still." And also on the same day, the Grand Lodge of Mississippi met in annual communication.

A report written on the 26th about a Mason named Christopher "Kit" Carson and his operations in New Mexico was highly complimentary of his actions. "Much of the credit is due to the perseverance and courage of Colonel Kit Carson, commanding the expedition," the report stated. Another Mason, Brigadier-General James H. Carleton, also praised Carson highly.

Sherman left Vicksburg on February 3, with the 16th Army Corps under command of the Mason, Stephen A. Hurlbut, in what was to become known as "Sherman's Mississippi Expedition." He was to write in March: "we staid at Meridian a week, and made the most complete destruction of railroads ever beheld." His troops marched over 400 miles in 30 days and "left so many terrible marks of its prowess in its tracks."

Some of the "terrible marks" appeared in Marion while Sherman's troops were encamped at Meridian, some five miles away. Richard N. Rea wrote of one phase for the *Confederate Veteran:*

Many years before the war my mother had been initiated into the side degrees of Masonry, similar to the Eastern Star of the present day, little thinking of the help it might be to her in later life. We had quite a quantity of silver and three thousand dollars in gold, which she packed in a box and buried under a beautiful water oak tree at a late hour in the night. All the valuables of our home having been also secreted, my poor mother, as a solitary sentinel, guarded these family treasures while my two little sisters slept in peace, no doubt dreaming of daddy and brothers far away in Georgia.

Shortly after the sun was up, the enemy entered our town with a regiment of Wisconsin troops in the lead, and a company of cavalry, without invitation, hitched their horses to the huge swinging branches of our beautiful oak tree. Just at this time my mother, Mrs. Margaret Rea, made her appearance with her two little girls. She was ready for the early callers, and very soon the skirmishing began. However, a vicious horse, hitched directly over our treasure box, uncovered it and the silver and gold flew in every direction. With great bravery, the Yankees charged our sole fortune, and were making fine progress in their heroic attack. At this critical moment, my mother made the Masonic sign of distress, and at once the Wisconsin captain and others drew their swords and pistols and surrounded the robbers.

This brave officer succeeded in getting every piece of silver and gold, and returned our treasure box intact to my mother. He then placed a guard around our home, and slept upon the gallery himself as long as the Federal army occupied our once pretty village, which was the county seat of Lauderdale County. My mother told this Wisconsin captain she would pray for his return to his home in safety, and that she never would forget his kindness. In three or four days, the Federal troops folded their tents and made a hasty retreat to Vicksburg.

As to whether Masonry is a protection in the hour of danger, I know it is from actual experience.

General William S. Smith was ordered to join Sherman at Meridian on the 10th, but for various reasons he did not make it. One of the reasons was Nathan Forrest, the man who was left without an army to command after Chickamauga. That had not daunted him. He recruited a new army from the Western parts of Tennessee and Kentucky. Then he captured Union supplies and arms to equip them, and on February 20 they faced Smith, fought him to a standstill, and finally sent him back to Memphis.

In Richmond on February 7, "there was all the evidence of such a panic as had never before been witnessed." The "panic" was caused by Butler who sent a large force as far as Bottoms Bridge hoping to raid the military prisons in Richmond and liberate the Union prisoners. A Federal deserter foiled that plan by giving the Confederate authorities information concerning the intended movement.

During February, 1864 another Confederate prison camp was hastily thrown together at Andersonville, Georgia. It was needed to help hold the vast number of Federal prisoners of war that the Union refused to exchange. It was filled even before it was completed, and before it was closed in April, 1865, 49,000 prisoners were confined within its boundaries. Close to 13,000 died of various diseases before it was abandoned. That prison became the subject of a controversy that still continues. As late as 1960 a Broadway play depicted what was purported to be life in Andersonville prison.

Joseph McElroy, who said he was not a Mason and he "was not beholden to a Rebel for a single favor of any kind," wrote a story about the Andersonville prison. In that story was this paragraph:

A comrade writes to remind me of the beneficient work of the Masonic Order. I mention it most gladly, as it was the sole recognition on the part of any of our foes of our claims to human kinship. The churches of all denominations—except the solitary Catholic priest, Father Hamilton—ignored us as wholly as if we were dumb beasts. Lay humanitarians were equally indifferent, and the only interest manifested by any Rebel in the welfare of any prisoner was by the Masonic brotherhood. The Rebel Masons interested themselves in securing details outside the stockade in the cook-house, the commissary, and elsewhere, for the brethren among the prisoners who would accept such favors. Such as did not feel inclined to go outside on parole received frequent presents in the way of food, and especially of vegetables, which were literally beyond price. Materials were sent inside to build tents for the Masons, and I think such as made themselves known before death, received burial according to the rites of the Order. Doctor White, and perhaps other Surgeons, belonged to the fraternity, and the wearing of a Masonic emblem by a new prisoner was pretty sure to catch their eyes, and be the means of securing for the wearer the tender of their good offices, such as a detail into the Hospital as nurse, ward-master, etc.

Not all of the Southern prison camps were infamous. Years after the struggle General J. Madison Drake wrote for the *Confederate Veteran:*

One afternoon in the prison inclosure at Savannah, which, by the way, was a paradise compared to others in the South owing to the large live oak trees whose luxuriant foliage protected the six hundred Union officers there confined from the burning sun by day and the heavy miasmatic dews at night, a Confederate captain of the 1st Georgia Regiment, the best set of men that ever guarded a prison, while walking about the inclosure, engaged in conversation with a comrade of mine, in the course of which they happily recognized each other as Masons.

"What can I do to render your situation more comfortable?" I heard the Confederate ask my friend.

"Well, captain," replied the Union prisoner, "if I could be provided with a couple of boards, I would be enabled to build a bunk for myself above the ground."

The Southerner, after extending his hand, which was promptly grasped and significantly pressed, took his departure, and a couple of hours afterwards a wagon-load of smooth, yellow pine boards was delivered to my companion, whose joy was so great that he divided the lumber among his friends, reserving scarcely enough to answer his own purposes.

I might tell of many instances of this character that came under my observation during the four years' war to show the love that true-hearted men, even though enemies, can bear toward one another.

The bill creating the first rank of lieutenant-general of the Army of the United States was signed by Abraham Lincoln on March 1 and he immediately nominated Grant for that rank. On the 9th Lincoln formerly presented him with his new commission; on the 12th the President stated: "Major-General Halleck is at his own request relieved from duty as general-in-chief of the Army, . . . Lieutenant-General U. S. Grant is assigned to command of the Armies of the United States." A new era was ushered in.

From New Orleans on March 22 Nathaniel Banks issued orders constituting a Board of Education, and Lew Wallace assumed command of the Eighth Army Corps with headquarters in Baltimore, Maryland.

Nathan Forrest, after fighting William Smith, moved to the Ohio River and on the 27th wrote:

I left Jackson on the twenty-third ultimo, and captured Union City on the twenty-fourth, with four hundred and fifty prisoners . . . about two hundred horses, and five hundred small arms.

I also took possession of Hickman, the enemy having passed it.

I moved north with Bufords' division, marching direct from Jackson to Paducah in fifty hours; attacked on the evening of the twenty-sixth, drove the enemy to their gunboats and forts, held the town for ten hours, and could have held it longer, but found the small-pox raging, and evacuated the place.

We captured many stores and houses, burned up sixty bales of cotton, one steamer in the dry-dock, and brought out fifty prisoners.

Among the men reported as fighting with Forrest was a Mason named Isham G. Harris, a former governor of Tennessee.

Forrest continued his raids in Kentucky and on April 12 attacked Fort Pillow. That attack resulted in a lengthy investigation by the Congress of the United States. The *Rebellion Record* devoted 98 pages to the report and testimony which "was political, for political consumption."

The Confederates reached the vicinity of Fort Pillow early on the morning of the 12th and by ten o'clock had forced the Federals to their main fortifications. Forrest describes it and the battle:

The fort is an earthwork, crescent-shaped; is eight feet in height and four feet across the top, surrounded by a ditch six feet deep and twelve feet in width; walls sloping to the ditch, but perpendicular inside; it was garrisoned by four hundred troops, with six pieces of field-artillery. [*Battles and Leaders of the Civil War* estimates 557 soldiers, half colored, of which about 400 were captured, killed, or wounded.] A deep ravine surrounds the Fort, and from the Fort to the ravine the ground descends rapidly. . . . After several hours' hard fighting, the desired position was gained, not, however, without considerable loss . . . being confident of my ability to take the Fort by assault, and desiring to prevent further loss of life, I sent, under flag of truce, a demand for the unconditional surrender of the garrison.

Major Booth refused to surrender and the Confederates stormed the fort. "In less than 20 minutes from the time the bugle sounded the charge," the fighting was over. The Federals did not surrender or lower the United States flag and it was not until some of Forrest's men cut the "halyard" that the firing stopped.

On the 18th, Lincoln said the "massacre" at Fort Pillow should be amply retaliated. Sherman was ordered to investigate. Of that R. S. Henry wrote: "Whatever Sherman's investigation may have shown, it evidently did not sustain the political findings of the committee of Congress, for no retaliation was ever ordered—and Sherman was not a man who would have hesitated to order it had he thought that the facts justified such orders."

Differences of opinion were not confined to the battle-field or political arena. In Louisiana the grand master took the members of his jurisdiction to task for refusing to admit Union Masons dressed in uniforms to the subordinate lodges. "It does not show a proper Masonic spirit, and, what is more, tends to destroy the universality of Freemasonry," he stated.

General Rosecrans, a Roman Catholic, did not like the "incendiary, disloyal, and traitorous character" of the *Metropolitan Record,* "called a 'Catholic family newspaper,' published in New York." He ordered the provost-marshal to seize those numbers which in his opinion, "no man having a drop of Catholic charity or patriotism in his heart could have written."

A war widow, whose name was not printed, wrote to the editor of the *Freemasons' Magazine:*

Dr. McMurdy—

Sir—I wish to inform you of the death of my husband, who was a subscriber for your paper. He died the 24th of March, of Chronic Diarrhea, in Cincinnati, Ohio. He contracted the disease of which he died while he was in the army, and was unable to attend to his business for a long time previous to his death.

I would even gladly continue the paper if I could afford it, for next to religion I think Masonry is the grandest and the most benevolent institution in the world. I wish I could command words to express to you how forcibly I realized the truth of what I have said when I went to Cincinnati to attend my husband during his last illness. Although among entire strangers, I found the warmest friends among the Masons. Their attentions, their sympathies, their prayers, and their money were all lavished. Not a want was unsupplied, and I was made to feel almost as though I was in my father's house. I have a little boy, nine years old, who feels deeply the loss of his father, and I hope if he is spared to grow to be a man that he will love the institution of Masonry as well as I do.

The same magazine carried another article with no signature:

My dear Brother—I received this morning a copy of the National Freemason, addressed to my poor dear Brother (fraternally) Capt. Wm. A. Collins, company F, 61st N. Y. Vol. Infantry. I have to inform you that at the battle of the Wilderness, May 5, he was killed by one of the sharpshooters while leading his company on the ever memorable morning! and previous to leaving camp near Stevensburg, he remarked to me that he had an idea that he should fall in this campaign, and wished me to receive his National Freemason in remembrance of him. I hope, and trust, in accordance with his bequest, you will forward it in due time, addressed to me. . . . I can testify that a nobler-minded, disinterested and worthy Brother Mason, in my age of twenty years' travel, I never met. Would to God we had more of the same Masonic spirit which actuated him in all his actions amongst us.

The *Masonic Monthly* carried an article, in which no names were mentioned, entitled, *How Freemasonry Saved My Life:*

After the hard-fought battle of Sabine Cross Roads, in Louisiana, where the gallant Nineteenth Corps saved from destruction the army of the Gulf, the Troops retreated to Pleasant Hill. Early on the next morning (April 9, 1864) the victorious Rebels, following up their advantages of the previous day, and flushed with victory, fell upon the thin and shattered ranks of the Union army, as they were sleeping on their arms, trying and expecting to secure a few hours' rest.

I was awakened from my slumber by the fierce hiss of an exploding shell, and on coming to my senses found that three of our men had been killed before they were fully aware of their perilous position.

Our brigade was immediately ordered to support the right, which showed signs of wavering; but before we reached the brow of the hill, we were entirely broken up by the batteries giving way in front; and riderless horses and rattling caissons rushed pellmell through our ranks. Every man had then to fight for himself, and many single-handed combats were the result.

The incident which I am about to relate took place in a small grove which laid between our corps and the Sixteenth Army Corps. The Rebels had planted a three-gun battery in the center of the only road running through the woods, which opened a galling fire, utterly preventing us from forming a connection with our comrades in the opposite side.

At first we knew not what to do. There being no commissioned officer with us, we conferred together, and decided upon driving them from their position, if possible, at the point of the bayonet.

There were some sixty of us all told, from different regiments, representing nearly every Union State. Each one of us took a tree, and then attempted to pick off the Rebels from our hiding-places, at the same time gradually approaching the battery. Before we had got within a hundred yards of it, we had lost nearly twenty of our crowd, and several others were wounded.

At this point a color-sergeant of one of the gallant Maine regiments sprang to his feet, and waving the fragment of the tattered banner which he had carried through many a bloody fight, shouted, "Come on, boys!"

The word was all that was wanted, and with a yell we approached the battery. When I had got quite near the guns, a lieutenant of an Alabama regiment sprang from a tree, and caught me by the shoulder.

Already weak from loss of blood, having been wounded twice during the day, I felt that I was no match for the powerful Alabamian. As I drew my revolver, a shot from him shattered my right wrist. With my wounded hand I grabbed him by the waist as well as I could, while with the other I held his hand and prevented him from again firing.

205

We stood transfixed, speechless, defiantly staring at each other, catching breath for a renewal of the deadly struggle. And as thus we stood, I happened to espy the square and compass on his breast.

My situation was one of extreme peril; with joy I discovered the brotherly emblems; and giving the grand hailing-sign of a Master Mason, he instantly relaxed his hold, and we grasped each other by the hand.

Suffice it to say in conclusion that the battery was captured, and that the Alabama officer surrendered himself, of his own free will, a prisoner of war of the United States. Thus Freemasonry was the means of saving my life.

It appeared that Grant, after being placed in charge of the Federal armed forces, determined to press the war on all fronts, and disregarding casualties, move forward toward Richmond.

On May 4, Grant crossed the Rapidan with 118,000 men and a string of trains that "would have reached from the Rapidan to Richmond," or 65 miles. The following day, as they entered a dense forest, to become known as "the Wilderness," Lee attacked.

The tangled thickets of pine, scrub-oak, cedar, and ravines made fighting difficult. It was impossible to see what was happening over a relatively short distance. Webb stated: "At times, our lines while firing could not see the array of the enemy, not 50 yards distant." To make matters worse, before the Battle of the Wilderness ended on the 7th, the men were fighting in dense smoke and a forest fire.

In conjunction with his move toward the Confederate capital, Grant sent Butler from Fort Monroe up the James to cut the railroads between Petersburg and Richmond. John Reagan, in his *Memoirs,* writes of an incident that resulted where the opposing commanders were Masons:

In May, 1864, Gen. B. F. Butler landed a force, about 40,000 strong, on the south side of the James River, above the mouth of the Appomattox, for the purpose of cutting the railroad connection of Richmond with the South. He actually reached and took possession of the railroad between Richmond and Petersburg. It devolved on General Lee then, with an inadequate force, to defend both Richmond and Petersburg; and he was perplexed with this difficult problem. If he should take soldiers from the north side of the James to enable him to repossess the railroad, it would endanger Richmond. If he should take them from the east side of the Appomattox this would endanger Petersburg; and the loss of either place would have been most unfortunate for the Confederate cause.

In this condition of things Gregg's [John Gregg, a Mason] brigade (formerly Hood's) was confronting the Federal forces which occupied the railroad. Suddenly, without orders, and as the result of an accidental movement of the brigade standard, it rushed forward and drove the Federals from the line of the railroad and thus relieved this embarrassing situation, by reestablishing communication between Richmond and Petersburg. I inquired of General Gregg how this came about. He told me they were expecting orders to advance; that he was at one end of his line and the standard of the brigade at the other; that the flag was moved forward, he did not know by whom or for what purpose, and that the men assumed the order to advance had come, and dashed forward, driving the enemy before them.

Later Reagan said of John Gregg, "There was no more sincere and truthful man than Gregg, who at last was killed [October 7, 1864] in advance of his command, in an assault upon a strongly intrenched line near Richmond."

The final year of war had started. Many a man was to die, and many more hearts would ache before the end was reached.

CHAPTER XVII

The Last Summer

◇◇◇

*The summer of 1864 was rapidly drawing to a
close. After the most determined efforts and the
most desperate fighting of the war, the Union
armies seemed to be as far as ever from effecting
the conquest of the South. The Virginia campaign had been to the North a dismal failure.
. . . Forrest held such control of the country
outside of the Union headquarters at Memphis
that the Confederate legislature held its sessions
in Jackson, Tennessee.*

JOSEPH T. DERRY

AFTER LEAVING the flaming Wilderness behind, both
armies raced for Spottsylvania Court House, a key road
junction to the rear of Lee. The Confederates won the race and
dug in.

For ten days Grant hammered at the line that he said he
would "fight it out on if it takes all summer." Lee let him attack and took a dreadful toll in Union lives. He refused to do
what Grant wanted; he kept the Confederates entrenched; he
would not fight the Federal troops in the open.

Captain J. M. Bosang was in command of Company C, 4th
Regiment, Stonewall Brigade during Ewell's thrust on Grant's
rear during the Battle of Spottsylvania Court House. During
the engagement he was separated from the main Confederate
column. Wandering, lost, he stumbled on Union pickets and
considered it wise to surrender, and did. His "Memoirs" tells
what happened then:

In the afternoon we came upon them and after getting as near as
we thought prudent I tied my handkerchief to a stick and stepped
out where they could see me with my flag of truce. Two of them

208

came over to me and I told them there were four of us who wished to surrender. We were taken back on the hill to headquarters and the Colonel was informed there were four Johnnies outside who had come in. The Colonel came out and gave us a friendly "hello." He noticed the dingy gold lace on the shoulder of my faded jacket, and said, "you are an officer and what command?" I gave him my name, Capt. of Co. C, 4th Regiment, Stonewall Brigade. We entered into general conversation and he asked me how we thought things were going generally. I tried to make him believe we were well pleased and very hopeful. Then he asked several questions about our members and other things. I asked him to excuse me for not answering and he commended my course and invited me into his little tent. Soon the lieutenant colonel and major came in and I was introduced to them. They were all three nice gentlemen and after a short while one of them noticed a ring I was wearing with a Masonic emblem. He asked me if I were a Mason and I replied I was. It so happened they were all three Masons and that made me at home at once, and we spent a pleasant evening. The Colonel said if I would give him my promise to not try to escape I would not be kept under guard but have the liberty of the camp, to which I agreed so long as in his camp, but no longer. I was expecting to be sent to Fredericksburg next day so let him know I could make him no promise as to this trip. That night after they had talked the matter over they asked if I had any money. I had not, so they asked me as a Mason to accept $5, which I did.

* * *

The next morning we started for Fredericksburg, I in a wagon, the other afoot. Upon arriving at Fredericksburg we were taken to the guard house. Soon one of the guards came to me and we struck upon a conversation and he asked me what command I belonged to and I replied, the 4th Virginia Infantry. "Why," he said, "you were in the fight at the Wilderness on the 5th." I told him I was and had a brother killed there. I then asked if he was in that battle. He replied he was and said, "our regiment, 153rd N. Y., was engaged with the 4th Virginia Regiment and on your second charge you cut our regiment up so badly that what few were left were sent back here for provost guard."

I was kept there about a week, taken from there to Bell Plain, a boat landing, where we remained one night. At Bell Plain we were formed in line to be searched, a big Yankee sergeant doing the searching. They would order the men to take everything out of their pockets and the sergeant would examine to see there was nothing left. When it came my turn I had nothing but a handkerchief and my five dollar greenback that had been given me. He asked how I came by the money. When I told it was a present he wanted to know from whom. I said I would rather not say. With an oath he said I could not have it. I could not let my money go if I could help it, so I said some officers who were Masons gave it to me. The lieutenant in command, who was standing by, told the sergeant to give my money back and make no further search. Ah, that was a relief; I not only had my money but another friend. He invited me up to his tent and it is hardly necessary to say he was a brother Mason.

He asked me to share his tent for the night, for which I thanked him but declined, telling him I preferred to stay with the other prisoners. He said if there was anything he could do for me he would gladly do it. I soon went down where the other prisoners were. They had some little tent flies to sleep under and they were preparing supper. After a while the lieutenant sent for me again and set out a large bottle of whiskey and asked me to drink. I told him I never drank, but if he had some to spare I thought some of the other prisoners would likely enjoy it. He poured a pint cup full for me and when I went I took it with me and let the men have a sip around which they seemed to enjoy.

Grant, finding he could not move through the center, flanked the Confederates to the left. Once more Lee beat him to his destination, Cold Harbor, and entrenched. Grant attacked, and again there was a tremendous loss of life.

Edward S. Ellis, in his *Masonic Stories,* writes one account of the battle that took place at the tavern, where there was no harbor, and where it was far from cold:

The Army of the Potomac, under Grant, assailed the Confederate line on June 1st to 3rd at Cold Harbor. The Union Army suffered the most bloody repulse of the war. For twenty minutes the losses in killed and wounded were at the rate of 500 a minute. The Union was fought to a standstill. An order to advance again was disobeyed.

One of the most gallant of the Confederate leaders, who was barely 27 years of age, was General Robert F. Hoke. He commanded a division at Cold Harbor, and had received his commission as major-general less than six weeks previous. Directly in front of his lines lay scores of Union dead and wounded. Loss of blood always causes a horrible thirst, and the cries of the sufferers were more than the Confederates could bear. Scores ran from the ranks, and kneeling among the poor fellows shared the water in their canteens with them. They had been thus engaged only a few minutes when the Federals opened fire on them not understanding the meaning of the charity. The bullets whistled so hotly about them they had to hurry

210

back. General Hoke was so indignant that he issued an order forbidding his men going out of his lines.

In the lull that followed he lay down at the foot of a tree to rest, for the day was insufferably hot, and he like his men was exhausted. While lying thus, two of his men approached, and saluting, said: "General, a wounded Yankee is lying out in front and he wanted to know whether there are any Masons among us. We told him there were, whereupon he gave the sign of distress and begged us to go out and bring him into our lines. We replied that we had been fired upon while helping his companions, and because of that you had issued strict orders against our passing outside."

General Hoke roused up and looked keenly at the two men. "Are you Masons?" he asked.

They told him they were.

"Do you know that it is almost certain death for you to try to give help to that poor fellow?"

"We do; but he has made the Masonic appeal to us, and we only await your permission to try to bring him in."

"Then go in God's name. I do not stand in the way of such courage as that."

As eagerly as if rushing to meet a returning brother the brave men ran toward the Federal who lay helpless on the earth. They had hardly started when the enemy, still failing to understand the meaning of the act, opened fire on them. They did not falter or show hesitation. Everyone expected to see one or both fall dead at every step, but they reached the sufferer, coolly held a can to his lips, and raised his limp body between them, walked deliberately back with their burden. Neither received a scratch.

The *Freemasons' Magazine* carried a story that was typical of what happened after a battle was over. Although the Federal soldier who wrote the letter was not aware the Confederate soldier was a Mason when he assisted him, it made him feel particularly proud when his identity was discovered:

I had the good fortune when at the battle of Coal [Cold] Harbor to fall in with a poor wounded rebel Brother, who had lain near one of their rifle pits for over two days and nights, suffering from a severe wound, from the effects of a piece of shell thrown from one of our batteries. He was on the point of death from the effects of his suffering, not only from the dreadful wound, but for the want of even a drop of water. I called one of our stretcher-bearers, a worthy Brother also, who happened to come up at the time, and had him carried to our division hospital, and while the surgeon was un-

211

dressing him we found a Masonic emblem, and though unable to speak by words, he did by signs. The surgeon being of high standing found that this poor Masonic Brother was a member of some Masonic Lodge in Richmond, and a Royal Arch Mason. Oh! did it not do my heart and soul good, though fighting under most disagreeable circumstances, that it laid in my power to alleviate my poor Brother's wants, and render him which I did, all the assistance that I could command. The poor fellow died in the course of a week, and I saw him properly interred, but not as I could wish, but I did all that possibly could be done under the circumstances.

General Halleck wanted to stay at Cold Harbor, about nine miles from the Confederate capital, and conduct a siege. Grant whittled away on a piece of wood and thought about the small city of Petersburg and the railroads running through there to supply Richmond. By cutting them off, and the railroads from the Shenandoah Valley, he could starve out the capital of the Confederacy and force Lee's army into the open where he could destroy it. So, on June 7, Sheridan's cavalry was on its way to Charlottesville.

On June 7, also, the Grand Lodge of New York met, and Grand Master Clinton F. Paige told that grand body:

The fond hopes, cherished by all, when we last assembled, that another year would restore peace to our unhappy country, have not been realized. Civil war, with all its attendant horrors, and of a magnitude hitherto unknown in the history of the world, is still raging over half the Union. The groans of the dying, the wail of the widow and orphan, the lament of the mother over the remains of the loved and lost, are borne to our ears upon each passing breeze; and throughout the land we see thousands who but yesterday went forth in all the strength and vigor of perfect manhood, returning maimed, diseased, and helpless, dependent upon the charities of a thankless world. Truly, the record of the year is written in blood. Yet, above the din of battle and the wail of the dying, from the prison and the hospital, the "still small voice" of Masonry is heard attesting the truth and power of Masonic love. The baser passions, inflamed by deadly strife, have vanished at the remembrance of former vows, and the firm grasp of the uplifted steel, given place to the warm grip of brotherly love. Thousands of our brethren who have been participants in these tragic scenes, bear testimony to many beautiful exemplifications of the noble tenets of our profession, and recount with pride and satisfaction many practical illustrations of

212

the nature and spirit of our teachings; that though civil strife may sever all national, political, and religious ties and associations, yet the *mystic tie* unites men of every country, sect, and opinion, in one common bond of allegiance which death alone can sever.

* * *

I have also received several applications for the formation of Military Lodges, to be attached to regiments in the field, and one to be located at the headquarters of one of the military departments in a Southern State. I have never regarded these organizations with favor, and my observation of the manner in which the majority of those heretofore granted by us, have conducted their affairs, has confirmed me in the opinion, that the objections far exceed any advantages resulting from their establishment. But aside from the question of expediency, there is an insurmountable objection in my mind in the fact, that when the military organization to which such a Lodge is attached removes beyond the limits of our own State, an infringement of the jurisdictional rights of other Grand Lodges is inevitable and unavoidable.

The right of exclusive jurisdiction within the political territory where there is a Grand Lodge already in existence is now universally recognized, and implies full authority and exclusive control over all Lodge organizations and labors of the Craft within the limits of that territory; and I can discover no principle of Masonic law nor equity that will justify us in sending one of our Lodges into another jurisdiction *temporarily,* that would not with equal propriety allow us to establish a Lodge *permanently* therein. Entertaining these views I declined granting such Dispensations, and submit the question to the better judgement of the Grand Lodge.

He went on to state that five of the military lodges that had received dispensations in 1861 had made no report to the grand lodge. There was no way to tell who had been made members of the lodges, nor anything about their transactions.

The committee on foreign correspondence commented on the "edict" that was supposed to have been issued by the Grand Lodge of Virginia outlawing all Union Masons. "Recent circumstances, however, have induced us to believe that no such edict was issued. Who has seen, or read it? . . . the extracts we have since seen, from the report of Grand Secretary Dove, do not indicate any such spirit, and confirm our impressions, that the statement is groundless." The committee was correct.

On the same day, the grand master of Iowa, Edward A. Guil-

213

bert, told his members about a military lodge that was anything but Masonic:

On April 23 of the current year, Bro. E. H. Warren, P.M. of Anomosa Lodge No. 46, called upon me. He has been spending the winter in Columbus, Ky., where was located Halleck Lodge U. D., acting under the authority of the Grand Lodge of Illinois. Bro. Warren informs me, and his statements are confirmed by those made by Bros. P.D.G.M. Col. Scott, P. Sr. Grand Deacon Major Olney, both of the 32d Iowa Infantry—and others, that this lodge paid its Master, who was imported from De Kalb Co., Ill., a salary of *one hundred dollars per month;* that profanes, without regard to the jurisdiction from which they hailed, where balloted for, entered, passed and raised, habitually, within a week or ten days; that the fee was twenty dollars, and that over *two hundred* masons were made by the two who "ran the machine," during its short lived existence. I am also informed, and know, that many persons from our jurisdiction were made masons contrary to all masonic custom, and without the permission of your Grand Master.

He goes on in scathing tones to condemn the Grand Lodge of Kentucky for permitting this lodge to exist on its soil, and claimed that many men were made Masons in that lodge who could never have passed the ballot box at home. "The proprietors of the Lodge also operated a R. A. Chapter," he added, "in which within a week, they would grind out as poor grists from the raw material, as they were wont to do in the lodge."

At Guntown, Mississippi, where Forrest defeated Sturgis on June 10, 1864, John Grim of the 7th Ohio Independent Battery was taken prisoner. While riding beside "a handsome lieutenant in the Confederate gray," he noticed the Masonic square and compasses on his captor's watch chain. Grim immediately let him know he was a Mason.

The lieutenant let his squad get several paces in front of him, then told his prisoner to make a dash for the Federal lines. He did. But the Confederates opened fire and he fell wounded. He started to get up when he heard a whisper, "Lie still; pretend you are dead." Grim's advisor then shouted, "You fixed him that time boys. Go ahead; we will leave him here. We have no time to bury Yanks."

Grim crossed the river a short time later to the safety of his

Federal friends. He never did learn the name of his benefactor.

On June 13 Grant finished his whittling and pulled his army away from the Cold Harbor stalemate and toward Petersburg. The Grand Lodge of Texas met on the same day, with only 34 out of better than 250 lodges represented. Grand Master William P. Brittain thanked God for His many mercies and blessings, and for the privilege to meet again. He then added:

We did hope, when together at our last Grand Annual Communication, that before this time this unholy war would have closed; but it still continues. Brethren, it will close; there has never been a night without a day; never a beginning without an end; and history shows that we have never had a war that did not close, and, with the evidences before us, this will close at an early day, when the South will be herself again, when the officers and members of this Grand Lodge and of the Subordinates will return to their families and Lodges; and we trust the day is not far distant when we, in Grand Lodge, will meet in communion, a full representation, as in former days.

Brethren, since we met last, the scythe of time has launched numbers of our brotherhood into eternity, where they will sleep until the resurrection morn. Among the number, Brother Sam Houston, one of the original members of this Grand Lodge, the general, the hero of San Jacinto, the statesman, has departed this life—has been translated from this to the Grand Lodge above, where the Supreme Jehovah presides . . . this Grand Lodge has lost one of the brightest ornaments, and the State her brightest jewel.

Sam Houston had died at Huntsville, Texas, on July 26, 1863.

Grand Master Alvin B. Alden of Wisconsin told his grand lodge on June 14:

The Lodge room is an asylum sacred to Brotherly Love, Relief and Truth, which should never be polluted by any controversy tending, in any degree, to interfere with those essential principles of Masonry, least of all by religious or political dissentions or discussions. Until human nature shall be recreated, men will conscientiously differ in opinion, but differences of opinion upon political or theological questions should never be made the subject of discussion in a Lodge room, or influence us in the discharge of our Masonic duties. When we assemble around the sacred altar, which we have all learned to love and revere, let us leave all exciting controversies outside the outer door, and exercising towards

215

each other that charity which "suffereth long and is kind," let us reverently thank God that there is one place left on earth where man may meet together as brethren, and dwell together in unity, and whence dissentions, strifes and bickerings are forever excluded.

The foregoing had been brought about by the expulsion of a member of Tomah Lodge, No. 132. The lodge had tried its member for desertion from the military service of the United States. The committee on appeals for the Grand Lodge of Wisconsin reversed the decision of the lodge and the member was restored to membership.

Beauregard, the Mason, in command of Confederate forces south of the James, with a small contingent of troops, had Butler, the Mason, "bottled up" at Bermuda Hundred. Beauregard was also expected to defend Petersburg with the 2,000 troops left over. He could call on another Mason, Governor Henry A. Wise, who was in the city in command of a mixed force armed with discarded equipment.

"Baldy" Smith attacked the small band of heavily fortified Confederates on June 15. For the next three days Beauregard fought to hold the Federals until Lee could bring the main army from Cold Harbor. For three days Beauregard sent message after message to Lee in an endeavor to convince him that the whole Union Army was knocking on the gates of Petersburg. So well had Grant out-maneuvered Lee, it was three in the morning of June 18 before Lee was convinced that his counterpart was at Petersburg.

Beauregard held back the Federal Army until Lee arrived and saved the Confederacy for nine more months. Again the center was to hold. Grant lay siege to Petersburg.

A graphic picture of one Federal unit that fought with the Army of the Potomac is told in a letter originally published in the *National Freemason* and reprinted in the *Freemasons' Magazine.*

Head Quarters 39th Mass. Vols. *July 9, 1864*
Rev. Dr. McMurdy:
Dear Sir: While reading "No. 2" this morning, I was reminded that I am indebted to you for my subscription to the second volume of the National Freemason; the amount of which please find enclosed.
One year ago to-day, after a three months' pleasant so-journ in

216

Washington, my regiment left your city to join the Army of the Potomac, and after much hard service, I have reason to feel grateful to Him who controls the destinies of men, that my life and health are spared.

We have lost in killed and wounded of our regiment in this campaign, more than two-fifths of our number; among them, connected with "Army Lodge, No. 8," were Lieut. Paull, and Sergt. Stevens, killed May 8, at Spottsylvania, and Sergt. Henry, May 10; Sergt. Fisher, wounded, May 5, at Wilderness; Sergt. Turner, Lt. Merrifield, Corp. Simpson, Corp. Trask, Sergt. Davis, and Corp. Tileston, wounded May 8, at Spottsylvania; Capt. Graham, Adj. Moulton, Sergt. Endesle, and Corp. Hill, wounded May 10, at Spottsylvania; Capt. Spear and Lt. Wyman, wounded June 18, at Petersburg; Priv. Blake, June 23, at Petersburg.

Three of the Brothers gone home! May we not hope that the number is complete? Sergt. Daniel Henry was our Senior Deacon; a young man of unblemished reputation, a grand soldier, a brave man, and bright Mason. He was Junior Warden of Mount Lebanon Lodge, Boston, when he entered the army.

On the 8th of May, our division formed the advance of the army on Spottsylvania, where we met Longstreet's and Hill's corps massed behind strong works—about two thousand of us against two corps of the rebel army—the audacity of the movement was all that saved us from annihilation or capture. Here Lt. Isaac D. Paull fell, mortally wounded and a prisoner, "he died half an hour after being carried within the enemy's lines, and was buried by a Brother Mason." On the same day Corp. Simpson of Company C, was badly wounded, and left on the field when the regiment retired from the enemy's works. He was recognized as a Mason by a rebel officer, who directed his men to fill his canteen, and placed him in a comfortable position, and said he could do no more for him—from which position, a few hours afterwards, we recovered him and carried him to the rear. Though very badly wounded, he yet lives.

Thus we perceive that Masonic obligations are recognized by our enemies. May it ever be so on both sides, and soften, somewhat, the rigors of war in this unnatural strife.

Fraternally yours,
P. S. Davis

The author of the letter, P. Stearns Davis, was master of Putnam Army Lodge, No. 8, under a Massachusetts charter. Three days after writing the foregoing, he was killed, so the "number" was not complete. His body was sent to East Cambridge, Massachusetts, where his funeral was held on July 19.

Daniel H. Wheeler, grand master of Nebraska, during his annual communication of June 23, 1864, prayed "that ere another anniversary of the *Annual Meeting* of this Grand Lodge . . . this cruel and unjust rebellion may be effectually crushed and our people become again united under one common flag." His prayer was answered and the following year he thanked "the Grand Master of all" for the "angels of mercy and peace" that had descended upon the nation.

The *Masonic Monthly* for July, 1864 contained an article entitled "Masonic Amenities" which it had reprinted from the *"New York Herald's* Hilton Head correspondent":

The remains of the rebel Captain W. H. Gladding, who was arrested a year ago and over, while attempting to run the blockade, who died in prison while detained as a spy by General Hunter, and who was buried by the Masons, were recently disinterred and carried across the line, under flag of truce, by a party in charge of Lieutenant-Colonel J. F. Hall, Provost-Marshal General. The party landed on a causeway opposite Port Royal ferry, and it was a notable circumstance that it was lined on both sides with the acacia, the funeral emblem of the Order. Near where the body was deposited to await transferal a large and fine one was growing. Colonel Hall plucked it, and has forwarded it to his lodge—Kane Lodge of New York. Captain Gladding's body was received by Capt. Walker, of the rebel army. A deputation of Masons from Savannah were to have received the remains, but by an inadvertence were not informed in season.

Mr. William H. Guernsey, of Duchess county, New York, a clerk in the Post Quartermaster's office, and a member of the Masonic Order, died very suddenly of fever. The members of the Fraternity here procured a burial casket and escorted the remains to the cemetery, where they were deposited in a tomb, with appropriate exercises, preparatory to being sent North when the season will admit. The beautiful service of the Order was read by Lieutenant-Colonel Hall in a most impressive manner.

While the major portions of two armies held each other at bay, Lee sent Jubal Early and the Masonic general, John C. Breckinridge, to attack the Federal capital. Another Mason, Lew Wallace, who fought against heavy odds, delayed the Confederates for one day; one day was all that saved Washington from being captured; one day that, perhaps, kept Breckinridge from keeping his promise to visit the White House.

On July 12 reinforcements arrived in time to stop the Confederate advance, but Lincoln, from a Fort Stevens rampart, saw men fall dead, riddled with bullets. Not three feet from where he stood, an officer fell and died.

The town of Chambersburg, Pennsylvania was burned on July 30 by McCausland. That caused no end of resentment in the North, and was condemned bitterly in the South. One kind act stood out during that atrocity. The Masonic Temple, recently renovated, was saved.

A Confederate officer, riding south on Second Street, thought he recognized the character of a building. He inquired in neighboring houses and found it was a Masonic Temple. He instructed guards to prevent its burning, then rode away.

On the day Chambersburg was burned, a plan originally suggested by a coal miner from Pennsylvania turned soldier and carried to fruition by Lieutenant Colonel Henry Pleasants, a mining engineer, reached its climax.

The plan was to dig a tunnel of better than 500 feet from the Federal lines ending under a Confederate fort in the defenses of Petersburg. There four tons of powder was to be planted, and at a given signal set off, blowing the Southern lines wide open.

Against odds, without assistance from the Federal engineers, and with only General Burnside appearing to be in favor of the plan, Pleasants worked. He accomplished what no one thought he could. Then Grant, still skeptical, but seeing an opportunity to break through to the city and practically end the war, set up a plan of battle.

The explosion was scheduled to go off at three-thirty in the morning of July 30. The Federals waited to pounce on the surprised Confederates. But a faulty splice in the fuse held up the attack for an hour and fifteen minutes. Then the blast struck—like great thunder. A hole—a crater—170 feet long, 60 feet wide, and 30 feet deep appeared containing all sorts of debris and bodies.

The first "sight-seers" arrived in the form of Federal troops. They were unable to pass by the awesome sight without stopping, and hours later the crater held many more Union bodies than Confederate. Because of a series of errors, the plans of

219

Grant went awry and the North lost the advantage of surprise. Grant was disgusted; Pleasants "was awful mad"; the siege was continued.

During the annual convocation of the Grand Chapter of Canada on August 9, the address of Douglas Harrington was read because he was in ill-health. He referred briefly to the war across his border.

The miserable civil war still exists in the neighboring states, causing ruin and grief throughout the land; but freemasonry, though it cannot prevent, has there proved its beneficient power to mitigate suffering and distress; and our Order will ever be found side by side with mercy and humanity, provided its numerous members are only true to their attributes and themselves.

Throughout the months of July and August, the Federal cavalry fought its way through Georgia to Atlanta. The *Masonic Monthly* carried one of the many stories that took place in that state:

In February of last year we met a genial brother who had been for four years an officer in a Wisconsin regiment. During the series of sanguinary battles which preceded the surrender of Atlanta, he was taken prisoner, and in due time was carried to Charleston. On the way thither he became ill, and when he arrived in that city he was so far gone in typhus as to be bereft of his reason. He was placed in a comfortless outhouse adjoining the prison, and there left unattended to await the coming of the hospital surgeon. This officer came at last, and hurriedly made his rounds. Reaching the cot on which our friend lay, his attention was at once arrested by the bare and attenuated fore-arm of the patient, on which had early in his Masonic career been painted in India ink a square and compass. Without a word of explanation to the attendant, the noble surgeon immediately ordered our friend removed to his own quarters, and there through a tedious and dangerous illness so fanned the flickering life-spark that in due time it grew into a steady flame. He lavishly supplied his wants, and in due season so successfully favored the effort made to secure an exchange, that our friend was at last sent home. Said the recipient of these benefactions to us:

Until that time I never had realized the force of Masonic ties, and now I almost worship them.

Another episode of Masonic significance occurred when Captain Rankin of Mississippi led a Confederate charge into the Federal lines in front of Atlanta. The *Confederate Veteran* contains the story of what happened next:

. . . The Confederates were repulsed, leaving the pale and lifeless form of the Captain in the enemy's hands. The Confederates fell back a pace, re-formed, and rested on their arms. During this lull the voice of song was heard within the Federal lines, and proved to be a Masonic funeral song which touched a sympathetic cord in the breast of every Mason within the Confederate lines, and they too joined in sweet accord and sang with their brother Masons in blue, for they knew that a brother Mason was filling a bloody grave. Soon after the funeral service was over the Federals sent in a flag of truce accompanied by the belongs of Capt. Rankin, consisting of his sword, watch, spur, etc., with an earnest request that there be a special committee appointed to carry those valuables to the poor, heart-broken widow. The service proved to be the burial of Capt. Rankin with Masonic honors.

Several days after the battle of Ezra Chapel (Church), Georgia, July 28, 1864, a group of Confederates was sent to try to find the body of Colonel Ben R. Hart of the 22nd Alabama. The day was hot and the men soon had to stop searching the shallow gully where most of the bodies had been lightly covered with brush and earth. The odor proved too sickening.

The Confederates began searching the field in the hope of finding the colonel's body in a single grave. They came across one marked by two cracker box boards and inscribed: "Here lies Captain Thomas I. Sharp, of the 10th Mississippi Regiment [Company G, Tucker's Brigade], buried with the honors of his brother Masons of the—New Jersey Regiment."

U. S. Grant, from his headquarters at City Point, issued several orders to his generals instructing them to destroy and lay waste the country-side through which they traveled. To Sheridan he wrote: "Do all the damage to railroads and crops that you can. Carry off stock of all descriptions, and negroes, so as to prevent further planting. If the war is to last another year, we want the Shenandoah Valley to remain a barren waste."

Another order that was to have repercussions was issued from "City Point, August 16, 1864, 1:30 P.M.:" to *Major General*

221

Sheridan, Commanding District Winchester, Va.: When any of Mosby's men are caught, hang them without trial. U. S. Grant, *Lieutenant General."*

A short time later General George Custer ordered six of Colonel John Mosby's men executed at Fort Royal, Virginia. Several weeks later, when Mosby had captured over 50 men from the commands of Custer and Powell, he retaliated. The prisoners were lined up and ordered to draw lots to determine which six would be hanged. On the first drawing a 16 year old drummer boy was chosen. Mosby ordered him released and another drawing to be made; then he left.

Captain Mountjoy took over the distasteful task. On the next round a Mason was among those selected. He was released by his fellow Mason, Mountjoy. The "success" of the drawing continued poor; two of the six finally ordered hanged escaped.

Under a flag of truce, Mosby sent a letter to Sheridan telling him that he had delayed retaliation waiting for men captured from Custer and Powell. While waiting he had not lost a man as a prisoner and had sent "some twelve hundred men of yours to Richmond. Now, if you want to fight under the black flag, I am ready."

Sheridan gave Mosby's Rangers the status of regular Confederate soldiers; there were no more hangings.

As the last summer for the Confederate States drew to a close, the situation for them was precarious. To all but the most ardent supporters of the Confederacy, the war was as good as over. The "hammering" by Grant and his generals was reaping results, but the loss in lives was terrific.

The blockade had grown tighter. Few blockade runners were able to penetrate the screen of Federal gunboats covering the entire Southern coast. When a load of goods managed to find its way to the market-place, the prices were outrageous. In Richmond a pair of boots sold for $200; a bushel of coal $3.60; cotton stockings $6.00 a pair; a merino dress $150. In many other cities the situation was even worse.

Mrs. Jefferson Davis had been forced to sell her carriage and horses. Self-sacrifice was common among the supporters of the

Confederacy, but greed and graft were also to be found throughout the beleaguered cities of the South.

While the dire situation that existed among the Confederate States was common knowledge in the North, the Democratic party pronounced the war a dismal failure. An immediate cessation of hostilities was demanded, and once again a Mason was nominated to oppose Abraham Lincoln. George B. McClellan was chosen to campaign for the presidency of the United States.

CHAPTER XVIII

The Last Fall

◇◇◇

As a class, no better men, either as officers or privates, can be found in the army than the worthy Freemasons there. Obeying implicitly, ordering considerately, faithful and true, always and everywhere. These are some of the observed effects of Masonry in the army.
Masonic Monthly, December, 1864

MASONS, as well as those who were not, were kept busy trying to win the war—the war that was not considered such by the government of the United States.

Among the Masons were: David Farragut, who captured the outer defenses of Mobile, and on the 23rd of August captured Fort Gaines; Nathan Forrest, who raided Memphis, Tennessee, and spent two months raiding and fighting in that state; John (or John Hunt) Morgan, killed at Greeneville, Tennessee, on September 4; Sterling Price, the Missourian fighting for the Confederacy in his native state; plus a multitude of others on both sides of the conflict.

A Mason, who later was to become a judge in Rhode Island, was involved in a "minor" skirmish at Waynesboro, Virginia. On September 28, Federal cavalry attempted to destroy a railroad bridge. They were almost successful, but the Confederates caught them and proceeded to drive the Federals back to the city. The Rhode Islander mounted a horse and led his provost guards into the fight.

A. D. Payne, "late Captain of the Black Horse Troop (Co. 4), Fourth Virginia Cavalry, C. S. A.," wrote about what then transpired:

. . . A single soldier, coming from the direction of the enemy, with

224

sword in hand, dashed into the Black Horse Troop, which composed one of the squadrons of the Fourth Virginia Cavalry, on that occasion was the color squadron, sabering the men right and left, wounding several . . . this bold assailant succeeded in forcing his way through the Confederate column, and might possibly have escaped, but a shot fired by a Confederate brought his horse down and he fell with it . . . in all probability he would have been slain on the spot, but the timely interference of Captain Henry C. Lee, an aid of Colonel Munford, who seeing the struggle, rode up and put an end to it. It is said that Captain Lee recognized in the prostrate man a brother Mason, through some sign or cry used by the Masonic order in time of distress or danger. The hero of this affair, which sounds like a romance, turned out to be Capt. George N. Bliss, of the First Rhode Island Cavalry . . . at Waynesboro.

Thomas T. Munford, "Brig.-Gen. Cav. A. W. V. Late War," confirmed the above by writing to George Bliss:

When I saw you at night, sitting behind a Confederate cavalryman, with blood streaming down your face, going to the rear, a prisoner, I said to Doctor Randolph, Brigade Surgeon, that you were one of the "widow's son party." He being one of the elder brothers, replied, "I will see your mother's son well taken care of this night," and as most of the staff officers were of the clan, they did the best they could for a brother in trouble.

I am not a Mason, but most of my staff were Masons and I know they frequently did many things that seemed to give them extra pleasure for the unfortunate on the otherside. I was sure the institution was full of good works, and although I was only a poor soldier who tried to do his duty, without being a Mason, I believed the organization was based upon Christian principles, and was always in sympathy with the work of the fraternity.

The siege of Atlanta ended on September 2 when Hood marched out and Sherman marched in. At Petersburg the siege continued, as it was to do until the final month of the war. In far off California, Grand Master William C. Belcher, on October 11, noted the devastation taking place in the South:

After a long separation, we again meet in Grand Lodge, and it gives me great pleasure to report that all is well with us, and that, from every portion of our widely extended jurisdiction, the brethren send up good tidings of peace, harmony and prosperity. We all know that we have fallen upon evil times: that our country is involved in civil war—a war of such magnitude and momentous import as the world never saw before. Every day we read of the march

225

of great armies, of great battles fought, and of thousands and tens of thousands slain. We know that the homes of our childhood have been made desolate, and are filled with sorrow and mourning, for their young men have gone forth in beauty and strength, and they come not back again. The sick and wounded, the maimed and helpless, the widow and orphan, in every village and hamlet of the land, give evidence of the dreadful character of the contest. We are far removed from the scenes of strife, yet with most intense anxiety do we watch the progress of events. As citizens, we feel deeply, and perhaps sometimes speak bitterly; but I am happy indeed to say that, as Masons, we have continued to gather around our altars; that no sound of confusion or strife has there been heard; and that our brethren appear to have remembered the ancient Charges, and have sedulously excluded from the Lodges all disputes and controversies about politics and political matters, "as what never yet conduced to the welfare of the Lodge, nor ever will."

Amidst the turmoil of civil war a happy note was struck in Boston, Massachusetts, for on October 14 the grand lodge held a special communication to lay the corner-stone of a new temple. The old one had been destroyed by fire on April 6, 1863. A guard of honor comprised of 755 members of the Grand Encampment of Massachusetts and Rhode Island escorted Grand Master William Parkman to the corner of Tremont and Boylston Streets, the site of the new temple. "The march began at about 12 o'clock, and the Procession, moving at quick step—rather too much so for comfort—passed over the route in a little less than two hours." After the ceremonies, 700 guests enjoyed "choice and tempting viands" at Faneuil Hall, which was decorated in a patriotic mode.

The annual communication of the Grand Lodge of Kentucky was held in Louisville on October 17. Grand Master Thomas Sadler spoke of the unhappy condition of the lodges in his state:

I regret to say that a large number of our Lodges have been deprived of the privilege of meeting with us as regularly as in former years, in consequence of the war that has been raging in many parts of our State; yet, through the blessing of God many of our Lodges have prospered and lived in comparative peace. It is to be much lamented that our once happy country has been engaged in a war in which brother is arrayed against brother, father against son, and

226

son against father, in deadly conflict, causing a wide separation between the best and warmest of friends—a state of things, which as a Mason I deeply regret, and hope and pray for a speedy reunion of true fellowship among all, but more particularly among brother Masons.

During the past year many of our friends have fallen in various battles that have been fought in our and sister States. I say sister States, for I am unwilling to give up a single one of them, and pray for a speedy reunion of all the States, by an honorable and satisfactory adjustment of all difficulties between the two contending parties: for this, let us all continue to send up our fervent prayers to Almighty God, so that in the future we may meet on the Level, act by the Plumb, and part upon the Square.

On the following day the Grand Lodge of Kansas was unable to hold its scheduled annual communication because the "State was threatened with invasion, and contending armies struggled on the border. The members were in the field with State militia to repel the advancing foe, and it was altogether impossible" to hold the scheduled communication. The grand master was present, but the attendance was so small he postponed the meeting until December.

The grand master of Ohio, Thomas Sparrow, told his members on October 18 that two members of a subordinate lodge had differences of opinion which threatened to destroy the peace and harmony of their lodge. The deputy grand master was asked to intervene and "by judicious management and fraternal admonitions, he succeeded in effecting an amicable adjustment of the difficulty. The two brethren met upon the level before the altar of Masonry, and there, with true Masonic charity, in the presence and amid the tears of their companions, reconciled their differences."

A convocation of a Royal Arch chapter located in a small town far from the major scenes of the war was abruptly halted on October 19, 1864. Concerning that occurrence, William Bridges wrote in the records of Champlain Chapter No. 1, St. Albans, Vermont:

. . . Being about to confer the degree of Past Master upon Brother Wilcox, when Satan, the Prince of Devils, commenced a raid upon the banks of St. Albans. (Money being the root of all evil.) And robbed them of many thousand dollars. About twenty of the infernal imps of the lower regions, cut and covered with impunity, killed Mr. Marrison, a worthy citizen, which created a great excitement in our quiet village for a half hour, until the troops of his Satanic majesty had departed, which was the reason for not conferring the degree upon our worthy Brother J. M. Wilcox.

The "infernal imps of the lower regions" were 21 Confederate soldiers, under the leadership of Bennett Young, who raided the three banks in St. Albans. The plan had been brought to fruition when the participants met at the Lafayette Hotel, Philipsburg, Quebec, on October 11, 1864. After receiving their orders, the young men (all were between 20 and 26, except one who was 38) separated to meet at an appointed time in the Vermont village.

In order to keep their purpose a complete surprise, the Confederates arrived in St. Albans two or three at a time; took rooms in the American Hotel, Albans House, and the Tremont Hotel; and kept apart until the appointed hour for the raid on the three depositories. During the interim, Young made the acquaintance of one of the young ladies of the town, much to the annoyance of his partners.

As the town clock tolled the hour of three on the afternoon of October 19, 1864, the Franklin County Bank, the First National Bank of St. Albans, and the St. Albans Bank, were simultaneously entered. The employees were dumb-founded to find themselves confronted by men, waving guns, and who were delighted to inform their unwilling listeners, "We are Confederate soldiers who have come to rob your banks and burn your town."

In less than 15 minutes the looting of the banks was completed. Then Young jumped on the steps of the American Hotel and shouted, "This city is now in the possession of the Confederate States of America." But less than a half hour later the Southerners had left the town, hotly pursued by a hastily organized posse. They left behind two wounded citizens of St. Albans, one of them mortally, and several burning buildings. One of the raiders was badly wounded but managed to escape. About the meanest thing they did was to pour Greek fire all

228

over the water closet of the American Hotel causing it to burn for a full day.

Young and his men managed to escape to Canada where they were placed on trial and subsequently released. The $208,000 they had taken, according to some accounts, was turned over to the Confederate authorities in Richmond.

Nearly 50 years later, Bennett Young, while visiting in Montreal, Canada, was entertained by a group of the leading citizens of the town in the Green Mountain state whose banks he had raided. The friendliness of the gathering indicates the forgiving nature and sense of humor of the American people. The group from St. Albans treated Young as though he was a conquering hero; he was no longer "the Prince of Devils."

The Grand Lodge of Colorado, on November 7, took note of the generous gesture of John G. Brandley, a soldier of Company C, First Colorado Cavalry, who deposited $105 with a friend, who was to give it to "the Masonic Fraternity" in the event of Brandley's death. He was killed during a battle with Indians the following June, and the money was turned over to his grand lodge.

Grand Master Henry M. Teller called attention to the lack of Masonic reading and urged the officers of the lodges to induce their members to subscribe to one or more Masonic papers.

The lack of reading material was the subject of an article in the *National Freemason* and reprinted in the *Masonic Monthly*, written by "Brother Shupe":

During a recent visit by myself and a friend, to the armies of the Potomac and the James, we were much impressed with the plentitude of Masonic pins, and also with their evident high appreciation. Particularly among the surgeons was the percentage of Masons large, and very happy are the results which flow from that fact, as many of the sick and convalescent bore witness.

A person who has never been in the army would find it difficult to understand how the finer and social feelings of the men are disregarded in necessary discipline—how completely machine-like, one of a large lot of the same sort, a soldier becomes and is. No antecedent relations of officer to privates is permitted to work disrespect of discipline; there is no bond of sympathy, no level upon which shoulder-straps and stoga-shoes meet, save one, and that one is not disregarded. The Masonic tent only is where men, without distinction of rank, "meet upon the level and part upon the square."

People who witness this in our national armies can understand why it has been remarked that in all times of civil commotion and turblence the institution of Masonry has flourished more vigorously than ever, and that all others during such periods have declined— even the Church. The present specially prosperous condition of the Fraternity in this country furnishes the most conclusive proof of the truth of the observation. It is because its teachings are uniform and simple, and practically inculcate principles of unity, equality, honor, Brotherly-love and truth.

In visiting the various hospitals it was surprising how quick invalid eyes detected our Masonic emblems, and how glad and relieved all who could read them seemed to be. At City Point we noticed a sick man upon his pallet so thin and wan that we did not think it proper to annoy him by conversation, and were walking past his bed when he spied a Masonic paper in our hand, and starting up to rest on his elbow he exclaimed, "What paper is that?" "Are you able to read?" we asked. "Yes, if I had anything to read," he replied. Handing him the paper he seized it with thanks, and oh, with what eager eyes did he scan it! He gave his name as Bro. Clark, of Worth Lodge, No. 210, of New York city. *Claiming of us his fraternal right,* he made known his immediate wants, and they were attended to.

In one case, at Point of Rocks' Hospital, we found a poor old German, who was so near death's door that he could not speak, but he pointed to a Masonic pin in the writer's neck-tie, and in Masonic language told us that he was one of us. Need we say that he was ministered to?

I might indefinitely add instances of such cases; a great number of truthful, unselfish, fraternal attentions on the part of surgeons, officers, and nurses are to be found at every hospital, and should be collated as part of the records of the war.

The great want with all the men, and more particularly the Masons, who, as a class, at home are much accustomed to reading, is the scanty supply of reading matter; nothing could be more grateful to all grades of men, particularly when in hospital or winter quarters, than a good supply of reading matter, to relieve the tedium, and prevent the irksome necessity of counting the pegs in their boots or the stitches in their shirts, for the want of something better to kill time.

Our errand to the army led us to particularly inquire into the condition and needs of the sick and wounded; and with this class more than any other was found evidence of the genuine work of Masonry, and the greatest need of reading matter. If you, Bro. Editor,

230

or the reader of this, could stand by the bedside of one who is compelled to lie upon his back for weeks and sometimes months, and see
no one but the regular nurses and physician, with an occasional
curiosity hunter, in the shape of a visitor, you could realize that
your old papers and read magazines would be by him a thankfully
received gift, more prized than a hundred times its value in green-
backs. If any reader has been away from his home and native
scenes for a long season, and by accident met one familiar with his
early haunts, he knows how much relief it afforded him to talk of
the old and perhaps common tramping ground, discussing various
scenes and remembrances, and how his heart warmed toward that
quasi-friend—that reader can, particularly if he be a Mason, understand how near, how warm and Brother-like, will be the intercourse
of those in the army who can commune upon the reminiscences and
scenes upon that checkered floor upon which both have been equals,
upon which all, from the prince to the peasant, must be equals. . . .

Every man who served in World Wars I and II can attest to
the correctness of that writer's plea for reading matter. Next to
letters from home, the soldier desired a good book, for in every
war the cry has always been "hurry-up—and wait." Much more
time is spent in waiting than in fighting.

The *Masonic Monthly,* in an article entitled, "Masonry on
the Battle-Field," gives a woman's viewpoint of what Freemasonry meant to the men in the war:

Numerous instances have occurred during the present war to show
the power of Masonry over the minds and actions of those who have
been initiated into its mysteries, even during the hottest conflicts
on the battlefield. Amid the confusion and strife of actual, present
war, while the fiercest of human passions are raging, and death and
wounds are being dealt on all sides, the Mason's mystic sign to whose
knowledge may have come instances of this power of Masonry
should make it a rule to record them, or take some method to have
the recollection of them preserved. Such recollections make Masonry
more dear to us, as being the evidence that our principles take a
deeper hold upon its disciples in times which try men's souls than
we are apt in periods of peace to suspect; that Masonry is in deed
and in truth a living power to help and bless all within its circle
of influence.

We have never met with a narrative which better illustrates what
Masonry is accomplishing on the battle-field than has been communicated to us by a young lady friend now employed in one of the
army hospitals. In making this communication to us the writer

remarks with emphasis, *"I can only say that Masons act more like Christians toward their brethren under difficult circumstances than Christians themselves do."*

Here is valuable testimony to the practical character of Freemasonry from a quarter which cannot be expected to know anything of the institution other than from the actions and conduct of its members. Without further comment we will permit the writer to tell her own story.

"In a charge made on the enemy during the great battle of Spottsylvania C. H., May 8th, 1864, our men were repulsed and compelled to leave their dead and wounded on the field. Among the sufferers lay one young Sergeant scarcely able to move, his life-blood flowing rapidly from three severe wounds in thigh, breast and ankle, while the rebels came dashing over the prostrate forms in pursuit of flying troops. Expecting death at any moment, he exerted himself to the utmost, and by means of the mystic sign was so fortunate as to succeed in attracting the attention of the Lieut. Col. commanding the rebel Regiment. The Col. at once ordered a man from the ranks to take him carefully to the rear and treat him kindly. After the rebels had fallen back to their line of defences the officer resumed his brotherly work by seeking out the Union soldier and giving him a letter recommending him to the care of Dr.——, Surgeon, in charge of a Division Hospital in Longstreet's Corps. To this hospital, which was about two miles distant, he was carried, and he soon had the satisfaction of knowing that his wounds had been cared for in the best possible manner, and that he would be provided with everything necessary to facilitate his recovery. Amputation of the left foot had been found unavoidable, and the wound in the breast was considered a dangerous one. But treatment more skilful or tender, his best friends could not have desired for him than he received during the fourteen days of his stay in this place. He was then transferred to Richmond with a special request to Dr.—— having charge of prisoners there, to be sent North by the first flag of truce that should arrive. In Richmond he experienced similar kind attention, was supplied with good and sufficient food, and was the first man paroled when the boat arrived to take our poor fellows back to the protection of the old flag. He reached Annapolis, Aug. 12th, with wounds nearly healed, and bringing with him all the valuables he had about him when captured."

During the annual communication of the Grand Lodge of Virginia a letter was addressed to the Grand Master:

Richmond, Dec. 14th, 1864

W. H. HARMAN:

Most Worshipful Sir and Brother: Just after the battle of the

232

Wilderness—fought last spring—it was my fortune to meet at a Federal field hospital a Federal surgeon, named (I think) McDermot —who represented himself to be the Deputy Grand Master of Pennsylvania—who informed me that he had in his possession the Jewels, Charter, Holy Writings, &c, belonging to the Lodge at Centreville, Va., which he would be pleased to forward to any one I would name, authorized to receive them. I thanked him, and requested him to forward them to your Most Worshipful Grand body, or to Most Worshipful James Evans, or Worshipful John Dove, Grand Secretary.

I visited the hospital in the capacity of surgeon, for the purpose of removing the wounded Confederates held by the Federals.

Very respectfully,
Yours fraternally,
C. W. P. BROCK

A devastating blow to the South occurred on December 21, for after eleven days of siege, Savannah, Georgia fell to the overwhelming strength of the Federal forces. A resolution adopted by the Masonic lodge in the city tells something of what happened after the city was turned over to a Mason from the North:

Solomon's Lodge, No. 1, AFM
Savannah, March 15, 1866

WHEREAS, upon the evacuation of this city by the Confederate forces on the morning of the 21st of December, 1864, the Masonic Hall Building (partly owned by this Lodge) together with the Regalia & furniture and many valuable mementoes of its past history, were placed in imminent danger, from the mobs who were plundering many places in the city, and which would have probably been greatly injured or perhaps destroyed, but for the prompt action of Major Gen. John W. Geary, Commanding the 2nd Division, 20th Army Corps, which constituted the advance of the U. S. Army, who upon being informed of the state of affairs as he marched into the city, promptly placed a strong guard at the disposal of the W. M. of the Lodge, which quickly dispersed the plunderers, before any material damage had been done to the building. Therefore be it,

Resolved: That Solomon's No. 1, AFM remembers with deep gratitude this truly masonic act of kindness on the part of Gen. Geary also other favors which he extended to it while comd'g officer of this post, and would assure him that his treatment of our fraternity, and the citizens of this place, in general, in those trying times gave relief to many anxious hearts, and will always be appreciated by them; and therefore be it further Resolved

That the thanks of this Lodge be and the same we hereby tender to P.G.H.P. Jno. W. Geary of Penn. and that the Secty. be instructed to forward a copy of these Resolutions to our esteemed Brother under the seal of the Lodge and that a copy be furnished to Bro. Mason of the Sav'h. Herald for publication at such time as he shall think proper.

When Geary learned about the resolution and the high esteem in which he was held, he was Governor of Pennsylvania, and wrote the following letter from the state capital:

Harrisburg, Pa.
July 13th, 1866

J. H. Estill, Esq.
    Secy. of Solomon Lodge, No. 1, A.F.M.
    Savannah, Ga.
    Dear Sir & Bro.

Through the politeness of brother A. Wilber Esq., I am in receipt of a printed copy of the proceedings relative to myself, at a meeting of Solomons Lodge, on Thursday evening March 15th, 1866. Your letter concerning the original copy sent me at the time, was not received.

Please return my most hearty thanks to the brothers of Solomon's Lodge for their kind remembrances, and still kinder expressions to myself, for the part I was permitted to take at the capture of Savannah, and in the management and government of the city while it was under my command.

When the City of Savannah was surrendered into my hands by your late Worthy Mayor, Hon. R. C. Arnold, it was done in the following language, "As Chief Magistrate of the city, I respectfully request your protection of the lives and private property of the citizens and of our women and children. Trusting that this appeal to your generosity and humanity may favorably influence your actions."

My actions under these circumstances is well known, and those who best understand it, have in almost every possible manner conveyed to me their thanks and gratitude for the manner in which the government of the city was conducted, and for the treatment which was meted to your citizens.

In the performance of those duties, I was actuated by no motives, but which were in every respect compatible with those of a soldier, dictated by the true principles of charity and humanity. For the spirit and action thus manifested, I am entitled to no extraordinary credit or praise; for they should pervade the human heart in every circumstance of life and should be particularly prominent in every action of those connected with Freemasonry. Since then the rude scenes of war have passed away and fratricidal strife has ceased, and peace again spreads her genial influences over common country. God grant we may ever rejoice under one Flag, and one destiny.

We have reason to be thankful that our lives and health have been spared amid the chances and changes of the stormy period it has been our lot to witness, and for the generally increasing harmony and prosperity which seems to prevail throughout the nation. And here I feel again justified in referring to our beloved institution, by saying that to Freemasonry the people of the country are indebted for many mitigations of the sufferings caused by the direful passions of war.

With hearty desires for the health, happiness and prosperity of the members of Solomons Lodge, and again thanking them for their kind expressions, I have the honor to be,

Yours truly and fraternally,
Jno. W. Geary

The year 1864 ended with much of the South in the possession of Federal forces. One bright spot for the Confederacy was the stalemate at Petersburg, where Grant was still being kept away from Richmond. That brightness was dimmed by the defeat of McClellan by the incumbent Lincoln for the presidency of the United States. Although the Confederate States did not realize it, the election of Andrew Johnson as vice-president would do much to eventually reunite the nation.

It was estimated that in the federal Army 11% were freemasons, and slightly over that figure in the Confederate forces. From Illinois alone, 774 officers were furnished for the Union. They comprised five major generals, Ransom, Hurlburt, Logan, McClernard, and Palmer; nine brigadier generals, Brayman, White, Paine, Cook, Ross, McCook, McArthur, Smith, and Ducat; 61 colonels; 42 lieutenant-colonels; 40 surgeons; 38 majors; 10 chaplains; 278 captains; 27 quartermasters; 264 lieutenants; and an untold number of enlisted men.

More Masons were to join the fight; more Masons were to die for the cause they felt just, before a welcome peace was restored and the states were united once again.

235

CHAPTER XIX

The Fighting Ends

◇◇

*So long as men love liberty more than life it-
self; so long as they treasure the priceless privileges bought with blood of our forefathers; so
long as the principles of truth, justice and charity for all remain deeply rooted in human
hearts, I shall continue to be the enduring banner of the United States of America. I AM
OLD GLORY!*
The Civil War Centennial Commission

WITH THE BEGINNING of a new year, President
Davis' troubles with his congress increased. Few of the
Confederate congressmen were satisfied with him or his cabinet.
To help save his president further embarrassment, Secretary of
War James A. Seddon resigned.

Edward S. Ellis, in his *Low Twelve*, relates a story about
Seddon that started on a passenger steamer on the Mississippi
River, ten years before the outbreak of hostilities. Seddon, a
passenger on the steamer, contracted small-pox. A Mason named
John Wilkins went to his aid, saved him from being thrown
overboard, and nursed him back to health.

During the war Wilkins was arrested, accused of burning
bridges in the Confederacy, and placed in prison. Some weeks
later he gave a Quaker, who visited the prison every day, a note
to deliver for him. It was answered on the day he was to be shot
when the provost-marshal handed him a yellow piece of paper.
The telegram read:

WAR DEPARTMENT, Richmond, Va.
Provost-Marshall, Knoxville, Tenn:
Release John Wilkins from custody at once and do not allow him
to be molested or disturbed in person or property. Allow him to

pass back and forth between the Confederate and Federal lines without question.

By Order of

JAMES A. SEDDON

Secretary of War, C.S.A.

Davis reluctantly accepted Seddon's resignation and called a Mason, John C. Breckinridge, to Richmond to become the sixth, and last, secretary of war for the Confederate States. As such he was to play an important part in the last days of his government.

A letter from a Mason to a friend describes the difficulty members of the Order had in finding lodge communications to attend:

Savannah, Georgia, *January 6, 1865*

Bro. Reynolds: It is known to many of my Illinois friends that I abandoned the publication of the Greene County *Loyalist,* and enlisted as a private soldier in Walker's famous Missouri Light Battery. I have written to various papers giving accounts of our marches and battles, and have also written to Masonic Brothers, of our great deprivation of Lodge privileges. But once within the last year have I beheld the "Great Light" or heard the sound of the Master's gavel calling the Craftsmen to labor, and that once was last night. In company with Bro. Curtis, of Illinois, I sought admission into Solomon's Lodge No. 1, and after patiently waiting until some hundred or so officers of the army (and some privates, too,) had passed through the hands of the examining committee, I was ushered into the most beautiful Lodge room it has ever been my privilege to enter, just in time to see the closing scene in the raising of a Brother to the sublime degree of a Master Mason. The chair (or rather, "throne",) was filled by the Master of the Lodge, Rich Turner, Esq., a venerable, intelligent and worthy Mason. The room was crowded to a degree of uncomfortableness, by citizens and soldiers, (Generals, Colonels, Majors, Captains and Privates, mingling together as if such a thing as *rank* existed not in the service). The work was beautifully executed, and everything seemed to conspire to render the evening one of pleasure and of profit. By my side sat a rebel prisoner, who had got permission to visit the Lodge without a guard, the word of a Master Mason being a sufficient guarantee that he would return promptly to his quarters when the Lodge should close. Rebels and Union men mingled in that throng as if no war was going on, and I doubt not each one prayed that the clangor of arms might soon cease. Oh! Masonry, thy influence over the human soul is truly wonderful! A little incident occurred worthy of record. An officer of the Federal Army brought into the Lodge a "collar and apron," both very beautiful, for the purpose of having them restored to the rightful owner. It seems that a party of our soldiers were pillaging the house of a rebel, carrying off, not eatables, (a soldier's lawful prize) but everything else that struck their fancy. The lady at the sight of the devastation of her household, exclaimed, *"Is there a Freemason here who will protect me?"* The words ran like an electric spark through the nerves of Capt.——, who instantly commenced an indiscriminate booting of the mob from the premises. Pursuing his way with the column, he was informed a soldier had carried off from the house alluded to, some articles pertaining to Masonry. The soldier was forced to give up his spoils, (of what use to him?) and the gallant and true Brother carried them safely to Savannah, and at the meeting last night, placed them in hands that will convey them to the rightful owner. This incident affected me more than anything that has ever come to my notice in our noble Institution. God bless Freemasonry.

I saw in this Lodge a Bible, presented to it by General Oglethorpe, which is highly prized.

Fraternally,   ISAAC H. BOYLE

The Grand Chapter of Florida met on January 9, 1865, and the grand secretary, Hugh A. Corley, reported the loss of the jewels, furniture, charter, and books of Tampa Chapter. Federal troops had plundered them during their raid on Tampa.

On the same day Grand Master Thomas Hayward, during the annual communication of the Grand Lodge of Florida, expressed concern over the type of members admitted:

Once more by the permission of Divine Providence we have assembled to review the action of the past and to consult in reference to the future. Many of our Masonic friends, instead of being with their Lodges and here to-day in attendance on this Grand Lodge, are far away, battling for freedom and independence. May God, in His infinite goodness, so dispose the hearts and minds of all concerned as to bring about a speedy and honorable peace, and all return home and enjoy the comforts and blessings of which they are now deprived!

But few of our Lodges have had the opportunity of assembling as heretofore, but some have been engaged more than usual, and have done much which I fear will not redound to advantage. Some have initiated members residing in other jurisdictions. Soldiers have been admitted, emergency declared, jurisdiction waived and degrees conferred without sufficient evidence of character. All this is calculated to create dissatisfaction and disturb the harmony among our sister Lodges.

Two days later, far removed from the sunny climate of Florida and the war, in the land of snow-crested mountains, the Grand Lodge of Vermont met for its annual communication. Grand Master Leverett B. Englesby told his members:

War still exists in our midst; and as war must necessarily be fierce, cruel, bloody. Our peculiar mission is a peaceful one, and yet obedient to the call of duty; recognizing the right of the government to the service of its citizens; many a brave one has gone forth from amongst us. The blood of many a noblehearted Mason has moistened the battle-fields of the contending hosts; in the silence of many a lonely grave, far away from their loved native hills, rests many a noble form. Scarred, mutilated forms are amongst us, bearing silent, eloquent testimony to all they have done, all they have suffered. Vacant chairs are in all our Lodges; eloquent voices will no more be heard. Of those who have thus passed away, nought but pleasant memories remain to us. These memories let us cherish, ever remembering that as we leave their perishable bodies amongst the lowly slain, that immortal part remains, with which, our Masonic teaching tells us, we shall, brethren, in some happier time meet again. Of many kindnesses conferred, courtesies extended, even while bitter feelings would seem to be most violently engendered and aroused, it may not, perhaps, be well to speak, lest we seem to magnify ourselves. It is pleasant, however, to know, that while in no particular have duties been neglected, or failed to be discharged to the uttermost that have been or could be required, Masonic vows have not lost their force; and brethren, when it was proper for them so to do, have not failed with kind words and kindlier acts to respond to the claims of Brotherhood.

In Michigan, on the same day, January 11, Grand Master Lovell Moore refused to recognize Masons who had received their degrees in a military lodge in the state of Mississippi, working under a dispensation from the Grand Lodge of Indiana. He claimed it was an "unjustifiable infringement upon the prerogatives of the Grand Lodge of Mississippi." He also took to task the Grand Lodge of the District of Columbia for invading the jurisdiction of Virginia.

Grand Master William S. Patton, on January 23, told his grand lodge about some of the damage done by invaders:

Since last we met, many scenes have transpired. Our beloved Mississippi has been shaken to its very foundation; our property destroyed, dwellings reduced to ashes and helpless women and children driven out and thrown upon the cold charities of the world and that too, by the people of the Northern States who profess Christianity. Nor is this all—the Masonic Temples of our State have been robbed and desecrated by the Vandals of the North.

Canton Lodge No. 28 was visited by the Yankees, the Charter stolen, together with most of the books, jewels and other property, and the greater portions of the Lodges of Madison County suffered the same fate. Oxford Lodge No. 35 lost its Charter and the hall was very much injured.

The Yankee soldiers dressed themselves in the stolen Royal Arch regalia and paraded the streets in mockery of our Institution, and in August last, during Smith's raid, the hall which cost $10,000.00 was burned by them.

Evergreen Lodge No. 77 and Sageville No. 186 were robbed of the Holy Bible, jewels and furniture, the torch applied to the buildings and burned to the ground. Scott No. 80, Iuka No. 94, Satartia No. 176, and many others have scarcely a vestige left. Many are not able to meet as a Lodge on account of the depredations committed by the Federal soldiery.

I am truly sorry, brethren, and regret exceedingly that our own troops, in some instances, have done worse than the friends of the North.

Information comes to me from John A. Quitman Lodge No. 204, that Colonel Scott's cavalry, whilst commanded by Captain Bryant, broke open a lodge, robbed it of its jewels, and did divers other injuries, all of which were duly reported to Colonel Scott.

Daleville Lodge No. 151 has twice been broken open by the Confederate cavalry, the books and furniture mutilated and part of it carried away.

It has been justly remarked by my predecessor, [P. G. M. Richard Cooper] that hitherto, it has been the custom of civilized nations at war to respect the property, jewels, furniture and records of Masonic Lodges.

President Lincoln and his secretary of state met three commissioners from the Confederate States aboard a steamer at Hampton Roads on February 3, 1865. The "peace conference" brought no results and the war continued.

The Confederacy may have asked for that conference because the Confederate soldiers at Petersburg, and everywhere else, had but little food. On December 14 Lee had telegraphed Davis that his army was without meat. The Confederate Congress was informed, in a secret session, that there was not enough meat in the South for the armies it had in the field; that meat had to be

240

obtained from abroad. As the days wore on the soldiers of the South were being starved into submission, for not only meat was scarce, or non-existent, so were all of the necessities of existence.

Sherman left Savannah on February 1 to march through the Carolinas. He left a trail of devastation and destruction, burning and plundering, in his wake. "The roads were covered with butchered cattle, hogs, mules, and the costliest furniture."

The Federal forces reached Columbia, South Carolina, on the 17th and it was surrendered in the hope that it would be spared. It was not. Even the Catholic convent, presided over by a nun who had educated Sherman's daughter, was burned, despite the Mother Superior's plea to Sherman. Eighty-four squares of buildings were destroyed, "the capitol building, six churches, 11 banking establishments, the schools of learning, the shops of art and trade, of invention and manufacture, shrines equally of religion, benevolence, and industry."

The Grand Lodge of Louisiana met on February 13 and Grand Master Fellows reported the deaths of "Thos. W. Peyton, P. M. Quitman Lodge No. 76, killed in battle in Tennessee; [and] Seith R. Field, P. M. Quitman Lodge No. 76, killed in the battle of Mansfield, La., in April 1864."

The grand secretary, Samuel M. Todd reported:

The 29th of July, I received a letter from Captain S. M. Thomas, member of Atchafalaya Lodge No. 163, of this State, a prisoner of war, on Johnson's Island, Ohio, stating that there were confined on that Island between five and six hundred members of our fraternity who were suffering for many of the necessaries of life, and appealing for assistance to their brethren of this city, also stating that a Masonic Association had been formed on the Island, of which Colonel L. M. Lewis, of Missouri, was president, that a considerable amount had already been disbursed by the Association in supplying the want of the sick and suffering among them, but that their funds had now become exhausted. Having laid this letter before the M. W. Grand Master, I, with his sanction, addressed letters to the Lodges then holding meetings in this city, nearly all of whom responded in the most liberal spirit.

For this cause, $854 was collected and later the grand secretary received another communication from Johnson's Island, that one from James Parker Irwin, Secretary of the Masonic Association there:

I am instructed by the President of our association, Bro. J. J. Davis, to thank you in the name of the association for the great material aid which has been afforded us, and to inform you that the necessity no longer exists for its continuance, as our treasury is well supplied by the noble Masonic kindness of the Craftsman residing inside of the Federal lines. From you we have received $600., from the Masons of St. Louis $165., of Nashville $165., of New York $20., and in Boston they have on hand, subject to our order, several hundred dollars. The Masons of the city of Louisville have supplied us with at least $300 worth of hospital stores and medicines, and those in St. Louis have supplied us with four boxes of hospital stores. You stated in your letter that the Masons of New Orleans would soon send us further aid; but, should it not have been already sent when this reached you, inform them of the contents of this letter, and so have the aid contemplated for us applied to the relief of situations of greater distress. I will not attempt to express our gratitude to the craft for their Masonic kindness to us in the dark hours of our distress; the heart of a Mason can feel it, but no tongue can express it. . . .

Todd also reported receiving the seal belonging to St. Joseph Lodge, No. 79 from the gunboat *Switzerland*. It had been picked up in the road near St. Joseph, in Tensas Parish. Concerning Atchafalaya Lodge, he wrote:

I received, in May, a letter from the former Secretary of this Lodge, Bro. F. H. Babitt, stating that the Charter and some of the property of the Lodge was in the possession of one of the members at Simmsport, but that the Lodge had ceased to work since its effects had been stolen and the Lodge room destroyed by fire. Lieutenant Swift of the 150th Regiment, New York Volunteers, instituted enquiries with regard to the plundering of this Lodge room. . . .

Before Beauregard evacuated Charleston a story unfolded that was reported in the *Masonic Monthly:*

The world knows well of the bombardment and partial destruction of the ancient city where treason was nurtured and matured as its chosen seat. The world has not, however, traced the fortunes and fate of a loyal youth wounded and made a prisoner in the storming of the fort where our National flag was first dishonored. Too young to be admitted to our Fraternity he knew that in the devoted city, was a skilful physician and surgeon, who had met his father at the Masonic altar. When the fortune of war threw him into that city a fatally wounded prisoner, he had only to make himself known as the son of a Mason whom the Grand Lodge had delighted to honor, to secure the most devoted care while life lingered, and then to receive Christian burial with the good physician and his family as mourners, and a flag of truce bears words of sympathy through rebel lines to the mourning ones at home.

Toward the end of February, Sheridan's cavalry began raiding almost at will in Virginia, while Sherman continued his destructive march, and Grant kept Lee's main force at Petersburg.

Mrs. W. P. McGuire, in the *Confederate Veteran*, wrote of an incident that involved Sheridan's cavalry, in March of 1865. Her father, the Attorney General of Virginia, sent her mother and her six children to Ivy, some five miles from Charlottesville, believing they would be safer there than in Richmond. Up until that time the only Federal soldiers they had seen were prisoners of war. That was soon changed.

The raiders arrived early one morning, pointed "their pistols at the heads of the 'damned women,' . . . and ordered them to give up everything in the way of provisions."

Our terror was beyond description, not knowing what would happen next [wrote Mrs. McGuire]. When we thought probably the house might be burned, Mrs. [Meriweather] Anderson turned to my mother and said: "My father and husband were both Masons, and I have taken a woman's degree, and I have a Mason's apron. I am going to get it and see what can be done with it." She took it from the bureau drawer and ran with it to a porch. The house was surrounded by cavalrymen, who were guarding it while the others were ransacking the inside. She stood up on a bench, holding this little apron in her hand, and cried: "Is there no one here who can protect the widow of a Mason?" Instantly a soldier dismounted, grabbed the apron, examined it, then went inside and ordered every soldier out. The house and place were cleared of them, and for three days that the army was there, although encamped in the field near the house, not a soldier came inside the yard gate.

It was the most thrilling scene that I ever witnessed, and one that we always felt should be told to show the power of Free Masonry. I have often wondered who that soldier was, and if the scene could have been as impressive to him as it was to us.

It was during one of Sheridan's raids on Waynesboro that the grand master of Virginia, William H. Harman, was mortally wounded. Twenty months later the Grand Lodge of Virginia took an unprecedented action when it adopted the following:

243

Whereas, in the providence of Almighty God our beloved and M. W. Bro. William H. Harman, Grand Master of the Grand Lodge of Virginia was suddenly and violently taken from us by the hand of death, in the spring of 1865, in the full prime and vigor of manhood, and with his armor on, leaving behind him a widow and six orphaned children to mourn his loss; and whereas, it is represented to this Grand Lodge that the pecuniary circumstances of Bro. Harman's family are embarrassed, and that, to support herself and little ones, his widow, in a noble spirit of self-reliance, has undertaken to conduct a school in the town of Staunton: Therefore,

Resolved, That this Grand Lodge deeply sympathized with her condition, and most earnestly commend the school to the support and confidence of the members of our fraternity, in the hope that its success will vindicate the affection with which the memory of our beloved Brother must be ever cherished by all Masons throughout the jurisdiction of the Grand Lodge of Virginia.

The committee to whom was referred the resolution of Bro. Covell, beg leave to report the following resolutions:

Resolved, That in view of the fact that his widow has undertaken a school for the support of herself and family, we, as Masons of the Grand Lodge of the State of Virginia, do most cordially accord to her our support.

Resolved, That this school shall be known by the name of the "Masonic Female Seminary of Staunton."

Resolved, That this Grand Lodge does most earnestly exhort and entreat that the fraternity generally throughout this jurisdiction shall aid and assist this enterprise as far as they can consistently with their duties as Masons.

Resolved, That in the performance of this our sacred duty, as Masons of Virginia, we will ever cherish him in our memory as an upright man and Mason.

Respectfully submitted.

> J. C. COVELL,
> JOHN P. LITTLE,
> WM. B. TALIAFERRO.

D. C. Gallaher, not a Mason, wrote an article for the *Confederate Veteran* magazine about "Masonic Loyalty and Chivalry in the War" with a doctor who was to become world renowned as the central figure.

General Jubal Early's cavalry was overtaken by the superior forces of General Philip Sheridan at Waynesboro, Virginia, on March 2, 1865. Although the Confederates fought valiantly, they were forced to retreat.

In the flight, Dr. Hunter McQuire, medical director of Early's staff (as he had been of Stonewall Jackson's), attempted to jump his horse over a rail fence. The horse fell sprawling, throwing its rider. When the doctor arose he looked squarely into a Federal carbine. McQuire made a Masonic sign. A Union officer rode up, knocked the gun down, and said, "This man is my prisoner."

Soon after the battle was over, it became cold and rain fell in torrents. Dr. McQuire suggested to his captor they seek food and shelter in the home of a friend of his. The officer gladly accepted his offer and a short time later they were sitting down to a hot meal served by Mrs. Gallaher.

While they were eating the Union officer eagerly inquired about a Knight Templar chart hanging on the wall. He was informed it belonged to his absent host. That is why the officer stopped the plundering and burning of the out-buildings of the Gallaher estate and stationed Federal troops around the grounds.

At Five Forks on April 1, Sheridan attacked Pickett with an overwhelming force and drove him from his entrenchments with a heavy loss in lives and prisoners. The following day Grant assaulted the whole Confederate line about Petersburg and A. P. Hill was killed. And on that second day of April 1865, Petersburg and Richmond were evacuated.

Sergeant J. B. Thompson of Company F, 16th Mississippi Regiment, years later, told of his experiences at Fort Gregg, near Petersburg on that day the Confederates started their last retreat. Early in the morning "the famous 29th Army Corps on the Federal side, or thirty Federals to one Confederate," attacked. The Southern forces managed to check two Union attacks while Lee's troops crossed the Appomattox River. Although the mission of the men in "Fort Hell" had been accomplished, Major Chew refused to surrender.

When the third assault came, the fort was quickly filled by the enemy [said Sergeant Thompson]. We had no time to load and fire. We broke our guns and used the barrels for clubs. But what could we do against so many? General Lee, seeing the work of extermination, sent a courier to a near-by battery with orders to open fire on

245

friends and foes alike. Shot and shell quickly rained into the fort, checking the slaughter. There were left of that three hundred Confederate heroes only twenty-seven alive, nineteen of them badly wounded. Among the eight unwounded was M. G. Turner, a Free Mason. He gave the Masonic sign of distress to a Federal colonel, who grasped him by the hand and drew him from the crowd and protected him from massacre.

While Grant, with his big guns, was knocking at the gates of Richmond, Mount Vernon Lodge, No. 4, in Providence, Rhode Island, held its 67th annual communication. About that the Providence *Evening Press* reported:

Major General Burnside, who was expected to be present, having been unavoidably detained, sent a brief note, enclosing the following, which was received with applause:

"Abraham Lincoln! His integrity, loyalty, courage, determination and faith in the great truths, enunciated by Saint Paul to the men of Athens, that 'God hath made of one blood all nations of men to dwell on the face of the earth,' and also by the signers of the Declaration of Independence, that 'all men are equal,' have made him a fit instrument in the hands of Providence to carry our people through the fearful struggle now being enacted, and we promise him and his officers, now leading our armies, our cordial support, confident they will succeed in establishing the authority of the government and in making it respected at home and abroad."

The article goes on to tell about the drinking of various toasts, and dwells at length upon the exercises of the evening.

On the Sabbath morning, April 2, the streets of Richmond were quiet; not a vehicle moved; not a single sign of war was visible; everything spoke of peace; the sound of church bells fell pleasantly on the ears of the church-goers; nothing was present to warn the citizens that the capital of a nation was about to crumple and fall.

One of the church-goers was President Davis, and while he sat in his pew in St. Paul's Church, he was handed a slip of paper. It contained the news that turned the city of Richmond into a bedlam. Not immediately, but gradually the disorder increased until, by nightfall, disorder, pillaging, mad revelry, and confusion ran rampant.

To make the devastation worse, the Confederate forces set fire to the four principle tobacco warehouses of the city, destroyed the bridges across the James River, and blew up the ships, *Richmond* and *Virginia*. The warehouses, located near the center of the city, soon spread the fire to other buildings, and continued to spread until the following evening, despite the efforts of the Federal troops to stop it.

While "groups of women and children crawled under shelters of broken furniture in the Capitol square; [and] hundreds of homeless persons laid down to sleep in the shadows of the ruins of Richmond," the North celebrated the downfall of the capital of the Confederacy. And while Davis and his cabinet were escaping, Lee was fighting toward Appomattox.

When Lee reached Amelia Court House he expected to find large quantities of supplies—supplies of food, arms, and ammunition his men needed badly. They were not there. The train carrying them had hurried to Richmond without bothering to stop.

On Sunday, April 9, General Grant's headache left him, for with all hope gone, General Lee sent the Federal commander a note agreeing to accept Grant's earlier terms of surrender.

In the home of Wilmer McLean at Appomattox Court House, Lee waited for General Grant and his aides to arrive. The owner of the house, McLean, had owned a home near Manassas which Beauregard had used as his headquarters for a time during the first full-scale battle of the war. To avoid further war activity he had moved to the quiet village of Appomattox, and once again found himself surrounded by soldiers.

Lee and Grant were friendly throughout the solemn discussions that took place, and when the terms were finally decided agreeably to both, Ely Parker, a Mason and full-blooded Indian, was given the task of writing the final draft (because "his handwriting presented a better appearance than that of any one else on the staff").

General Lee bid his command a sorrowful farewell the following day and left for his home in Richmond. Grant took most of his staff to Washington. He left the Masonic general, Joshua L. Chamberlain to accept the surrender.

Three days after the terms of surrender had been agreed upon, the soldiers of the Army of Northern Virginia walked up the hill from the tiny mouth-formed waters of the Appomattox River. The remnants of the Old Stonewall Brigade, hating to lay down their arms, were in the lead. Then Chamberlain, whom even Southerners years later termed "a great Yankee general," ordered his men to give the surrendering Confederates a full military salute!

The complexion changed. Instead of a humiliating "walk up the hill," the Confederates regained their pride, snapped to smart military routine, and responded to Chamberlain's dignified honor. Late that day the last arms were stacked.

Before Lee's surrender, Charleston had been forced to capitulate. Shortly after its fall, the following order was issued:

GENERAL ORDERS NO. 50
WAR DEPARTMENT, ADJUTANT-GENERAL'S OFFICE, Washington, March 27, 1865

Ordered: *First,* That at the hour of noon, on the 14th day of April, 1865, Brevet Major-General Anderson will raise and plant upon the ruins of Fort Sumter, in Charleston harbor, the *same* United States flag which floated over the battlements of that fort during the rebel assault, and which was lowered and saluted by him, and the small force of his command, when the works were evacuated on the 14th of April, 1861.

Second, That the flag, when raised, be saluted by one hundred guns from Fort Sumter, and by a national salute from every fort and rebel battery that fired upon Fort Sumter.

Third, That suitable ceremonies be had upon the occasion, under the direction of Major-General William T. Sherman, whose military operations compelled the rebels to evacuate Charleston, or, in his absence, under the charge of Major-General Q. A. Gilmore, commanding the Department. Among the ceremonies will be the delivery of an address by the Rev. Henry Ward Beecher.

Fourth, That the naval forces at Charleston, and their commander on that station be invited to participate in the ceremonies of the occasion.

Official.

By order of the President of the United States.

EDWIN M. STANTON, *Secretary of War.*
E. D. TOWNSEND, *Assistant Adjutant-General.*

Among the men who were honored by being invited to attend the ceremonies at the Fort was Peter Hart, a member of Park Lodge, No. 516, New York City. It was he who risked his life during the bombardment in April, 1861, to nail the American flag to the top of the staff from which it had been shot. His heroism was appreciated even by the Confederates on the shore, who cheered him heartily.

Once again Hart fastened the same battle-scarred flag he had rescued four years earlier to the halyards while the spectators cheered. Then at noon on April 14, Robert Anderson raised the tattered flag that he had lowered four years before. The salutes were tumultuous. The Reverend Beecher made an oration that was interrupted repeatedly by thunderous applause, and after the benediction was pronounced "six deafening cheers were given for the old flag replaced upon Sumter; and three times three for President Lincoln, General Robert Anderson, and the soldiers and sailors."

That night "nothing could be seen in the darkness until, as if by magic, at a signal from the flagship, the entire harbor for miles around was brilliantly illuminated. Every vessel and transport and monitor was ablaze with many-colored fires. Each mast and sail and rope was aglow with light. From every deck came the roar and glare of rockets, darting in quick procession to the sky, then turning and descending in showers of golden rain."

"Old Glory" was once again to fly over every state that had earlier comprised the United States of America and who were to become once again united.

CHAPTER XX

An Assassin Strikes

<><><><><><><><><><><><><><><><><><><><><><><><><><><><><><><><><><><><>

> *"A great man has fallen in Israel." The Chief Magistrate of this mighty nation has fallen— not upon the battlefield, amid the thunder of hostile cannon, the clashing of the sword and bayonet, and the discharge of death-dealing musketry, but by the hand of an assassin—his work unfinished, and his kind and genial nature extinguished forever.*
>
> JOHN F. HOUSTON

WHILE THE celebration of the raising of the flag of the United States was at its height in Charleston, President Abraham Lincoln was shot. In a theatre Lincoln had not wanted to attend, John Wilkes Booth turned a rejoicing nation into one of sorrow.

Although Lincoln was not a Mason, many of the grand lodges and their subordinates could not let his death pass unnoticed.

The grand master of the grand lodge in the nation's capital, George C. Whiting, told his members on May 2:

The Lodges in this jurisdiction are in a prosperous condition and entire harmony prevails among the craft, and but for the great sin which has culminated in the assassination of the Chief Magistrate of our nation, this meeting would have been one of universal pleasure and rejoicing. "Grim visaged war hath smoothed his wrinkled front," and the birds and flowers of genial spring were inviting us forth to rejoice in anticipation of the glorious resurrection from the tomb, which reviviscence of nature so beautifully exemplifies. Peace had begun to shed her gentle and healing influence over a land long cursed with the rude blasts of war. But an all-wise and inscrutable Providence had decreed that our joy should not be unmingled with grief.

On the evening of the 14th of April—a day which had been

piously observed by the Christian world as the anniversary of the cruel murder of the Prince of Peace—our honored and beloved President, whilst enjoying a brief relaxation from the responsibilities and cares of his high official station, was stricken down by the hand of a wretched and misguided man. His crime no mortal thought can measure, and none but Him who hath said 'vengeance is mine, I will repay,' can adequately punish. He stands before the bar of the Judge Eternal, and our just though puny anger is hushed in the awful wrath of offended Deity.

As members of a loyal and order-loving association, peculiarly bound to be peaceable subjects to the civil powers, and never to be concerned in plots of conspiracies against the peace and welfare of the nation, nor to behave undutifully to magistrates, are called to share in the deep and universal sorrow, it is meet that we should recognize that amiable and virtuous conduct, and the inflexible fidelity to his trust, which so marked him as the fit successor to our illustrious brother—the great and good Washington—and in some appropriate form give expression to our sense of the loss our country has sustained—for, in the language of the great poet, he

> "Hath borne his faculties so meek hath been
> So clear in his great office, that his virtues
> Will plead like angels, trumper-ton'g, against
> The deep damnation of his taking off;
> And pity, like a naked, new-born babe,
> Striding the blast, or heaven's cherubim, hors'd
> Upon the sightless couriers of the air,
> Shall blow the horrid deed in every eye
> That tears shall drown the wind."

Before the communication ended a lengthy resolution was adopted praising Lincoln, and the grand lodge was ordered into mourning for a period of six months.

Grand Master John F. Houston, of the border state of Missouri, on May 22, said:

Brethren . . . how true it is, "that in the midst of life we are in death." . . . Is there a crime "beneath the roof of Heaven that stains the soul of man with more infernal hue than damn'd assassination?" Who can foresee the consequences of this cruel and most dastardly act? When peace, descending with "healing on its wings," was about to enfold this bleeding country in its angelic embrace, a demon from hell, in the likeness of a human being, by one fell blow shattered the hopes and expectations of nearly thirty millions of freemen, and for a time left them in despair.

251

But the Republic still lives; lives in all that constitutes freedom under and by virtue of law; lives in the affection of a free people, purified by much suffering; lives in the hopes, the aspirations and yearning of the hearts of the millions of the down-trodden of every clime, country, language, and religion; lives, and will live, until the Archangel of God shall pronounce, in trumpet tones, that time shall be no more, until,

> Wrapt in flames, the realms of ether glow,
> And Heaven's last thunder shakes the world below.

On June 6, Grand Master Edward A. Guilbert of the Northern state of Iowa told his members:

. . . Truly, the cloud has turned a "silver lining" to the light, but yet like a scintilliant diamond in a setting of jet, that "silver lining" is bordered with the emblems of mourning. Even in the hour of victory, while the glad Io! rang over the jubilant north and *the recreated south,* "there was death in the White House;" the head of the nation—the wise and pure—the clement and faithful president was "done to death" by the assassin's bullet, and he who was fast becoming the idol of his countrymen, was not! . . . Mason's hands assisted to bear him to the "equal grave," Mason's Lodges were clad in the emblems of mourning for departed worth, and Masons mingled their laments with those of the nation. . . . And it was fitting that Masons should thus evince their love of country and their regard for its murdered ruler, who, though he was not a Mason, revered the order, and was himself composed of the stuff out of which the most capable, the most benignant fraters are made. . . .

A Northern Grand Royal Arch Chapter took note of the death of the President when the grand high priest of New Hampshire, John R. Holbrook, on June 13, told his Companions:

. . . And now the whole nation mourns the loss of our honored chief magistrate, Abraham Lincoln, stricken down by the hand of an assassin; and well may the nation mourn, for he has been the leader in the midst of all our perils, has safely guided our ship of state through its storm of war unto the haven of peace. We mourn for him as an honest, Christian man—as one who inspired the people with his confidence, and who exercised his power with "malice towards none, and with charity for all."

The grand secretary of the Grand Chapter of Alabama,

Daniel Sayre, felt called upon to defend the South, as far as the assassination of Lincoln was concerned, for on December 5, 1865 he wrote:

Your committee regret to perceive, that there is still a spice of bitterness prevailing in the hearts of some of our northern Companions, and tincturing their actions and expressions. This fact is the more observable in the proceedings of the Grand Chapter of Indiana. The Grand Chapter met on the 17th of May last. At that time the Confederacy had virtually ceased to exist. Petersburg had been evacuated, Richmond given up to the victors, and General Lee had surrendered. Under these circumstances it might have been thought that a better feeling would have taken hold of the hearts of our northern Companions; that kindness would have rooted out all disposition to hate; and that the olive-branch would have been extended for our acceptance, and not that the waters of Marah would have been offered to our lips. But instead of exhibiting this friendly and masonic spirit towards us of the south, the Grand High Priest, Solomon P. Bayless, although writing from a bed of sickness, which he was not able to leave to attend the convocation of the Grand Chapter, does not hesitate to declare, in speaking of the murder of President Lincoln, that he fell by the hand of an assassin, instigated by the same spirit that inaugurated and carried on the rebellion against the government. And the committee, to which was confided the duty of reporting suitable resolutions in regard to the same matter, speaks of his homicide as "one of the natural and legitimate results of this ill-conceived and unnatural rebellion." Now, we do not propose to inaugurate any discussion upon the subject of the late unhappy war; we desire, on the other hand, that it should be forgotten as soon as possible; that all traces of it should be wiped out; and that a spirit of masonic and friendly comity should be cultivated. But when the people of the south are put upon the same footing, are said to be imbued with the same spirit, and actuated by the same motives, with assassins and cut-throats, we are compelled to enter our indignant protest. We are neither. We fought honorably, and fairly, and we may be permitted to say, bravely, for the achievement of certain results. We have been disappointed in our calculations, and we submit to our fate with the spirit of men. The death of President Lincoln could neither help the cause of the south, nor retard the progress of the north, consequently upon his decease, as a base, we have erected no superstructure, least of all had we contemplated it as occurring in the manner in which it took place. He died not by the hand, or at the instigation (as far as we know) of any citizen of the late Confederacy. For his death we are

253

not responsible. Our skirts are clear. Our hands are clean. There is no blood upon them, and therefore we need not implore, the language of the great poet, "out, damned spot."

An innocent victim of the tragic happenings in the Ford Theatre was a Mason who would rather confer the Master Mason's Degree than "receive the plaudits of the people in the theatres of the world." Edwin Booth was the brother of the man who mortally wounded Lincoln. In order to reassure him of their esteem, his lodge wrote him a letter which was published in the *New-York Times,* Sunday, June 4, 1865:

New-York Lodge No. 330, F&A.M.
New-York, 1865

Edwin Booth, Esq.:

DEAR SIR AND BROTHER: The undersigned, at a regular communication of New-York Lodge No. 330, were appointed a committee to draft a letter of fraternal greeting, in consideration of recent occurrences not unknown to the public.

They approach the subject with much delicacy of feeling, and would at the threshold beg you to believe that they are actuated only by those high and holy motives which constitute Masonic intercourse.

Your recent communications which have been given to the public through the medium of the press, relating to the mournful calamity which has lately befallen our common country, have impressed us with a sense of solemn duty to one whom, as a brother of our lodge, we owe especial consideration.

While, as Masons, we are not called upon to take part in, or espouse any political cause or object, we cannot refuse the expression of our long-tried and continued confidence in your loyalty and good standing as a citizen of the United States, and as men and Masons fully indorsing your status throughout the Masonic and civic world. It affords us distinguished pleasure to be the organ of the New-York Lodge in making this communication, and to assure you in fullest personal and Masonic confidence, of the complete and entire reliance of the Lodge, and of all those who know you best, that your political condition and fealty to the laws and constitution of the United States, has been firm and steadfast.

Your noble heart, generous nature, and liberal disposition, have ever contributed to the common advancement of our fraternity, and we feel a just pride in being thus permitted to respond to the sentiments which you have so recently publicly announced. With the most extreme delicacy we indulge the hope that the future may prove that no "private woe" may be realized by you by reason of the recent occurrences at the National Capitol; and should our thoughts in this respect result in contradiction, it may not be improper to say that the members of the New York Lodge, in common with the country at large, will most enthusiastically join in a loud acclaim to the Great Master of the Universe, in grateful thanks for the merciful relief that must result to you and yours; and if, on the contrary, it should appear that our hopes are unsubstantial, we tender you our delicate sympathies and most sincere condolence in the domestic affliction which must necessarily follow.

In any event, dear brother, we can from personal and fraternal knowledge of you, and your private and public career in our midst, most sincerely and earnestly indorse you as a good man, a true friend, a loyal citizen and faithful brother; and if advice were needed, we might very properly add in the words of the poet:

"Honor and shame, from no condition rise,
Act well your part, there all the honor lies."

In conclusion, dear brother, permit us in the discharge of this fraternal duty to add to our official communication our individual sympathies and renewed confidence under the trying circumstances which now appear to surround you, and should our hopes fail of realization we can but commend you to the beneficent goodness of the all-wise and merciful Being who "tempers the wind to the shorn lamb."

We subscribe ourselves with very high personal and fraternal regards, your friends and brothers,

WILLIAM J. BUNCE, THOMAS E. MORRIS, JAMES R. ELSEY, THOMAS J. LEIGH, WILLIAM W. PADDEN, J. H. HOBART WARD, WILLIAM B. SMITH, WILLIAM R. BREWSTER,
Committee of New-York Lodge No. 330

Edwin Booth's reply was also printed in the same newspaper:

No. 28 East Nineteenth-Street.
BROTHERS: Your fraternal and consoling letter has come to me at the hour of my greatest need. It is very comforting, amid the dreadful darkness which shrouds my present and my future.

If there can be compensation for such a calamity as has overtaken me, it is to be found in the sentiments which you so gracefully express, and, as I believe, sincerely entertain for me.

I thank you, brothers, for the great relief your cheering words convey.

It has pleased God to afflict my family as none other was ever afflicted.

The nature, manner and extent of the crime which has been laid at our door have crushed me to the very earth; my detestation and abhorrence of the act, in all its attributes, are inexpressible; my grief is unutterable, and were it not for the sympathy of friends such as you, it would be intolerable.

You bear witness to my loyalty; you know my persistent and, to some extent, successful efforts to elevate our name, personally and professionally. For a proof of this, I appeal to the records of the past.

For the future, also, I shall struggle on in my retirement, bearing a heavy heart, an oppressed memory and wounded name—dreadful burdens—to my too welcome grave.

Your afflicted friend and brother.

(signed)   EDWIN BOOTH.

On the front page of the same paper there was an extensive account of the "Trial of the Assassins" covering the court-room drama of the day before. In headlines, the national debt was recorded at "$2,635,205,753.50" and the "cash in treasury" was stated at $25,000,000.

The last engagement East of the Mississippi was fought two days after Lincoln was shot. Colonel Oscar H. LaGrange, under the command of General Edward M. McCook, who in turn was under the command of General James H. Wilson, captured West Point and LaGrange, Georgia. Concerning that battle, the deputy grand master of the third Masonic district reported to the Grand Lodge of Georgia on October 25.

While the blasting influence of war has laid waste our fair country, and especially that portion embracing the Third Masonic District, some things have transpired worthy of notice, to the honor of Masons in the Federal Army. I desire to record the fact that where it was within their power so to do, Masons and masonic property were protected, and in some instances defended by order of leading Generals. The citizens of West Point and La Grange will not soon forget the General who led the Federal forces that captured those two places. The victory was complete, (although heroically defended,) yet not more complete than the place won in the memory and affections of a grateful people, for the humane and generous treatment meted out to them by their conquerors. The symbols of the craft on buildings indicating that they were dedicated to the work of brotherly love and charity, were sufficient passports to the affections of those who had bowed at the altar of our sublime institution. Notwithstanding a national quarrel at the time made us political enemies, yet in their zeal to serve their country, their

256

love of, and respect for, the "Ancient and Honorable Order" was not forgotten. In many instances, looking out over the wreck and ruin of surrounding buildings, stands one bearing on its front the *compass* and *square,* those permanent jewels of the Lodge, teaching virtue and circumspection in thought and action.

During that same communication, the constitution of the grand lodge was changed. "United States" was substituted wherever "Confederate States" appeared.

A letter, which is now a prized possession of the Grand Lodge of Virginia, was written to a lodge in Massachusetts on April 20, highly commending a former "enemy":

Richmond, Va., April 20th 65.

To the W.M., Wardens & Brether of Putnam Lodge, F. & A. Masons, East Cambridge, Mass:

Gentlemen & Brethern:

Thanks unto the allmighty for having sent unto us a man, a man in reality but yet an angel in imagination, whose first inquiry was for the Masonic Hall, to save the same from Pillage & fire; it was in the very middle of confusion when women & children old & young ran to & fro & knew not, whither, it was in the very midst of when half the city of Richmond enveloped with smoke & fire the other half being pillaged & destroyed that a miracle occured which I am about to relate to you, it was one of your members, but yet also a Bro. of ours through whose hand our Masonic hall was saved, it is A. H. Stevens Major & Provost Marshall of Richmond whose name will ever be a pleasant recolection by many one of us Here; nay, He has made an everlasting impresion on our minds & hearts which can *never* be forgotten! (and it is at his request that I am sending these few syllables to your Fraternal Body!) The Union forces had not bin in the city more than a few minutes when Maj. Stevens raised the first Union flage over the Capital that had been absent for the last 4 years, but he was not unmindful of other dutys, still of no less importance, he dashed from [blotted] in full speed and passing through a Private Str. where one of my daughters resides; he wheeled his horse stopped & made the immediate inquiry, *"Can you tell me Sir where the Masonic Hall is"* Yes sir I replied here is one of its [members] who has guarded against the approach of Cowans & Eavsdropper for the last 25 years, also that I had bin Grand Stewart of the G.L. of the State of Va. he immediately sent me a guard and selected for the officer of the guard another Mason whose name I dont recolect, but who deserves the honor of being called a good & true man. On arriving at the Hall met the G. Sec., [John Dove], Gr. Treasr. [Thomas U. Dudley] all of us met about one &

the same time, the guard was placed immediatly about the Hall, and all danger was at an end. This did not suffice the Major, he sent me a guard for my own house & also one for my daughters, and a good many other Masons who were treated in like manner. It was the will of the Supreme Architect that the Temple of Love should not be poluted by the hands of the mob; For it is So Sacred an Edifice; and there fore he sent us an angel in our midst to save that from destruction which has bin the refuge of so many, where no words are uttered than save those which links and unite us in to one Band of Friends & Brothers that indissoluble chain which is not easily severed.

Brethern I am proud to say that not only such men as Maj. Stevens, but many & many other, who came on the same errand must be an example to the world to show them that their intention were kind, their motive to make peace, and not to wage war as a great many of Southern People had anticipated. Only such men as Maj. Stevens for inst. can be proven to the world that he was a messenger of Peace; & further more I am proud to take him by the hand that I can call him brother, which is true material to adorn & beautify that Temple of Everlasting Spirits where the Supreme Architect alone in his Glory Presides. Accept my many heartfelt thanks for the services rendered by Maj. Stevens and believe me to be your everlasting

Friend & Brother
EMANUEL SEMON

The Masonic lodge in Winchester, Virginia, had been through many trying experiences. The town had changed hands over 70 times during the conflict. On March 12, 1862, the Federal forces drove out the Confederates for the first time. No communications were held by the lodge until April 20, 1863, and then it only met until June 12. On September 19, 1864, the Federal troops captured the town for the last time and held it until the war was over.

After it became apparent that Winchester would remain under Union control, a group of Masons from Winchester Hiram Lodge, No. 21, requested and received an audience with General Sheridan. Their plea to reopen the lodge fell on a deaf ear until Dr. C. H. Allen, a member of Sheridan's staff, told the general he would be present at all communications and report anything of a rebellious nature to him. With that assurance, Sheridan granted permission on a trial basis.

The lodge held its first meeting under that arrangement on November 28, 1864. From then until June 24, 1865, 231 men were made Master Masons in Winchester Hiram Lodge; 207 were connected with the Federal troops. Among them was a captain from Ohio, William McKinley, who was destined to become president of the United States and die by an assassin's bullet. He received his degrees on May 1, 2, and 3. John B. T. Reed, who had been master all through the war, conferred the last degree on him.

McKinley petitioned Masonry because he had been greatly impressed by the many Masonic episodes of brotherly love and affection he had witnessed throughout the war. Many other men were to follow him for the same reason.

CHAPTER XXI

Peace

◇◇◇

And ours be it now, my brethren, to bury in the grave of the dead past the heart-burnings and animosities that have been engendered in the strife; ours to extend the hand of conciliation and forgiveness to the repentant; ours to win back to the household of the faithful our erring brethren; ours, by precept and example, to hasten the day when faults shall be forgotten, and replaced by a generous emulation for the good of our whole country.

CLINTON F. PAIGE

AFTER THE PRESIDENT of the Confederate States left Richmond, he went to Danville, Virginia, taking his cabinet with him. Upon the surrender of Lee, he moved the government to Greensboro and from there to Charlotte, North Carolina. John H. Reagan relates an incident that happened during that period:

While General Johnston was with us at Greensboro he told President Davis that General Sherman had authorized him to say that he (Davis) might leave the country on a United States vessel and take with him whoever and whatever he pleased. To this the President replied, "I shall do no act which will put me under obligations to the Federal Government." This was not given to the public by any member of the Cabinet, so far as I know, as we did not know whether General Sherman was authorized to make such an offer, until he made it public in an after-dinner speech in New York in the summer of 1866. In that address he said he had inquired of President Lincoln whether he should capture Mr. Davis or let him go; and that Mr. Lincoln replied by an anecdote about a temperance lecturer in Illinois, who, when cold and wet, had stopped for the night at a wayside inn. The landlord, noting his condition, inquired whether he would have a glass of brandy. "No," came the

260

reply; "I am a temperance lecturer and do not drink." However, after a pause, he said to the landlord, "I shall be obliged to you for a drink of water, and if you should put a little brandy in it unbeknownst to me, it will be all right."

When we had gotten about half way to Charlotte, the President received a dispatch from General Johnston, informing him that he was in communication with General Sherman, and requesting that some one should be sent to assist in the negotiations [of surrender]. Mr. Davis requested the attendance of General Breckinridge [John C.] and myself, and stating the substance of the dispatch, observed that as I had proposed the basis for the negotiations, he desired me to go, and that as there might be a refusal to treat with the civil authorities of the Confederacy, he wished General Breckinridge to go to represent the Army.

Breckinridge and myself left at once, traveling that night, the next day and the second night until near daylight, when we reached the headquarters of General Johnston. (Much of the railroad track had been torn up and a number of bridges burned, which caused this delay.) General Hampton was with him. We had breakfast toward sun-up; and shortly afterward General Johnston suggested that he and General Breckinridge would go to the place of meeting and entertain General Sherman until I could put in writing our proposed terms. This programme was followed and I sent the paper to General Johnston, who subsequently stated that it contained with slight variations the terms of the armistice agreed on by those generals. I did not join the negotiations beyond this, because objections had been made to the recognition of the civil government of the Confederacy. But the Federal Government refused to recognize the terms of surrender as proposed between Johnston and Sherman; and so an arrangement was drawn up similar to that effected at Appomattox, and General Johnston's army was surrendered.

Even before the complete surrender of the Confederacy, Masonry was getting back to normal. On May 2, Grand Master George C. Whiting told the Grand Lodge of the District of Columbia: "It is gratifying to know that the Lodges in Alexandria, under the jurisdiction of the Grand Lodge of Virginia, are again in successful operation, and that Masonry in that city has returned to its normal condition, and that a kind and fraternal feeling prevails among the craft." Later, all of the money it had collected from Union Lodge was turned over to the Grand Lodge of Virginia; the furniture became the property of Alexandria Washington Lodge, No. 22.

The Confederate government continued to move. When it was near Washington, Georgia, Reagan called upon his Masonic brother Robert Toombs at the latter's home. Toombs, who had become dissatisfied with President Davis early in the war, offered to furnish horses and men, as well as money, to help Davis and Reagan. Reagan informed him that they were not needed as he had one of the best saddle horses in the country, and Davis "had his fine bay horse, Kentucky, and . . . General Lee had sent him at Greensboro, by his son Robert, his gray war horse, Traveler, as a present." Reagan then wrote:

After a moment, General Toombs observed, "Mr. Davis and I have had a quarrel, but we have none now; and under the terms agreed to between Johnston and Sherman he is entitled to go anywhere he pleases between here and the Chattachoochee River, and I want you to say to him that my men are around me here, and that if he desires it I will call them together and see him safely across the Chattachoochee River at the risk of my life." I was much impressed with so noble a sentiment, because it was so different from the conduct of some others who had pretended to be the President's close friends, and who were then getting away as far as they could from him, and were base enough to malign him, no doubt with the hope that such abuse would secure them the favor of our enemy.

At a small creek, a mile or two from Irwinsville, Georgia, Davis, his family, Reagan, and other members of the Confederate party were captured by Federal cavalry, commanded by Colonel Benjamin D. Pritchard. That happened on May 10 and immediately after his arrest Davis was imprisoned at Fort Monroe. A year later he was indicted on the charge of treason. Two years after his arrest, he was released on a bail-bond of $100,000 signed by Cornelius Vanderbilt, Gerrit Smith, and Horace Greeley.

General Breckinridge along with Colonel Wood escaped, made their way to Florida, then sailed in an open boat to Cuba.

On the day the Confederate government ceased to exist, the Grand Lodge of Connecticut passed resolutions extending its thanks and gratitude "to Brother Albert G. Mackey and our Brethren of South Carolina for their many deeds of Masonic love and fraternal feeling extended so fearlessly and so faithfully to the 'widows' sons' of the North who found themselves prisoners in an enemy's country."

The death of "P. D. Grand Master Thomas Holliday Hicks, U. S. Senator and formerly Governor of Maryland" was noted by Grand Master John Coates during a session of the Grand Lodge of Maryland. He gave Hicks credit for keeping his state from "the horrors of civil war."

The "by-laws" of Montgomery Lodge, No. 11, of Alabama, prove that Masonry was not divided by the conflict. This paragraph is recorded for May 15, 1865:

At the regular communication of the lodge, there were present twenty-four visitors from the Federal Army then occupying the city. There were two Army Lodges here which by invitation held their meetings in the hall while encamped at this place and their members were frequent visitors.

On May 22 John F. Houston, Grand Master of Missouri, pleaded with his members to be truly Masons during the trying days ahead:

In December last, I visited Lafayette Lodge, No. 32, [Lexington] to contribute an humble part in the conferring of Degrees. I found a most unfortunate and deplorable feeling existing in consequence of a difference of political opinions. Members of the craft of one political party would not meet, nor affiliate with, members who differed with them in opinion. In fact, the estrangement was so great that they refused to speak to each other on the streets. In view of the unfortunate difficulties existing, I directed the Secretary to peremptorily summon every craftsman who had not been legally suspended or expelled, living in the county of Lafayette, to meet me in Lafayette Lodge Room, on the 3d Saturday in January. And, although the weather was very inclement, a snow storm raging, the Lodge Room was filled, many of whom then present had not visited a Lodge for three years. In my humble efforts to restore peace and harmony, I was most ably and efficiently seconded and sustained by P. G. M. Ryland, to whom, for his noble and praise worthy efforts to bring about a perfect reconciliation and good feeling among the craft, I must return my most sincere and heartfelt thanks. The result of the labors of that evening was, to use the language of a distinguished brother present, "a regular old-fashioned Masonic love feast," each brother plighting his faith anew, over our sacred altar, to live in future as a society or band of friends and brothers, "amongst whom no contention should ever arise, except that noble contention, or rather emulation, of who can best work and best agree." However much we may differ outside the Lodge room, in our religious, political or other views, upon assembling there, within the sacred precincts of our Lodge, our feelings should be merged into the objects of Masonry. It matters not with us whether a man is Jew or Greek, American or German, Aristocrat or Plebian, Democrat or Republican, the moment he enters the Lodge, as a Master Mason, that moment he is equal; all are on a level, and the only strife or emulation ever allowed is, "who can best work and agree." The ties of brotherhood are for life, and each member feels, or should feel, a common interest in the advancement and perfection of his brother in Masonic Light and Knowledge.

* * *

The prospect of a substantial and permanent peace becomes brighter every day, and it is not too much to say that in a few months at furthest, "swords will be beat into ploughshares and spears into pruning hooks." When this great blessing is bestowed on us, many, very many, of our absent Brethren, whom we used to greet in former times, will return to Missouri, broken in health and spirit, and may be utterly destitute, and scarcely able, from the wreck of their remaining property, to sustain themselves and families, if they satisfy the requirements of the civil law. If they are permitted, by legal authority, to drag out a few short months or years in view of the graves of all most dear to them, and of their desolate hearths, do not, I entreat you, my Brethren, add to their misery by failing to recognize them as Brethren. Remember that none of us are free from faults, moral, social, or political, and, remembering this, let us bear with their infirmities of our erring Brethren, pardon their errors, and be kind and considerate to them; remember that a cup of cold water given in a kind and forgiving spirit, a gentle word fitly spoken, will fall upon the human heart like music wafted over a calm and placid lake, on a bright summer's eve, and will revive all the generous emotions and noble aspirations of former years. Then, my Brothers, let us do unto our returning Brethren all kind and affectionate acts as become Masons, and make them feel, if they never felt before, that the mysterious chain of Masonry, though tried in a thrice-heated furnace, is as strong and enduring as the immutable laws of truth and justice.

Among the many interesting reports of the district deputy grand masters of Missouri was one by Thomas B. Howe:

Owing to the unsettled state of the country, and difficulties arising over which I had no control, and believing then as I believe now, that Masonry did not compel or require me to risk my life in the open field before a vastly superior force of the enemy, I felt warrented and justified in abandoning the field; so, on the 6th of July, 1864, I left the bounds of the district (Macon County) and have not been in it since. . . . We keep whiskey and politics out of its precincts [a Lodge in his district], and harmony is the result. . . . I find all the difficulty and lukewarmness in the different lodges result from allowing political prejudice to rule the hour. I have, as far as possible, rebuked the argument of some *superlatively loyal* brethren, that if a brother is charged with disloyal feelings, he is not entitled to their Masonic esteem. . . . An institution that has stood aloof from political and religious strifes; that has rode triumphantly over the waves and billows of time (time and other institutions have perished with their folly), and now stands a proud monument of its own antiquity, ought not, must not, allow politics to enter its portals and mar its beauty.

The Grand Lodge of Indiana met on May 23 and Grand Master William Hacker was thankful for peace:

Many who are now present, and with us at our annual assembly in 1861, will remember how, during our deliberations, we were startled, from time to time, as we progressed in our labors, by the sound of the fife and the drum, those tocsins of war and of strife, coming up from the streets below—the tread of the marshaled hosts —the rumbling of the wheels of baggage trains, and the engines of war, as they rolled over the streets of the city. Four dark, terrible years of war, strife and bloodshed have passed away, during which time not one ray of light, or even of hope, appeared visible.

We are again assembled in Annual Communication, and as we look out from our "Temple of Peace," over the streets of the city below us, we behold much of the same proceedings going on. From over there comes the shrill sound of the fife and the rattling of the drum; there comes the regular step of a long line of well drilled soldiers; yonder, we behold the baggage trains, and hear the rumbling of those terrible engines of war, as they pass along. But here, thank God, the comparison ends. While those scenes to which I have above referred, were caused by the organizing of troops, collecting munitions of war, and hurrying them off to the field of deadly strife, those of to-day are caused by the return of those veterans from the bloody field, with victory perched upon their banners. The rebellion is subdued! The leaders are fugitives fleeing from justice, with a price upon their heads! Peace, with all its happy influences is returning to our afflicted land, and our noble veteran Hoosier boys are coming home, again to enter upon the pursuits of civil life. A

265

large number of these gallant boys are Masonically our brethren, of whom we may well be proud; for most gloriously have they sustained the honor of our State, and upheld our national banner on every battlefield. And then our sons are there! Our brothers and fathers, too, are coming! With what a thrill of joy can we welcome them to their homes, knowing and realizing that they bring with them Victory, Honor and Peace! Who, on this occasion, does not feel like swelling the angelic anthem of "Glory to God in the highest, on earth peace, good will to men."

The Grand Master added that if he had his two years to serve again, he did not know whether or not he would issue dispensations to organize lodges connected with the Army. He felt few of them would prove to be of credit to Freemasonry.

The grand high priest of Iowa, Lewis S. Swafford, was highly critical of army chapters of Royal Arch Masons. His decision prohibiting any Mason exalted in any of them from visiting, or becoming members of, any Iowa Chapter was upheld by his grand chapter. That action was not endorsed by the Grand Chapter of New Hampshire, however. Its Foreign Correspondence Committee wrote:

We admit that Grand Lodges and Grand Chapters committed a great error in granting dispensations for army Lodges and army Chapters, but we cannot agree with the Grand High Priest of Iowa that those having received the degrees in such Lodges and Chapters are to be treated as clandestine masons. Such received the degrees in good faith, the Lodges and Chapters conferring those degrees acted in good faith, having legal authority for so doing, and we see no other just course than to treat such as nonaffiliated, and receive them as visitors or members as they would other non-affiliated masons when applying as visiting brethren or for membership. One strong argument against army Lodges and army Chapters is that they encroach upon and violate other jurisdictions.

Complaints by Lodges and Chapters, grand and subordinate, for encroachments of jurisdiction are of common occurrence, but we never yet heard it asserted or even intimated that the recipients of masonic honors under an encroachment of jurisdiction were clandestine or needed healing before they could be admitted into full fellowship, although the Lodges and Chapters thus violating other jurisdictions deserve severe censure and are often obliged to make restitution.

Grand Master Guilbert of Iowa, on June 6, praised Albert G. Mackey and other Masons who "remained true to their

[Union] government . . . 150 men kept patriotism alive in Charleston." Guilbert hated the Confederacy, calling it the "Sodom of America," meriting "the fate of the Sodom of old." The *Proceedings* of his Grand Lodge listed 71 "Patriotic Dead." Twenty-eight died in battle, or as the result of wounds sustained while fighting; 43 died from various types of disease, notably, diarrhea.

The Grand Lodge of New York met on the same day with the Grand Master, Clinton F. Paige, presiding. He was also thankful for peace:

Under Providence, the truth and the right have come out of the fierce trial undimmed and triumphant. No longer will the soil of the republic tremble beneath the shock of contending armies; no longer will brother meet brother upon the battle-field; nor the misguided children of our common country be formed in hostile array against the government of our fathers. The angel of peace has at last unfolded her spotless wings, and as her gentle influence resumes its wonted sway, the reunited millions, forgetting their animosities and remembering only the glory and perpetuity of our free institutions, will hail the standard of the republic as the symbol and token of trials and difficulties overcome in the past, of concord, amity, and union in the future.

Discussion of the various topics connected with public affairs would, of course, be utterly irrelevant here; but I may be permitted to remind you that, in the immediate future as in the dark days now happily past, there is a work peculiarly Masonic in its character, and therefore peculiarly devolving upon Masons to perform.

Masonry is the daughter of peace; striving always and ever to promote conciliation and friendship, to unite men in acts of benevolence, to turn their minds from the bickerings and strife of the world, and to prepare them for the coming of that day when there shall be no war, and she bows only in sorrow before the inevitable necessities that call for the cannon and the bayonet to vindicate national authority, and preserve national existence. If her sons point the instruments of death, or apply the torch of desolation, it is because God and the country ordain the sacrifice; and scarce a battle-field of our civil war but what will attest that Masons have been the first to bind up the wounds of the fallen, and to accord the rites of sepulture to the dead.

John L. Lewis, chairman of the correspondence circle, was joyful as he started his report:·

. . . Our hearts are full as we enter upon the discharge of our annual duty. The glad news of approaching peace should inspire us with joy, and we hail, with the deepest emotions, the common blessing. It is the blessing which we, as craftsmen, most highly prize, fraught as it is with a great leading principle of our Institution; but it is alloyed with a sorrow which we cannot repress, at the remembrance of those for whom the olive branch brings not this wide-spread gladness, but who slumber on where they fell, or have laid them down to die upon mount and plain, in the woodlands, and by the river, to wake never again in time. Brethren cherished, fathers revered, sons beloved, went away from us in the pride and flush of their manhood, and will come to us no more forever. . . . But peace is at hand, and already the great arena of strife, bloodshed and death is becoming hushed in a Sabbath stillness and calm serenity, such as follows the wrathful outbursts of a tempest, when its whirlwinds have ceased, and its thunders have died away in the distance.

Every patriot heart rejoices in this glad consummation, but with this feeling of congratulation should come, also the sterner calls of duty. There are burning embers of passion to be quenched; there is brotherly love to be inculcated; there is widowhood to be relieved; there is orphanage to be protected; there is want to be supplied; there are bleeding hearts to be tenderly and gently healed; there are the calls of mercy to be heeded; there is need of the sympathizing heart, the pitying hand, the melting eye. By whom should such duties be practically taught, encouraged and performed, more than by Free and Accepted Masons? We boast ourselves builders; let us not forget that it is our vocation to *build up,* and not to *tear down;* and let us gird up our loins and address ourselves to the work, like men, and we shall call down upon our heads the priceless blessing of those ready to perish.

The Grand Chapter of North Carolina was told that the effects of Union Chapter, No. 17, "had been ruthlessly destroyed by the invading army." Most of the chapters in the state had shared the same fate. Almost all of them were not in a position to purchase new equipment; even the grand chapter had "not the means to defray its ordinary expenses."

Only 25 lodges were represented at the annual communication of the Grand Lodge of Texas on June 12 when the committee on finance asked that the more than $10,000 in Confederate securities "be filed with the archives and the amount be placed to the account of profit and loss upon the books of the grand treasurer." That was approved; the treasurer was left with a zero balance.

John R. Holbrook, the grand high priest of New Hampshire, on the 13th, while happy about the restoration of peace, reminded his members of the preceding four years:

The past year has been one of exciting events. For over four years our nation has been plunged in civil war; but looking forward through the smoke and din of battle, above party passion, we see, through the hand of Divine Providence, the golden boon of peace restored to our distracted land, and our glorious old flag now floats proudly over an undivided country. But amid all our joy and prosperity, how much sorrow and mourning! Alas, how many of our noble brothers have fallen as martyrs upon the altar of liberty! Upon the banks of the fair Potomac, in the loathsome swamps of the Chickahominy, upon the white sands of South Carolina, with the ever restless sea to chant their final requiem; upon every hill and vale—in short, upon every spot where our armies have met in conflict, there may their graves be found. Rest, fallen brothers! Though no marble may mark your last resting place, though no kind friend may shed the tear of pity over your graves, still your memory is enshrined in every patriot heart.

Throughout the Masonic world the end of the war was greeted with quiet rejoicing. Masons were looking to the future. Little could they realize what a great future they were to help bring forth.

CHAPTER XXII

A Grand Lodge Is Born

◇◇

The separation of the Craft in the old State of Virginia, which was the Mother of so much in America, into Virginia and West Virginia came about as quietly and as naturally as the stealing of dawn across the sky . . . [and] the older Grand Lodge welcomed its younger sister with a gesture, the full meaning and beauty of which can be understood by veteran Masons only. . . .
H. L. Haywood

WHEN VIRGINIA, "the Mother of Presidents," the state that had done much to preserve the Union it had helped form, adopted an "Ordinance of Secession" on April 17, 1861, the citizens in the Western part refused to break their ties with the Federal government.

A majority of the people of the whole state of Virginia ratified the Ordinance on May 23, but the residents of 31 Western counties, after two weeks of bitter debate, formed the "Restored Government of Virginia" and elected Francis Pierpoint as governor.

When hostilities began, communication by many lodges with the Grand Lodge of Virginia was impossible, particularly for the lodges in the Western counties. As the war progressed, and feelings became more bitter, other lodges refused to submit returns, or otherwise hold allegiance to the grand lodge in Richmond. Most of the lodges ceased to work because of the war and unsettled conditions.

On May 13, 1862, 48 counties formed the state of West Virginia. The legality of that formation was questioned for years after, even though the bill admitting it as a state was passed

270

by Congress and later, December 31, 1862, signed by Abraham Lincoln. The secretary of state, William H. Seward, put enough "ifs" in his proclamation to prove he had his doubts as to its legality. All of which was to be a troublesome factor to many grand lodges by the time the war had ended.

Gradually the fighting in West Virginia was transferred to its borders, leaving large districts in comparative peace. The Masons in those areas were eager to commence their work again, and the necessity for some central authority became eminent. Consequently, Fairmont Lodge, No. 9, sent a circular to the lodges of West Virginia requesting that a convention be held in Grafton, December 28, 1863. That convention, as well as the following one, was unsuccessful in its purpose, as reported in the *Proceedings* of the Grand Lodge of West Virginia:

This convention met during a period of great excitement, occasioned by events of the war which prevented the attendance of delegates from some parts of the State. Although more than a constitutional number of Lodges were represented, it was thought best to adjourn the convention to meet in Fairmont, on the 22nd day of February, 1864.

At the second convention, there was an increased attendance. A still larger representation of the working Lodges of the State was greatly desired, and it was again decided to postpone immediate organization. The convention was adjourned to meet in Fairmont, on the 24th of June, 1864.

Eight working lodges were represented at the meeting on June 24. Grand officers were elected and a date set for their installation, but those grand officers met and, claiming the election was not legal because of an informality in the proceedings of the convention which elected them, refused to be installed.

Fairmont Lodge, which took the initiative in the formation of the Grand Lodge of West Virginia, sent another circular to the subordinate lodges in the area informing them that the grand master and grand secretary elect refused to be installed, and their reason for that decision. As a result of the circular, a committee met and after due consideration drafted a letter to be sent throughout the state:

BRETHREN: In again inviting you to assemble in Convention

for the purpose of organizing a Grand Lodge of the State of West Virginia, we feel that it is unnecessary for us to argue at length the *right* or *expediency* of Subordinate Lodges of this State to establish a Grand Lodge, as the very fact that we live under what is beyond all doubt a *de facto* State government, determines, according to the usages of the order, the legality of such a proceeding; and your own experience, since communication with the Grand Lodge of Virginia has been destroyed, must have convinced you of the necessity of a Grand Lodge.

We, therefore, respectfully and earnestly invite you to send regularly appointed delegates to a Convention to be held in Fairmont, on Wednesday evening, April 12th, 1865, for the purpose of electing officers of a Grand Lodge. It is also hoped that brethren belonging to Lodges not active, will attend.

Brethren, please give the subject early attention in your Lodges, and let us meet and consummate the work before us, in the spirit of brotherly love and affection.

> F. J. FLEMING, W.M.
> C. A. SWEARINGTON, *Sec'y*
> J. N. BOYD

Fairmont, February 21st, 1865.

Eight lodges, all with Virginia charters, were represented at the convention of April 12: Fairmont, No. 9; Marshall Union, No. 37; Morgantown Union, No. 93; Ohio, No. 101; Wheeling, No. 128; Fetterman, No. 170; Cameron, No. 180; and Wellsburg, No. 108. Not only those eight were lost by the Grand Lodge of Virginia, but eventually 45 were to become part of the new grand lodge.

After E. C. Bunker was elected president and Ellery R. Hall, secretary, J. N. Boyd offered the following resolution: *"Resolved,* That it is expedient at this time to proceed to the election of the officers necessary to constitute a Grand Lodge for the State of West Virginia."

The *Proceedings* of that grand lodge further state: "After full discussion, in which brethren present from lodges not active were invited to participate, the resolution was adopted." The convention then elected a man who was to prove one of the most able and well informed Masons in that state as the first grand master of the Grand Lodge of West Virginia. He was William J. Bates, a past master of Wheeling Lodge, No. 128. He served in that position until November 15, 1871, when Thomas

H. Logan, who was elected grand secretary during the convention of April 12, 1865, succeeded him.

The members of the convention set the second Wednesday in May as the date for the installation of the grand officers; then, perhaps to prove they were about to become a grand lodge, the following resolution was adopted:

Resolved, That the Grand Secretary elect, be authorized to call on the several Subordinate Lodges within this State for a contribution, equal to fifty cents for each contributing member of the same. . . .

On May 10, 1865, the last convention of Ancient Free and Accepted Masons of the state of West Virginia was held in the Masonic Temple, Wheeling. Past Grand Master William B. Thrall of Ohio, who was present to install the grand officers elect, stated in his address:

It is no every day occurrence, my brethren, nor even of transient interest, that has caused our assembling here to-day. . . . But a nation like ours—however blessed of Heaven, and endowed with all the elements of human happiness—does not cast aside these advantages and see land deluged in blood; does not behold its beauty turned to ashes, and its oil of joy to mourning, without leaving some enduring mementos, as *waymarks* of the progress of such fearful career.

And such has been the experience of the people of West Virginia. At the very commencement of the civil contest, the alternative was forced upon them, either to take up arms for the subversion of the government of their common country—embrue their hands in fraternal blood—and fight for the overthrow of that which makes us one people, with one constitution, and one destiny; or else, by severing the ties which has long connected them with their *trans-montagne* fellow-citizens, maintain their fealty to the government, and assume to themselves that separate and equal stations in the community of States to which, as they believe, the laws of nature, and of nature's God, entitle them.

Ready at the prompting of truth, justice and patriotism, they did not hesitate in the path of duty; but when the "Old Dominion" parted the cable that secured her safe and quiet moorings in the haven of the Federal Union, and drifted on the shoals of Secession and the breakers of Treason, beyond their power to rescue her, they lost no time in casting about for their own security, and the permanent welfare of those to come after them. To this end they organized the government of West Virginia, and resumed their nationality. The existence and functions of the civil government of West Virginia, having been distinctly recognized by the several departments of the Federal government, as well as those of the other States of the Union, a distinct Masonic jurisdiction succeeds, as an appropriate sequence. The necessary preliminaries having been observed, the business of the present hour is to give form and consistence to such jurisdiction. And I gladly avail myself of the occasion in behalf of the brethren "on the other side of the river," and indeed of the whole fraternity, wheresoever dispersed, to tender to the Grand Lodge of West Virginia, and the Lodges and Masons constituting the same, most cordial and fraternal salutations.

At the conclusion of his address, Thrall installed the officers of the Grand Lodge of West Virginia, "in solemn and AMPLE FORM." On motion, the convention was then dissolved.

Mt. Olivet Lodge, No. 113, joined the other eight for the first communication of the new grand lodge a short time later, when all of them heard the grand master deliver his first annual address:

Brethren: I am deeply grateful for the evidence of your regard and confidence manifested by your selection of me for the honorable position of Grand Master of this Most Worshipful Grand Lodge.

. . . And let us humbly invoke the Divine blessing on the new career upon which we are about to enter, praying that in all our labors we may ever manifest an unwavering devotion to the cause of morality and virtue, and thus be enabled to "reflect true dignity on the character of our profession"—advance the usefulness and promote the happiness of the brethren, and "convince mankind at large of the goodness of our cause."

Some doubts have been expressed as to the right of the Lodges in the State of West Virginia to establish a Grand Lodge. These doubts appear to have arisen from the particular views taken of the circumstances under which the State of West Virginia came into existence.

It would not be proper, in this place however, to enter into a discussion as to the regularity or irregularity of the proceedings, by which the State of West Virginia was created. Nor indeed, if proper, would it be necessary, since, with that proceeding, we as Masons, have nothing whatever to do; and therefore, it cannot in any manner, affect the legality of this Grand Lodge.

* * *

West Virginia is now a separate State, and it has been recognized

274

by the different departments of the general government, as having all the rights, powers and privileges of the other States of the Union.

The change in the political relation of the district out of which West Virginia was formed, to the State of Virginia, being thus fixed and determined, it was in accordance with the custom adopted in such cases throughout the country, and was, indeed, necessary in order to insure the regular and efficient working of the Masonic system within our territory, that the Lodges in the new State should sever their allegiance from the Grand Lodge of Virginia, and establish a Grand Lodge for themselves.

But this procedure was rendered still more necessary by the fact, that for four years the Lodges in West Virginia have been cut off from all intercourse with the Grand Lodge of Virginia and, therefore, subject to all the evil consequences which must result from the absence of the controlling and regulating authority of a supreme government. Many of the Lodges, by reason of the absence of their officers, or from the existence of discord among the members, have discontinued their meetings. Others have been deterred from pursuing their labors, in consequence of being located near to military encampments. In some instances, Lodge rooms have been taken for military purposes, records mislaid or lost, and jewels and Lodge furniture carried away or destroyed. And even in some of the Lodges which have continued in active operation, many irregularities have been introduced, which require speedy correction, but which, from the absence of any "settled authority," it has hitherto been impossible to effect.

Such was the condition of Masonic affairs in the counties now composing this State; when, the General Government having formally recognized West Virginia, and the tide of war having transferred military operations to the extreme border, restoring a large part of the State to comparative tranquility, the brethren felt that the time had come for a movement towards the organization of a Grand Lodge. And (after due notice to all the Lodges in the State) it was at length effected by the Convention, which assembled in Fairmont, on the 12th of April last; which Convention was composed of the representatives from a majority of the Lodges, that (so far as we have information) were at the time in active operation in the State.

* * *

It has been hitherto impracticable to have any correspondence with the Grand Lodge of Virginia, in reference to the organization of this Grand Lodge. But now that communication is again open. I deem it important that your first business should be to forward to them a statement of the circumstances and reasons which have led us to sever our connection with that Grand Lodge, and to constitute a Grand Lodge for West Virginia. For this purpose, I would recommend the appointment of a special committee to prepare an address to the Grand Lodge of Virginia, embodying a statement such as I have suggested. And also, that the Grand Master be authorized to appoint a special representative as the bearer of the address, who shall be empowered on behalf of this Grand Lodge, to settle and adjust all matters in relation to which difference could arise; so that all our obligations may be faithfully observed, and the most cordial fraternal relations may be established with the Grand Lodge of Virginia.

Bates went on to cite several Masonic authorities for the action taken by the Masons of his state. After he had finished his address, resolutions were adopted requesting the subordinate lodges to submit their charters for endorsement by the grand master; for the appointment of a committee to prepare a constitution; and for the "Constitution and General Regulations of the Grand Lodge of Virginia" to be continued in the meantime for the government of the Grand Lodge of West Virginia.

No time was lost by the new grand lodge in going to work, for on July 4 the grand master assembled the Craft for the purpose of laying the corner-stone of a monument to be erected in the Soldiers' Burying Ground in Wheeling.

During the annual communication of the Grand Lodge of Virginia on December 11, 1865, Grand Master Edward H. Lane commented on the newly formed grand lodge:

It has come to my knowledge in the form of a circular, that some of the Lodges holding charters from this Grand Lodge, located in what is styled "West Virginia," have met and formed a Grand Lodge for that State. As to the number of Lodges claiming to belong to that jurisdiction, I am ignorant. It appears they have elected their Grand Officers, and I am informed they have been installed by the Grand Master of Ohio. It is not the province of Masonry to inquire into the political status of West Virginia. Whether that State has been rightfully formed according to fundamental law of the land, is a question with which we have nothing to do as Masons. It is believed to be sound Masonic law, that the political boundaries of a State being definitely given and decided upon, fixes the Masonic jurisdiction, and this by common consent. Such Lodges as have been previously chartered within such geographical boundaries being desirous of forming for themselves a Grand Lodge, have an undoubted right to do so. . . . [But] how far the Lodges located in "West Virginia" have violated (if at all) their duty and obliga-

276

tions as Masons, I leave for your consideration. All the information I have on this subject is in the hands of the Grand Secretary, and to which you are respectfully referred.

A special committee was appointed to look into the matter and report at the next annual communication.

Grand lodges throughout the country took note of the action of the Masons in West Virginia. New York welcomed "the advent of the 40th Grand Lodge within the boundaries of the United States"; Ohio said, its formation "cannot be otherwise than gratifying to the Craft throughout Ohio"; Kansas claimed "this 'State of West Virginia' seems to have a doubtful existence, and we trust our brethren there will not urge their claim too strongly until their political boundaries are fully established"; Pennsylvania refused to "recognize" the Grand Lodge of West Virginia until Virginia had done so.

There were 14 lodges, all holding Virginia charters, represented during the first annual communication of the Grand Lodge of West Virginia, January 17, 1866. Grand Master Bates informed his members that he had appointed a committee of one to attend the communication of the Grand Lodge of Virginia. He was received by "the venerable and eminent brother, John Dove, grand secretary" and was most cordially and kindly attended by all whom he contacted. The committee reported that Virginia would insist that all of the lodges in West Virginia would have to pay their back dues and return their charters to the grand secretary of Virginia. The latter requirement upset the Masons of the new jurisdiction greatly; they wanted to retain their original charters.

During 1866 hundreds of words were again written by the grand lodges in the United States; again many more of them approved the formation of the Grand Lodge of West Virginia than disapproved the action. New Hampshire said, "the right of such lodges to unite and form a grand lodge, must, we think, be regarded as indefeasible." The Masonic scholar from Maine, Josiah H. Drummond, wrote a report of several hundred words defending the formation of the new body. He concluded his report by stating:

From a careful examination, we are convinced that the Grand

277

Lodge of West Virginia is regularly formed and has exclusive jurisdiction in that State; and we doubt not that all questions of detail will be arranged between the two Grand Lodges, in that Masonic Spirit for which the Grand Lodge of Virginia has been so justly celebrated.

The committee appointed by Virginia to look into the matter of West Virginia reported during the annual communication of 1866 that it did not consider the formation of the new grand lodge legal, but desiring peace and harmony would be willing to "recognize" it if the following resolution was complied with:

Resolved, That this Grand Lodge is willing to recognize the Grand Lodge of West Virginia, whenever we shall be satisfied that a full majority of the thirty-three active Lodges in the boundary of West Virginia, holding charters from this Grand Lodge, shall desire to separate from us and unite with the Grand Lodge of West Virginia, and shall return their charters and pay up their dues to this Grand Lodge to December, 1865.

During the 1867 session of the Grand Lodge of West Virginia, the "Working Committee" reported it had, during the day, exemplified the work in the first and second degrees in accordance with the Virginia ritual. In the evening the Virginia ritual was again followed when the Master Mason's degree was conferred.

Again other jurisdictions commented on the differences between the two Virginias. Oregon stated: " 'There was neither hammer, nor axe, nor any tool of iron heard in the house while it was building.' We recommend action of this Grand Lodge in this case"; Illinois claimed "those who object to a recognition for a political reason, would, as it seems to us, do well to waive that point until it is clear that a political reason exists"; Missouri denied the right of recognition by West Virginia, and the committee on foreign correspondence wrote:

We trust, for the sake of Masonic integrity and independence before the world, that the Grand Lodge of West Virginia will relinquish her control over Lodges not her own, but resolve them back to their mother, and then let the division be made amicably and with adherence to "Masonic usage."

On November 10, 1868, the grand master of West Virginia

told his members that the Grand Lodge of Virginia was willing to recognize their body provided certain terms were met. Among those terms was the requirement that the subordinate lodges in West Virginia return their original charters to the grand secretary of Virginia. He strongly suggested they comply with that request even though they did not want to. He pointed out that recognition by the Grand Lodge of Virginia was necessary in order for the new grand body to be acknowledged as legitimate by every other grand lodge in the country. He told his members that Masons from West Virginia had been refused admittance to lodges in Pennsylvania as well as Virginia. Toward the close of his address he said:

I desire also, to express my sense of the very great benefit which our Grand Lecturer and many of our members have derived from the instructions received from R. W. James Evans, Grand Lecturer of the Grand Lodge of Virginia, who recently came to this city, in response to an invitation from Lodges here, to teach the lectures to a class of brethren. His extensive knowledge of Masonry, and his kind and courteous manner, gave us not only a high opinion of his Masonic abilities, but a feeling of strong affection for him personally; and his visit will be long remembered with pleasure by the Masons of Wheeling.

That visit helped cement the ties between the two grand bodies, for it was alluded to by Grand Master William Terry a month later when the Grand Lodge of Virginia met in its annual communication. Terry told his members he thought it was time to finally dispose of the "vexed and perplexing question of our relations to that Grand Lodge." He went on to add:

Whilst thus maintaining the rights of the Grand Lodge of Virginia, I have further decided and hold that all do not regard the Masons who recognize the Grand Lodge of West Virginia, or even those who have been initiated under its authority, as clandestine, but on the contrary, they are to be held and treated with all the courtesies and respect due to visiting brethren from any other jurisdiction. . . . And in support of this view, we have the fact that this Grand Lodge did, in December 1866, during its session, receive and admit upon this floor, Bro. Bunker, who came as a representative from the Grand Lodge of West Virginia for the purpose of conferring with this Grand Lodge in relation to the recognition of the Grand Lodge of West Virginia. We have further confirmation of this view in the fact that our most worthy and well-informed Grand Lecturer, who, it is but fair to presume, is properly advised of the action and purposes of this Grand Lodge, has, during the past year, been on a tour of instruction to Lodges within and recognizing the jurisdiction of the Grand Lodge of West Virginia. Surely our Grand Lecturer did not regard these Lodges as beyond the pale of Masonic recognition.

The grand master went on to ask his body to recognize West Virginia, and "in deference to the feeling expressed by our brethren of West Virginia, of surrendering with reluctance the charters they hold from us—and it is a feeling all can appreciate and should respect—I would respectfully recommend to this Grand Lodge to recede from the requirement that the charters held from this Grand Lodge be surrendered."

On December 16, 1868, the "difficulties" between the two grand lodges ended with the adoption of the following:

The committee appointed to confer with the Commissioners from the Grand Lodge of West Virginia, to this Grand Lodge in reference to the differences existing between these Grand Bodies, beg leave to report, that they have had a full and free conference with said Commissioners, and take great pleasure in stating that the spirit manifested by the Grand Lodge of West Virginia towards this Grand Lodge is fully appreciated by your committee; and while it is a source of deep regret, that circumstances have occurred which, in the opinion of our brethren of West Virginia, justified them in forming a Grand Lodge, yet, in the spirit of Fraternal feeling, and with an ardent desire to cultivate peace and harmony with all Grand Bodies, we are willing to recognize the Grand Lodge of West Virginia as a legally constituted body upon their complying with the conditions heretofore prescribed by this Grand Lodge; and the said Commissioners being present and having satisfied this Grand Lodge that the Grand Lodge of West Virginia has fully complied with the conditions aforesaid, or is now ready and willing to comply with the same; be it therefore

1st resolved, That this Grand Lodge hereby recognizes the said Grand Lodge of West Virginia, and extends to her our Fraternal and Masonic recognition, and cordially recommend her to all other Grand Masonic Bodies in correspondence with this Grand Lodge.

* * *

4th, That inasmuch as the original Charters which emanated from this Grand Lodge to the Subordinate Lodges in West Virginia,

280

have been formally surrendered to this Grand Lodge, but the said Subordinate Lodges having earnestly asked that they may be returned to them to be laid up in their archives as mementoes of the past; therefore,

Resolved, That the said Subordinate Lodges be permitted to retain the said old Charters.

5th Resolved, That this Grand Lodge recommend to all of its Subordinate Lodges in the territorial limits of West Virginia, to surrender their present Charters to, and ask new Charters from the Grand Lodge of West Virginia.

The Grand Lodge of Virginia had concurred with Grand Master Terry and the deed which Harry LeRoy Haywood thought so beautiful was carried out—the subordinate lodges of West Virginia were permitted to keep their Virginia charters!

The recognition of the new body by the mother grand lodge brought its recognition by every other grand body. Everyone was happy, including W. C. Penick of Alabama, who wrote:

Surely these brethren can and will separate in peace, and each will go to his place. But the farewell will rend the heart of each, and the bitter tears of sorrow will course their manly cheeks. We, too, are a Virginian, and while we write this, in sympathy, we are weeping as a child. May the genius of Masonry, with justice in one hand and truth in the other, guided by friendship, still write you— a band of brothers.

While the Civil War cost one grand lodge several thousand members, it brought it, and the whole Masonic world, a beautiful lesson in the first tenet of Freemasonry—Brotherly Love!

CHAPTER XXIII

Reconstruction

◇◇◇

> *. . . I have long labored to ameliorate and alleviate the condition of the great masses of the American people. Toil and honest advocacy of the great principles of free government, have been my lot. The duties have been mine—the consequences are God's. This has been the foundation of my political creed.*
>
> ANDREW JOHNSON

THE TRAGIC DEATH of Abraham Lincoln placed a Mason once again at the head of the government of the United States. The four years he was to serve his country were to be the most trying during the history of the young republic.

The debate about Andrew Johnson and his policies was to continue throughout the years. Some claim he was a great president; a few say he was the greatest; others believe he was the poorest the country ever had; and the debate started even before ten o'clock on the morning of April 15, 1865, when he took the oath of office.

E. A. Pollard, the war-time editor of the *Richmond Examiner,* despised both the North and Jefferson Davis. He believed Johnson was a "scrub," a man who "was sprung from a low order of life"; a man who "had the shallowness and fluency of the demagogue."

Pollard later reversed his opinion and stated Johnson had changed from the hour he became president. "The man who had been twitted as a tailor and condemned as a demagogue, proved a statesman, measuring his actions for the future, insensible to clamour and patient for results."

282

Johnson had been a tailor. He began that career at the age of ten, when the child of today is in school. The education he received was through his own perseverance and started while he was working in a tailor shop in Raleigh, North Carolina. A man in the town, who had admired the heroism of Johnson's father (he had died of injuries received while saving the life of Thomas Henderson, editor of the Raleigh *Gazette,* five years before), visited the boy almost daily to teach him to read.

Johnson learned rapidly, particularly after his marriage, and from early manhood became an able advocate of the working man. That led to his election as alderman in Greenville in 1828, at the age of 20. From then until his death, July 31, 1875, he remained in politics.

Johnson's philosophy was clearly stated in a speech he made in the House of Representatives on December 19, 1846. While supporting Polk's administration in regard to Mexico, he stated firmly: "But, sir, I care not whether right or wrong, *I am for my country always."*

With a civil war brewing, he proved that even though he was a Southerner he wanted no part in a dissolution of the Union. He spoke to the senate on December 19, 1860:

I am opposed to secession. I believe it is no remedy for the evils complained of. Instead of acting with that division of my Southern friends who take ground for secession, I shall take other grounds while I try to accomplish the same end. I think that this battle ought to be fought, not outside but inside of the Union, and upon the battlements of the Constitution itself. I am unwilling voluntarily to walk out of the Union, which has been the result of a Constitution made by the patriots of the Revolution. They formed the Constitution; and this Union that is so much spoken of, and which all of us are so desirous to preserve, grows out of the Constitution . . . if anybody is to leave this Union, or violate its guaranties, it shall be those who have taken the initiative, and passed their personal liberty bills.

Johnson's loyalty to the Union brought him the military governorship of Tennessee, and in 1864 he was chosen as Lincoln's running-mate. At the inauguration on March 4, 1865, Johnson's critics found something else to criticize him for, as he was obviously intoxicated during the ceremony. The proof is ample that he was not at fault. He was recovering from typhoid fever, and although he had not wanted to be present, Lincoln insisted. He went, and because he was still weak and ill, a friend gave him a drink of whiskey to bolster him for the ordeal ahead. The newspapers spread the news of his intoxication far and wide, but few of them printed the explanation. That it was never to happen again was proved during his impeachment trial when the charge of "drunkenness" was not brought up. In fact, Hugh McClullock wrote, "there were few public men whose character and conduct would have sustained as severe a scrutiny" as Johnson's during the impeachment proceedings.

Andrew Johnson became a member of Greenville Lodge, No. 119, Greenville, Tennessee, in 1851. From the first he was an ardent Mason. Throughout his life he worked for and with Masonry. There are those who believe that fact, more than any other, led to his impeachment trial. The ringleader in those proceedings was Thaddeus Stevens, a violent anti-Mason, who was one of the strong leaders against Freemasonry during the Morgan affair. He fought the organization at every opportunity.

Throughout his term as president, Johnson was to fight for the preservation of the Constitution of the United States. To do that he had to withstand the slurs, slanders, and threats of the men who have become known as "radicals."

President Johnson was present and spoke when, with an "immense procession, numbering several thousands," he saw the Grand Lodge of Pennsylvania and Grand Master Lucius H. Scott lay the cornerstone of the monument to be erected in the Soldiers' National Cemetery in Gettysburg on July 4, 1865.

The restoration of peace was to be the subject most prevalent in all grand bodies for the next several months. James Seymour of the Grand Chapter of Canada wrote on August 8, 1865:

The fiery ordeal through which our Companions in the neighboring states have been called to pass, has indeed been a trying one; and as they received our heartfelt sympathy in their season of affliction, so now we extend to them our sincere congratulations on the happy return of peace. War's devastations having ceased, Companions north and south, as members of the same mystic family, can once more exchange their fraternal greetings, and mingle with each other as in the past, their mutual feelings of friendly solicitude and good will. Happily, throughout the unnatural struggle, masonry exercised a sacred power and a benign influence that perhaps its most ardent supporters could scarcely have anticipated, in view of the merciless rancor too often shown. That influence will now tend in a great degree to bind those cherished principles still closer to their hearts, and give them greater confidence in the stability and truth of its venerated and immutable teachings.

The presiding officer of that grand chapter, Douglas Harrington, was equally enthusiastic:

My second subject of congratulation is the restoration of peace in the United States, and a return to friendly relations, so long interrupted between all our brethren and Companions, citizens of that powerful and important republic. In all the proceedings I have had the pleasure of studying, there is a general expression of satisfaction among freemasons at the changed condition of affairs, and let us hope now that the demon of discord and civil war, the worst of scourges, will be banished, and that men will look their fellow men in the face as they should do, without wishing to take from each other, what they never did or could give, life and light.

William F. Jefferys of the Grand Chapter of New Jersey wrote on September 13 about Freemasonry's mission in the months ahead:

The "tidings from the craft" come to you this year as Noah's dove came to the ark with the olive branch of peace; "the roar of cannon," "the din of musketry," and the "clash of arms" have ceased. We have no longer to inquire, "what is the cause of all this confusion in and about the temple?" but our appropriate work now is to "search among the rubbish," find "the lost keystone," place it once more into the Royal Arch of National Union, and seek to restore harmony.

Freemasonry has now to perform its great mission in this country which is to "spread the cement of Brotherly Love and Union."

We believe there is a Divine Providence in the fact that our Order is at this time so powerful and numerous, for its influence in the present crisis must prove most salutary.

Such are its laws, rules, and landmarks, that there is more to be expected of it, in wiping out the memory of our civil war, and in restoring national harmony, than can be reasonably expected of any other organization in the land. The secret history of its silent workings while the conflict was raging proves that men who were open enemies with deadly weapons in their hands were, by its mysterious power, transformed into bosom friends. If such was its in-

285

fluence in actual war, what can it do under the reign of peace?

There is now no civil or military restraint upon its action; we are free to correspond as masonic brothers and Royal Arch Companions with the members of our fraternity in all sections of our common country; and shall not these open avenues of masonic intercourse become grand channels through which the old union feeling shall again flow, and may not our beloved Order thus become a mighty instrument in the hands of an All-wise Providence in removing the effects of past discord, and restoring national harmony and brotherly love. . . .

It is a proud thought for our fraternity that the future historian will be able to record the fact that while during the struggle of conflicting elements and opinions which produced actual war and bloodshed, all the great national organizations of societies and churches throughout the country were broken up, divided or dissolved, the one national organization of Royal Arch Masons, although severely tried, withstood the shock, and still remained undivided and undissolved amid the jarring elements of discord and civil war.

The General Grand Chapter which Jeffreys referred to, was convened in Columbus, Ohio, in September, 1865, by Albert G. Mackey, the General Grand High Priest, for the first time in five years. He called upon his companions for love and understanding:

In the fratricidal contest which for four years has deluged our country with blood, freemasonry, if it has not done all it should have done, has at least done more than any other organization of men towards ameliorating the horrors and inhumanity of war. On the field, in the hospital and the prison, masonry has been seen exerting her beneficial influences and saving life, comforting the sick and wounded, and lessening the evils of captivity. For what she has done in this way we should be proud of our noble institution. Her teaching has always been, like that of her great Patron, the Evangelist, "children, love one another." There have been, alas! for the infirmity of humanity, too many instances in which this teaching has been, for the time, forgotten. But it has never been repudiated. There is no mason living who will deny that love is the chief corner-stone upon which the edifice of masonry is erected. In theory we are all right. In practice we are too often wrong.

But if the theory be there—if the doctrine be admitted—what remains for us, the chiefs of the Order, but to insist upon the practice and to give life and energy to the doctrine.

286

At the first outbreak of the rebellion, attempts were made by many distinguished masons to stem the tide of approaching war. The attempts were noble but the advice was unheeded. Passion had closed the ear and dethroned the judgment. Yet that the attempt was made is a proud record for the men who made it and for the institution whose principles had prompted it.

The war is now over. The sword is to be turned into a ploughshare. But although there is no longer a battle of arms, dissensions still exist. Bitter feeling is not altogether allayed. Some men will remember the past with revengeful or unforgiving thought. Now, then, is the time for masonry again to raise her warning voice, to say unto her children that they are of one household and of one faith. To beseech them to lay aside all bitter animosity, to remember that they have a common language and a common altar, and throwing the veil over the cruel struggles of the past to seek in the future every opportunity of doing good to each other. Let them cultivate that spirit of forbearance and of kindness which will make them say, "Behold, how these masons love one another."

If masonry is good for anything it is good for this. If it is capable of accomplishing anything it is capable of accomplishing this. If our professions are not mere words—if our obligations and charges have any weight—if our symbols and allegories contain any meaning, then does masonry oblige us to the law of love, and then it is our duty, when hatred lingers in the land, to seek to overcome that hatred with love, and to inaugurate a new era, when every American shall exhibit to his fellow citizens who are beyond our pale the great fact that American Masons know no north, no south, no east, no west, but only one common country, undivided and indivisible.

Charles F. Dana of the Grand Chapter of Vermont wrote on October 4:

We avail ourselves of this opportunity to tender to all our Royal Arch brethren throughout the land our sincere and hearty congratulations upon the termination of the deadly struggle that has raged with such fury for four years past, and we hope to renew, ere long, with our southern Grand Chapters, the pre-existing cordial and fraternal relations which marked our intercourse. It is the earnest prayer of our hearts that next year we shall be once more in the receipt of those interesting transcripts from the sunny south, which have always given us so high an opinion of the masonic virtues and qualifications of the Companions in that part of the union.

On October 9, the Grand Chapter of Tennessee voted to appeal to "Companion A. M. Hughes, General Claim Agent for the State of Tennessee, at Washington City" for reimbursement for damages sustained when their Masonic Temple was used as a Federal hospital.

The Grand Chapter of Massachusetts, on the following day, prayed "that by no act of ours, as citizens or as masons, shall the nation's future be put in jeopardy."

William C. Belcher, grand master of California, on October 10, mildly boasted that Masons remembered their teachings during the war:

> . . . More than for all our immediate personal blessings are our hearts made glad by the return of peace to our country. Her fields shall no more be drenched with the blood of her children. She is no longer divided against herself. For four years we have endured the miseries of civil war, and now we are at peace. For four years fraternal intercourse with our brethren of one-half of our country has been suspended. It is true, and we are proud to say it, that the kindly relations which Masons should sustain toward one another, everywhere, were not forgotten. They did not cease to remember, though arrayed under hostile banners, the command— "love ye one another"; and their love went forth into acts—acts of the most disinterested, generous charity—acts which will be remembered when all the bitterness and animosities engendered by the strife in which they were then engaged shall be forgotten. Again our fraternal relations and intercourse with them are restored.

Grand High Priest William E. Robinson of Kentucky told his members on the 16th:

> Since our last convocation the terrible struggle through which our country has been passing has been brought to a close, and with the return of peace new responsibilities devolve upon us as citizens, but more especially as Royal Arch Masons. As such it is our duty, with "purity of heart and rectitude of conduct," to use every means to reconcile our brethren and Companions. There is an effort now being made in the masonic world to restore the fraternal regard which formerly existed between the various portions of our country, and already has an address been made through the public prints by the grand officers of the Grand Lodge of Pennsylvania.
>
> I hope that this Grand Chapter will also take steps to aid in the great work of reconciliation. We should extend the hand of "fraternal love and affection" to all who desire to discharge their masonic duties, without any other inquiry than, are they "worthy and well

qualified?" Then we will have peace and harmony throughout our borders.

Grand Master J. D. Landrum of the same state, on the same day, told his members that politics and Masonry are separate items:

Many brethren seem to have forgotten that Masonry does not conflict with political or religious sentiments. I have received not a few letters touching this subject. Some wish to know whether, as Masons, they should celebrate the funeral obsequies of deceased members who took service in the rebel cause. Others have asked whether resolutions of condolence and respect should be adopted in such cases, and whether the widows and orphans of such deceased brothers are entitled to masonic charities. To all these inquiries my answer has been substantially: Brethren, let not politics be mentioned in your Lodges, and know no difference in men because of political or religious distinctions. Masonry unites men of every country, sect and opinion, upon the broad basis of universal charity. Our institution is not sectional, and our Lodges should not be converted into courts-martial. Alleged crimes against the civil government should be tried and punished only by the civil authority. Masonry should take no part in civil strife, except to throw the broad mantle of masonic charity over the faults of our brethren, succor the needy, and apply the oil of consolation and the wine of joy to the afflicted, especially to those of our own household.

Concerning the fratricidal war he stated:

When last we met here the lurid cloud of civil war threatened swift destruction to our dearest earthly interests. Belligerent armies of kindred people, marshaled in dread array, engaged in mortal strife, and all the elements of destruction were at their deadly work. But now peace sheds abroad her benign influences, the storm of war has ceased, the fell passions which raged so madly are hushed, and universal gladness is diffused throughout the length and breadth of our beloved land. It is the mission of our divine art to minister to the afflicted, to bind up the wounds of the captive, and speak words of comfort and peace to the troubled heart, as well as to teach the grand principles of Masonry. Let us be true to our calling, and aid in restoring that fraternal love that should animate the hearts of all the citizens of our common country. Let us wipe away the tear from the widow's eyes, and minister to the wants of the bereaved orphan.

Congratulate yourselves, that amidst all the convulsions that have so deeply agitated our country, when destruction threatened all our loved institutions, Masonry—venerable with the hoary antiquity of ages—still, like a lofty rock whose foundations were laid deep in the earth, towered above the storm of civil strife, the howling waves of discord beat in vain upon her elevated crest. Amid subsiding kingdoms and crumbling empires, our Mystic Brotherhood still stands, the great beacon of life in ages, the friend of justice, the preserver of peace and humanity.

The Grand Lodge of Georgia met on October 25. Grand Master John Harris feelingly alluded to the devastation that followed the train of hostile armies, and was thankful that they were assembled under more favorable conditions than the preceding year. He called upon his members to "meliorate the condition of our fellow-men, to relieve the distressed and needy—to wipe away the widow's tears, support the orphan, and relieve the distressed from want and destitution."

On November 6, Grand Master A. J. Van Deren of Colorado made one of the few references to the war that had been made in that grand lodge:

I also congratulate you that since our last Grand Communication, peace has been restored to our beloved country, and that it is fast resuming its former happy and prosperous condition. Let us exercise due Masonic charity towards those who have been separated from us by the recent national difficulties, and promptly stretch forth the hand of fellowship, and give them every facility and offer them every inducement to return to their former relations of friendship, fraternity and union, and enjoy with us the prosperity and blessings of our Ancient Order, and of a free and united people.

E. H. English, grand master of Arkansas, on November 6, told his grand lodge of the unity of Freemasonry:

The terrible storm of war is over, the last faint echoes of its awful thunders are hushed, its angry clouds are drifting away, and the sun of peace once more smiles upon our desolate country. Desolated though it be, yet time, patience, and perseverance in the pursuit of peaceful and industrial occupations of life will restore it to its former prosperity.

Many of our brethren who met with us here in former years, and whose faces were familiar to us, now sleep the long sleep of death in their quiet resting-places, and their homes are left in mourning. They may have erred, but to err is incident to the frailty of human nature, and to forgive is not only Masonic but Divine. Let the broad mantle of Masonic charity be thrown over their errors, whatever they may have been, and let their virtues be cherished in the memories of those who survive them.

In the unfortunate and deplorable civil commotions, which for four gloomy years afflicted our country, fortunately for Masonry, it has no schism—the Masons of the United States, now, as before the national troubles, constitute one great, individual Fraternity. Leading Masons, from every section of our extensive country, have assembled at Columbus, Ohio, in the General Grand Chapter, and in the General Grand Encampment, since the close of the war, and, as in years gone, treated each other as brothers and companions, transacted their Masonic business in peace and harmony, renewed their social and fraternal obligations around a common altar, and have thus demonstrated to the world that Masons are bound together by ties which can not be severed by civil strife or political conflicts. So the unity of Masonry has survived the political revolutions of all ages and all countries, and so, in the very nature of its Constitutions and Landmarks, it will continue to maintain its unity. It came down to us from the infancy and cradle of the human family, and so it will go down from us to the old age, final doom, and grave of the human race! Nay, more, we are taught in the symbolism of the Ladder, which the patriarch Jacob in his vision saw, while his head was pillowed on a stone, beneath the watching stars, that the virtue most revered by Masonry, will survive the final wreck of all matter, and doom of all worlds, and continue through the ages of an everlasting eternity! I need not to say to the intelligent craftsman that the sublime and immortal virtue is—Charity! Masons, as such, have never created wars in any age or in any country. They have been drawn into them, as men, in consequence of their connection with the civil institutions of the country, as citizens; but the principles of the Order are tolerant, conservative, peaceful and law-abiding, and tend to prevent war and blood-shed. Masonry never persecuted for opinion's sake. Her skirts are guiltless of the blood of martyrs. She never erected a stake, forged a chain, or kindled a fire for a human victim! I am willing, this night, to take by the hand as my brother, any man on the globe, who is in spirit and truth a Mason, no matter what his country, his claim or his creed; and I will never go to war with him if I can help it! And such, I am sure, are the sentiments of all of you, my brethren. It is fortunate for our country, as well as for humanity, that there is one venerable, old institution, organized upon social and moral principles, which furnishes a common platform and a common altar, where all men who have been intrusted with its sublime mysteries, and assumed its imposing obligations, may meet, and kneel, and mingle the better and nobler feelings and sentiments of our nature, in perfect unity and concord, regardless of all external distinctions and differences in matters of opinion. There is no human organization upon the globe that ever has, or ever will, harmonize in one body so many elements which are in external conflict, as the Masonic organization. Its wise founders, if it ever had any, organized it upon a few simple, but cardinal Landmarks, which command the approbation, and lay fast hold upon the affections of all its initiates, and which furnish no grounds of controversy, admit of no improvement, and tolerate no change. The laws of Masonry are fixed, immutable, and eternal as the laws of mathematics. The old patriarch, Enoch, inscribed them upon a pillar of stone, and transmitted them through the mighty flood. Noah taught them to two of his sons upon the summit of the sacred mountain, where his Ark rested when the flood subsided, and the green earth bloomed and blushed again with vine and fruit under the general sun. Moses learned them from the old priests on the banks of the Nile. The men of Gibal carved them on the rock-ribs of the Mediterranean Sea. Solomon and the two Hirams collected them in a brief code at Jerusalem, and the builders and rebuilders of the Temple spread them over the globe; and they were transmitted to us in legendary lines, as well as to the Indian chiefs who inhabited and claimed to own this great country, before our forefathers discovered it.

His grand lodge adopted a resolution that would forgive all Masons who had political differences during the war.

For the committee on foreign correspondence of the District of Columbia, William G. Parkhurst wrote on November 7:

Silently, noiselessly, but at the same time steadily and successfully, has Masonry been pursuing her great mission, "to soothe the unhappy, to sympathize with their misfortunes, to compassionate their miseries, and to restore peace to their troubled minds." Thus may it ever be, until the arrival of that period, foretold on prophetic vision, when there shall be no want to relieve, no sorrow to assuage.

E. L. Stevens of the Grand Chapter of Maryland and the District of Columbia, six days later, summed up what had transpired among Freemasons during the four years of war:

In taking a retrospective view of the terrible scenes of bitter strife and carnage through which our nation has passed, we can with pride and pleasure point to what our Order has accomplished—its benign influence upon those arrayed against each other—its missions of mercy on thousands of battle-fields, in camps, in hospitals, in prisons, towards the dying and the dead—everywhere its voice of mercy and kindness has been heard, and its charities distributed with a liberal hand. In allaying the animosities of the heart, in uniting those who are enemies and estranged from each other, it has accomplished what no other organization or institution has ever been able to do. And now, as the dark clouds of war have rolled away, and the dawn of a more glorious day is ushered in, it is found in the front rank of the foremost division of all other benevolent societies and agencies, in its heaven-descended mission of charity— in uniting hearts hitherto severed by the cruelties of war—in imparting joy and consolation to homes made desolate—in feeding the hungry, clothing the naked, and binding up the wounds of the afflicted.

We have the most cheering tidings from all portions of the country; brethren and Companions from the north and from the south are again gathering around one common altar and renewing their fraternal vows towards each other, and in that spirit of charity and brotherly kindness, so characteristic of the Order, willing to forget and bury animosities of the past, and seek aid and strength from above, to labor harmoniously in the future for the advancement and welfare of our noble craft. While the same happy results are not realized in ecclesiastical bodies, the outside world may well look in wonder and ask what mysterious power it is that has such a happy influence upon the hearts and affections of these men? Could not the iron hand of pride and of war sunder the ties and break the knot of love and friendship that united them in strong fraternal bonds, as it has in religious bodies and other societies?

The grand high priest of Alabama, James B. Harrison, on December 5, explained what happened in his state when it was struck by an invading army:

Previous to our last convocation the southern portion of our jurisdiction had not felt or experienced the horrors of war in all its bearings; since which we too have been made its victims. Wherever the army penetrated the country was devastated, atrocities of every kind were committed, many were reduced to want, and now the crumbling walls, the isolated chimneys of once happy dwellings, are but monumental evidences of how well the work of destruction was executed; again, after the cessation of hostilities, crops that had been but just planted were abandoned, some in part, others altogether; some were left only for a time through want of labor, a large portion of those that were worked was not properly cultivated, and the yield was therefore very short. I speak not of these things politically, but simply with a view to impress your minds with the present condition of our people, and the want and distress that must inevitably follow. Many of our Companions and brethren have returned home after years of suffering in the army or in prisons. They return with impaired health and broken constitutions, many of them maimed and crippled for life, utterly incapable of physical labor. They return to find the little property upon which they depended for support for their families and themselves all gone—all destroyed; and such are dependent upon the charity of friends. Again, an equally distressing picture is presented by the widows and orphans of our gallant soldiery; they have been made so by the chances of war, and are now left destitute and without even a protector, by its cruel and destructive hand. Among these, doubtless, will be found many who are the widows and orphans of Companions and brethren beloved. These are emphatically widowhood and orphanage, who are to find in every true-hearted mason a friend that sticketh closer than a brother. In view of these facts and the situation of our people, if ever there was a time when masons should practice the beautiful tenets of our Order as taught in our Lodges and Chapter, that time is now. Let us begin the work immediately. Let us take counsel together and see if some means cannot be devised by which timely assistance can be rendered, and thus a large amount of privation and suffering be, if not entirely relieved, so ameliorated as to avoid a want of the necessities of bare subsistence. By a firm, persistent and united effort on our part we can go still farther, and comfortably feed, clothe and educate many of those wards of masonry, to whom we stand in the relation of guardians.

Edward H. Lane, who had become grand master after William H. Harmon had died of the wounds he received at Waynesboro on March 2, spoke to the Grand Lodge of Virginia on December 11:

The "All-seeing eye of Jehovah" has rested upon us. And notwithstanding we have for the last four years passed through an ordeal which it seldom falls to the lot of any people to undergo, yet we may with truth say, that as a Masonic Body, we have preserved our Institution from all those inroads and innovations which have unfortunately found their way into too many of the institutions of our country. And to-night we practice the same rites, and recognize the same principles, as did those noble Worthies who founded our glorious Order. As a Grand Lodge, our integrity is as unsullied as it was on the 17th day of October, 1778, the day of its formation. We have never for one moment lost sight of the tenets of our profession. Actuated by "Brotherly Love, Relief and Truth," we have gone forth on the heavenly mission of relieving the distressed, sympathizing with the unfortunate, and restoring peace to the troubled. . . .

The evils and misfortunes of war have been felt all over our land; and nowhere more than in our Fraternity. Many of our most flourishing Lodges, both in the towns and country, that five years ago were almost all that could be desired of them, have fallen prey to the "devastations of war." In many instances, all their jewels and furniture were destroyed or carried off, and in not a few instances, nothing is left but the naked walls. Not even their charters escaped; but they, together with that "Great Light in Masonry"; which it was fondly hoped would have thrown the panoply of protection around them, escaped not the unsparing ravages of ruthless hands. To supply the place of lost and destroyed charters, will be one of the duties of this Grand Lodge. . . .

The shooting war had been over for six months when the year 1865 drew to a close, but a different type of "war" had taken its place. In the words of the President: "before our brave men have scarcely returned to their homes to renew the ties of affection and love, we find ourselves almost *in the midst of another rebellion.*" He was referring to the men who did not want the Southern states returned to the Union. A war of words had begun.

CHAPTER XXIV

The Year of Crisis

◇◇◇

*Now that the unhappy conflict is ended, it is
gratifying to observe that our noble Brotherhood, everywhere, like the good Samaritan, are
binding up the wounds of the nation, and
soothing them with the oil and wine of charity
which "Hopeth all things." Let us . . . with
stout hearts and ready hands participate in this
noble work, and remove, as far as we can, all
obstacles that may lay in the way.*

CHARLES A. FULLER

WITH FEW EXCEPTIONS, Freemasonry throughout
the country was advocating "forgiveness." On the political scene, with few exceptions, the politicians were demanding retaliation—revenge against the people of the South who
had seceded from the Union.

Andrew Johnson told a large audience in Washington on
February 22, 1866, his version of what the politicians were
doing:

. . . You denied in the beginning of the struggle that any State had
the right to go out. You said that they had neither the right nor the
power. The issue has been made, and it has been settled that a State
has neither the right nor the power to go out of the Union. And
when you have settled that by the executive and military power
of the Government, and by the public judgment, you *turn around
and assume that they are out and shall not come in.*

The laughter and cheers that greeted that statement indicated the people were in agreement with the President even
though the politicians were not. He concluded his extempo-
raneous remarks by pleading with the citizens to read and study
the Constitution of the United States—then stand by it. *"I will*

be found standing by the Constitution as the chief rock of our safety, as the palladium of our civil and religious liberty," he promised them.

In Masonic circles the temperament was entirely different, according to a report submitted by J. Eastman Johnson, the grand secretary of the Grand Chapter of Michigan, on January 8, 1866:

Masonry north, as appears by the uniform tenor of the proceedings received, moves on in peace, unity and plenty. Great prosperity and entire harmony prevail, without exception; and the only ground of solicitude arises from too rapid growth.

The Grand Chapters are now rejoicing at the return of peace. All are anxious to aid in bringing about the most fraternal feeling toward those who have gone astray. They exhort us to extend the broad mantle of masonic charity over all the erring, and to welcome home returning Companions.

Many of the Grand Chapters attest to the kindly power of the mystic tie in the midst of battle; and this power, ever active cannot but materially aid in reuniting the hearts of our countrymen, that never should have been estranged. This reunion being truly and fully consummated by the aid, in part, of our Order, our country—great in the past—becomes greater in the future—one in heart, one in power, one in its elevating influences, and one in its grand destiny.

On the same day a former governor of Florida, Thomas Brown, submitted his report on the correspondence the Grand Lodge of Florida received. He took Guilbert of Iowa to task in no uncertain terms, following the example of most grand lodges, both North and South. He wrote at length about the "conquered" citizens of Florida:

When this Grand Lodge met at its last Annual Communication, war and desolation marched without restraint and, unchecked by any rule of civilized warfare, over our devoted country. Conquering armies swept over our adjacent sister States like the locusts of Egypt, leaving only ruin and nakedness behind them, devastated fields, blackened chimneys, smoking villages and demolished cities. A dark cloud of gloom and despair hung over the Southern horizon like a death pall beneath whose ample folds no ray of light appeared to inspire hope in the stoutest heart. Today we meet with the full assurances that the iron rule of war is over, war destructive to the prosperity of our order, and abhorrent to all our fraternal teachings, and in the place of grim war, the angel of peace spreads her protecting wings and inspires hope and confidence amid our surrounding ruins. In the prospect of returning peace, amid our ruins, let us pause and ponder the course that wisdom would dictate to us to be adopted under the surrounding circumstances. I am aware that as Masons we have nothing to do with the turmoils of war and the strife of partizans and politicians, that our vocation is peace, brotherly love, relief and truth. But so closely and intimately are these duties connected with war and political strife and human suffering, that it will be found often very difficult to avoid drawing profane subjects into our reports, particularly in matters involved in the past civil conflict. I shall endeavor to avoid all exciting subjects except when forced to notice them in self-defence, and to repel injurious charges.

My Brethren, our rulers submitted our national difficulties to the award of the God of Battles, and the issue has been against us. As Masons, our influence was exerted on the side of peace. When war came, our duty was to be true and faithful to the Government under which we lived and found protection; and all those obligations were truly and faithfully discharged, and by our defeat we have lost all but our honor, which no earthly power can take from us, if we are true to ourselves and to God. Then, let us meet the stern issue like men. Let there be no murmurings, no despair, no faintings by the way-side. Let there be no crimination or recriminations, or charges of who erred, or who acted wisely, but like brothers rally together, and show the world how a brave and magnanimous people can meet adversity and rise above calamity. Yes, my brethren, it needs not for me to admonish forbearance and manly perseverance; we see evidence of it wherever we cast our eyes around us. We hear no repinings among the people, but everywhere a determination to meet the issues and make the best of the situation, by firmness and honest perseverance; and like our captive brethren of old, gird ourselves and come up to the great and glorious undertaking of restoring the waste place of our beloved land, with the hope that under the guidance and blessing of our Great Grand Master, and our own labors, the wilderness will again blossom like the rose, and peace and prosperity will again smile over our country.

We witness daily manifestations of Divine Providence to our people, and evidences of hope and confidence on their part, that the Great Architect of the Universe has not forgotten us; but He will, in His good time, restore order out of chaos. The people of the South are now rehearsing one of the most sublime moral spectacles the world has ever witnessed. All classes of the community, men, women and children, of high or low degree, without murmuring or repining, all suiting themselves cheerfully to the new state of things which war has wrought in their several and domestic relations, and gracefully coming down from high positions of refinement and elegance, to a state of poverty, labor and menial service, with grace, ease and cheerfulness. The whole South having submitted their cause to the arbitrament of the sword, are now determined to meet and abide by the issue in good faith and honor, and freely and contentedly return into a reconstructed Union, such as our fathers constructed for us assured—the one great cause of discord having been removed—that it will be as permanent, lasting and prosperous as they contemplated, and that never again will our favored land be disturbed by civil commotions or sectional strifes and jealousies, and that the Government, administered upon the great principles of the Revolution, will work out her destiny as the home and asylum for the oppressed, and the example of liberty and free Government to the whole earth.

With these cheering prospects before us, let us, my brethren, renew our sacred vows to the Giver of all Good, and set our hearts to the work before us with zeal, perseverance and fortitude, believing that He who has set a good work before us, will enable us to accomplish it.

Brown continued his report with several remarks about "Negro Masonry," a question that was to plague Freemasonry continuously. He wrote:

The slave is now as free as his former master, and, in justice, entitled with him to equal protection in his civil, religious and political rights, and in person and property. . . . But as to the question of their social equality, it is a subject in which we are, as Masons, most vitally concerned. . . .

Most foreign grand lodges have lodges comprised of colored men, but with the lone exception of Alpha Lodge, No. 116, under the Grand Lodge of New Jersey, there are none in the United States. The Negroes have their own lodges and appendant rites known as "Prince Hall Masonry." The name is derived from their first Grand Master.

The controversy concerning Prince Hall Masonry dates back to the Revolutionary War. Some say it started on March 6, 1775, when it is claimed Prince Hall and 14 other Negroes were made Master Masons in an army lodge of white Masons attached to General Gage's British Regiment, during the time that regiment was stationed in Boston, Massachusetts. There appears to be no certainty as to which military lodge initiated them, but Harry Davis, a well-informed Prince Hall Mason, believes it was No. 441, Irish Registry.

According to Davis: "The first organized body of colored Masons in America was African Lodge, No. 1—not No. 459, as is generally supposed." *The Prince Hall Year Book* claims that lodge was organized on July 3, 1776. On June 30, 1784, Prince Hall and his lodge formally petitioned the Grand Lodge of England for a charter, which was received on April 29, 1787. In 1791 they formed a Grand Lodge in Massachusetts. Today, all but 11 states have a Prince Hall grand lodge.

It was not until the Civil War erupted that Negro Masonry became a "problem." They were content to practice the rites among the men of their own color, until, with the changing times, Negroes began petitioning for membership in lodges not of Prince Hall ancestry.

Many grand lodges, both North and South, spoke on the subject. Josiah Drummond of Maine, in a lengthy report in 1868, states: ". . . it is useless to undertake to say that the law of Masonry excludes a man . . . because of his race or color. Lodges may not choose to receive a man of another race; that is their prerogative." He also concluded that Prince Hall Masons "can receive '*no countenance*' whatever, not because of their race or color, but because they are, at best but clandestine Masons. . . ."

In 1898, under the leadership of William H. Upton, who was to be elected grand master during the same communication of the Grand Lodge of Washington, resolutions were adopted by that jurisdiction which in effect recognized Prince Hall Masonry as "legitimate." It also agreed to recognize Negro lodges if they were established in Washington under another grand lodge. The wrath of most of the grand lodges in the United States was aroused, and it took three years before everyone appeared to be satisfied that the Grand Lodge of Washington was not "recognizing" Negro Masonry, and that it would continue to maintain its "exclusive jurisdiction" over Freemasonry in its state.

The question of the "legitimacy of Prince Hall Masonry" was again brought up when Melvin H. Johnson, a past grand master of the Grand Lodge of Masachusetts, led a movement in 1947 for his grand lodge to state that a particular colored grand lodge was "legitimate." Massachusetts so voted, but rescinded its action two years later. And the controversy continues today.

During the communication of January 8, 1866, of the Grand Lodge of Florida, the committee on accounts reported it had "examined the books and accounts of the grand treasurer and grand secretary. The account books of the grand secretary have been lost. Those of the grand treasurer we find neatly and correctly kept. We find in the hands of the grand treasurer $469.18 in Confederate Treasury Notes, which we recommend be burned and expunged from the books. . . . We find in the hands of the grand secretary, not paid over to the grand treasurer at the commencement of this grand communication, $75."

All of the jurisdictions and their subordinates in the former Confederacy had the same financial difficulties. The report of George T. Stainback, grand high priest of Mississippi, on January 18, was typical:

The Grand Secretary's and Grand Treasurer's reports will inform you of the condition of the finances of the Grand Chapter, which is indeed, deplorable enough. By a regulation of the Grand Chapter, enacted many years ago, nothing but gold and silver could be received in payment of dues. Two years ago this regulation was for the time changed, and the officers required to receive confederate money, which legislation at that time was wise, and the money so received answered every purpose then; but that cause has gone down, and with it the money, so that the coffers of the Grand Chapter are now empty. In view of these facts, I earnestly recommend that you devise some means to meet the exigencies of the case; and the very reason, Companions, that I do not indicate the policy to be pursued in this matter is, that I am utterly at a loss to suggest a remedy. The subordinate Chapters are in the same deplorable condition. They have received confederate currency in payment for degrees and dues, and are now impoverished, many of them I fear, to such an extent that they will not be able to meet their liabilities to the Grand Chapter. For all I bespeak your indulgence.

* * *

The terrible war just closed has left the land full of widows and orphans. Those to whom they formerly looked for support now sleep in their bloody graves, and the eyes of their surviving loved

301

ones are longingly turned to you. Shall they look in vain? I know they will not. To see that they are fed, clothed and educated you will esteem, I am confident, your duty, as well as inestimable privilege. I urge you, Companions, and through you the subordinate Chapters, to the discharge of this God-like mission.

Before the convocation was closed, resolutions were adopted thanking the Masons of the North for their "brotherly love and kindness."

The appreciation of the Grand Chapter of New York of the Masons of the South was extended by the grand high priest, Horace S. Taylor, on February 6, 1866:

During the progress of the war now so happily ended masonry has done its full part in ameliorating its horrors. In the midst of battle the masonic recognition has often turned aside the messenger of death; and when the battle was over, and darkness overshadowed the field, masons from each army have sought out the wounded and dying brother; binding up his wounds, supplying his wants, and receiving the last messages from dying lips, to be transmitted to loved ones at home.

*　*　*

The masons of the north will ever remember with gratitude the many acts of kindness of their southern brethren towards unfortunate prisoners of war who were placed in their power. Many instances of their kindness have come to our knowledge; prominent among them is the noble conduct of a Grand Master [Fellows] of one of the southern states, who, during the early period of the civil war, went through the prisons of the city in which he dwelt, supplying the wants of his brother masons among the prisoners, at the risk of his own life. Many a family at the north was unknowingly indebted to him for information concerning those whom they had supposed dead.

The grand master referred to, John Q. A. Fellows, called the Grand Lodge of Louisiana to order on February 12, and told his members:

It is one of the landmarks, that masonry only flourishes in times of peace. The Masonic world had, it seems, almost forgotten this trite maxim. It is now known to us, so as never to be forgotten by this generation, and we hope not by the succeeding. The Fraternity has suffered, but, at the same time, has learned lessons which could only be learned by such experience. We have learned another thing: that there exists a virtue in our Institution, which is superior to all the trials of life, to all the vicissitudes of time and the world. We may, now that it has not only survived the storm of fanaticism aimed at itself, but also this last storm aimed at good government, safely assume that the origin of our Institution is Divine, that its principles of morals, as well as its form of government, is such as the Grand Master of us all has devised, or rather inspired, as that best suited to man. So firmly convinced am I of this, that in case of doubt, either on the subject of morals or government, I unhesitatingly refer to the practical teachings of our Order, and never fail in finding a practical solution of every doubt.

Amos Kent, the district deputy grand master of district 2, of Louisiana, reported the instructor of St. Helena Lodge, No. 96, John T. Spencer, had been killed at Vicksburg, and it was in dire straights because "in the fall of 1864, a large body of troops, under Gen. Davidson, occupied Greensburg and ransacked the Lodge."

George A. Pike, of the third district, reported on St. James Lodge, No. 47:

. . . without any interruption except that occasioned by the movements of the military, during the siege of Port Hudson, [it] has labored up to the present moment, and is now in a more flourishing and prosperous condition than ever before in its history. Situated, as it was, on the very border of the conflict, it had a delicate mission to perform, and by the practice of the precepts of our orthodox and catholic religion, this Lodge earned the respect and esteem of those in authority, of both sides of the line, and was the only power here instrumental in mitigating the horrors of war. That this confidence was never betrayed or misused, I think we may safely call on all in authority during that time to bear testimony.

Further reports from the districts contain much information about the trials of lodges in the path of the fighting. DeSoto Lodge, No. 55, after the Battle of Mansfield, was occupied as a Federal hospital. In the confusion the furnishings were destroyed. The master of the same Lodge, N. A. Sutherlin, was killed on December 3, 1862, during the Battle of Fredericksburg. Plains Lodge, No. 135, situated near Port Hudson, was stripped of its furnishings and the building destroyed.

W. C. Driver had been appointed a special district deputy

grand master by Fellows to receive the papers of Army Lodge, U.D., when the members were separated from the service. At the close of his report he wrote:

I cannot close this report without adding my testimony to the harmonizing influence exerted by our Institution, not only on its own members, but on every class of society. The box containing the papers, returns, etc., through the care of the W.G. Secretary, had been marked "Masonic Documents," and sealed with the Seal of the M.W. Grand Lodge. In my journey from New Orleans to Natchitoches, I necessarily came in contact with many officers and privates of the U.S. army, who were not Masons. Yet I was treated by them all with not only every mark of attention, but was forwarded in my progress by the transmission of my baggage, without examination or delay, to the Confederate lines. I could adduce many instances brought within my observation of the benefits derived by Masons from their connection with the Order—instances the more remarkable from the time and circumstances of their exhibition.

Louisiana Relief Lodge, No. 1, during the year 1865 assisted Masons from ten Southern states, eight Northern states, and three foreign countries.

Early in 1866 a report was received by the Grand Lodge of Massachusetts about the activities of Bunker Hill Army Lodge, No. 5, which had worked under a dispensation granted on November 4, 1861:

William Parkman, Esq.
M.W. Grand Master of Masons in Massachusetts.

Sir:

I have the honor to return to you the Dispensation granted in 1861 to Colonel George H. Gordon and brethren of the Second Regiment of Massachusetts Infantry. I surrender also the records. Their imperfect state is due to the fact that the first Secretary, Capt. Edward G. Abbott, was killed at Cedar Mountain; and his acting successor, Surgeon William H. Heath, died in front of Atlanta of disease contracted in the faithful and untiring discharge of his duty. His minutes I have copied and attested. Of the history of this Lodge, I take the liberty to make the following report:—Speedily after the receipt of the Dispensation, Colonel Gordon assumed his office with the Wardens named, Chaplain Alonzo H. Quint, Senior Warden; Major Wilder Dwight, Junior Warden. Measures were taken to perfect the officers and members in the work, the necessary furniture was procured, and in the winter of 1861-2, the Lodge at Frederick, Maryland, kindly allowed us to hold a meeting. Charles Wheaton, Jr. (Adjutant), and Lieutenant Charles R. Mudge and Lieutenant Robert B. Brown, were received as Entered Apprentices, and passed to the degree of Fellow Craft. Lieut. Wheaton leaving the regiment did not proceed further; Lieut. Mudge fell as Lieutenant-Colonel commanding at Gettysburg. Lieut. Brown subsequently was raised.

In the winter of 1861-2, much brotherly intercourse was had with other brethren. On St. John's day, the Lodge in Frederick held a public installation, and our Lodge formed a part of a large procession. I was asked to deliver an address in the Lutheran Church, which was well filled, upon "Masonry and the State." The banquet which followed was attended by over five hundred Masons. In our Army Corps, after consultation, a Committee of Relief was instituted; our Senior Warden was one of seven to serve under Major-General Banks, Colonel Murphy of Pennsylvania, and others. In the active campaign many changes followed: our W.M. Colonel Gordon was promoted to Brigadier-General and transferred; Captain Tucker resigned; Captain Underwood was promoted and sent to the Thirty-Third Massachusetts, the fall of Captain Abbott at Cedar Mountain, the wounding and resignation for disability of Surgeon Leland, and the fall of Lieutenant-Colonel Dwight at Antietam. Thus two of the original eight remained. But, in the winter of 1863-4, in Tennessee, the Lodge again prosecuted its work and resumed meetings. Other Masons in the regiment assisted, and suitable accommodations were had, and the Lodge became a centre of great interest. John F. George, Charles W. Thomas, James W. Cook, Edward A. Phalen, Theodore K. Parker, and Nathan D. A. Sawyer, were severally received, passed and raised. The Lodge was organized as follows: the Senior Warden as Master; Brother James A. D. Sawyer (Lieut.), S.W.; Bro. W. H. Heath (Surgeon), Secretary and Treasurer; Bro. R. B. Brown (Capt.), S.D.; Bro. Whitney (Capt.), J.D.; Bro. Miles (Sergeant), and Bro. A. W. Mann (Lieut.), Tyler. Great numbers of visitors were habitually present. The care of rigid examinations was thoroughly performed, with much labor.

Generals and enlisted men met together not only with no detriment to discipline, but to its advantage. Masons of low military position were only the more careful to show due respect. As an illustration of the extent of visiting, on one evening I noticed present brethren from Maine, New Hampshire, Massachusetts, Rhode Island, Connecticut, New York, New Jersey, District of Columbia, Ohio, Indiana, Illinois, Michigan, Iowa, Colorado, Tennessee, Alabama, and Georgia. Citizens as well as soldiers were visitors; and it is evident that in the work of harmonizing the country, Masonry has a powerful mission to fulfil. The active campaign which fol-

305

lowed, never ceasing until Sherman's army was at Washington, forbade all effort to meet as a Lodge. The intercourse with Masonic brethren was always good. Masons were found to give a brotherly welcome everywhere. The intercourse, even with enemies, was never in the slightest degree prejudicial to loyalty, yet it proved often valuable. The courtesies and helps to prisoners, and to wounded men, were often touching. The hand of the wounded on the field felt a safeguard even those just before in conflict, when it found a brother; and the wounded prisoner on the operating-table felt relieved when he knew that a brother's hand held the knife of the surgeon. Of those eight, originally mentioned in the Dispensation. I will recapitulate with those who were subsequently under the Craft's care.

Col. Gordon became Brevet Major-General; Chaplain Quint left service in Georgia by the advice of the Surgeon; Lieutenant-Colonel Dwight fell at Antietam, nobly; Captain Tucker resigned; Surgeon Leland wounded at Cedar Mountain and resigned; Capt. Underwood, maimed for life at Wauchetchie, became Brevet Major-General; Lieutenant Sawyer resigned from ill health, in front of Atlanta; Captain Abbott was killed at Cedar Mountain—a brave soldier. Of those who received degrees—Lieutenant Colonel Mudge fell at Gettysburg, bravely leading his men; Lieutenant Wheaton is still in service; Captain Brown served with gallantry until the close of the war. Of the other five, four have been wounded. Of other Masons working with us, Surgeon Heath died of disease in front of Atlanta—a true and noble man. I believe none of the enlisted men were wounded; except that George H. Ide, a Fellow Craft (though not sitting with the Lodge), was killed at Cedar Mountain. The lamented Shaw, then a Captain in the Second Massachusetts, had expressed his determination to offer himself at the first opportunity; but he left to take that position in which he fell at Wagner. Accompanying this report, will be forwarded to the proper official the fees due. Other funds have been used in assisting needy brethren; and some help was also rendered to a poor widow and large family of fatherless and suffering children in Georgia; that her husband had fallen in the Confederate army did not seem a reason why assistance should hesitate.

With gratitude I have the honor to be

Fraternally yours
ALONZO H. QUINT
(Late chaplain Second Mass. Inft.)
Senior Warden

That letter answered many questions about the numerous military lodges established during the war.

President Johnson vetoed Senator Lyman Trumbull's civil

rights bill on March 27, because in his opinion, it was unconstitutional and violated the rights of the several states. Before two weeks had passed, Congress, for the first time in history, overrode a Presidential veto of a major measure. There were to be many more before Johnson's term had ended.

The animosity prevalent in Congress toward the vanquished nation, added to the destruction sustained in whole areas of the Southland, caused harsh feelings toward Northerners who had settled in the South. The rule of the "carpetbaggers" did not help matters any.

Among the thousands of Federal soldiers who had found new homes among their former enemies, were a group of Masons in New Bern, North Carolina. Many of them were unhappy with the manner in which they were received when they visited St. Johns Lodge No. 3. They felt "that they were looked upon as intruders" and not as visiting Masons. Although there were many notable exceptions, they decided their best course of action was to request a dispensation to form another lodge in the city.

On the evening of April 10, 1866, several Northern Masons met for the purpose of forming a new lodge in New Bern. Of the 26 who signed the petition, six were from New York, two were native North Carolinians, one each were from Connecticut, Illinois, Indiana, Iowa, Maine, New Hampshire, Ohio, and Pennsylvania. The largest number, ten, were from Massachusetts. Federal troops from that state occupied New Bern during most of the war, which may account for the large number of New Englanders who settled in the city after hostilities had ceased.

Many questions of Masonic law were encountered by the petitioners, although St. Johns Lodge did approve their request. The master, C. C. Clark, declined to sign the recommendation until he was satisfied all of the objections he had raised were removed. Among them was his belief the signers should demit from the lodges in which they held membership before they could apply for a dispensation to form a new lodge.

Letters asking for a clarification of the many questions raised were sent to Albert Mackey of South Carolina, John W. Simons of New York, and C. W. Moore of Massachusetts. All but Simons claimed it was not necessary to obtain demits in order to form a new Lodge. But at least eight of them did request and obtain demits from their Northern Lodges; then they applied to St. Johns Lodge for membership. All eight were rejected! "Proving," stated James O. Whitemore, "there were men who forgot the teachings of the order and allowed sectional feeling to prevail."

When the members of the proposed New Bern lodge held their next meeting, it was determined to submit another petition for its formation to St. Johns Lodge. The new one was signed by only the eight who had been rejected for membership. It was done, and the members of the original lodge approved the request. The Grand Master issued a dispensation on September 7, 1866. The Northerners had found a Masonic home.

During the annual communication of the Grand Lodge of Missouri in May, the grand secretary, George F. Gouley, reported:

We find the Craft, generally, throughout the United States and Canada, in an exceedingly flourishing condition. . . . We have also found, on the other hand, that some of the Grand Lodges, during the past years of war and passion, have "fallen into the hands of the Philistines"—the politicians—and these, at our hands, are entitled to no quarter, and received none. If there is one creature on the face of God's earth, that is more of an intolerable curse to vital and legitimate Free Masonry than another, it is a politician, who has not the common decency to keep his political or sectional views to himself, without intruding them into the sanctity of the Lodge room, Grand or Subordinate, either in public addresses or private discussions.

The days and circumstances which brought these blatant reformers upon the stage have providentially passed away, and we may also hope that the effects will disappear with them. Let us, therefore, hope for a more exalted tone of Masonic sentiment—one that is never carried away from the haven of conservative peace out into the stormy sea of contending passions, but ever adhering to the immovable anchor of *Truth*—will bid defiance to all the storms of revolutionary or civil hate. The Free Mason who forgets his solemn obligations to *"Brotherly Love, Relief and Truth,"* in the dark nights of disaster, is unworthy the name of a *Mason* in the bright days of peace, when the temptations of our nature are at rest. We have found this idea to be the controlling line of action in this Grand Body since its formation, and from which it has never deviated, even during the last five years, when she rode majestically and calmly over a gulf of rapine, murder, arson, and kindred outrages such as no State or nation has ever suffered before in the same space of time. This idea has been our guide in these brief reviews, and from it we have measured the proceedings of our sister Grand Bodies.

The President's efforts for the South, and actually for all of the United States as future generations were to learn, did not go unrewarded, for the University of North Carolina gave him an honorary LL.D. degree on June 7.

Four days later, Grand Master Robert M. Elgin of Texas, happily reported to his grand lodge:

In looking over the proceedings of those Lodges for the last few years, I have been gratified to find that amid the turmoil and bloodshed, the bitter feeling and hatred outside, the genuine principles of Freemasonry have governed the action of our sister Grand Lodges. Even in those jurisdictions where the strife was most bitter, and partisan hatred most intense, we find that, although the feelings of a brother or the action of a particular Lodge has occasionally gone beyond the teachings of the Order, and caused them to forget for a moment the time-honored regulations of the Craft, the Grand Bodies have stood, almost without exception, as I trust they ever will, the great conservators of the Institution, and have checked every movement calculated to degrade the Order into a participation in political and partisan affairs.

The committee on foreign correspondence for the Grand Lodge of Texas, headed by W. B. Botts, was not happy about the statements made by Edward A. Guilbert during his reign as grand master of Iowa. It claimed he had "polluted the records of his grand lodge with political rhapsodies akin to the first effort of a school boy at a 'Fourth of July' oration."

The grand treasurer of Texas submitted the following report:

1865
June — To Balance in treasury, as per last annual report,
      nothing $0.00
1866
June 11. — Received from grand secretary, nothing 0.00
      Paid out, nothing 0.00
      Amount in the treasury, nothing, ... 0.00
GALVESTON, June 11th, 1866.

JAMES SORLEY, *Grand Treasurer*

309

The grand master of Wisconsin, John T. Wentworth, on June 12, commented on the large number of men petitioning for the degrees in Masonry:

This increase of material may probably, to a large extent, be attributed to the termination of the civil war, whereat a large number of our young men returned to their homes. These men had, during their soldier-life, witnessed on many occasions, the beneficent influence of the Order. On the wearisome march, in the loathsome prison, and in the deadly strife, they had beheld the practical exemplification of the three great tenets of the Mason's profession: Brotherly Love, Relief, and Truth. He had seen the hand of the dying soldier clasped, his parched lips moistened, the death sweat wiped from his brow, and his last dying message to his distant home and friends intrusted to one against whom he had just been contending in the terrible conflict. Is it strange, therefore, when generous, noble-hearted men have been called to witness all this and more, on many occasions, and have been brought into direct contact with the practical workings of an Institution "which unites men of every country, sect, and opinion, and conciliates true friendship among those who otherwise would have remained at a perpetual distance," that they should be drawn almost irresistibly toward it, desiring, through its sublime and mystic ceremonies, to study its teachings and share in its benefits. Hence, we find a large number, on return to their homes, seeking admission into our Order, thus causing an unusual increase of membership in the various subordinate Lodges within this jurisdiction.

On the same day, Grand Master T. Douglas Harrington of Canada told his members:

No political struggles can affect the standing of a brother, nor interfere with the mission of Masonry, which is to try to mitigate suffering and alleviate distress. I have been particularly struck with Missouri, where many Lodge rooms have been robbed of all furniture, jewels, records, everything of the slightest value. The Committee on Grievances report thus nobly and Masonically: "It is not for us, who have preserved relations of loyalty, to pronounce sentence of outlawry upon brothers, who, wherever they may be, are as conscientious in their action as we claim to be in ours. We may grieve that so many of our brethren entertain conflicting sentiments, that lead to civil war and carnage; but, as Masons, we hope the day will never come when our Lodge rooms will be closed against a worthy brother on account alone of political opinions."

In the political arena charges and countercharges were being made during the congressional campaign of 1866. Johnson took an active part in an endeavor to gain men who believed in his policies. Two of his staunchest friends were Union heroes of the war, Grant and Farragut. The opposition did everything possible to break up that friendship, but with no success.

Although Johnson had been elected in 1864 along with the Republican Lincoln, he was a Democrat. But during the campaign of 1866 he worked for a conservative congress, asking the people to rise above party differences. He pleaded for the Constitution, peace, and conciliation; he explained his policies, and begged for a complete restoration of the Union.

During that campaign, rumors of threatened violence were spread everywhere. Before the election thousands of guns were shipped to such places as Illinois and Indiana. Riots broke out in many places.

The "Radicals" won a decisive victory which some observers credit to the non-secrecy of the ballot, and the fear of reprisals. Each party had its own type of ballot, easily discernable at the polls. The secrecy enjoyed today was over two decades away.

Howard K. Beale closed his account of "The Critical Years" by writing: "A study of that campaign shows that the Radicals forced their program upon the South by an evasion of issues and the clever use of propaganda. . . ." The results were to cause Johnson no end of trouble.

Troubles for the Grand Lodge of Arkansas had lessened on November 5 when its grand master, Elbert H. English, told his members:

Twelve months ago, Masonry in Arkansas was . . . in the condition of a *fallen tree*. Out of *one hundred and seventy* chartered Lodges upon our Register, but fifty were represented at your last Annual Communication. The Register itself had been destroyed by fire, with the Masonic Hall of this city [Little Rock], which contained it. Many other Lodge-houses had been consumed by flames kindled by the war. A number of Lodges had been plundered. . . . The masters and wardens of other Lodges were dead. They had fallen upon distant battlefields, or died from the exposures of the march and the camp, and slept in unmarked graves far from their homes and their much loved Masonic altars. The membership of many of the Lodges were also dead, or scattered. Communities were broken up, houses left tenantless, and abandoned fields uncultivated. The destitute widow and the helpless orphan were in want of bread, and, in many instances, there was but little to supply them.

But at the close of the war no class of our population returned more readily, quietly and cheerfully to the peaceful pursuits of life than the Masonic Fraternity. . . . Lodges have been rebuilt and re-furnished . . . the surviving Craftsmen have reassembled and re-sumed their labor. . . . *Masonry* can never die, because her laws are immutable and everlasting.

Charles A. Fuller of the committee on foreign correspondence for Tennessee took a dim view of the few lodges in the South who asked for monetary assistance:

The Grand Lodge [Pennsylvania] donated the sum of one thou-sand dollars to the Grand Lodge of South Carolina. We regret very much the undignified spectacle presented by many of the subordi-nate Lodges in our sister jurisdiction, in flooding the country with clamorous appeals for pecuniary aid. Undoubtedly our brethren of the Palmetto State suffered severely in the closing scenes of the late war, and we deeply sympathize with them in the partial but terrible desolations of her people; but she endured not so much the "brunt of the contest" as Virginia, whose soil was deeply dyed with the blood of the contestants, and for years was the theater of more hard-fought battles than were fought in any other State; nor more than Georgia, in the sweeping destruction following in the train of mov-ing armies, and so of other States, where the brotherhood suffered equally as much, if not more, in the destruction of their halls, furni-ture, and property of every description, leaving them "houseless and homeless, and subject to the peltings of the pitiless storms of heaven;" but from all these we have seen no like piteous appeals for aid as have come to us from various portions of South Carolina. Not withstanding our condemnation of these numerous begging applications, we take pleasure in recording the noble responses made to many of them by our Northern brethren, who, casting aside the ascerbities naturally engendered by the frightful contest—forgetting the trials and tribulations of the past—dropping all political feel-ing—seeing nothing, knowing nothing, except that brethren of the same mystic family were overwhelmed with dire distress, came promptly to the rescue by individual and collective appropriations of their substance, freely contributing of their means toward reliev-ing the wants of brethren in distress. Nevertheless, we like not the spirit of mendicancy lately so publicly manifested, and, while we applaud the noble responses to the appeals made, we feel con-strained to condemn the appeals themselves, as tending to bring the brethren of the South into contempt.

Fuller had opened his report on a happier note:

Since our last Communication the country has experienced a great and important change. The din of arms and shout of battle are measureably silenced; the smoke of the fires laying waste our country has passed away, leaving the gleam of returning peace and the hope for better days for the future. In the crisis through which our country is passing, Masonry has high and responsible duties to perform.

As the great and sublime mission of our Order is "Peace on earth and good will to men," we should hail with pleasure the restoration of peace to our afflicted country. During the late reign of terror, violence, and suffering, the power and divinity of Masonic principles were often thoroughly tested and beautifully illustrated on many sanguinary battle-fields and in hospitals; mitigating the fierceness of strife on the field of carnage and soothing the sufferings of its mutilated victim on the couch of pain.

The grand secretary of the Grand Lodge of Massachusetts received a letter from West Virginia signed by "Adme." The writer pleaded with Charles W. Moore to write a history of Freemasonry during the Civil War while the events were fresh in the minds of everyone. He went on to give the Grand Secretary some material with which to work:

... In 1862 I was appointed a chaplain to the hospital at this place [name not given]; and during my connection therewith, I was brought into close contact with the sick portion of the Federal prisoners, of which there were at different times, at this fort, about 15,000. There were usually from three hundred to five hundred in the hospital. These I visited almost daily. I was also, by request of the party interested, the chaplain to one house of well prisoners, of about 450 officers, during the years 1864 and 1865. I thus had an opportunity of freely meeting the common soldier as well as the officer. Until the fall of 1864, I do not think I saw any evidence that there was a Mason in the whole crowd. Then, however I saw the signal of want, which was relieved by me from day to day as well as I was able, by a supply of such food as the sick needed, and which could not be prepared in the culinary department of the hospital. On inquiring of him why he had not hailed me before, he replied that, before leaving home, he had been told that the Grand Lodge of Virginia had passed an order not to recognize Masons of the Federal army who should be found on our soil. I replied to him, that I had been a member of that Grand Lodge for years, and could assure him that the statement had not the slightest foundation. After

313

this time I found many Masons, and received many calls for help; and in every case they were answered by personal conversation with the applicant, and with the relief demanded. What I was able to do was done. That the Mason was better off than others I freely acknowledge; for, while I tried to do my duty to all, the masonic tie of brotherhood caused that they receive the friendly, in addition to the official, attention. My duty as chaplain had no reference to the temporal condition of the sick; but I felt it my duty to labor in either capacity whereby the greatest good might be produced, and the greatest comfort given to the sick. [He also stated he loaned vast sums of money to destitute Masons].

. . . I should also state that I knew several of the members of my Lodge, who, when prisoners in the North, received favors from the brethren there. When the Sixth Corps was in our town, we had several meetings of our Lodge, at which members of the corps were present. Our hall was in very bad condition, having been used and abused as a hospital, and by other causes; and we had done nothing of importance toward furnishing it, as we had just paid off the debt of its erection, and had not the means either to re-roof it or furnish a suitable regalia for the officers. But we had very neat jewels as a beginning. While the officer of the Provost Marshal's office had possession of our ante-room, the lodge-room was forcibly entered and our jewels removed. It was with some unpleasant feelings that we were to be seen, with our W.M. having a piece of tin, our J.W. with a piece of wood, and other officers similarly decorated, by representations of city and well-furnished Lodges; but we did what we could, and gave them a cheerful, if not a pleasing reception. Our feeble lights and dingy walls formed a heavy contrast to the brilliantly-lighted and handsomely-furnished halls which awaited their presence at their homes. As our jewels were taken by some member of the corps, the Masons of that body promised to send us a new set, but we have heard nothing of the fulfillment.

The following incidents have come to me in so direct a line, that I will mention them. The first was in this State. The Federal soldiers had taken possession of a neighborhood, and were freely helping themselves to whatever could be found that suited their purpose. Among other yards they entered, was that of a Methodist preacher, who was absent. His wife seeing her pigs and poultry rapidly fall, and that the soldiers were entering her house, sprang to the door, and, in a loud and alarmed voice, asked if there was not a Mason who would relieve the wife of a Mason? In a few moments the house and yard were empty of soldiers. Of such incidents I have heard many. The other case was this: an officer, a Mason, having occasion to go out on the bloody field of Gettysburg, on the night after the battle, had not gone far before he heard sounds of words

314

which at once arrested his attention. The voice was gradually becoming fainter. He could do nothing alone and in the dark, and seeing a light in the field hospital, went there and asked the use of a light. A very stern refusal was the reply. Failing to get the assistance he desired, and feeling bound to attend that cry, and afford, if possible, the desired relief, he, as the last resort asked in a loud voice, if there was a Mason within? The officer, who had so sternly refused him a light, came to him and asked, why the question? He was told to take his lantern, and come and see. After a private word, they went out. The sounds soon fell upon the old Surgeon's ear, and he passed on until he came to a Confederate colonel, with a piece of shell in the groin, and rapidly sinking. The attendants with the stretcher were soon there, and the wounded Mason was taken to the hospital, cared for, nursed, and restored to health, and was in active service at the surrender of Lee. What more could have been done by an own mother's son?

When we see what Masonry has done to bless our race, are we not forced to believe it, next to the Church of God, the greatest Institution of the world?

Many grand lodges during 1865 and 1866 were sorrowed by the announcement from the Grand Lodge of Pennsylvania of the death of George Mifflin Dallas. He was a past grand master of that grand lodge and had been vice-president of the United States under James K. Polk from 1845 to 1849. Dallas was to endear himself forever to Masons for his defense of the Fraternity when Thaddeus Stevens and his anti-Masonic legislature of Pennsylvania tried to force him to betray Freemasonry. In January, 1836, he was "arrested and brought before that tribunal, like a criminal," but in a masterly address he refused to be sworn. The legislature finally became disgusted with Stevens and his tactics, and released Dallas and the other Masonic "prisoners."

The year 1866 ended with harshness, bitterness, and hatred in the political arena. In Masonic circles the actions were completely different. Every effort was being made by the Masons of the North and South to reunite the still un-united states.

CHAPTER XXV

The Years After

◇◇

> *The object . . . is simply to impress upon Masons their duty in the broad, the liberal, and the charitable exercise of the Masonic virtues towards our brethren in the South . . . and thereby perfect a complete restoration of fraternal relations, which may lead in the end to a harmonious political re-union. The former of these are the elements of the latter, and without them the latter can never take place.*
>
> S. C. COFFINBURY

THE FORTUNES of all Masonic bodies began to increase in 1867, and they were to continue to prosper throughout the years. There were to be no more major setbacks in the United States, but the Masons in some foreign countries were not to fare so well. Wars on their soil were to prove more disastrous than the one between the North and South, insofar as Masonry was concerned.

When the Grand Chapter of Mississippi met in January, 1867, the grand treasurer reported a balance of almost $3,000; the grand lodge reported a balance of more than $4,000.

Grand Master S. C. Coffinbury of Michigan, on January 9, spoke feelingly about Masonry's mission in the years after the war:

At the present juncture of events in our country, it may be considered that our Order stands in a most responsible position. A war has terminated, leaving many of the ties and bonds which once united the people, dissevered and broken. There is no power, or effort of power, which can exert so succcssful an cffort in reuniting these ties and bonds as the offices and influences of Masonry. The political issues which have separated, and still in a measure separate the North and the South, we ignore. With these, as Masons, we have

316

nothing to do. All we can see as our duty in this most interesting crisis of our common country, is the humanitarian duty of diffusing brotherly love, peace and harmony, and a restoration of our Union to its former strength and integrity. It is our duty by this means to give strength where political issues weaken the bonds. The officers of Masonry are fraught with harmony and peace; political questions and their discussion harrass the mind, create discord and arouse animosities. It is our duty to pour oil and wine to sooth the rankling heart-aches of a disappointed, a conquered, and a submissive people. If they have been in fault, a reopening of the wounds by retrospection will but keep alive the animosities and widen the breach which separates us, thus defeating the great object —an affectionate re-union, upon which alone can a political re-union be successfully founded. To re-establish those bonds of affection rests with the Order of Free Masonry, North and South, and if through this element they cannot be re-established, then is our Confederacy forever broken, for the tendency of every other effort is to fan the fires of discord between us. But, you ask, what can Masonry do? It can, in the true spirit of its original design and its sublime lessons, forgive the past where it was at fault; it can, in the superabundance of its charity, sympathize with our unfortunate brethren of the South—it can mourn with them over their devastated plantations, their razed mansions, and the smoking ruins of their cities and villages; it can drop the tear with them over their bloody battle-fields, and the graves of their sires, their sons, and their brethren, albeit they fell in arms against the North. This last it is human to remember, but not to cherish is Masonic. To forget, it is noble; to forgive, it is divine. Perhaps, if in the pure spirit of Masonry we were to put ourselves under the same stringent rule of accusation and condemnation to which we subject others, we might in many respects become supplicants for forgiveness. Have we all so far satisfied our own consciences individually as to enable us to look up to the Throne of God with confidence and hope of forgiveness and say, Forgive us our trespasses as we forgive those who trespass against us? Then let us not reprehend too severely our brethren of the South.

The South began to rebuild as soon as hostilities had ended, but for years it was to be hampered by the politicians of the North. The former Confederate states had almost no champions in the congress of the United States. Only President Johnson and his supporters stood between the South and complete subjugation by Northern political and unscrupulous business leaders.

Thaddeus Stevens, the anti-Mason, was the clever political leader who opposed the President's moderate course in dealing with the conquered Southern states. The fact that there were thousands of empty places in the homes of the North where fathers, sons, husbands, and brothers would have been had there been no war, did not help matters any. The South appeared to feel it had been the only section to suffer; that feeling kept what appeasement there might have been from crystallizing.

Johnson's plan for the South considered no basic changes, nor did he believe in taking advantage of the confusion to increase the powers of the Federal government. The Republicans in congress felt differently and passed laws that, in the opinion of Southerners, and many Northerners, were unconstitutional; they even tampered with the Constitution, it was claimed.

They were referring to what has come to be known as "The Fourteenth Amendment." The ground work for that was laid early in 1866. Its ratification by Tennessee resulted in congress admitting that state to the Union on July 24, 1866. Tennessee was the first of the former Confederacy to accept that amendment. Within eight months after the amendment had been submitted to the states, all of the other Confederate states had rejected it; three of them unanimously; the others almost so. It was also rejected by three border states, Kentucky, Maryland, and Delaware. The latter was never to ratify the Fourteenth Amendment, and it never ratified the Thirteenth.

California neither ratified nor rejected the amendment. Three states, New Jersey, Oregon, and Ohio, accepted it during 1866, but in 1868 withdrew their earlier assent. All of which was to be most confusing to Secretary of State Seward.

In spite of the plea of Governor Murphy of Arkansas for the citizens to accept their lot, his state rejected the amendment during December, 1866. The senate committee of Arkansas reported "the Amendment had not been Constitutionally proposed, nearly one-third of the States being excluded from all participation in it," and "it had not been submitted to the President for his approval."

Although, mathematically, three-fourths of the states had not ratified the Fourteenth Amendment, in July, 1868, Congress

318

directed the secretary of state to declare it adopted. The confused Seward did so on July 28.

The great battle over, Thaddeus Stevens died two weeks later. He was buried, by his own direction, in a Negro cemetery in Lancaster, Pennsylvania. The stone over his grave bears an inscription in his own handwriting:

I repose in this quiet and secluded spot, not from any natural preference for solitude, but finding other cemeteries limited as to race by charter rules, I have chosen this, that I might illustrate in my death the principles which I advocated through a long life, Equality of Man before his Creator.

As far as the South was concerned, their arch-enemy had gone to join the devil. One editor in Louisiana, Daniel Dennett, formerly a citizen of New Hampshire, wrote: "With Thad Stevens in his [the devil's] Cabinet, and [Benjamin] Butler in Washington, he can manage things in both Kingdoms to his liking."

President Johnson, committing political suicide, continued to speak for moderation in dealing with the former Confederacy. His speeches, when read, appeared to many people to be those of a demagogue, according to William H. Crook, but Crook went on to say: "He had a calm, assured way of talking. . . . His bearing was quiet and dignified, his voice low and sympathetic. . . ." Even his enemies agreed that he was a great orator.

The continued opposition of the many "reprisal" acts of Congress by Johnson, brought about a resolution of impeachment on February 24, 1868. "That Andrew Johnson, President of the United States, be impeached of high crimes and misdemeanors in office," read the resolution of the committee on reconstruction of the House. The "high crimes and misdemeanors" were proved to be simply a disagreement with Congress over what punitive action should be taken against the South. Benjamin Butler, the Mason, joined with the anti-Mason Stevens, and others, to oust the president.

The "trial" opened on March 30 and the first vote was taken on May 16. When the voting was over, it stood 35 guilty; 19 not guilty. One vote stood between Johnson and impeachment. The opposition did not give up; the senate was adjourned for ten days; for ten days the senators who had voted against impeachment, particularly the seven Republicans, were subjected to the worst sort of pressure. "The Radical press raged and clamored, the pulpit thundered, while the practical politicians put on the pressure," wrote Henry.

The impeachment trial ended on May 26 with the vote exactly the same as ten days earlier. Nineteen men had saved the Congress of the United States from performing a disgraceful act.

Congress was not through, however. It declared "the Johnson states" illegal and set up new state governments. They became so corrupt that many Northern newspapers began to realize that Johnson had not been completely wrong; too late for his salvation, but in time to save the country.

Johnson was not a candidate for the presidency in 1868. U. S. Grant became the Republican candidate and won over Horatio Seymour, the ex-governor of New York, who had opposed Lincoln's policies throughout the war. For the next eight years the South suffered.

About the time corrupt legislatures were taking control of the Southern states in 1868, Nathan Bedford Forrest organized the Ku Klux Klan into "the Invisible Empire," becoming its "Grand Wizard." He "dropped out" of Masonry about the same time. Before 1870 he attempted to disband the Klan, and the "respectable element of Southerners who had widely joined the order" withdrew, but the organization remained active and has continued its existence to the present time.

While many of the politicians of the day were taking every means at their disposal to win votes no matter who was hurt (a situation that still exists), the Masons of the day were doing everything in their power to heal the wounds that were the result of the war. The Grand Lodge of Wisconsin, on June 11, 1867, adopted the following report and recommendation:

Your Committee are well satisfied, that, in very many localities in the Southern States, Master Masons, and the widows and orphans of Master Masons, are in state of almost destitution, not having at the present time, the common necessaries of life, which appeals loudly and earnestly, for the exercise of Masonic charity.

And disregarding all questions, differences, and conditions of a civil or political character, and governed only by Masonic obliga-

320

tion, your Committee recommends a donation of ten hundred dollars by this Grand Lodge, out of the charity fund, for the purpose herein contemplated; and that the sum be drawn, by the Grand Master, Deputy Grand Master and Grand Secretary, and so disposed of as shall in their opinion reach the true objects of Masonic Charity in the Southern States.

Your Committee reports further: that we find, from the best evidence within our reach, that the subordinate Lodges of this State have donated the sum of $823.50, for the same purpose, $793.50 of which has been paid in to the Grand Secretary, and by him disbursed as directed by the Grand Master. The balance sent directly, from the several Lodges donating, to the South.

On the following day, the Grand Lodge of New Hampshire appropriated a sum "for the benefit of necessitous Lodges in the Southern States." Almost every other grand lodge and chapter in the North, East, and West, did the same. The plea by the grand master of Minnesota, C. W. Nash, was typical of many during that period:

In this case, their great hour of need, we should fulfill that great mission that Masonry teaches, which is to feed the hungry and destitute; to clothe the naked; to soothe and cherish the disconsolate; to bind up the wounds of the broken-hearted; and, in the spirit of Masonry, forgive the errors of the past, remembering that to forget is noble, to forgive, divine; that indiscretion in them should not destroy humanity in us.

His appeal resulted in donations for the South totalling $2,292.65.

The appreciation of such kind acts was noted by all of the recipients. The comments of Grand Master Wilson Williams of Alabama, whose grand lodge had received some $3,500 by December 2, 1867, is symbolic:

Just emerging from a long and disastrous civil strife, in which clouds and darkness were round about us, with the war echoes and their wail of woe still tingling in our ears, and longing for peace and tranquility, we gathered our clans of scattered craftsmen to comfort those that mourned, and give aid to the destitute; we could not give aid to the afflicted, for *they* mourned those that were not, and exhausted our means ere the work of relief was well begun. Thus, powerless to succor, the voice of cheer comes to us from our northern brethren—enemies in war, in peace, friends—and the hand of charity is extended to a fallen foe. They bid us welcome to their hearts and give of their substance to relieve our necessities. We accept, with grateful hearts, the aid thus tendered, and in these acts of fraternal sympathy we recognize the influence of that noble tenet of our time-honored order—"Brotherly love, relief and truth." By it the gulf of strife is bridged over, and we enter a land of peace and harmony, where our feet tred the sacred pavement of the Lodge. Would that Masonry were universal; then would all enemies be subdued, and the nations learn war no more. . . .

One of the few grand masters who had let his political feelings overcome his Masonic teachings received much criticism from all sides. He was Edward A. Guilbert of Iowa who, among other deeds, removed John S. Breckinridge as Iowa's representative near the Grand Lodge of Kentucky, terming him a "self-convicted traitor and a fugitive from justice."

Phillip C. Tucker of Texas did not like that. "We always thought that conviction should come through regular channels of justice and through forms prescribed by law," he wrote. "Grand Master Guilbert has not convinced us of our error although he has constituted himself judge, jury, witness and prosecutor."

The chairman of the foreign correspondence committee for the Grand Lodge of New York, John L. Lewis, did not appreciate Guilbert's "flowery" speeches, for he wrote "The Grand Master opens his address on a key so far up in the scale of harmonies, that we confess our inabililty to follow him. We take it for granted, however, that it is all right, because it is full of poetry, which we never could understand."

Many Northern Masons moved to the South during and after the war. The same was true in reverse. The migrating Masons were responsible in a large measure for soothing the unhappiness and ill-will engendered during and after the conflict. The story of one is an excellent example of many of them.

Alexander G. Babcock was born in Princeton, New Jersey, April 18, 1835, and was educated in the schools of that state until, at the age of 13, he was apprenticed to a banknote printer in New York City. He worked at that trade until 1862 when he moved to Richmond, Virginia. Upon his arrival in the Confederate capital, he offered his services to the government and was assigned to the Treasury and Post Office departments, two agencies in dire need of experienced assistance.

Babcock became a captain of Company H, Third Battalion, on February 19, 1864, after the war had taken a turn for the worst for his adopted country. Under special orders, he joined Colonel John S. Mosby as a first sergeant on May 23. While in charge of an artillery unit of Mosby's Rangers, he was surprised and captured by a company of the 16th New York Cavalry on October 15, 1864.

Hohenlinden Lodge, No. 56 (now St. Albans), Brooklyn, New York, made Babcock a Master Mason on March 6, 1862. He affiliated with Dove Lodge, No. 51, Richmond, Virginia, on August 26, 1864, and from the first took an active interest in Virginia Freemasonry. He proved his interest in 1889 when he gave the Grand Lodge of Virginia 44½ acres of excellent farming land, a ten room dwelling, large barn and stable, and all of the other necessary outhouses; in addition he added a further gift of $5,000 "in a perfectly solvent bond"; all to be used to start a Masonic Home.

It is generally conceded that Babcock, the Northerner whose sympathies were with the South, hastened the day of the establishment of the Masonic Home of Virginia by many years.

Twenty-two years after his gift, a group of Masons in the community of which the Masonic Home is a part perpetuated his memory when they formed a new Lodge and named it "Babcock Lodge"—to which the Grand Lodge of Virginia added, "No. 322."

Acts similar to Babcock's became so commonplace after the war that they were taken for granted in far too many instances. Through Masons like him goodwill was spread throughout the North and the South.

During the years after the war, many of the ornaments and furniture that had been stolen when Masonic temples were ransacked, were returned. Many items were found in shops, purchased by Northern Masons, and sent to their rightful owners.

On October 4, 1861, Relief Lodge, No. 284, Pierpont, Ohio, made Sylvester B. Brown a Master Mason. The following day he moved south with the Union army, his whereabouts to remain a mystery for the next 50 years. Then a letter sent from New Orleans by a Mason named David T. Weill, was received by Relief Lodge:

A couple of years after cessation of hostilities between the states, one of my laborers in plowing a field, turned up an old grave whose indications pointed to its being that of a soldier, and in this grave was found a medallion, or charm, made out of a silver half dollar, having engraved on one side a square and compass in the center, and the following engraved around the Bible, which was the base of the coin, "Relief Lodge No. 284" and the letters "S. B." at the base. This grave is about 20 miles from Fort Hudson, La., which during the war, as you doubtless know, was a fort, and around which many a man, both Federal and Confederate, paid the price for his devotion to his country. I mentioned the find to a number of Masons who showed interest in the matter and tried to trace the lodge in question, but so far as I know never did.

I was very desirous of returning the charm to some member of the family, satisfied that it would prove an heirloom if the grave was in fact that of a soldier as I surmised. But time went on. No information was vouchsafed me, and I forgot all about the matter and in the meantime I had mislaid the charm. A few days ago in rummaging over an old trunk of effects I found the charm and I made up my mind to endeavor to find out where Relief Lodge No. 284 was located, and for that purpose I wrote to Mr. Johnson, Grand Secretary, and he furnished me your name and address. If there are any members of the family of the late S. B. B. have them communicate with me, if not, and your lodge wants the charm, let me know.

That medallion now hangs on the wall of Relief Lodge, along with a copy of the foregoing letter.

That Masons, both North and South, had remembered and still practiced the teachings they had received in their lodges, was evident from the many reports made by grand masters and committees. Henry J. Stewart of Florida told his grand lodge on January 13, 1868:

The condition of our once happy country is deplorable indeed. We have passed through a severe and trying ordeal. But the din of musketry is no longer heard on the tented field, the clash of arms has ceased, and although there may still be strife in the political arena, yet our Northern brethren have reached forth their hands

for fraternal fellowship, saying, "Peace be unto you!" Not doubting, as Thomas did the Savior, we eagerly grasped those hands thus extended, and bid them welcome into our holy temples and around our sacred altars. Thus has the wound been healed, the widow's heart made to rejoice, and the orphan's tear wiped away. How pleasing, then, and delightful the thought to him who can claim to belong to an Order fraught with so much influence, and so wonderful in its character. . . .

A. J. Buird, D.D., summed up what many were saying in October, 1868:

In all the fury and rage of evil passion, not a single voice charged this institution of deviating from its true sphere. In prison, on the field, and along the desolate and cindered walks of destroyed homes, full many a sufferer found rest, refreshment, shelter, and a friend beneath its old ivy-grown arch. Who does not rejoice to know that there is a bow of sympathy and hope too high to be reached by the evil thunders of human passion; or obscured by the gloom of the sin of men! "We speak that we do know, and testify that we have seen."

One of the most respected Masons of his day, William C. Penick, a past grand master of Alabama, explained the Southern Masons' position during the war:

We cannot realize that we have at any time been traitors or rebels against the Government of the United States. We know that we had no intention to do anything which would make us traitors or rebels. My brethren, are you fanatics and knaves? Neither are we traitors or rebels, and never have been. We differed as to the principles of the Government, our States also; an issue was made, that issue has been fought out, the end has come, and we have been beaten. We have accepted the condition, and intend to act in good faith. We hope that through a returning sense of justice in you, we may yet obtain our rights; until then, and always, we expect to be quiet and peaceful citizens—as good Masons should be. In Christianity we are taught to provoke each other to good works. Let us, as Masons, teach each other and practice in truth the moral and social virtues; instead of criminations and recriminations. These virtues, the moral and social, after a belief in God, are the great levers by which Masonry expects to influence the world, and by which to govern its membership. They are distinctive and cardinal. Dispense with them, and Masonry dies.

Masonry has not died. To the contrary, it has grown from

325

about 400,000 members when the war ended to more than 4,000,000 in the United States in 1960. Its tenets and precepts are practiced more widely in the free world now than at any other time in its long history.

Unfortunately, the mistakes of the past have often been forgotten. Too many are still "stepping-on" their fellowman for a dollar or a vote. The old proverb "live and let live" is being constantly violated. Freemasonry's first tenet—Brotherly Love —is considered by far too many as so much sentimentality. Group is fighting group; religion is opposing religion; section is antagonizing section; competing ideologies are running rampant.

The Civil War ended before the summer of 1865, but its repercussions have been felt ever since. The North has opposed the thinking of the South; the same is true in reverse. Politically, the Republican party, with rare exceptions, has made no headway in the former Confederacy. The treatment by members of that party almost a century earlier has never been forgiven. The North has not been forgiving either; no Southerner has been nominated by either of the two major political parties for the presidency since the surrender.

In Masonic circles the opposite has been true. Masons have been quick to help, not only their own, but everyone deserving of assistance. They remember the charge that "every human being has a claim upon your kind offices." The living proof is plentiful.

The house that was never divided, has remained a house undivided!

—So Mote It Be—

Bibliography

◇◇◇

Angle, Paul M. (ed.) *The Lincoln Reader.* (New Brunswick: Rutgers University Press, 1947.)

Avirett, Rev. James B. *The Memoirs of General Turner Ashby and His Compeers.* (Baltimore: Selby & Dulany, 1867.)

Beale, Howard K. *The Critical Year.* (New York: Frederick Ungar Publishing Co., 1958.)

Benedict, G. G. *Vermont in the Civil War.* (2 Vols.: Burlington: Free Press Assoc., 1866-88.)

Bosang, J. M. "Memoirs of a Pulaski Veteran of the Stonewall Brigade."

Botkin, B. A. (ed.) *A Civil War Treasury of Tales, Legends and Folklore.* (New York: Random House, 1960.)

Brooks, R. P. "Conscription in the Confederate States of America, 1862-1865," Bulletin of the University of Georgia: Reprinted from *The Military Historian and Economist,* Vol. 1, No. 4, Harvard University Press.

Catton, Bruce. *A Stillness at Appomattox.* (New York: Doubleday & Co., 1953.)

Claudy, Carl H. (ed.) *Little Masonic Library.* (5 Vols., Kingsport: Southern Publishers, 1946.)

Cochran, Hamilton. *Blockade Runners of the Confederacy.* (Indianapolis: Bobbs-Merrill, 1958.)

Confederate Veteran. (40 Vols., Nashville: 1893-1932.)

Coulter, E. Merton. *The South During Reconstruction 1865-1877.* (Vol. VIII of *A History of the South.*) (Louisiana State University Press, 1947.)

Dame, George W. (D.D.) "Historical Sketch of Roman Eagle Lodge, No. 122, A.F. & A.M." (Danville, Virginia: 1895.)

Denslow, Ray V. *Civil War and Masonry in Missouri.* (Grand Lodge of Missouri, 1930.)

Denslow, Ray V. *The Masonic Conservators.* (Grand Lodge of Missouri, 1931.)

Denslow, William R. *10,000 Famous Freemasons.* (4 Vols., Missouri Lodge of Research, 1957-61.)

Derry, Joseph T. *Story of the Confederate States.* (Richmond: Royal, 1896.)

Dodrill, J. Bernard. "Chartered Lodges in West Virginia." Reprinted from the Proceedings of the Grand Lodge of West Virginia, 1953.

Douglas, Henry Kyd. *I Rode With Stonewall.* (Chapel Hill: University of North Carolina Press, 1940.)

Dowdey, Clifford. *The Land They Fought For*. (New York: Doubleday and Co., 1955.)

Ellis, Edward S. *Low Twelve*. (New York: Macoy Publishing and Masonic Supply Co., 1927.)

Faulkner, Harold Underwood. *American Political and Social History*. (New York: 7th Ed., Appleton-Century-Crofts, 1957.)

Fay, Bernard. *Revolution and Freemasonry*. (Boston: Little, Brown & Co., 1935.)

Foster, Lillian. *Andrew Johnson, President of the United States: His Life and Speeches*. (New York: Richardson & Co., 1866.)

Franklin, John Hope (ed.) *The Diary of James T. Ayers*. (Illinois State Historical Society, 1947.)

Gay, Archer Bailey. *A History of the Grand Chapter, Royal Arch Masons in the Commonwealth of Virginia*. (Highland Springs: Masonic Home Press, 1958.)

Goodwin, S. H. "Freemasonry in Utah Rocky Mountain Lodge No. 205, A.F. & A.M." Printed by order of the Grand Lodge of Utah, 1934.

Gould, Robert Freke (ed.) *The History of Freemasonry, Its Antiquities, Symbols, Constitutions, Customs, etc., Derived From Official Sources Throughout the World*. (New York: John C. Yorston & Co., 1886-89.)

"The Great Locomotive Chase." Louisville & Nashville Railroad, 1961.

Green, Charles E. *History of the Grand Lodge of A.F. & A.M. of Delaware*. (Grand Lodge of Delaware, 1956.)

Hammond, Otis G. (ed.) *The Utah Expedition*. (Concord: New Hampshire Historical Society, 1928.)

Haywood, H. L. *Well Springs of American Freemasonry*. (D. C.: The Masonic Service Association, 1953.)

Henry, Robert Selph. *The Story of the Confederacy*. (Indianapolis: Bobbs-Merrill, 1931.)

Henry, Robert Selph. *The Story of Reconstruction*. (Indianapolis: Bobbs-Merrill Co., 1938.)

Hesseltine, William B. *Lincoln's Plan of Reconstruction*. (Tuscaloosa: Confederate Publishing Co., 1960.)

Hillman, James Noah. "A List of the Charters Issued by the Most Worshipful Grand Lodge A.F. & A.M. of Virginia. (Virginia Research Lodge, No. 1777, 1955.)

Hillman, James Noah. "Botetourt Lodge, No. 7, A.F. & A.M." (Gloucester, Virginia, 1957.)

Hillman, James Noah. *Kilwinning Crosse·Lodge Number 2-237 A.F. & A.M.* (Bowling Green, Virginia, 1955.)

Hoge, Peyton H. *Moses Drury Hoge, His Life and Letters*. (Richmond: 1909.)

Horan, James D. *Confederate Agent*. (New York: Crown Publishers, 1954.)

Hunter, Frederick M. *The Regius Manuscript*. (Grand Lodge of Oregon, 1952.)

Jasperson, Robert O. *The First One Hundred Years*. (Grand Lodge of Wisconsin, 1944.)

Johnson, Robert Underwood, and Buel, Clarence Clough (eds.) *Battles and Leaders of the Civil War*. (4 Vols., New York: The Century Co., 1884-88.)

328

Johnston, Joseph E. *Narrative of Military Operations.* (New York: D. Appleton & Co., 1874.)

Leach, Jack Franklin. *Conscription in the United States: Historical Background.* (Vermont: Charles E. Tuttle Publishing Co., 1952.)

Mallory, Daniel (ed.) *The Life and Speeches of the Hon. Henry Clay.* (2 Vols., New York: A. S. Barnes & Burr, 1860.)

Martin, Clarence R. "Traveling Military Lodges." Reprint of an article presented at the Conference of Grand Masters of Masons in the United States, 1943.

McElroy, John. *Andersonville, A Story of Rebel Military Prisons.* (Toledo: D. R. Locke, 1879.)

Mitchell, Edward L. (ed.) *Masonic Monthly.* (Massachusetts: Vols. I, II and III, 1863-66.)

Moore, Frank. *The Rebellion Record.* (11 Vols. and Supplement: New York: D. Van Nostrand, 1861-68.)

Newman, Ralph, and Long, E. B. *The Civil War, the Picture Chronicle.* (New York: Grosset and Dunlap, 1956.)

Newton, Joseph Fort. *River of Years.* (New York: J. B. Lippincott, 1946.)

"Nocalore." Proceedings of North Carolina Lodge of Research, No. 666, A.F. & A.M., Vol. 5, 1935.

Patton, John S. (ed.) *Poems of John R. Thompson.* (New York: Charles Scribner's Sons, 1920.)

Personal Narratives. Soldiers and and Sailors Historical Society of Rhode Island, Sixth Series, 1903-05. Providence, 1903; "Battle of Waynesboro, Virginia, 1864."

Pittenger, William. *Capturing a Locomotive: A History of Secret Service in the Late War.* (Philadelphia: J. B. Lippincott & Co., 1882.)

Pollard, Edward A. *The Lost Cause.* (New York: E. B. Treat & Co., 1866.)

Proceedings, Grand Chapter of Missouri, New Hampshire.

Proceedings, Grand Lodge of: Colorado, District of Columbia, Florida, Iowa, Kansas, Louisiana, Massachusetts, Michigan, Nebraska, New York, Pennsylvania, Texas, Vermont, Virginia, West Virginia.

Reagan, John H. *Memoirs.* (New York: Neale Publishers, 1906.) Walter F. McCaleb (ed.)

Roberts, Allen E. "A Daughter of the Grand Lodge of Virginia." Virginia Research Lodge, No. 1777, 1958.

Roberts, Allen E. "The Controversy Concerning Prince Hall Masonry." Virginia Research Lodge, No. 1777, 1959.

Roberts, Charles C. (ed.) *Masonic Monthly.* (Massachusetts, Vol. IV, 1867.)

Sandberg, Carl. *Storm Over the Land.* (New York: Harcourt, Brace and Co., 1942.)

Schneider, Kurt O., Sr. "History of Ozaukee Lodge, No. 17, F. & A.M." Port Washington, Wisconsin, 1947.

Shannon, Fred Albert. *The Organization and Administration of the Union Army 1861-1865.* (2 Vols., Cleveland: Arthur H. Clark Co., 1928.)

Wadman, Theoph. G. (ed.) *Masonic Monthly.* (Massachusetts, Vols. V, VI, VII, 1868-70.)

Walthall, David K. "History of Richmond Lodge, No. 10, A.F. & A.M." (Richmond: 1909.)

Whitridge, Arnold. *No Compromise!* (New York: Farrar, Straus and Cudahy, 1960.)

Williams, T. Harry. *Lincoln and His Generals.* (New York: Alfred A. Knopf, 1952.)

Willis, Dr. F. Milton, adapted by, *Fort Sumter Memorial.* "Replacing the Flag Upon Sumter, From the Narrative of an Eye Witness." (New York: Edwin C. Hill, 1915.)

PERIODICALS

Charleston *Courier*
Cincinnati *Commercial*
The *Empire State Mason*
Freemasons' Magazine
The *Freemason* (Pennsylvania)
Grand Lodge Bulletin (Iowa)
The *Indiana Freemason*
Milwaukee *Sentinel*
The *Ohio Mason*

Providence *Evening Press* (R. I.)
Richmond *Whig* (Virginia)
The *Square and Compasses* (Louisiana)
Virginia Masonic Herald
The *Wisconsin Freemason*
Various publications of the United States Government.

Appendix A: Annual Communications During the War

<<<<<<<<<<<<<<<<<<<<<<<<<<<<<<<<<<<<<<<<<<<<<<<<<<<<<<<<<<<<<<

COMMENCEMENT OF ANNUAL COMMUNICATIONS OF GRAND LODGES DURING THE CIVIL WAR YEARS

Grand Lodge	1861	1862	1863	1864	1865
Alabama	Dec. 2	Dec. 1	Dec. 7	Dec. 5	Dec. 4
Arkansas	Nov. 4	Nov. 3	Nov. 2	Nov. 7	Nov. 6
California	May 14	May 13	May 12	Oct. 11	Oct. 10
Canada	July 10	July 9	July 8	July 13	July 12
Colorado[1]	Dec. 10	Nov. 3	Nov. 2	Nov. 7	Nov. 6
Connecticut	May 8	May 14	May 13	May 11	May 10
Delaware	June 27	June 27	June 27	June 27	June 27
District of Columbia	Nov. 5	Nov. 4	Nov. 3	Nov. 1	Nov. 7
Florida	Jan. 14	Jan. 13	Jan. 12	Jan. 11	Jan. 9
Georgia	Oct. 30	Oct. 29	Oct. 28	Oct. 26	Oct. 25
Illinois	Oct. 1	Oct. 7	Oct. 6	Oct. 4	Oct. 3
Indiana	May 27	May 26	May 25	May 24	May 23
Iowa	June 4	June 3	June 2	June 7	June 6
Kansas	Oct. 15	Oct. 21	Oct. 20	Dec. 20	Oct. 17
Kentucky	Oct. 21	Oct. 20	Oct. 19	Oct. 17	Oct. 16
Louisiana	Feb. 11	Feb. 10	Feb. 9	Feb. 8	Feb. 13
Maine	May 7	May 6	May 5	May 3	May 2
Maryland	Nov. 18	Nov. 17	Nov. 16	Nov. 21	Nov. 20
Massachusetts	Dec. 11	Dec. 10	Dec. 9	Dec. 14	Dec. 13
Michigan	Jan. 9	Jan. 8	Jan. 14	Jan. 13	Jan. 11
Minnesota	Oct. 22	None	Oct. 27	Oct. 25	Oct. 24
Mississippi	Jan. 21	Jan. 20	Jan. 19	Jan. 25	Jan. 23
Missouri	May 27	May 26	May 25	May 23	May 22
Nebraska	June 4	June 3	June 23	June 23	June 22
Nevada[2]					Oct. 10
New Hampshire	June 12	June 11	June 10	June 8	June 11
New Jersey	Jan. 16	Jan. 22	Jan. 21	Jan. 20	Jan. 18
New York	June 4	June 3	June 2	June 7	June 6
North Carolina	Dec. 2	Dec. 2	Dec. 7	Dec. 5	Dec. 4
Ohio	Oct. 15	Oct. 21	Oct. 20	Oct. 18	Oct. 17

Oregon	Sept. 16	Sept. 15	Sept. 21	June 20	June 19
Pennsylvania	Dec. 27	Dec. 27	Dec. 28	Dec. 27	Dec. 27
Rhode Island	June 24	June 24	May 25	May 30	May 29
South Carolina	Nov. 19	Nov. 18	Nov. 17	Nov. 15	Nov. 21
Tennessee	Oct. 7	None	Oct. 5	Oct. 3	Oct. 21
Texas	June 10	June 9	June 8	June 13	June 12
Vermont	Jan. 9	Jan. 8	Jan. 14	Jan. 13	Jan. 11
Virginia	Dec. 9	Dec. 8	Dec. 14	Dec. 12	Dec. 11
Washington	Sept. 2	Dec. 1	Nov. 24	Nov. 29	Nov. 28
West Virginia[3]					May 10
Wisconsin	June 11	June 10	June 9	June 14	June 13

[1] Organized August 2, 1861.
[2] Organized January 16, 1865.
[3] Organized May 10, 1865.

332

Appendix B: Masons Connected With the War

◇◇◇

THIS LIST of Masons connected with the Civil War is by no means all inclusive. Thousands could be added. In this group are generals and privates, statesmen and writers, government officials and politicians. While only one lodge is listed beside the name, many were connected with several others. Where "q.v. FFM" appears, refer to *10,000 Famous Freemasons;* for "q.v. B.I." see the Boyden Index of the Scottish Rite (SJ).

Name	*Masonic Affiliation*	*Location*
Alden, Alvin B.	Tomah, No. 132 (GM)	Wisconsin
Alden, R. S.	Grand High Priest	Minnesota
Alger, Russell A.	Corinthian, No. 241	Michigan
Allen, James M.	q.v. FFM	
Allison, William B.	Mosaic, No. 125	Iowa
Anderson, George T.	q.v. FFM	
Anderson, Robert	Mercer, No. 50	New Jersey
Anderson, Robert H.	Palestine, K. T., No. 7	Georgia
Anderson, Thomas McA.	St. John's, No. 11	Washington
Archer, P. C.	Paris, K.T., No. 9	Texas
Armistead, Lewis A.	Alexandria Washington, No. 22	Virginia
Armstrong, George	Grand Master	Nebraska
Ashby, Turner	Equality, No. 136 (now No. 44, W.Va.)	Virginia
Atkins, Smith D.	Excelsior, No. 97	Illinois
Bailey, Joseph E.	Columbia, No. 124	Wisconsin
Bailey, Theodorus	Washington, No. 21	New York
Balloch, George W.	Stansbury, No. 24	District of Columbia
Ballou, Ariel	Grand Master	Rhode Island
Bankhead, John H.	Grand Master (1881-85)	Wisconsin
Banks, Nathaniel P.	Monitor Lodge	Massachusetts
Barnum, Henry A.	Central City, No. 305	New York
Batchelder, Richard N.	Lafayette, No. 41	New Hampshire
Bate, William B.	King Solomon, No. 94	Tennessee

Name	Masonic Affiliation	Location
Beadle, William H. H.	Montezuma, No. 89	Indiana
Beal, George L.	Oxford, No. 18	Maine
Beauregard, Pierre	q.v. FFM	
Bee, Bernard B., Jr.	q.v. FFM	
Bee, Hamilton P.	Austin, No. 12	Texas
Balcher, William C.	Grand Master	California
Bell, John	King Solomon, No. 6	Tennessee
Benton, Thomas H.	Bluff City, No. 71	Iowa
Benton, William P.	Webb, No. 24	Indiana
Berry, Hiram G.	Aurora, No. 50	Maine
Berry, John S.	Grand Master	Maryland
Birney, David B.	Franklin, No. 134	Pennsylvania
Black, John C.	Olive Branch, No. 38	Illinois
Blake, John A.	Amity	Massachusetts
Blanchard, Stillman	Grand Secretary	Michigan
Blair, F. M.	Grand Master	Illinois
Bramlette, Thomas E.	q.v. B.I.	
Brayman, Mason	Springfield, No. 4	Illinois
Breckinridge, J. C.	Des Moines, No. 41	Iowa
Breckinridge, R. J.	Lexington, No. 1	Kentucky
Breckinridge, Wm. C. P.	Lexington, No. 1	Kentucky
Brooke, John R.	Columbia Chapter, No. 21	Pennsylvania
Brown, Albert G.	Gallatin, No. 25	Mississippi
Brown, Egbert B.	Toledo, No. 144	Ohio
Brown, John Calvin	Pulaski, No. 101	Tennessee
Brown, John M.	Naval, No. 87 (GM)	California
Buck, Ira W.	Grand Master	Iowa
Buchanan, James	Lodge, No. 43 (PM)	Pennsylvania
Buckner, Simon B.	q.v. FFM	
Butler, Benjamin F.	Pentucket	Massachusetts
Butterfield, Daniel	Metropolitan, No. 273	New York
Caldwell, Robert P.	Trenton, No. 86	Tennessee
Cameron, Simon	Perseverance, No. 21 (PM)	Pennsylvania
Campbell, Alexander	Jackson Commandery K.T.	Tennessee
Campbell, Jacob M.	Cambria, No. 278	Pennsylvania
Campbell, John	Unity, No. 12	Ohio
Canby, Edward R. S.	q.v. FFM	
Cantey, James	Kershaw, No. 29	South Carolina
Carleton, James H.	American Union, No. 1 (GM)	Ohio
Carson, Christopher	Lebanon, No. 98	Tennessee
Caruthers, Robert L.	Montezuma, No. 109	New Mexico
Cass, Lewis	Montezuma, No. 109	New Mexico
Chamberlain, Frank	q.v. FFM	
Chamberlain, Joshua	United, No. 8	Maine
Chetlain, August L.	Washington, No. 43	Illinois
Chivington, John M.	Grand Master	Colorado
Chrysler, Morgan H.	St. John's, No. 22	New York
Clay, Cassius M.	Davies, No. 22	Kentucky
Cleburne, Patrick R.	Lafayette, No. 16	Arkansas

334

Name	Masonic Affiliation	Location
Clemens, Samuel L.	Polar Star, No. 79	Missouri
Cleveland, Chauncey F.	Eastern Star, No. 44	Connecticut
Coates, James H.	Acacia, No. 67	Illinois
Cobb, Howell	Mt. Vernon, No. 22	Georgia
Cody, William F.	Platte Valley, No. 32	Nebraska
Cocke, Richard	Waco, No. 92	Texas
Coleman, William T.	Holland, No. 8	New York
Collamer, Jacob	Rising Sun, No. 7	Vermont
Commager, Henry S.	Northern Light, No. 40	Ohio
Conner, James	Landmark, No. 76	South Carolina
Cook, John	q.v. B.I.	
Cooper, Richard	Past Grand Master	Mississippi
Corley, Hugh A.	Grand Secretary	Florida
Corson, Thomas J.	Grand High Priest	New Jersey
Cowdin, Robert	q.v. B.I.	
Cox, William R.	William G. Hill, No. 218	North Carolina
Crawford, Samuel J.	Orient, No. 51	Kansas
Crittenden, John J.	Lexington, No. 1	Kentucky
Crittenden, Thomas L.	q.v. FFM	
Crittenden, Thomas T.	q.v. FFM	
Crocker, Marcellus M.	Pioneer, No. 22	Iowa
Cross, Edward E.	North Star, No. 8	New Hampshire
Croxton, John T.	q.v. FFM	
Cruft, Charles	Terre Haute, No. 19	Indiana
Curtin, Andrew G.	Belleforte, No. 268	Pennsylvania
Curtis, N. Greene	Grand Master	California
Curtis, Newton M.	DeMolay Commandary No. 4	Virginia
Curtis, Samuel R.	q.v. B.I.	
Dahlgren, John A.	q.v. FFM	
Daniel, John W.	Marshall, No. 39	Virginia
Darrow, Francis	Grand Master	Michigan
Dawkins, D. C.	Grand Master	Florida
DeBray, Xavier B.	Austin, No. 12	Texas
DeLaey, William	Independent Royal Arch, No. 2	New York
Desaussure, Wilmot G.	Grand High Priest	South Carolina
Dix, John A.	q.v. B.I.	
Dodge, Moses	Grand High Priest	Maine
Douglas, Stephen A.	Springfield, No. 4	Illinois
Dove, John	Grand Secretary	Virginia
Draper, William F.	Montgomery	Massachusetts
Drum, Richard C.	Oriental, No. 144	California
Drummond, Josiah H.	Grand Master	Maine
Dubois, Theo. B.	California, No. 1	California
Ducat, Arthur C.	Blaney, No. 271	Illinois
Duncan, Samuel A.	Franklin, No. 6	New Hampshire
Dustin, Daniel	Sycamore, No. 134	Illinois
Dyer, Elisha	St. John's, No. 1	Rhode Island
Edgerton, Alonzo J.	Grenada Lodge, No. 31	Mississippi

Name	Masonic Affiliation	Location
Egle, William H.	Perseverance, No. 21	Pennsylvania
Ehlers, Edward M. L.	Continental, No. 287	New York
Elkins, Stephen B.	Montezuma, No. 109	New Mexico
Elliot, I. H.	Bureau, No. 112	Illinois
Ellis, John W.	Fulton, No. 99	North Carolina
Engleshy, Loverett	Grand Master	Vermont
English, Elbert H.	Grand Master	Arkansas
Evans, James	Grand Master	Virginia
Ewers, Ezra P.	Sackets Harbor, No. 135	New York
Fairchild, George H.	Hiram, No. 50	Wisconsin
Fairchild, Lucius	Grand Master	Kansas
Farragut, David G.	(Buried by St. Johns No. 1, N. H.)	
Faulkner, Charles J., Jr.	Equality, No. 136 (now No. 44, W.Va.)	Virginia
Faulkner, Charles J., Sr.	Equality, No. 136 (now No. 44, W.Va.)	Virginia
Fellows, John Q. A.	Grand Master	Louisiana
Fessenden, James D.	q.v. B.I.	
Field, Stephen J.	Corinthian, No. 9 (formerly Lavely)	California
Fitzgerald, A. L.	Rockwell, No. 600	North Carolina
Fitzsimmons, Charles	Yonnondio, No. 163	New York
Fletcher, Thomas C.	Joachim, No. 164	Missouri
Floyd, John B.	St. John's, No. 36	Virginia
Foraker, Joseph B.	Walnut Hills, No. 483	Ohio
Forrest, Nathan B.	Angerona, No. 168	Tennessee
Forsyth, James M.	Union, No. 121	Pennsylvania
Fowler, Edward B.	Lexington, No. 310	New York
Frizzell, John	Cumberland, No. 8	Tennessee
Furnas, Robert W.	Capitol, No. 3 (GM)	Nebraska
Gamble, Hamilton R.	Missouri, No. 1 (GM)	Missouri
Garfield, James A.	Magnolia, No. 20	Ohio
Gary, Franklin F.	Grand High Priest	South Carolina
Gatling, Richard J.	Center, No. 23	Indiana
Geary, John W.	Philanthropy, No. 255	Pennsylvania
Giddings, Joshua R.	Jerusalem, No. 19	Ohio
Gilder, William H.	Kane, No. 454	New York
Gillette, Lee P.	Western Star, No. 2	Nebraska
Gilmore, Joseph A.	Thirty Third Degree	New Hampshire
Gobin, John P. S.	Williamson, No. 307	Pennsylvania
Goff, Nathan, Jr.	Hermon, No. 6	West Virginia
Goldsborough, John R.	Federal, No. 1	District of Columbia
Gordon, George H.	Bunker Hill, No. 5	Massachusetts
Gordon, John B.	q.v. FFM	
Gorman, William A.	Federal, No. 1	District of Columbia

336

Name	Masonic Affiliation	Location
Gorringe, Henry H.	Anglo Saxon, No. 137	New York
Gray, William	Grand Master	Rhode Island
Greely, Adolphus W.	St. Marks	Massachusetts
Green, Thomas	Austin, No. 12	Texas
Greenly, W. L.	Grand Master	Michigan
Gregg, John	Fairfield, No. 103	Texas
Gregg, William M.	Union, No. 95	New York
Gurney, William	Continental, No. 287	New York
Hadley, Henry H.	Progressive, No. 354	New York
Halderman, John A.	Leavenworth, No. 2	Kansas
Hale, Stephen F.	Grand Master	Alabama
Hall, Charles B.	Hancock, No. 311	Kansas
Hall, Cyrus	Jackson, No. 53	Illinois
Hall, James F.	Kane, No. 454	New York
Halpine, Charles G.	Holland, No. 8	New York
Hamblin, Joseph E.	Kane, No. 454	New York
Hancock, Winfield S.	Charity, No. 190	Pennsylvania
Hanson, Roger W.	Good Samaritan, No. 174	Kentucky
Harlan, John M.	Hiram, No. 4	Kentucky
Harllee, William W.	Clinton, No. 60	South Carolina
Harman, William H.	Staunton, No. 13 (GM)	Virginia
Harriman, Walter	St. Peters, No. 31	New Hampshire
Harris, Isham G.	Paris, No. 108	Tennessee
Harris, Nathaniel E.	Macon, No. 5	Georgia
Harrison, George P.	Grand Master	Alabama
Hart, John E.	St. George's, No. 6	New York
Hart, Peter	Park, No. 516	New York
Hartranft, John F.	Charity, No. 190	Pennsylvania
Haskins, Kittredge	Social, No. 38	Vermont
Hayes, Isaac I.	Kane, No. 454	New York
Haywood, Thomas	Grand Master	Florida
Hayne, Paul H.	Landmark, No. 76	South Carolina
Hays, Harry T.	Louisiana, No. 102	Louisiana
Heiman, Adolphus	Cumberland, No. 8	Tennessee
Helm, John L.	Morrison, No. 76	Kentucky
Henderson, David B.	Mosaic, No. 125	Iowa
Henderson, Howard A. M.	Hiram, No. 4	Kentucky
Hepburn, William P.	Nodaway, No. 140	Iowa
Herbert, Paul O.	Iberville, No. 81	Louisiana
Herron, Francis J.	Mosaic, No. 125	Iowa
Heth, Henry	Rocky Mountain, No. 205	Utah Territory
Hodges, Henry C.	Willamette, No. 2	Oregon
Hofmann, John Wm.	Lodge, No. 51	Pennsylvania
Hoge, Moses D.	Dove, No. 51	Virginia
Hollbrook, John R.	Grand High Priest	New Hampshire
Holliday, John H.	Mystic Tic, No. 398	Indiana
Horner, Joseph P.	Marion, No. 68 (GM)	Louisiana

Name	Masonic Affiliation	Location
Houston, John F.	Grand Master	Missouri
Houston, Sam	Cumberland, No. 8	Tennessee
Hoyt, Henry M.	Number 61	Pennsylvania
Hubbard, Lucius F.	Red Wing, No. 8	Minnesota
Hubbard, Richard B.	St. Johns, No. 53	Texas
Hughes, Aaron K.	Union, No. 95	New York
Hughes, Aaron P.	Grand Master	New Hampshire
Humphrey, Lyman U.	Fortitude, No. 107	Kansas
Hurlbut, Stephen A.	Belvidere, No. 60	Illinois
Hyde, Alvin P.	Grand Master	Connecticut
Imboden, John D.	Staunton, No. 13	Virginia
Ingalls, Rufus	Williamette, No. 2	Oregon
Ireland, John	Guadalupe, No. 109	Texas
Iverson, Alfred	Columbian, No. 108	Georgia
Jackson, Conrad F.	Number 45	Pennsylvania
Jackson, James S.	Hopkinsville, No. 37	Kentucky
Jilton, John M.	Grand Master	Maryland
Johnson, Andrew	Greeneville, No. 119	Tennessee
Johnson, Eastman J.	Grand Master	Michigan
Johnson, George W.	Mt. Vernon, No. 14	Kentucky
Johnson, Robert W.	Union Chapter, No. 2	Arkansas
Johnson, Stephen H.	Grand High Priest	Mississippi
Johnston, Albert S.	q.v. FFM	
Jones, Daniel W.	Mount Horeb, No. 4	Arkansas
Jones, Edward F.	q.v. FFM	
Jones, George W.	Dubuque, No. 3	Iowa
Jordan, Thomas J.	Perseverance, No. 21	Pennsylvania
Judah, Henry M.	North Star, No. 91	California
Kavanaugh, Benjamin	Grand Master	Wisconsin
Kemper, James L.	Linn Banks, No. 126 (PM)	Virginia
Kenly, John R.	Maryland Commandry, No. 1	Maryland
Kennedy, John D.	Kershaw, No. 29 (GM)	South Carolina
Kershaw, Joseph B.	Kershaw, No. 29	South Carolina
Kimball, Nathan	Mt. Pleasant, No. 168	Indiana
Kimberly, Lewis A.	St. Johns	Massachusetts
King, Finlay M.	Grand Master	New York
King, Horatio C.	Winchester Hiram, No. 21	Virginia
King, Thomas Starr	Oriental, No. 144	California
Kirkwood, Samuel J.	Iowa City, No. 4	Iowa
Knipe, Joseph F.	Perseverance, No. 21	Pennsylvania
Landram, Lewis	Grand Master	Kentucky
Lanham, Samuel W. T.	Phoenix, No. 275	Texas
Lawrence, Samuel C.	Hiram (Arlington)	Massachusetts
Lawton, Henry W.	Summit City, No. 170	Indiana
Leake, William W.	Feliciana, No. 31	Louisiana
Leggett, Mortimer D.	Amity, No. 5	Ohio

338

Name	Masonic Affiliation	Location
Lindsay, William	Hickman, No. 131	Kentucky
Livingston, Robert R.	Plattsmouth, No. 6	Nebraska
Logan, John A.	Benton, No. 64	Illinois
Lounsbury, Phineas C.	Jerusalem, No. 49	Connecticut
Lovell, Mansfield	Holland, No. 8	New York
Lowry, Robert	Brandon, No. 29	Mississippi
Lubbock, Francis R.	Holland, No. 1	Texas
MacArthur, Arthur, Jr.	Magnolia, No. 60	Arkansas
Mackey, Albert G.	St. Andrews, No. 10	South Carolina
Magruder, John B.	San Diego, No. 35 (E.A.)	California
Majors, Thomas J.	Monitor, U.D.	Nebraska
Mallery, Garrick	Columbia, No. 91 (PM)	Pennsylvania
Manderson, Charles F.	Nebraska, No. 1	Nebraska
Manson, Mahlon D.	Montgomery, No. 50 (PM)	Indiana
Marmaduke, John S.	Rocky Mountain, No. 205	Utah Territory
Marshall, Humphrey	q.v. FFM	
Martin, John A.	Washington, No. 5	Kansas
Martin, William T.	Harmony, No. 1	Mississippi
Mather, Samuel	Grand Master	Texas
Maxey, Samuel B.	Paris, No. 27	Texas
McArthur, John	Cleveland, No. 211	Illinois
McBride, Robert W.	Waterloo City, No. 307	Indiana
McCallum, Daniel C.	Valley, No. 109	New York
McCallum, James	Grand Master	Tennessee
McClellan, George B.	Willamette, No. 2	Oregon
McClernand, John A.	Central, No. 71	Illinois
McCook, Alexander	Lancaster, No. 106	Illinois
McCook, Edwin S.	Naval, No. 69	New York
McCreary, James B.	Richmond, No. 25	Kentucky
McCullock, Robert	Natural Bridge, No. 64	Virginia
McDaniel, John R.	Grand Master	Virginia
McFarland, Marcus H.	Grand Master	Missouri
McKenzie, James A.	James Moore, No. 230 (GM)	Kentucky
McKinley, William	Canton, No. 60	Ohio
McLeod, Hugh	Holland, No. 1	Texas
McMalron, John B.	Grand Master	Texas
Mead, John A.	Rutland, No. 79	Vermont
Meade, Richard K.	Blandford, No. 3 (PM)	Virginia
Meredith, Solomon	Cambrodge, No. 105	Indiana
Merrill, Samuel	Capital, No. 110	Iowa
Miles, Nelson A.	Southern California, No. 278	California
Miller, Stephen	North Star, No. 23	Minnesota
Mills, Robert Q.	Corsicana, No. 174	Texas
Mitchel, Charles B.	Mount Horeb, No. 4	Arkansas
Mitchell, John I.	Ossea, No. 317	Pennsylvania
Moore, Andrew B.	Marion Fraternal, No. 34	Alabama
Moore, Jesse H.	Macon, No. 8	Illinois
Morgan, John Hunt	Daviess, No. 22	Kentucky

Name	Masonic Affiliation	Location
Morrill, Edmund N.	Hiawatha, No. 35	Kansas
Morrill, John	Occidental, No. 40	Illinois
Morris, Robert	Grand Master	Kentucky
Murphy, John K.	Montgomery, No. 19	Pennsylvania
Neal, John R.	Rhea Springs, No. 310	Tennessee
Negley, James S.	Lodge Number 45	Pennsylvania
Newberry, Walter C.	Sanger, No. 219	New York
Nichol, Bradford	Cumberland, No. 8	Tennessee
Nicholson, Alfred O. P.	Columbia, No. 31	Tennessee
Orahood, Harper M.	Chivington, No. 6	Colorado
Ormsbee, Ebenezer J.	St. Paul's, No. 25	Vermont
Orr, James L.	Hiram, No. 68	South Carolina
O'Sullivan, Anthony	Grand Secretary	Missouri
Otey, James H.	Hiram, No. 7	Tennessee
Owens, Joshua T.	William B. Schnider, No. 419 (PM)	Pennsylvania
Paige, Clinton F.	Grand Master	New York
Paine, Eleazar A.	Monmouth, No. 37	Illinois
Palmer, George W.	Bunting, No. 655	New York
Palmer, John M.	Mt. Nebo, No. 76	Illinois
Palmer, Joseph B.	Mt. Moriah, No. 18 (PM)	Tennessee
Parker, Ely S.	Miners, No. 273	Illinois
	Valley, No. 109 (PM)	New York
Parkman, William	Grand Master	Massachusetts
Patterson, Robert E.	Kadosh Commandery, No. 29 (PC)	Pennsylvania
Patton, William S.	Grand Master	Mississippi
Pearl, Cyril	Grand Chapter	Missouri
Peck, George W.	Wisconsin, No. 13	Wisconsin
Peck, Theodore S.	Grand Marshal	Vermont
Penick, William R.	Grand Master	Minnesota
Perry, Edward A.	Escambia, No. 15	Florida
Phelps, John S.	United, No. 5	Missouri
Philip, John W.	Catskill, No. 468	New York
Phillips, Henry M.	Grand Master	Pennsylvania
Pickett, George E.	Dove, No. 51	Virginia
Pierce, Samuel C.	Genesee Falls, No. 507	New York
Pierson, A. T. C.	Grand Master	Missouri
Piggot, Robert	Grand Chaplain	Maryland
Pike, Albert	Western Star, No. 2	Arkansas
Pinckney, Joseph C.	Eureka, No. 243	New York
Pleasonton, Alfred	Franklin, No. 134	Pennsylvania
Plumb, Preston B.	Emporia, No. 12	Kansas
Porter, James D.	Paris, No. 108	Tennessee
Porter, William D.	St. John, No. 11	District of Columbia

Name	Masonic Affiliation	Location
Postles, J. Parke	Eureka, No. 23 (PM)	Delaware
Price, Rodman M.	Union, No. 11	New Jersey
Price, Sterling	Warren, No. 74	Missouri
Quarles, William A.	Clarksvill, No. 89	Tennessee
Quay, Matthew S.	St. James, No. 457	Pennsylvania
Quitman, John A.	Harmony, No. 18 (GM)	Mississippi
Randall, Alexander W.	Waukesha, No. 37	Wisconsin
Randall, Samuel J.	Montgomery, No. 19	Pennsylvania
Ransom, Matthew W.	Johnson-Caswell, No. 10	North Carolina
Ransom, Thomas E. G.	St. John's, No. 13	Illinois
Rawlins, John A.	Miners, No. 273	Illinois
Read, John Meredith, Jr.	St. John's, No. 1	Rhode Island
Reagan, John H.	Palestine, No. 31	Texas
Rees, R. R.	Grand Master	Kansas
Revere, Joseph Warren	St. John's	Massachusetts
Rex, George	Grand Master	Ohio
Reynolds, George D.	Potosi, No. 131	Missouri
Reynolds, James A.	Shenandoah Valley, No. 109	New York
Reynolds, William	q.v. FFM	Pennsylvania
Rice, Benjamin F.	Hyperian, No. 48	Arkansas
Rice, Edmund	Cataract, No. 2	Minnesota
Rice, Henry M.	St. Paul, No. 3	Minnesota
Richardson, David P.	Western Union, No. 146	New York
Richardson, James D.	Mt. Moriah, No. 18	Tennessee
Richardson, Robert M.	Central City, No. 305	New York
Richardson, William A.	Rushville, No. 9 (PM)	Illinois
Rinaker, John Irving	Mount Nebo, No. 76	Illinois
Roberts, Horace S.	Grand Master	Michigan
Roberts, Oran M.	McFarland, No. 3	Texas
Robie, Edward D.	Binghamton, No. 177	New York
Robie, Frederick	Harmony, No. 38	Maine
Robinson, Charles	Lawrence, No. 6	Kansas
Robinson, James F.	Mt. Vernon, No. 14 (PM)	Kentucky
Robinson, John C.	Binghamton, No. 177	New York
Rockwell, William S.	Benevolent, No. 3	Georgia
Roe, Francis A.	Union, No. 95	New York
Rogers, James C.	Sandy Hill, No. 372	New York
Roome, Charles	Kane, No. 454 (GM)	New York
Ross, Edmund G.	Topeka, No. 17	Kansas
Ross, Lawrence S.	Waco, No. 92	Texas
Ross, Leonard F.	Lewistown, No. 104	Illinois
Rousseau, Lovell H.	q.v. FFM	
Routt, John L.	Union, No. 7	Colorado
Rowan, Stephen C.	Montgomery, No. 19	Pennsylvania
Rowley, William R.	Miners, No. 273	Illinois
Ruggles, Daniel	Fredericksburg, No. 4	Virginia
Rusk, Jeremiah M.	La Belle, No. 85	Wisconsin

Name	Masonic Affiliation	Location
Sadler, Thomas	Grand Master	Massachusetts
St. Vrain, Ceran	Montezuma, No. 1	New Mexico
Sala, George A. H.	Drury Lane, No. 2127	England
Salmon, William C.	Eureka, No. 80	Washington
Samford, William J.	Auburn, No. 76	Alabama
Sanders, Wilbur F.	Virginia City, No. 1 (GM)	Montana
Sanno, James M. J.	Mansfield, No. 36	New Jersey
Saqui, Jacob	Grand Master	Kansas
Saxton, Rufus	St. John's, No. 11	District of Columbia
Sayers, Joseph D.	Gamble, No. 244 (GM)	Texas
Sayre, Daniel	Grand Secretary	Alabama
Schley, Winfield S.	q.v. FFM	
Scott, Winfield	Dinwiddie Union, No. 23	Virginia
Screws, William W.	Andrew Jackson, No. 173 (PM)	Alabama
Shafter, William R.	Pairie, No. 92	Michigan
Sharkey, William L.	Vicksburg, No. 26	Mississippi
Sharps, Christian	Meridian Sun, No. 158	Pennsylvania
Shepherd, Oliver L.	Clinton, No. 140	New York
Sherman, Buren R.	Vinton, No. 62	Iowa
Shields, James	Faribault, No. 9	Minnesota
Shoup, George L.	Denver, No. 5 (GM)	Colorado
Sickel, Horatio G.	St. John's, No. 115	Pennsylvania
Slocum, John S.	Mt. Vernon, No. 14	Rhode Island
Small, Michael P.	York, No. 266	Pennsylvania
Smith, Caleb B.	Warren, No. 15	Indiana
Smith, Charles E.	Rising Sun, No. 126	Pennsylvania
Smith, Green Clay	Richmond, No. 25	Kentucky
Smith, Gustavus W.	Keystone, No. 235	New York
Smith, John Corson	Miners, No. 273	Illinois
Smith, John Eugene	Miners, No. 273	Illinois
Smith, Joseph B.	National, No. 12	District of Columbia
Smith, Robert W.	Oriental, No. 33 (PM)	Illinois
Smyth, Thomas A.	Washington, No. 1	Delaware
Sparrow, Thomas	Grand Master	Ohio
Spaulding, Oliver L.	St. John's, No. 105 (GM)	Michigan
Stannard, George J.	Franklin, No. 4	Vermont
Stansbury, Charles F.	Grand Master	District of Columbia
Stanton, Edwin M.	Steubenville, No. 45	Ohio
Steedman, James B.	Northern Light, No. 40	Ohio
Stevens, Walter H.	Richmond, No. 10	Virginia
Stevenson, Carter L.	Rocky Mountain, No. 205	Utah Territory
Stone, William M.	Coshocton, No. 96	Ohio
Stoneman, George	Benicia, No. 5	California
Strickland, Silas A.	Capitol, No. 3	Nebraska
Taliaferro, William B.	Botetourt, No. 7 (GM)	Virginia

342

Name	Masonic Affiliation	Location
Teller, Henry M.	Central City, No. 6 (GM)	Colorado
Thacker, George W.	Grand High Priest	New York
Thayer, John M.	Capitol, No. 101	Iowa
Thomas, Bryan M.	Rocky Mountain, No. 205	Utah Territory
Thomas, George H.	q.v. FFM & B.I.	
Thomas, Lorenzo	Potomac, No. 5	District of Columbia
Thompson, Hugh S.	Grand Master	Pennsylvania
Thomson, John	Richland, No. 39	South Carolina
Throckmorton, James W.	St. Johns, No. 51	Texas
Timby, Theodore, R.	Rising Sun, No. 103	New York
Todd, Samuel M.	Grand Secretary	Louisiana
Toombs, Robert	Lafayette, No. 23	Georgia
Torbert, Alfred T. A.	Temple Chapter, No. 2	Delaware
Tracy, Benjamin F.	Friendship, No. 153	New York
Travel, John B.	Grand Master	Indiana
Truxtun, William T.	Owen's, No. 164	Virginia
Tucker, Philip C.	Grand Master	Vermont
Turner, Thomas J.	Excelsior, No. 97 (GM)	Illinois
Underwood, Adin B.	Montgomery	Massachusetts
Vance, Zebulon B.	Mt. Hermon, No. 118	North Carolina
Vandever, William	Dubuque, No. 3	Iowa
Van Sant, Samuel R.	Snow, No. 44	Iowa
Van Wagner, Isaac	Grand Master	New Jersey
Vaux, Richard	Lodge, No. 3 (GM)	Pennsylvania
Veatch, James C.	Rockport, No. 112	Indiana
Vest, George G.	Sedalia Chapter, No. 18	Missouri
Viele, Egbert L.	Kane, No. 454	New York
Voorhees, Daniel W.	Fountain, No. 60	Indiana
Voorhies, William M.	DeMolay Commandery, No. 3	Tennessee
Vrooman, John W.	Grand Master	New York
Wagner, Louis	Harmony, No. 52 (PM)	Pennsylvania
Wallace, Lewis	Fountain, No. 60	Indiana
Wallace, William H. L.	Occidental, No. 50 (PM)	Illinois
Walthall, Edward C.	Coffeeville, No. 83	Mississippi
Ward, John H. H.	Metropolitan, No. 273	New York
Warren, Francis E.	Cheyenne, No. 1	Wyoming
Weber, Max	Trinity, No. 12	New York
Weitzel, Godfrey	q.v. FFM & B.I.	
Welles, Gideon	St. John's, No. 4	Connecticut
Wheeler, Joseph	Courtland, No. 37	Alabama
White, Julius	Oriental, No. 33	Illinois
Whiting, George C.	Grand Master	District of Columbia
Whitthorne, Washington C.	Columbia, No. 31	Tennessee

343

Name	*Masonic Affiliation*	*Location*
Wilcox, Samuel M.	Grand High Priest	New Hampshire
Williams, John S.	Winchester, No. 20	Kentucky
Williams, Lewis L.	Grand Master	North Carolina
Williamson, James A.	Pioneer, No. 22	Iowa
Wilmot, David	Number 108	Pennsylvania
Wise, Henry A.	Northhampton, No. 11	Virginia
Wistar, Isaac J.	Franklin, No. 134	Pennsylvania
Withers, Robert E.	Marshall, No. 39 (GM)	Virginia
Wolf, Simon	Lafayette, No. 19	District of Columbia
Wood, Fernando	Eastern Star, No. 227	New York
Woodbury, Urban A.	Mount Vernon, No. 8	Vermont
Woodford, Stewart L.	Continental, No. 287	New York
Woods, William B.	Newark, No. 69	Ohio
Worden, John L.	Lexington, No. 310	New York
Yates, Richard, Sr.	Harmony, No. 3	Illinois
Young, Thomas L.	McMillan, No. 141	Ohio
Yulee, David L.	Hayward, No. 7	Florida
Zollicofer, Felix K.	Cumberland, No. 8	Tennessee

344

Index

Booth, Edwin: brother of John Wilkes Booth, 254; letter from N. Y. *Times,* 254; thanks publication, 255

Booth, John Wilkes: shoots Lincoln, 250

Bosang, Capt. J. M.: at Battle of Spottsylvania, 208; quoted, 208

Boston Tea Party: 6

Boyle, Isaac H.: letter from, 237

Bradley, Wm. H.: member of a military lodge, 108

Brame, Frank: incident, 152

Brandley, John G.: donation to fraternity, 229

Breckinridge, Gen. John C.: attacked Baton Rouge, 117; last Confederate secretary of war, 237; sent to attack Federal capital, 218

Breckinridge, Rev. Robert J.: in favor of the Union, 63

Bridges, Wm.: and Capitular work, 227

Brittain, Wm. P.: GM Texas, quoted, 215

Britton, Wilie: quoted, 91

Brock, C. W. P.: letter to GM Va., 232-33

Brotherhood in Action: Chapter XII, 145-155

Brown, Albert G.: Southern secessionist, 7

Brown, Lt. Stephen F.: arrested and released, 164; at Gettysburg, 164

Brown, Sylvester B.: received degrees, 323; letter from, 324

Brown, Thomas: correspondent GL Fla., quoted, 297; Negro Freemasonry, 299

Buchanan, Com. Franklin: commanded the "Virginia," 91

Buchanan, James: dedicates Washington statue, 15; orders troops to Utah Territory, 25

Buck, Ira W.: GM Iowa, quoted, 64

Buckner, Gen. Simon B.: chief of brigade, 85; commanded State Guard, 63; mentioned, 86, 87

Bull Run: disaster at, 47-54, 118

Burnside, Gen.: writes R. I. lodge, 246

Butler, Gen. Benjamin: issued General Order No. 28, 98; opposed Pres. Johnson, 319; ordered gas plant seized, 193; report to Secretary of War, 98; sent to cut railroads, 206; ordered Southern sympathizer out of Norfolk, 198; unpopular, 98; unsuccessful attempt to free prisoners, 200

Cahill, Col. Thomas W.: repulses attack, 117

California: 85, 225, 288; and the 14th amendment, 318; war effects felt, 69

Camp Floyd: commandered by Mason, 25

Camp, James H.: wounded, 126

Canada: 115, 171, 220, 284, 285, 310

Carleton, Gen. James H.: praises Carson, 199

Carrick's Ford: Confederate troops at, 46

Carson, Christopher (Kit): actions highly complimentary, 199

Cass, Lewis: a Freemason, 7; resigns as Secretary of State, 27

Chamberlain, Joshua L.: accepts Lee surrender, 247

Chambersburg, Pa.: burned by McCausland, 219

"Charleston Courier": quoted, 198

Charleston, S. C.: harbor entered, 24; newspaper report, 27; U. S. troops surrender, 27

Chase, Horace: quoted, 149

Chase, J. H.: saves lodge property, 72

Chase, Salmon P.: anti-slavery politician, 7

Chattanooga: conditions in, 185; under siege, 185

Chivington, J. M.: GM Colo., absent annual communication, 183

Church: split, 44

"Cincinnati Commercial": quoted, 113

"Cincinnati Masonic Review": quoted, 79

Civil Rights Bill: vetoed, 307

Civil War Centennial Commission: quotation by, 236

Clark, Col. Thomas Scott: saves Masonic jewels, 154

Clarksville Lodge No. 17 (Mo.): situation in, 69

Clay, Henry: a Freemason, 7; believed in compromise, 21; favors General Grand Lodge, 129

"Cleveland Herald": quoted, 173

Coffinbury, S. C.: GM Mich., quoted, 316; quotation by, 316

Coleman, Wm. T.: quelled riots, 139

Colorado: 127, 183, 189, 229, 290

Committee of Thirteen: killed, 21

"Confederate Veteran": quoted, 199, 201, 221, 243, 244

Connecticut: 100, 262

Conservators: see "Masonic Conservators"; Chapter X, 129-136

Coolidge, Wm. D.: GM Mass., issued military lodge dispensation, 109

Cornerstone: 226, 276, 284

Cornwell, Love S.: GM Mo., quoted, 10

Corson, Thomas J.: GHP N. J., quoted, 59

Crane, John J.: GM N. Y., quoted, 156

Crisis, Year of: Chapter XXIV, 296-315

Crittenden, John J.: a Freemason, 7; believed in compromise, 21

Cross, Col. Edward E.: aids Mason in distress, 125

Curtin, Andrew G.: issued call for more troops, 102; stops three months enlistments, 102

Curtis, Gen. Samuel R.: arrived in Missouri, 91; defeated Sterling Price, 91

Custer, Gen. George: orders men executed, 222

Dallas, George Mifflin: PGM Pa., death, 315

Dame, George W.: quoted, 53

Dana, Charles F.: Vt. Grand Chapter quoted, 287

Darrow, Francis: GM Mich., refused petitions to form military lodges, 82

Daughters of Confederacy: appeal for help, 174; tended Hart's grave, 160

Davis, Jefferson: and Bragg's removal, 181; President of Confederate States, 88; free to go any place, 262; indicted for treason, 262; leaves Richmond, 260; letter from Lee, 139; receives news of attack, 246; receives welcome, 41; troubles increase, 236; Unionist, 7

Davis, P. Stearns: killed, 217

Dawkins, D. C.: GM Fla., quoted, 24, 83, 147

DeBray, Col. H. B.: attends Masonic funeral, 146

Dedication: of book, v

Delahay, E. H.: petitions GL of D. C. for dispensation, 36

Delaware: 29, 318

Denslow, Ray V.: author of "Masonic

Conservators," 130; quotation by, 129; quoted, 130, 132, 135

Derby, Joseph T.: quotation by, 208

Dimmick, Capt. Robert A.: wounded, 118

District of Columbia: 36, 37, 68, 76, 92, 128, 261, 262, 292, 296; and Negro Masonry, 300; issued lodge dispensation, 37; General Grand Lodge considered, 129; Washington statue dedicated, 15

Dodd, David O.: executed as spy, 195

Dodge, Moses: GHP Maine, quoted, 55

Douglas, Henry K.: describes Ashby, 103; relates Manassas episode, 53

Douglas, Stephen A.: a Freemason, 7; backs Crittenden, 21

Dove, John; quoted, 9, 17

Draft: Masonry blamed for, 137-144; riot, 138

Drake, Gen. J. Madison: article on prisons, 201

Drummond, Josiah: and Negro Masonry, 300; defends formation GL W. Va., 277; GM Maine; opposes military lodges, 107; quoted, 152

Dubey, Corp. Edward A.: wounded, 118

Dubois, Theo. B.: aboard USS Albatross, 159; describes funeral service, 159; letter to Hart family, 160

Dyer, John: quotation by, 78

Early, Jubal: sent to attack Federal capital, 218; retreated, 244

Eisenhower, Dwight D.: quotation by, 29

Elgin, Robert M.: GM Texas, reported, 309

Ellis, Edward S.: quoted, 210

Ellis, John W.: telegraphs President, 29

Englesby, Leverett B.: GM Vt., quoted, 130, 196, 239

English, Elbert H.: GM Ark., quoted, 16, 290, 311

"Essex": Wm. D. Porter commanded, 84

Evans, Joseph D.: PGM Va., 39

Ewell, Richard S.: commanded Jackson's second corps, 161

Fairchild, George H.: letter to GL Kansas, 65

347

348

out maneuvered by, 216; not a Mason, 170; orders destruction of countryside, 221; orders hanging without trial, 222; report on Chattanooga, 185; set up plan of battle, 219; without funds, 87

Gray, Capt.: ordered to counter attack, 151

Gray, Wm.: GM R. I., quoted, 41

Greeley, Horace: signs Davis bail bond, 262

Greenly, W. L.: GM Mich., quoted, 23

Gregg, John: killed, 207

Grim, John: taken prisoner, 214; wounded, 214

Grover, Col. Benjamin W.: PGM Mo., wounded, 60

Guerillas: story of attack, 175; under command of Quantrell, 178

Guernsey, Wm. H.: death, 218

Guilbert, Edward A.: condemns GL Kentucky, 214; criticised, 297, 322; GM Iowa, quoted, 214, 252; praised Mackey, 266

Guild Masons: 3

Hacker, Wm.: GM Ind., quoted, 265

Hahn, Conrad: poem by, ii

Hale, Stephen F.: GM Ala., absent GL, 73; death, 74

Hancock, Gen. Winfield: friend of Armistead, 163; repels attack, 114, 162; wounded, 164

Hardee, Wm. J.: Tennessee army turned over to, 186

Harman, Wm. H.: GM Va., death, 192, 244; wounded, 243

Harrington, T. Douglas: GM Canada, quoted, 115, 171, 220, 285, 310

Harris, Isham G.: Governor of Tennessee, 29; with Gen. Forrest, 202

Harris, John: GM Ga., quoted, 290

Harris, S. P.: delivered address, 161

Harrison, James B.: GHP Ala., quoted, 293

Hart, Col. Ben R.: hunt for body of, 221

Hart, Capt. John E.: aboard USS Albatross, 159; DAR tends grave of, 160; death, 159; Louisiana dedicated grave marker, 160; Masonic service, 159

Hart, Peter: at Ft. Sumter ceremonies, 248

Hayward, Thomas: GM Fla., quoted, 195

Haywood, H. L.: quotation by, 270

Herron, Gen. Francis J.: wounded, 91

Heth, Gen. Henry: met Meade forces, 162; senior warden Rocky Mtn. Lodge, 26; wounded, 163

Hicks, Thomas Holliday: death, 263

Hill, Ambrose P.: killed, 245; moves north, 161; stays at Fredericksburg, 162

Hill, D. H.: 113, 114; author of petition, 181; quotation by, 173

Hoge, Moses Drury: degrees conferred as he was dying, 143; used blockade runners for mail, 142

Hoke, Gen. Robert F.: at Cold Harbor, 210

Holbrook, Col. Charles L.: member of military lodge, 108

Holbrook, John R.: GHP N. H., quoted, 252, 269

Hooker, Gen. Joseph (Fighting Joe): drove Union army back, 151; removed from command, 162

Hospitals: conditions in, 176, 177; building used for, 36

Hough, Daniel: killed, 28

House Undivided: story of Freemasonry and Civil War; volume issued in 1961

Houston, John F.: GM Mo., quoted, 263; quotation by, 250, 251

Houston, Sam: death, 215

Howe, Thomas B.: DGM Mo., quoted, 264

Hughes, Aaron P.: GM N. H., quoted, 111

Hurlbut, Gen. Stephen A.: in command Ft. Donelson, 87

Huston, John B.: GM Ky., quoted, 172, 181

Hyde, Alvan P.: quoted, 100

Illinois: 7, 181, 235

Indiana: 40, 154, 239, 265; GM prepares list of military lodges, 106

Indians: under command of Albert Pike, 91

Ingersoll, Col. Robert G.: termed, "The Great Agnostic," 84

Iowa: 17, 36, 45, 57, 64, 157, 213, 252, 266, 297, 309, 322

Iverson, Col. Alfred: cited for bravery, 114

Jackson, Gen. Clairborne: at Manassas, 53; attends secession meeting, 62

349

350

nied recognition W. Va. GL, 278; Rocky Mtn. Lodge, 25, 26

Missouri Compromise: 7

Mitchell, Edward L.: published Masonic Monthly, 186; quoted, 186

M'Jilton, John M.: GM Md., quoted, 183

Monticello Lodge No. 16: baby born in Mo. lodge room, 62

Moore, Charles W.: to write Civil War history, 313

Moore, Lovell: GM Mich. and military lodge masons, 239

Morgan, Gen. John Hunt: captured, 173; cavalry defeated, 100; death, 91; escape from prison, 174; raided Nashville suburbs, 91; raids in Kentucky, 116, 172; raids in Ohio, 172; 224

Mormons: burn court records, 25

Morris, Rob: and the Conservators, 129, 130; begins Conservator movement, 14; honorary member GL Mich., 133; known as Poet Laureate, 133

Mosby, Col. John S.: orders men executed, 22

Mosscrop, Capt. Thomas D.: wounded, 118

Mozeille Mills, Mo.: bridge destruction threatened, 57

Mulligan, Col. James: forced to surrender, 61; Lexington College bldg. fortress of, 60

Mumford, Gen. Thomas T.: letter to Bliss, 225

Mumford, Wm. B.: condemned to death, 98

Murray, Lt. Col.: commanded Ohio cavalry, 92

Myers, Charles W.: quoted, 163

Nash, C. W.: GM Minn., quoted, 321

"National Freemason": letter published, 216; quoted, 229

Nebraska: 43, 218; and Masonic Conservators, 134, 135

New Hampshire: 46, 111, 125, 158, 252, 266, 321

New Jersey: 59, 148, 285; and the 14th amendment, 318; Negro lodge in, 299

New Mexico: Kit Carson in, 199

Newton, Joseph Fort: father a military lodge member, 107

New York: 12, 36, 37, 105, 118, 149, 156, 160, 212, 213, 267, 302, 322; and the draft, 138-139; edict against members of, 38; military lodges, 106; W. Va. grand lodge, 277

"New York Times": Booth thanks, 255; letter to Booth, 254; report, 100; trial of assassins, 256

"New York Tribune": quoted, 21

North Carolina: 17, 24, 29, 30, 36, 107, 108, 143, 181, 241, 268, 307, 308, 309

Ohio: 7, 36, 67, 79, 172, 173, 227, 273, 323; and 14th amendment, 318; GG Chapter meets in, 286; W. Va. Grand Lodge, 277

Operative Masons: 3

Oregon: and the 14th amendment, 318; comment on W. Va. GL, 278

O'Sullivan, Anthony: quoted, 41, 101, 102; quotation by, 43

Otey, James H.: Tenn. Episcopal Bishop, 28

Paige, Clinton F.: GM N. Y., quoted, 212, 267; quotation by, 260

Palmer, Theodore G.: petitions GL D. C. for dispensation, 36

Parkhurst, Wm. G.: quoted, 292

Parkman, Wm.: GM Mass. lays cornerstone, 226

Patton, Wm. S.: GM Miss. described damages, 239

Payne, Capt. A. D.: quoted, 224

Peace: Chapter XXI, 260-269

Pearl, Cyril: quoted, 56

Pelot, J. M.: quoted, 13

Penick, Wm. C.: quoted, 281, 325

Penick, Gen. Wm. R.: GM Mo., quoted, 44

Pennsylvania: 8, 15, 33, 75, 102, 141, 161, 162, 164, 192, 234; death of PGM Dallas, 315; lays cornerstone National monument, 284; refused recognition W. Va., 277

Periodicals: 330

Peyton, Thomas W.: death, 241

Philip, John W.: commanded naval blockade, 55

Philips, Wendell: abolitionist, 21

Phillips Grand Lodge: formed, 37; members to be healed, 38

Phillips, Henry M.: GM Pa., quoted, 8

Phillips, Isaac: assisted in formation Phillips GL, 37

Pickett, George E.: charge led by, 163

Pierpont, Francis: Governor of Va., 270
Pierson, A. T. C.: GM Minn., quoted, 182
Piggot, Robert: offers prayer, 176
Pike, Gen. Albert: 157; addressed GL Ark., 16; guard placed about home of, 45; Indians under command of, 91; Masonic Library saved, 17
Pillow, John B.: jealous, insubordinate, quarrelsome, 85; mentioned, 86
Pinkerton, Allan: 112
Pittenger, Wm.: quoted, 97
Pittsburg Landing: see "Battle of Shiloh"
Poem: "Men Must Brothers Be" by Hahn, ii
Pollard, E. A.: disliked Davis, 282; quoted, 145, 282
Pony Express: utilized on daily basis, 143
Pope, Gen. John: quoted, 118; resists attack, 118
Porter, Gen. Fitz John: mentioned, 114
Port Hudson: siege, 159
Pratt, Col. George W.: Masonic funeral, 84
Preface: by Allen E. Roberts, vii
Price, Gen. Sterling: 117; a Mason, 224; at Battle of Lexington, 61; attacked Union forces, 126; defeated by Curtis, 91; evacuated Little Rock, 180; moved to Neosho, Mo., 62
Prince, Col. Edward: tries to stop Forrest, 192
Prince Hall Masonry: controversy concerning, 299
Pritchard, Col. Benjamin D.: commanded Federal cavalry, 262
"Providence Evening Press": quoted, 246
Publications: need for, 229; see "Periodicals"

Quitman, J. A.: Southern secessionist, 7

Ramsey, David: GM S. C., quoted, 88
Rankin, Capt.: funeral, 221
Rawlings, Gen.: at Vicksburg celebration, 168
Raynor, Col. W. H.: at Bull Run, 47
Rea, Richard N.: quoted, 199
Reagan, John H.: calls on Toombs, 262; control of mail in the Confederacy, 142; quoted, 142, 206, 262

"Rebellion Record": reports Masonic funeral, 119; quoted, 44, 95, 117, 202
Reconstruction: Chapter XXIII, 282-295
Relief Lodge: in Louisiana, 150-151
Rees, Richard R.: GM Kans., quoted, 12; visits Kansas GL, 66
Regius Manuscripts: oldest Masonic document, 4
Rex, George: quoted, 67
Rhett, Barnwell: Southern secessionist, 7, 21
Rhode Island: 5, 41, 100, 111, 154, 224, 226, 246
Richmond, Va.: fall of, 247
"Richmond Dispatch": reported Masonic celebration, 117
"Richmond Examiner": quotation by, 185; quoted, 193, 282
"Richmond Whig": quoted, 126
Roberts, Allen E.: author of "House Undivided"; preface by, vii
Robinson, Gen. John C.: first master Rocky Mtn. Lodge, 25, 26
Robinson, Wm. E.: quoted, 288
Rockwell, Wm. S.: GM Ga., quoted, 14
Rocky Mountain Lodge: members scattered, 26; organized, 25
Rosecrans, Gen.: commanded Union forces, 126; a Roman Catholic, 203
Ross, Marion A.: executed, 97
Rousseau, Gen. Lovell H.: issued Special Order No. 54, 117
Royal Arch: degree conferred, 170-171; work halted, 227
Ruffin, Edmund: Southern fanatic, 21

St. Albans, Vt.: raided, 228; raider entertained, 229
St. John's College: building used as hospital, 36; closed, 36
St. John's Day: celebration, 161
Sadler, Thomas: GM Ky., quoted, 226
Saqui, Jacob: GM Kans., quoted, 178
Saunders, Samuel H.: GM Mo., 25
Sayre, Daniel: defends South in Lincoln assassination, 253
Schley, Winfield Scott: amusing episode, 99
Scott, Lucius H.: GM Pa., lays cornerstone, 284
Scott, Sir Walter: quotation by, 137
"Scranton Republican": quoted, 163
Seal, Confederate: description of, 126

Seddon, James A.: resigned as Secretary of War, 236; story concerning, 236

Seward, Wm. H.: antimason, 7; Whig governor, 7

Seymour, James: quoted, 284

Shackleford, Gen.: Union forces commanded by, 173

Sheridan, Geo. Philip: Va. raids, 243, 244, 245

Sharp, B. W.: PGM Mo., death, 44

Sharp, Capt. Thomas I.: grave located, 221

Sherman, Gen. Wm. T.: left devastation, 241; left Vicksburg, 199; to investigate Ft. Pillow battle, 203

Ships: Arkansas, 117; Bayou City, 145; Cincinnati, 166; Congress, 91; Cumberland, 91; Dacotah, 100; Harriet Lane, 145, 146; John H. Groesbeck, 166, 167; Maratanza, 100; Monitor, 92; Neptune, 145; Octorora, 117; Richmond, 246; Star of West, 24; Susquehannah, 100; Switzerland, 242; Tubal Cain, 117; USS Albatross, 159; Virginia, 91, 246; Wachusett, 100; Wyoming, 161

Simmons, John W.: GM N. Y., comment, 38

Skelly, Daniel: quoted, 163

Slocum, Col. John S.: Masonic funeral, 111

Smith, Gen. E. Kirby: troops attack, 119

Smith, Gerrit: signs Davis bail bond, 262

Smith, Joseph B.: death, 92

Smith, Gen. Wm. S.: ordered to join Sherman, 200; sent back to Memphis, 200

South Carolina: 20, 21, 88, 105, 24 262; and Masonic Conservators, 130; secedes, 8

"Southern Confederacy": quoted, 139

Sparry, Thomas: GM Ohio, quoted, 227

Spaulding, James K.: death, 177

Stainback, George T.: GHP Miss., on finances, 301

Stamps: bid to manufacture postal, 142

Stannard, Gen. George J.: ordered Brown release, 164

Stansbury, Charles F.: GM D. C., quoted, 68, 128

Stephens, Alexander H.: elected Vice President Confederate States, 26

Stevens, E. L.: quoted, 292

Stevens, Thaddeus: anti-Mason, 284; clever political leader, 318; death and burial, 319

Stevenson, Carter L.: member of Rocky Mtn. Lodge, 25

Stewart, Henry J.: issued dispensation Regimental Traveling Lodge, 83; quoted, 324

Stewart, O. C.: DGM Kansas, 13

Stoneman, Gen. George: makes balloon reconnaissance, 100

Stribling, C. K.: reported, 110

Strickland, F. P., Jr.: quotation by, 95

Strong, Capt. G. A.: wounded, 93

Stuart, J. E. B.: sent to learn enemy strength, 112

Substitute Wanted: to serve in army, 139

Sumner, Charles: antislavery politician, 7

Swafford, Lewis S.: GHP Iowa, criticises army chapters, 266

Taliferro, Col. Wm. B.: sends help to Carrick's ford, 46

Taylor, Horace S.: GHP N. Y., quoted, 302

Taylor, Rev. Thomas: quoted, 15

Tecumseh: mentioned, 13

Tennessee: 7, 15, 29, 30, 64, 91, 92, 96, 100, 101, 116, 127, 180, 185, 192, 202, 287, 312, 313; admitted to Union, 318; letter from GL of, 31; Andrew Johnson military Governor of, 87, 283

Tennyson, Alfred: quotation by, 156

Terry, Wm.: asks recognition of W. Va., 280; quoted, 279

Texas: 36, 45, 106, 109, 145, 146, 147, 157, 180, 215, 268, 309, 322; secedes, 24

Thacher, George H.: GM N. Y., quoted, 149

Thomas, Gen. B. M.: described Camp Floyd lodge building, 25

Thomas, George H.: at Mill Springs, Ky., 83; called "Rock of Chickamauga," 180; ordered to hold Chattanooga, 185

Thomas, Capt. S. M.: prisoner, 241

Thomason, John: GM Pa., quoted, 75

354

Thompson, J. B.: experiences at Ft. Gregg, 245
Thoreau: quotation by, 112
Thrall, Wm. B.: PGM Ohio, installed W. Va. grand officers, 273, 274
Tilghman, Gen. Lloyd: commanded Ft. Henry, 84
Todd, Samuel M.: quoted, 150, 241, 242
Toombs, Robert: backs Crittenden, 21; offered to furnish horses, men, money, 262; Secretary of State, 88; Unionist, 7
Tracy, Henry W.: member of Rocky Mtn. Lodge, 25
Traveling Lodges: dispensation issued for, 83; GM Tenn., comment, 64
Tucker, Philip C.: criticised Guilbert, 322; GM Vt., quoted, 22; on Magruder's staff, 147

Union Lodge No. 7: (Colo.) charter granted, 189
United Daughters of Confederacy: see "Daughters of Confederacy"
Utah Territory: Camp Floyd at, 25; unrest in, 26

Vanderbilt, Cornelius: signed Davis bail bond, 262
Van Deren, A. J.: GM Colo., quoted, 290
Van Dorn, Gen.: attacked Union forces, 126
Van Vleck, George W.: GM Texas, quoted, 109
Van Wagoner, Isaac: GM N. J., quoted, 148; quotation by, 195
Vaux, Richard, GM Pa., writes GL Tenn., 33; quoted, 141
Vermont: 22, 24, 80, 164, 196, 227, 228, 229, 239, 287
Vicksburg: and Gettysburg, 156; GL meets at, 24; Masonic meeting in, 168, 169; story of capture, 170
Virginia: 5, 9, 17, 29, 30, 36, 37, 38, 46, 74, 78, 100, 101, 102, 103, 106, 108, 113, 118, 119, 126, 141, 143, 152, 191, 206, 213, 232, 239, 243, 244, 245, 246, 247, 248, 257, 258, 260, 261, 270, 294, 323; Davis received in Richmond, 41; fighting becomes more tense, 46; letter from GL Mass., 17; lodge property saved, 71; military lodges, 106;

new GL formed, 272; objected to formation two grand lodges, 37; secession ordinance adopted, 270; resolution by General Assembly, 22; troops abandon Alexandria, 36; West Virginia GL, 272, 275, 276, 277, 278, 279, 280, 281
Virginia, Grand Chapter of: meets in Richmond, 17

Wainwright, Capt. I. W.: killed, 146; Masonic funeral, 146, 147
Walke, Adm. Henry: quoted, 84
Walker, Wm.: GM N. Y., quoted, 12
Wallace, Gen. Lew: at Ft. Donelson, 84; author of "Ben Hur," 84; headquarters in Baltimore, 202; quoted, 85, 86; saved Federal capital, 218
Warren, Joseph: mentioned, 9
War Incidents: Masonic Monthly publishes, 197
Washburn, G. W.: quoted, 110, 111
Washington, George: birthday celebrated, 88; mentioned, 9; quotation by, 145
Washington Statue: dedicated, 15
Wearengen, Capt. T. B.: wounded, 140
Wentworth, John T.: GM Wisc., comment on number of petitioners, 310
West Virginia: 30, 270, 271, 272, 273, 274, 275, 276, 277, 279, 280, 313; degrees conferred, 278; permitted to keep Va. charters, 281
Wheeler, Daniel H.: GM Nebr., quoted, 218; and Masonic Conservators, 134
Whiting, George C.: GM D. C., quoted, 251, 261
Whitney, James M.: member of military lodge, 108
Whiton, Col. John C.: member of military lodge, 108
Whytal, Capt. Thomas G.: gift to lodge, 109
Wilcox, Samuel M.: GHP Texas, quoted, 158
Wilkins, John: arrested and released, 236
Williams, Lewis B.: GM Va., quoted, 141, 191
Williams, Lewis L.: GM N. C., quoted, 17
Williams, Wilson: GM Ala., quoted, 321

355

Wilson, Major James: in prison, 174; mentioned, 256
Wilson, Richard: member of Rocky Mtn. Lodge, 26
Wisconsin: 137, 215, 310, 320; anti-Masonic feeling in, 69, 110, 149, 170
Wise, Henry A.: commanded mixed force, 216
Withers, Col. Robert E.: GM Va., commanded regiment, 54

Wood, Col. Benjamin: wounded, 54
Worden, John L.: ship commander, 92
Wyler, Wm.: directed filming of "Ben Hur," 85

Yancey, Wm. L.: Southern fanatic, 21
Year of Crisis: Chapter XXIV, 296, 315
Years After: Chapter XXV, 316-326
Yorktown: evacuated, 100; siege begins, 92

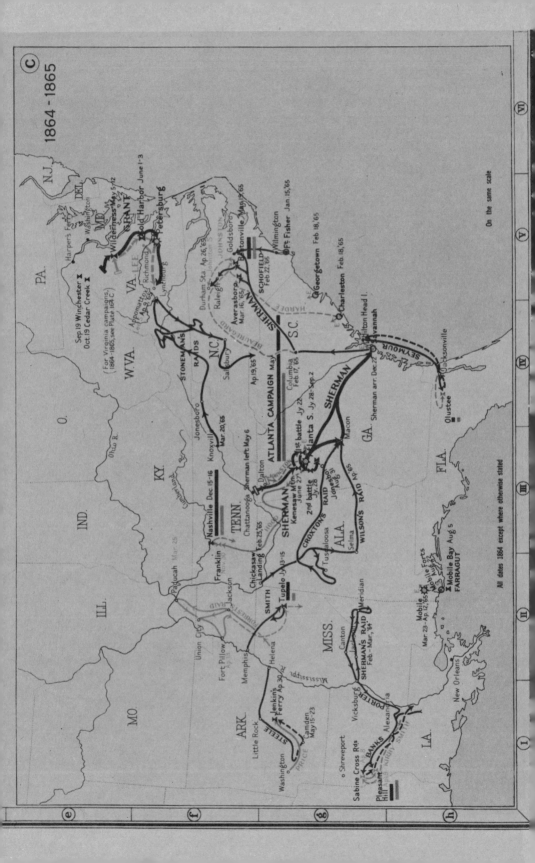

© 1864 - 1865